BLACK MOVEMENT

BLACK MOVEMENT

African American Urban History since the Great Migration

EDITED BY JEFFREY O. G. OGBAR

The University of North Carolina Press | Chapel Hill

This book was published with the
assistance of the John Hope Franklin Fund
of the University of North Carolina Press.

© 2025 The University of North Carolina Press
All rights reserved

Manufactured in the United States of America

Designed by April Leidig
Set in Garamond Premier Pro and Muller by Copperline Book Services

Complete Library of Congress Cataloging-in-Publication Data
is available at https://lccn.loc.gov/2024048189

ISBN 978-1-4696-8433-8 (cloth: alk. paper)
ISBN 978-1-4696-8434-5 (pbk.: alk. paper)
ISBN 978-1-4696-8435-2 (epub)
ISBN 978-1-4696-8755-1 (pdf)

Portions of the essays "Black Mecca or Black Dystopia? Race, Class, and Power in Atlanta" and "The Black Mecca: Atlanta and Twenty-First-Century Black Movement" appeared earlier, in somewhat different form, in Jeffrey O. G. Ogbar, *America's Black Capital: How African Americans Remade Atlanta in the Shadow of the Confederacy* (New York: Basic Books, 2023).

This book will be made open access within three years of publication thanks to Path to Open, a program developed in partnership between JSTOR, the American Council of Learned Societies (ACLS), the University of Michigan Press, and the University of North Carolina Press to bring about equitable access and impact for the entire scholarly community, including authors, researchers, libraries, and university presses around the world. Learn more at https://about.jstor.org/path-to-open/.

*To the ancestors who continued to
move and work toward greater freedom*

CONTENTS

xi   List of Illustrations

JEFFREY O. G. OGBAR
1   Introduction: Making Sense of African Americans and the City since the Great Migration

Part I

TOM ADAM DAVIES
29   A Piece of the Action: Black Mayors, the Black Business Class, and Black Progress in Urban America, 1965–1995

JEFFREY O. G. OGBAR
55   Black Mecca or Black Dystopia? Race, Class, and Power in Atlanta

Part II

MAURICE J. HOBSON
79   Greetings, Earthlings, Take Me to Your Leader: A Post-1968 History of Black Atlanta through the Prism of Black Sci-Fi

SCOT BROWN
97   Bands to Make You Dance: Dayton, Ohio, Black Bands, and Popular Music

Part III

TATIANA M. F. CRUZ
119   We Are All in the Same Boat Now: Mel King and the Origins of Boston's Rainbow Coalition

BRIAN PURNELL

137 Living and Working in a
World of Overlapping Diasporas:
Black New Yorkers' History in the
Metropolis since the 1970s

FIONA VERNAL

177 Unmooring and Tethering African American,
Puerto Rican, and West Indian Lives:
New Conceptual Frameworks for
Interrogating Three Great Migration
Traditions in Hartford, Connecticut

Part IV

SHANNON KING

199 What Did Rockefeller Do about the
Crooked Cop Who Sell You Drugs?
Black Protest and the Politics of Safety
in the Early 1970s

LASHAWN HARRIS

219 They Chained Me to a Refrigerator Like a Dog:
New York Black Women, Police Violence,
and Resistance during the Reagan Era

MELANIE D. NEWPORT

241 A Bigger, Better Jail:
From Jail Overcrowding to the Shackling of
Black Chicago during the War on Drugs Era

J. T. ROANE

259 Topology of Flames:
The Political Ecology of Fire in
Late Twentieth-Century Philadelphia

Part V

STEFAN M. BRADLEY

281 Chasing Angels:
Black Life in Los Angeles since 1965

CHANELLE ROSE AND BENJAMIN H. SARACCO

299 Camden Rising?
The Black Struggle for Racial Justice, Equity, and
Inclusion in the Age of Urban Revitalization, 1971–2020

JEFFREY O. G. OGBAR

321 The Black Mecca:
Atlanta and Twenty-First-Century Black Movement

341 Acknowledgments

343 Contributors

345 Index

ILLUSTRATIONS

Figures

- 9   Harlem block of row houses
- 17   A view from Baldwin Hills
- 220   Reverend Al Sharpton, Tawana Brawley, and attorney C. Vernon Mason outside the New York State Supreme Court
- 225   A fur-clad woman and cops wait for a matron to search her at a social club in Bedford-Stuyvesant, Brooklyn, 1982
- 333   Atlanta skyline

Tables

- 146   1. Total Black population (and as percentage of total county population) in New York metropolitan area counties, 1970–2010
- 154   2. Total Black population (and as percentage of total population) in Suffolk County (Long Island) sample towns, 1960–2010
- 156   3. Black populations (and as percentage of total population) of Nassau County (Long Island) sample towns, 1960–2010
- 161   4. Total foreign-born population from the African continent (and as percentage of all foreign-born) in New York metropolitan area counties, 2000, 2010
- 162   5. Total foreign-born population from the Caribbean (and as percentage of all foreign-born) in New York metropolitan area counties, 2000, 2010

BLACK MOVEMENT

JEFFREY O. G. OGBAR

Introduction

Making Sense of African Americans and the City since the Great Migration

At the dawn of the twentieth century, as the eminent historian, sociologist, and activist W. E. B. Du Bois penned his landmark text, *The Souls of Black Folk* (1903), about 90 percent of African Americans lived in the South, in largely rural communities. Any sociological or historical exploration of Black people at that time would have, accordingly, defined them in that context: largely a rural, southern people. They were inexorably shaped by the political, social, cultural, and economic forces that pervaded the rural South. From the songs that Du Bois discussed, through religion and other cultural characteristics, the people were definitively nonurban and overwhelmingly southern. Moreover, any serious comprehensive study of the South would necessarily devote considerable attention to the relationship between whites and Blacks in the region. The latter were either the majority or nearly half of the populations of several states. One of every three southerners was Black. Simultaneously, as Jacob Riis wrote *The Battle with the Slums* (1902), he centered his focus on New York City and its horrifyingly decrepit tenements. A follow-up to his classic *How the Other Half Lives* (1890), the book provided a photographic inquiry into the insalubrious conditions of the poorest of the country's largest city and the effort to improve those conditions. In exploring the tenements in either book, especially the earlier one, Riis gave vivid detail of how various European ethnic groups, particularly those from eastern and southern Europe, struggled in crime-ridden, unsafe, diseased, and cramped spaces. Corruption, greed, filthy conditions—inside and outside of apartments—and crushing poverty marked the inhabitants' lives. Black people, as subjects in the exploration, were mostly absent. Similarly, studies of slums in Boston, Chicago, and other cities at that time cast no attention to the plight of those cities' Black residents. Although disinterest may have shaped some of this inattention, these cities—and their slums—were nearly all-white. In 1900,

Chicago and Boston were 97 and 98 percent white, respectively. African Americans were not much of a political, cultural, or economic force in northern or western cities.[1]

A generation later, the Great Migration helped transform the country and its demographics in important ways. In two stages, the first starting around 1915 until 1930, and again from 1940 to 1970, over 6 million African Americans (and even more whites) migrated from the South to the North and West. Pouring into cities and towns, African Americans sought employment, greater freedom, and a range of opportunities denied them in the South. The Great Migration fundamentally affected American cities in the twentieth century in substantive ways. The mass movement of millions of Black people from the rural South into cities like Chicago, New York, Detroit, Los Angeles, and Philadelphia was transformative. It was the largest peacetime migration in history. A massive corpus of scholarship from historians, political scientists, sociologists, and others has explored the ways in which African Americans established communities in cities during the Great Migration.

One of the most significant studies of African Americans in the city is St. Clair Drake and Horace R. Cayton's *Black Metropolis: A Study of Negro Life in a Northern City*, published in 1945. Sociologists from the University of Chicago, the authors offered a sweeping look at the diversity, challenges, successes, and agency of Black Chicagoans. Called a "foundational text in African American history, cultural studies, and urban sociology," the book offered a nuanced look at the Black community.[2] Far from being an undifferentiated mass acted upon by a wider, hostile white society, the book laid bare the complexities of class and ideological diversity among Black people. While detailing the institutional forces of discrimination in every facet of life in the city, from housing through employment, policing, and education, the authors, who were Black, also provided insight into the variegated social worlds of Black people. Most Black people were, as anticipated, working class and poor. They lived in cramped homes in neighborhoods with the highest population densities. Legally sanctioned housing discrimination prevented Black people from securing federally insured housing loans; and private efforts, including mob violence, threatened families who could, somehow, circumvent legal barriers. Yet, even under these conditions, a Black middle class and even upper class had formed. As a class of professionals, they belonged to exclusive clubs, lived in grand homes, owned businesses, and managed to forge a remarkable space of comfort amid a wider space of racism and hostility. This social ecology was replicated in every major Black community in the country. From Philadelphia to Cleveland to Los Angeles, African Americans were constricted—by law and custom—

in their political, residential, and economic spaces. Still, they forged diverse urban spaces with newspapers and financial, religious, and social institutions that were critical to the community and its advancement. For decades, the opportunities afforded Black people in these cities attracted migrants from underdeveloped, poor, and rural sectors of the South. In addition to fleeing poverty, Black people left areas bereft of basic civil and human rights. They left communities that lacked paved roads, running water, electricity, and public schools available to Black people. In many cities in the South they were barred from using public libraries or public parks or from gaining municipal employment. Black people were barred from every public high school in the state of Georgia when the Great Migration began. They were prevented from voting and serving on juries across the South. This massive movement forged a new world with new and incredible possibilities.

Because of the Great Migration, the city, generally speaking, had become an essential locus for profound cultural contributions to the country in literature, music, film, and other creative projects. Political movements, from Black nationalist groups like the Universal Negro Improvement Association and the Nation of Islam, to revolutionary organizations like the Black Panther Party, made indelible marks on radical politics and philosophy. From Motown through the Philadelphia sound, the funk bands in various Ohio cities, and New York City's hip-hop, cities were incubators to new African American cultural expressions that transformed music globally.

What has always been clear in the study of urban African Americans across the decades of the Great Migration is the degree to which the very Black community itself, even in its privileged components, was a consequence of racist constrictions. In part, federal, state, and local laws politically, socially, and economically shaped the communities of Black people in those cities. They were relegated to segregated residential areas and barred by laws and private policy from accessing employment, leisure, or education. Bank loans, municipal employment, and private sector white-collar jobs were almost totally closed to them—often by explicit law or policy. Even as the country emerged from World War II and entered a new prosperity, most Black people languished in poverty, hemmed into ghettos across the country in a way that European immigrants had never been. As sociologists Douglas S. Massey and Nancy A. Denton argue, "Middle-class and affluent African Americans were legally constricted to urban spaces in close proximity to deep poverty. Institutionalized racism formed . . . a distinct class gradient in the ghetto, with the poorest families being concentrated toward the center . . . and the middle and upper classes progressively increasing their share of the population as one moved from the core toward the periphery."[3]

Unlike Italians, Poles, European Jews, or Irish, who had languished in slums, Blacks were prevented by laws to move out of these segregated spaces. The new middle-class suburbs that flowered around Chicago, New York, and Philadelphia offered homes to white veterans with surnames from every corner of Europe. White exoduses transformed cities. From Los Angeles to Baltimore, brand-new suburbs were nearly exclusively white when Martin Luther King Jr. was assassinated, twenty-one years after Jackie Robinson's integration of baseball. When Black people were able to circumvent housing restrictions, racist mob violence proved a powerful barrier to open housing across the country. Consequently, the percentages of Black people in major cities rose exponentially as whites left.[4]

The result of these sweeping demographic changes was stark. A confluence of middle-class white flight, deindustrialization, falling tax bases, declining city services, federal housing policies, and discriminatory bank loans made cities that were once nearly all-white mostly of color by the end of the twentieth century.[5] The transformations of the cities were consequential in many ways. By the third decade of the twenty-first century, although none of the twenty largest cities was majority-Black, all but four (Indianapolis, Fort Worth, San Diego, and San Jose) had elected a Black mayor and sent hundreds of African Americans to Congress, state houses, school boards, and city councils since 1970. Black people have often been at parity or overrepresented in municipal jobs, which became one of the most effective routes to the middle class. From New York and Washington to Los Angeles, Portland, and Houston, scores of cities, large and small, have had Black chiefs of police. For most cities, this had been nearly unthinkable decades earlier. African Americans have been superintendents of school districts across the country and occupied every stratum of local, state, and federal government. Despite enduring higher poverty rates than whites, most Blacks have not been in poverty since the 1960s—in cities or elsewhere. Since the end of the Great Migration, Black poverty rates have fallen to the lowest rates in history, while graduation rates from high school, college, and postgraduate school have reached new records.[6]

Cities across the United States emerged as critical sites for Black advancement and uplift during the Great Migration and witnessed an impressive expansion of Black opportunities in the decades following its end. But, as discussed throughout this volume, progress has never been neat, predictable, or linear. Black control of the city, even in the best of circumstances, cannot completely ameliorate the long national history of deprivation, injustice, and intergenerational white wealth accumulation that has unfolded over centuries. Individuals, families, businesses, and other entities may achieve extraordinary success, but the city and what it can offer has inherent limitations on a macro scale. The Black middle class expanded considerably in the first two decades after the decline of the civil rights movement. Yet, by the late 1980s, a number of cities had become, in many estimations, increasingly dystopian landscapes of crime and deprivation and pockets of acute poverty. Notwithstanding this, the expanding class diversity in the African American community also provided an alternative Black experience in the city.

Cities were also spaces for the ascension of the Black middle class. In major cities, Black-elected officials were palpable examples of Black political power. Through new policies and practices, new leadership expanded Black participation in the public sector job market, from police officers and teachers to jobs in public transportation, parks, city management, and more. No city better demonstrates the power of Black influence over the political economy than Atlanta, where its first Black mayor, Maynard H. Jackson Jr., heralded aggressive affirmative action policies, opening opportunities for Black firms. At the time Jackson was elected, 99.5 percent of contracts went to white firms, comparable to rates in the city during slavery. But by his last year in office, the percentage of Black firms represented over a third of city contracts. The Atlanta Plan became the gold standard for cities nationwide.

It has become evident to any scholarly endeavor that any history of African Americans since the Great Migration has been largely a history of city dwellers. Over the last half century, Black people in the United States have produced a remarkable and indelible imprint on the social, cultural, and political arenas of America. Much of this has been realized in the context of urban-based people in the post–civil rights and Black Power eras. An explosion of African American artistic expression in the last generation has offered an unprecedented, nearly panoptic, look at Black experiences in the United States. In films, television, and literary fiction, the city is generally the creative backdrop. The American city has had an ineffaceable impact on the African American experience, and cities have been essentially shaped by those experiences as well. Popular and critically acclaimed television shows, from *The Jeffersons* (1975–85) and *The Cosby Show* (1984–92) through *The Wire* (2002–8), *Insecure* (2016–20), and *Atlanta* (2016–22), have centered and explored the varieties of Black life through refractions of class, gender, sexuality, policing, and more. In every way, the city has been an essential component of this artistic exploration. Moreover, the most widespread musical art in history—hip-hop—is unequivocally urban-centered. One cannot be a real fan of Jay-Z and not know from which part of New York City he hails. Similarly, since Grandmaster Flash and the Furious Five's "The Message" (1982), everyone from André 3000 to Kendrick Lamar and Nicki Minaj has detailed the provincial landscapes of their upbringing. The city has emerged as a ubiquitous trope in the poetic narratives of art.

In the 1980s and 1990s, academics who studied cities explored the economic downturns and challenges as a consequence of demographic shifts including white flight, middle-class Black flight, and the decline of the manufacturing economy. Historians, sociologists, political scientists, and other observers across the ideological spectrum identified the effects of job loss due to deindustrialization, declining tax bases, and the social, economic, and political isolation of concentrated Black poverty. Multiple studies have demonstrated the deleterious effects of this new inner city: food deserts, declining city services, decreased racial and class diversity, increases in crime, and, importantly, huge wealth gaps due to Black real estate values growing at significantly lower rates than those in white or integrated neighborhoods. Then, by the 1990s, cities across the country experienced a reversal of these forces: gentrification. And yet, many bemoaned the very reversal of the trends that had so alarmed them earlier.[7]

Gentrification

Despite the tendency to facilely conflate race and class in these discussions, gentrification can unfold intra-racially. It is defined as the influx of higher socioeconomic status (SES) residents into a neighborhood. Defined by class, not race, it does not require that low SES inhabitants be pushed out—even if it does occur sometimes or often.[8] In 1964, the term "gentrification" was coined by British researcher Ruth Glass exploring the influx of higher SES whites into lower SES white areas in British neighborhoods. Over the last twenty-five years, one of the most gentrified cities in Europe has been Berlin, where higher SES artists and others moved into previously lower SES areas in formerly Communist East Berlin.[9] Given very broad, generalized notions of SES, there is no definitive set of criteria to identify the process of gentrification. *Governing* magazine identifies increases in home values and in the number of residents with college degrees as more specific criteria for analysis. "To be eligible to gentrify, a tract's median household income and median home value needed to fall within the bottom 40th percentile of all tracts within a metro area [in 2000]. Tracts considered to have gentrified recorded increases in the top third percentile for both inflation-adjusted median home values and percentage of adults with bachelors' degrees."[10] Using these standards, gentrification has emerged in diverse ways across the country, with Black gentrifiers among the agents of these changes. One of the most studied spaces of gentrification has been the most famous Black community in the country, Harlem, in New York City.

In the first wave of the Great Migration, Harlem emerged as an icon of Black urbane cosmopolitanism—even though most Black Harlemites were poor and lived in slum conditions. It was the center of the New Negro Renaissance (1919–35), a hub of Black cultural, intellectual, and political explosion. The percentage of Harlemites who were Black jumped from 32.4 percent in 1920 to 70 percent in 1930. By 1950, Central Harlem was 98 percent Black. Between the 1960s and 1990, Harlem saw a remarkable decline as middle-class Black families took advantage of the eradication of racist housing laws and policies that constricted them into ghettos. This process is illustrated in the sharp drop in numbers of residents (mostly Black) from Central Harlem between 1950 and 1970 from 233,000 to 157,178 (95.4 percent of which was Black). Hundreds of thousands of African Americans across New York City moved from low-income areas in Harlem, the Bronx, and Brooklyn into middle-class swaths of Queens and farther into Long Island, from Uniondale and Roosevelt to Freeport. Many others poured into New Rochelle, Mount Vernon, White Plains, and New Jersey. The decline was sharp, as people left areas burdened by high crime, high poverty, slumlords, and arson-for-profit, leaving shells of abandoned structures. The 1970s, which promised unprecedented mobility (in every way) for African Americans, saw disinvestment in the putative capital of Black America, Harlem. In Harlem, real estate taxes had been so delinquent that New York City had taken title to nearly 70 percent of the private rental units in the area.[11] By the mid-1980s, the city auctioned Harlem real estate in efforts to widen access to local people. The city even repaired shells and other dilapidated properties before sale. Black churches and civic groups hoped to encourage investment and revitalization (especially from Black families) in the community. In 1990, Central Harlem's population dropped to 101,026—lower than at any point since the nineteenth century. The 1990 population was 87.5 percent Black, around the Black proportion in 1940.[12] Banks had been fiercely resistant to investing in the area, providing "a paltry $2 million of mortgage money into Central Harlem" in the early 1980s.[13] The following decade, however, witnessed a dramatic reversal of this decline.

Between 1990 and 2000, thousands of new, more affluent residents purchased theretofore abandoned apartments and dilapidated homes. By 1998, Upper Manhattan (largely Greater Harlem) received $686 million in mortgages, up from $163 million five years earlier.[14] The city's intervention helped turn around the decline. By the early 1990s, Black flight continued but had slowed, and investment increased as non–African Americans, primarily Latinx, Black immigrants, and whites, moved in. The demographic shifts were a consequence of various forces. Subsequent studies have found that the iconic Black community had attracted hundreds of thousands of new residents as gentrification swept the area, making it more appealing. Many of these newcomers have been Black. According to a 2005 study in *The Crisis*, Harlem, after more than a decade of gentrification, had the highest rate of Black homeownership in its history.[15] The turnaround of the area was palpable, even if it remained one of the Manhattan neighborhoods with the lowest average income and lowest average home value. One report found that "Victorian mansions have been gutted, and refitted with intricate wooden staircases and period chandeliers; black professionals, white gays, students and many others have followed the developers, desperate to find a place to live in [an expensive] borough."[16] Indeed, the concentration of economic, racial, social, and political isolation had been disrupted with new demographic diversity.

By 2010, the Latinx population in Central Harlem increased from 10 percent in 1990 to 23.6 percent, while the white population jumped from 1.5 percent in 1990 to 11 percent. The Black population, meanwhile, dropped to 58.6 percent.[17] City services, new restaurants, shops, and supermarkets opened in the area. Unemployment, poverty rates, and violent crime (which had been dropping nationally and in New York City) continued a steep decline in Harlem. Harlem's Thirty-Second Precinct reported that all categories of crime decreased by 71.4 percent between 1990 and 2021. Homicides saw the most dramatic drop, not only in Harlem but across the city. Whereas 2,245 people were murdered in New York City in 1990, the city—with over a million more people—saw only 292 homicides in 2017. Note that the percentage of people of color had increased to the highest in New York's history, while homicides were lower than at any point since at least 1928, when the city was over 95 percent white.[18]

Black professionals were part of the wave of new homeowners and entrepreneurs. One thirty-nine-year-old Yale-educated business owner even found inspiration in quoting Black nationalist Marcus Garvey to underscore the importance of his work and investment in the community: "I chose Harlem not just as a business opportunity, but also because winning within this market meant more to me as a black entrepreneur." A business-networking organization, Harlem Park to Park, formed in 2009 with eight of its nine original businesses Black-owned. Two years later, a full 80 percent of fifty businesses in the network were Black-owned. By 2015, the number of Black businesses increased to sixty-seven, while the percentage dropped to 63 percent, due to a faster increase of non-Black businesses.[19] By 2015, Harlem's gentrification, in many ways, appeared to be what many social scientists and civil rights activists had desired decades earlier: an iconic Black enclave with safer streets, more amenities, and class, racial,

By 2005, Harlem's black homeownership rates reached record highs. Gentrifiers, many of them Black, increased the area's population after decades of Black flight. (Photo by Momos, courtesy Creative Commons)

and ethnic diversity; growing Black business enterprises; and increasing Black homeownership and growing home values, which would address the yawning racial wealth gap. Yet, the dominant sentiment toward gentrification has generally proved to be hostile.

"Displacement" has been a common refrain from critics who see gentrification as a process to push out native residents. Researcher Neil Smith argues, "Gentrification, the buying up and rehabilitation of land and buildings, whether by families or developers, occupied or abandoned means a rising rent tide for all, leading inevitably to displacement next door, down the block, or two streets away." The data clearly show that Black people are leaving Harlem. Yet, the data also reveal surprising dynamics regarding population shifts. As discussed in this volume, across the country, in ungentrified areas in Chicago and Camden, Los Angeles and New York, hundreds of thousands of African Americans have taken part in a "reverse migration" south.[20] Scott M. Stringer, Manhattan borough president, argues that "it's a mistake to see this only as a story of racial change.... What's interesting is that many African-Americans are living in Harlem by choice, not necessity."[21] And while Black people across class are moving out of major cities in the North, Midwest, and West, Lance Freeman, professor of city and regional planning and sociology, details that poor people (regardless of race) are more itinerant than affluent families. Across multiple New York City lower-income areas, poor residents were *less likely to move* when their neighborhood gentrified than those who lived in neighborhoods of concentrated poverty that did not gentrify. His research found that when communities were deprived of class diversity, city services, shopping options, and grocery stores and were marked by high crime, residents were likely to relocate once their financial resources granted them the ability to find housing that was more amenable. By studying data on residential longevity in several gentrifying communities in New York City (Chelsea, Harlem, the Lower East Side, Morningside Heights, Fort Greene, Park Slope, and Williamsburg), Freeman and Frank Braconi found that low-income households were "19% less likely to move than poor households residing elsewhere" in areas that were not gentrifying. Kathe Newman and Elvin Wyly, two scholars who have been critical of gentrification, researched arguments around displacement and conceded that, "although displacement affects a very small minority of households, it cannot be dismissed as insignificant." The team found that in the city of millions of people, across scores of neighborhoods in five boroughs, up to an estimated 10,000 people may be displaced by gentrification annually. Though much lower than many critics anticipated, that amount, they insisted, "should not be ignored, even in a city of eight million."[22]

One of the many complexities of gentrification is the degree to which middle-class and upper-middle-class African Americans have been drivers of it. Each year, over 150,000 Black people earn bachelor's degrees, and several thousand more earn MBAs, JDs, MDs, and PhDs. When these Black professionals move into gentrifying communities, they evade the same suspicion directed at their white counterparts, even as they also help drive up prices of real estate and rents. From Petworth in Washington, DC, to Castleberry Hill, the West End, and Atlantic Station in Atlanta, higher SES Black people have largely avoided scrutiny or stigma as gentrifiers as they melt into the undifferentiated mass of Blackness. In a myopic race-only analysis, the class privileges of higher-income African Americans are obfuscated in most debates over gentrification. Freeman explains that, given the long history of white supremacy in the United States, a "cynicism" regarding white people and their actions has developed. White interlopers, therefore, are viewed differently from Black ones. Yet, the material effects are the same: higher rents, higher property values, more city services, and more resources.[23] In addition, as evidenced in the declining proportions of whites in cities, gentrification cannot be viewed in a context that ignores class among Black people or other people of color. Few examples illustrate this point better than the three most gentrified cities in the country: San Francisco, Denver, and Boston.

Interestingly, patterns of gentrification do not take the same form across the country. The majority-white communities of San Francisco and Denver have witnessed widespread gentrification since 1990. Over the past two decades, cities have become sites of greater diversity with influxes of Latinx, Asian, and white populations, as well as non–African American Black populations. In 1990, San Francisco's white population stood at 46.9 percent, while Denver's was 61.4 percent. By 2020, the proportions were 39.1 percent and 54.9 percent, respectively. In the same period, the Black population of San Francisco dropped from 10.7 percent to 5.1 percent, while the African American proportion witnessed a more modest decline in Denver, from 12.8 percent to 9.8 percent.[24] Note, however, that although the percentage of Black people declined in the highly gentrified Denver, the actual numbers of Black people *increased* by more than 10,000 over the same period. The city had expanded (and racially diversified) over thirty years. In contrast, San Francisco witnessed a net loss of more than 30,000 African Americans.

For years, gentrification has swept Boston, including the majority-white sections Charlestown, South Boston, and Jamaica Plain, as well as heavily Black Roxbury and the diverse South End. It has never been as simplistic as wealthy whites moving into a Black or Brown community and displacing the residents. In fact, while Boston has been significantly gentrified, its percentage of whites in the city *declined* from a 1950 high of 94.7 percent to a historic low of 44.7 in 2020. Boston, like most major cities east of the Mississippi River, peaked in population in 1950 before witnessing an exodus of whites and an influx of African Americans from the Great Migration. Still, by 1970, Boston remained one of the whitest large cities in the country, at around 80 percent white. Over the last half century, however, waves of immigrants from Asia, the Caribbean, and Latin America have diversified Beantown. The Black population in Boston has become significantly more heterogeneous since 1970, when the overwhelming number were US-born. Those born in Cape Verde or in the Dominican and other parts of the Caribbean, especially Haitian populations, make up over a third of what used to be historically African American areas like Roxbury. The rates of non–African American Black people are higher, when considering Black residents whose parents are foreign-born. While the Black population was around 25 percent in Roxbury in 1950, it peaked at 79 percent before declining to 46 percent in 2020. Like in other cities, people of color, no longer legally barred from living in white-majority areas, have fanned out across heretofore segregated sections.[25]

Desegregation had never been an easy process, but it was especially difficult in Boston. In the 1970s, in an effort to desegregate public schools, a federal judge ordered busing of Black and white students between extraordinarily segregated

Boston neighborhoods. The backlash was immediate and extreme. Racist mobs swept across the city. Packs of women, children, and men hurled bottles, rocks, and hateful epithets at Black children entering white neighborhoods on school buses. The Boston busing crisis captured national attention and unfolded most acutely in areas like Charlestown and South Boston. These white areas offered strident opposition to racial integration of any sort—including education and housing. The all-white Charlestown public housing project in Bunker Hill made national news when the first Black tenants moved there in 1984. The area was called "the poorest part of Charlestown: passionate, close-bound, sometimes violent, and white Irish Roman Catholic to the core."[26] As late as 1990, Charlestown remained 95 percent white. By 2020, a largely white-on-white gentrification of areas like Charlestown and South Boston transformed formerly working-class and poor white communities. In addition to lower rates of poverty, increased education levels, and home values, both communities have become more racially diverse. Each community contains between 20 and 25 percent people of color today.

As many Black, Asian, and Latinx professionals join white counterparts as gentrifiers, the wider landscape in the city reveals stark differences of wealth along racial lines. While whites earn more than Blacks in Boston (and nationally), per-capita incomes between whites and Blacks narrow when controlled for education and marital status. In 2010, data revealed that among white, Black, Asian, and Latinx married couples, whites had the highest median income, followed by Blacks and Asians, earning 69 percent and 57.5 percent of white incomes, respectively. Latinx married couples earned 55.1 percent of comparable white family incomes.[27] Yet, when wealth was measured (net worth of all assets against debt), a glaring difference laid bare significant chasms. A 2015 report from the Federal Reserve Bank of Boston found that the average net worth of white households in Boston was $247,000, while the median net worth for the heavily immigrant Black households and Latinx households was just $8.00 and $28.60 respectively.[28] A staggering wealth gap in Boston complicates how income and even neighborhood integration does not always reflect household wealth.

Across the country, as detailed in this volume, cities are rife with class, racial, and ideological diversity. Gentrification, as a process, embodies these tensions and nuances. Despite proclivities to evade class analysis for simple racial ones, the measurable differences in class are striking within the Black community, where higher SES Black people are healthier, are more likely to have two-parent households, own homes, graduate college, and live longer. They are also less likely to be arrested or be victims of violence and report less depression than their poorer counterparts. While this may seem obvious, too many conversations avoid the complexities of class when discussing gentrification, instead offering typically gross assumptions that not only are Black people poor, but Blackness and poverty are nearly inextricable. To ignore these factors when considering the "Black community" undermines essential questions about policy interventions, as it would when viewing class more broadly. Yet even as some African Americans have been gentrifying cities, many more have moved away from them.

Suburbanization

Despite African Americans' profound ties to cities, there have been accelerated movements to suburbs over the last sixty years. In 1960, only 5 percent of African Americans lived in the suburbs. Due to federal housing laws that prevented guaranteed loans that would disrupt "the racial integrity" of the neighborhoods, racial mob violence, and other methods, suburbs were virtually all-white. Moreover, because of centuries of codified forms of racial oppression, the suburbs were more affluent than the more racially diverse cities. In 1970, after two decades of massive white flight from cities, the average household income in American cities was 80 percent of suburban counterparts' income. A decade later, that percentage dropped to only 74 percent of suburban households' income. The gap was much larger in some cities than in others. Baltimore's median household earned just 58 percent of what its suburban households earned.[29]

The 1968 Fair Housing Act, which outlawed housing discrimination, was consequential in reshaping Black communities. Often heralded as the last major legal achievement of the modern civil rights movement, the legislation helped open new housing opportunities to Americans of all races. It still had limits in scope. Discrimination in mortgage lending remained rampant. Six years later, the Equal Credit Opportunity Act made racial discrimination in mortgage lending illegal. Finally, in 1977 the Community Reinvestment Act outlawed redlining—a practice where banks often used a red marker to identify neighborhoods of color as areas to avoid investment. The movement of Black people to theretofore restricted white suburbia accelerated movement out of cities with the dismantling of racist housing laws, practices, and policies. In the first half of the 1970s, the number of African Americans living in suburbs increased by 19.5 percent. By 1980, nearly a quarter of Black people lived in suburbs, often those that immediately bordered cities.[30]

Since the last decades of the twentieth century and the first three decades of the twenty-first century, Black movement has continued to demonstrate the demographic mutability of the city with steep Black population declines. The largest decreases in the Black population between 2000 and 2020 occurred in

Detroit, Chicago, New York, Los Angeles, and Washington, DC. These declines, however, are currently slowing in comparison to the prior decade. Southern cities, such as Atlanta, Dallas, and Houston, increased the numbers of Black residents, 2000–2020, even as their proportions in each city declined because non-Black populations increased at higher raw numbers. For many larger cities, however, there were declines in both numbers and percentages of Black populations, as many moved to the suburbs.

In 2023, 40 percent of African Americans lived in the suburbs, as they left large and small cities alike. Some cities have seen much steeper exoduses than others. Over a quarter of Black Chicagoans have left that city since 2000. Many have escaped areas of high crime and poverty, like Englewood and Fuller Park, for safer communities in the suburbs or other parts of Chicago. Meanwhile, affluent Black Chicagoans have moved to the south and western suburbs, establishing thriving majority-Black communities, like Flossmoor and Matteson, with average family incomes of $119,836 and $111,754, respectively. One area, Olympia Fields, has a Black homeownership rate of 98 percent, far exceeding most of the wealthiest white communities anywhere. In fact, it ranks in the top 5 percent of highest average household incomes in the country.[31] Many others across Chicagoland have moved to the South in the reverse migration. In patterns that are similar to the Great Migration, people have followed employment opportunities in a dynamic economy. The South, with lower costs of living, has drawn Black migrants, but its veritable capital, Atlanta, has outpaced every city in the nation in attracting Black newcomers. While more Black people have migrated to the Atlanta area than to any other city over the last thirty years, most have settled in its suburbs, where over seven times as many Black people reside compared with the number in the actual city of Atlanta. African Americans are the majority, or plurality, in surrounding counties and dozens of towns near Atlanta. Despite rhetoric that Black people have been "pushed out" and are too poor to live in central cities, the average household incomes of suburban Blacks continue to exceed those in the cities—in many cases, significantly so.

Inasmuch as manufacturing jobs attracted people to Chicago, Gary, Detroit, and other cities generations ago, the high-tech economy has been a partial attraction for highly educated Black migrants to Atlanta's suburbs, where more African Americans live than in any other metro area other than New York City's. In addition to robust technological job growth, the metro area ranks number six among all metropolises for technology degrees awarded and is second only to New York City in digital supply chain rankings.[32] The rate of Black college degree holders is higher in the Atlanta metro area than in every metropolis but the Washington, DC, area. Black people are agents of their fates, not simply acted upon by putatively omnipotent forces of racism. They have sought better homes, safer communities, and stronger schools as they have achieved greater means to access them. This process has played out across the country. Few areas demonstrate this point more than the nation's capital.

In 1970, scores of thousands of Black people departed Washington, DC, to Prince George's County, east of the District. Middle-class Black families transformed the county, more than tripling the Black proportion in a generation. By the late 1990s, the previously white county had become the richest majority-Black county in the United States. The median income of $86,000 is over 25 percent higher than the national median income. By 2023, Charles County, Maryland, adjacent to Prince George's County, became majority-Black. It is even more affluent, with a median household income of $106,000, making this Washington suburb the new most affluent majority-Black county in the country.[33] Far from simply being "too poor" to live in the District, many Black people, at a historic moment with the lowest poverty rates on record, have chosen to relocate rather than be forced to do so. Again, Black agency has revealed itself in these demographic shifts.[34] This does not mean, of course, that poverty no longer disproportionately burdens the Black community in the city or elsewhere. As discussed throughout the volume, Black movement and the experiences in the city are significantly shaped by class, as access to capital is generally determined by where one chooses to live, and freedom to move anywhere has expanded since 1970.

The Black communities in the country's second-largest city, Los Angeles, have been substantially transformed since the Great Migration. My childhood neighborhood, formerly named South Central Los Angeles (renamed South Los Angeles in 2003), was one of the largest Black communities in the country. It has not been majority-Black for over twenty years. For decades, there were more people in South Central than in most cities, including the populations of Atlanta, Boston, Cleveland, and New Orleans.[35] By the early 1990s, increasing waves of Black Angelenos with means relocated to newer homes in desert communities such as Palmdale, Lancaster, and Victorville. Others settled in neighborhoods in other parts of the city or left the state altogether, often to southern states, in pursuit of safer areas, more affordability, and better employment opportunities. While I lived in eight different neighborhoods in Compton and Los Angeles as a child, I lived the longest in South Park, located in South Central. It was over 80 percent Black in the 1970s and 1980s. It is now less than 20 percent Black. The community, which is nearly 80 percent Latinx, has an average household income of $29,518, making it one of the poorest sections of the city. Watts, once synonymous with Black LA, is now only 37 percent Black, slightly lower than Compton's 39 percent. Although the areas have transitioned racially, they remain low-income, with regionally low average real estate values.[36]

A look at Black LA and suburban Washington, DC, forces one to resist tendencies to lazily conflate race and class, where Black communities are an undifferentiated mass of poor and working-class people. Today, of the city of 272 communities in Los Angeles County, only 11 are majority-Black.[37] View Park–Windsor Hills, which is 86.5 percent Black, is the Blackest neighborhood in the largest county in the United States. Its average home is worth around $1.2 million, and average household income is over $100,000. Nearly 60 percent of adults have at least a college degree—higher than the national averages for all racial groups.[38] An adjacent community, Ladera Heights, is nearly 70 percent Black and has an average household income of $139,415, higher than any race's local or national average. Homes in the hilly community often enjoy stunning views of the LA basin and sight lines of the Hollywood sign; many have pools and tennis courts. Some are more modest on small plots of yardage. The average Ladera Heights home is valued at $1.6 million.[39] Among the eleven communities that are majority-Black in LA, all but three have average incomes that are either high or average for the city.[40] While many have left the city, the Black exodus from LA has been complicated by class in the most fascinating ways.

For some, the Black movement from LA may appear to echo the pattern of middle-class whites who left cities in the 1960s for suburbs. Unlike the actions of white residents generations earlier, however, there were no systemic efforts to prevent racial newcomers from moving in. Redlining, restrictive covenants, legal barriers, and mob violence were absent from these demographic transitions. Instead, the movement evinces the increased mobility afforded Black people following the Fair Housing Act. Since the Great Migration and the removal of laws constricting Black housing opportunities, African Americans with the most resources stayed in Los Angeles's more affluent, historically Black communities. When incomes increased, Black families tended to leave the poorest Black sections as immigrants, mostly from Mexico and Central America, moved in.

The presence of these wealthy Black communities suggests that Black people who can afford to live anywhere are often inclined to live in majority-Black communities—in the city or in the suburbs. They, like most people, prefer safe communities with resources and financial security. Achieving this in an overwhelmingly Black space has been appealing for many who could afford it. These patterns are not always replicated across the country, but movement away from high-poverty centers is a common pattern for any ethnic or racial group. Finally, the socioeconomic conditions for African Americans in Los Angeles have been

In addition to expansive vistas of downtown Los Angeles, Ladera Heights, Baldwin Hills, Windsor Hills, and View Park have the highest concentrations of Black residents in Los Angeles area neighborhoods They are also some of the most affluent neighborhoods in the city. Meanwhile, older and poorer areas, such as Compton, Watts, and Historic South Central, have not been majority Black for more than a generation. (Photo by Alek Leckszas, courtesy Creative Commons)

nuanced by significant class diversity and challenging homeownership options. For those who could purchase homes in upscale communities like View Park–Windsor Hills and Ladera Heights, the surge in property value has been financially gratifying. For new homeowners, however, the chasm between average incomes and average home price is gaping and prohibitive.

Rust Belt cities as well as others like LA that once attracted scores of thousands of African American migrants each year have seen their Black populations decline after deindustrialization. The departure of Black citizens from high-poverty, high-crime areas with declining resources and services repeats the pattern of exodus from the South generations earlier. In many ways, the same drivers that caused the Great Migration a century earlier have inspired movement today. Yet in these pursuits, some, such as *New York Times* journalist Charles Blow, have argued that the reverse migration to the South is an important stage in securing new Black political power. Blow, one of the hundreds of thousands of Black migrants to Atlanta, insists that, with voting power that did not exist decades earlier, African Americans can transform the political landscape in several southern states, should they either become the majority or near majority.[41] Ultimately, people have sought for themselves and their families safer communities and greater economic—and political—opportunities. They have been drawn to opportunities, proving that communities are rarely static sites but dynamic spaces that, across generations, adapt to changing social, political, and economic forces.

Moving to the South or living in majority-Black cities is no nostrum for some of the same problems that have burdened people in the North and West. The complexities of policing, power, and government are underscored when exploring cases of police abuse against Black citizens in cities with either very diverse or even mostly Black police departments. In January 2023, a group of five Black Memphis police officers beat an unarmed Black motorist, twenty-nine-year-old Tyre Nichols, so savagely that he died of his wounds days later. In a majority-Black city, with a Black chief of police, the killing was a sobering reminder that Black police cannot guarantee protections against abuse of Black people. The swift firing, arrest, and murder charges against the officers, however, reflected a departure from similar abuses in the past. Few could imagine an all-white Memphis municipal structure arresting white officers for a comparable offense in the 1950s. In many cases, as in Los Angeles and New York, twenty-first-century police departments have become majority–of color by 2020. Not only are charges of police brutality significantly lower than they were decades earlier, but in these two cities, homicide rates have plummeted by over 80 percent since 1990, while other violent crimes have precipitously decreased as well.

· · · · · · · ·

What do these continued movements augur for the sense of a Black community as an ethnic formation or spatial one shaped by race? In what ways has the suburbanization of large numbers of African Americans affected the development of those spaces? As cities emerged as sites of Black political power in the 1970s, the dispersion of the Black population suggests new political alliances in an increasingly multicultural landscape. What is this significance? This volume explores these questions and others. It investigates the degree to which urban centers across the United States have been transformed since the Great Migration. Scores of books and journal articles and several documentaries have given attention to the transformative effect of the Great Migration. Interestingly, no historical volume has focused on the transformation of cities since that migration has ended. Since the early 1970s, those cities witnessed transformative events that indelibly affected their political, cultural, economic, and social landscapes.

Municipal power in the form of mayors, city councils, and heads of school systems and public safety came under the control of African American leaders. And even as a Black middle class became increasingly visible and significant in the machinations of power and governance, a widening chasm between them and the Black poor has drawn attention to the limitations of Black municipal power.

These chapters explore various facets of urban Black history since 1970. Movements into cities and then suburbs, as well as the reverse migration into southern cities, are points of investigation here. In other studies, historians have analyzed the rise of racial and ethnic diversity within urban centers, which inherently disrupted the largely binary racial politics in most cities before 1970. The rise of mass incarceration and the "War on Drugs" affected Black life in cities as much as deindustrialization, suburbanization, and gentrification did. This book assembles historians who review and interrogate a half century of history that has yet to be sufficiently captured in historical scholarship. Though sociologists and political scientists have studied various facets of the city (and American Americans in them) over the last fifty years, an investigation through the critical lens and disciplinary approach of historians has not been realized until now.

Part 1 looks at the rise of Black municipal power in the early years of the post-1970 era. Tom Adam Davies and I explore the significance of Black mayors and other city administrators, as well as the public policies and political economies that followed. The rise of Black elected officials centers this section, highlighting—as do most of these chapters—the extent to which political power has affected the quality of life, access to resources, and more in cities.

Part 2 surveys the role of popular culture and social space. It investigates the development of Black social institutions and sites of leisure and cultural production. Maurice J. Hobson looks at the discursive world of Atlanta hip-hop and the extent to which artists have explored science fiction tropes in their music. Scot Brown details the emergence of funk music in Ohio cities, with special focus on Dayton.

Part 3 examines suburbanization of African Americans in the last two decades. Millions of Black people have left cities for nearby suburbs, as aforementioned. Many others have moved from cities in the North and West for those in the South. Additionally, immigrants from Africa and the Caribbean have diversified the Black communities in many cities. What were once ethnically homogeneous groups with generations of Black families in the United States, many communities—such as Hartford and New York City—have swaths of Black populations that do not have more than two generations in the country. Brian Purnell and Fiona Vernal explore these processes in this section. In terms of demographic shifts, few have been more palpable than the increased populations of Latinx people in the United States. During the Great Migration, national conversations on race were largely fixated on a binary of Black and white. It was not until 1970 that there was a census category for Hispanic or Latino populations. Over a half century later, Latinx populations (some of which include Afro-Latinx people) have surpassed African Americans to become the largest community of color in the United States. Relations between African Americans and Latinx play out differently in different cities, but Tatiana Cruz excavates some of that history from Boston.

Part 4 considers the grassroots organizations, criminal justice system, and policing that shape cities. Histories of police brutality against African Americans in the decades leading up to the 1970s centered a nearly myopic focus on the racism endemic in a system burdened by a nearly all-white power structure of police, city officials, and broader political power. As Shannon King, LaShawn Harris, Melanie D. Newport, and J. T. Roane, detail, diverse policing, a diverse political class, and a diverse judicial system do not guarantee equity and justice. These chapters all draw connections to the daunting forces of the carceral state and its reach through policing, trials, sentencing, and more.

Part 5 centers its focus on three cities in flux, giving readers a glimpse into contrasts of a wide variety. Los Angeles, which Stefan M. Bradley explores, is the nation's second-largest city, with a county with more Black people than all but one US county (Cook County). Chanelle Rose and Benjamin H. Saracco examine Camden, New Jersey, a small industrial city across the country from the glow of Hollywood. In the generation since the end of the Great Migration, no municipal area has witnessed more Black migrants than Atlanta, which I explore in the last chapter. Its transformation has consequences on the national landscape in a range of ways. African Americans have forged essential institutions and created a significant political legacy to meet challenges in all three cities, but still, despite extraordinary achievements in various spaces, the future remains uncertain, except that the movement of Black people—like any people—will continue to be dynamic, transformative to the people and the environments that they call home.

Notes

1. See *1890 to 1960 Historical Statistics of the United States, Volume 1*, 22–23, accessed October 8, 2024, www.census.gov/library/publications/1975/compendia/hist_stats_colonial-1970.html; US Bureau of the Census, *Statistical Abstract of the United States: 1970* (Washington, DC: Government Printing Office, 1973), 27; US Bureau of the Census, *Statistical Abstract of the United States: 1980* (Washington, DC: Government Printing Office, 1985), 31; US Bureau of the Census, *Statistical Abstract of the United States: 1990* (Washington, DC: Government Printing Office, 1995), 31.

2. David A. Spatz, "Drake, St. Clair," in *Encyclopedia of African American History (1896-Present)*, ed. Paul Finkelman, vol. 2 (New York: Oxford University Press, 2009), 90.
3. Douglas S. Massey and Nancy A. Denton, *American Apartheid: Segregation and the Making of the Underclass* (Cambridge, MA: Harvard University Press, 1993), 39.
4. Richard Rothstein, *The Color of Law: A Forgotten History of How Our Government Segregated America* (New York : Liveright Publishing Corporation, 2017) is an outstanding history of the process of unfettered white access to the suburbs, especially through the GI Bill. As the author explains, prior to the GI Bill (passed in 1944), local and state laws prevented Black homeowners from moving into white areas in every section of the country. In other cases, mob violence—including the use of bombs and firearms—against new homeowners, from New Jersey to Michigan, Illinois, and California, made national news. Rothstein's remarkable book is part of a broader body of scholarship that includes Ira Katznelson, *When Affirmative Action Was White: An Untold History of Racial Inequality in Twentieth-Century America* (New York: W. W. Norton, 2005); and Keeanga-Yamahtta Taylor, *Race for Profit: How Banks and the Real Estate Industry Undermined Black Homeownership* (Chapel Hill: University of North Carolina Press, 2019). In some cases, wealthy African Americans were able to purchase homes without bank loans yet were confronted with homeowner groups that fought the purchase.
5. There is a well-documented history of this process, particularly from sociologists and political scientists. See William J. Wilson, *When Work Disappears: The World of the New Urban Poor* (New York: Vintage, 1997); William J. Wilson, *The Truly Disadvantaged: The Inner City, the Underclass, and Public Policy* (Chicago: University of Chicago Press, 1990); Massey and Denton, *American Apartheid*; Thomas J. Sugrue, *The Origins of the Urban Crisis: Race and Inequality in Postwar Detroit* (Princeton: Princeton University Press, 1996); Robert O. Self, *American Babylon: Race and the Struggle for Postwar Oakland* (Princeton: Princeton University Press, 2005); Donna Jean Murch, *Living for the City: Migration, Education, and the Rise of the Black Panther Party in Oakland, California* (Chapel Hill: University of North Carolina Press, 2010); N. D. B. Connolly, *A World More Concrete: Real Estate and the Remaking of Jim Crow South Florida* (Chicago: University of Chicago Press, 2016); Paige Glotzer, *How the Suburbs Were Segregated: Developers and the Business of Exclusionary Housing, 1890–1960* (New York: Columbia University Press, 2020); and Gene Slater, *Freedom to Discriminate: How Realtors Conspired to Segregate Housing and Divide America* (Berkeley: Heydey Books, 2021).
6. John Creamer, "Inequalities Persist Despite Decline in Poverty for All Major Race and Hispanic Origin Groups," US Census Bureau, September 15, 2020, www.census.gov/library/stories/2020/09/poverty-rates-for-blacks-and-hispanics-reached-historic-lows-in-2019.html. This census report finds that the Black poverty rate in 2020 is the lowest on record. This measurement does not take into account cash and in-kind benefits, such as Medicaid, Medicare, and public housing, which did not exist in measuring poverty many decades earlier. Jennifer Cheeseman Day, "88% of Blacks Have a High School Diploma, 26% a Bachelor's Degree," US Census Bureau, June 10, 2020, www.census.gov/library/stories/2020/06/black-high-school-attainment-nearly-on-par-with-national-average.html.
7. Mary Pattillo, *Black on the Block: The Politics of Race and Class in the City* (Chicago:

University of Chicago Press, 2008); William J. Wilson, *The Declining Significance of Race: Blacks and Changing American Institutions* (Chicago: University of Chicago Press, 1978); Wilson, *Truly Disadvantaged*; Wilson, *When Work Disappears*; Elijah Anderson, *Streetwise: Race, Class, and Change in an Urban Community* (Chicago: University of Chicago Press, 1992); Sugrue, *Origins of the Urban Crisis*. For information on how racial wealth gaps are accelerated by vastly different home values between Black and white neighborhoods, see "Wealth Inequality and the Racial Wealth Gap," Federal Reserve, October 22, 2021, www.federalreserve.gov/econres/notes/feds-notes/wealth-inequality-and-the-racial-wealth-gap-20211022.html.

8. The Centers for Disease Control and Prevention's study *Health Effects of Gentrification* defines "gentrification" as "the transformation of neighborhoods from low value to high value. This change has the potential to cause displacement of longtime residents and businesses ... when long-time or original neighborhood residents move from a gentrified area because of higher rents, mortgages, and property taxes." "Health Effects of Gentrification," Centers for Disease Control, March 24, 2015, http://medbox.iiab.me/modules/en-cdc/www.cdc.gov/healthyplaces/healthtopics/gentrification.htm.

9. According to Rowland Atkinson and Gary Bridge, Ruth Glass coined the term in her 1964 book, *London: Aspects of Change*. See Rowland Atkinson and Gary Bridge, introduction to *Gentrification in a Global Context*, ed. Rowland Atkinson and Gary Bridge (London: Routledge, 2005), 4; Jonathan Rock Rokem, "In Berlin, Hyper-Gentrification Has Proved Just How Fast Conflict-Torn Cities Can Change," *The Conversation*, November 11, 2019; and Noe Padilla, "Berlin: A City Plagued by Gentrification," *Medium*, July 29, 2019.

10. *Governing* magazine quoted in Tom Acitelli, "Boston Gentrification since '00: Some Parts More Than Others," Curbed Boston, February 1, 2016, https://boston.curbed.com/2016/2/1/10871802/boston-gentrification.

11. "The Evolution of New York City's Black Neighborhoods," Métropolitiques, May 9, 2017, https://metropolitics.org/The-Evolution-of-New-York-City-s-Black-Neighborhoods.html.

12. "Harlem's Shifting Population," *Gotham Magazine*, September 2, 2008, www.gothamgazette.com/demographics/4077-harlems-shifting-population. See also *Central Harlem*, NYC Landmarks Preservation Commission, May 29, 2018, http://s-media.nyc.gov/agencies/lpc/lp/2607.pdf.

13. Neill Smith, "Harlem the New Frontier?," First of the Month, April 1, 2001, www.firstofthemonth.org/harlem-the-new-frontier-2/.

14. Central Harlem, the name of Harlem proper, is roughly bounded by the Hudson River on the west, the Harlem River and 155th Street on the north, Fifth Avenue on the east, and Central Park North on the south. Greater Harlem extends west and north to 155th Street and east to the East River and includes many other neighborhoods, such as East Harlem and West Harlem. Greater Harlem has always had a lower Black population than Central Harlem. See K. Hinterland et al., "Manhattan Community District 10: Central Harlem," Community Health Profiles 2018, 10, Official Website of the City of New York, accessed October 2, 2024, www.nyc.gov/assets/doh/downloads/pdf/data/2018chp-mn10.pdf.

15. Tatsha Robertson, "Harlem on the Rise," *The Crisis*, May/June 2005, 21–24.

16. "Harlem Lost 10K Black Residents, Gained 18K Whites Decade," Patch: Harlem, NY, August 17, 2021, https://patch.com/new-york/harlem/harlem-lost-10k-black-residents-gained-18k-whites-decade; Smith, "Harlem the New Frontier?." See also "Urban Gentrification Beats Alternative of Deterioration," Pacific Research, March 23, 2023, www.pacificresearch.org/urban-gentrification-beats-alternative-of-deterioration/.
17. "Neighborhood Indicators," Central Harlem, MN10, NYU Furman Center, last updated May 21, 2024, https://furmancenter.org/neighborhoods/view/central-harlem.
18. "Overall Crime in New York City Reaches Record Low in 2020," NYPD website, January 6, 2021, www.nyc.gov/site/nypd/news/p0106a/overall-crime-new-york-city-reaches-record-low-2020. The homicides increased to 319 in 2019, still a significantly lower rate than in 1928. "Fewest Annual Murders and Shooting Incidents Ever Recorded in the Modern Era," NYPD press release, January 5, 2018, Government Publications Portal, https://a860-gpp.nyc.gov/concern/nyc_government_publications/05741v36b?locale=en.
19. "What Will Happen When Harlem Becomes White?," *The Guardian*, May 13, 2015, www.theguardian.com/us-news/2015/may/13/harlem-gentrification-new-york-race-black-white.
20. "Still Looking for a Black Mecca: The New Great Migration," *Washington Post*, January 14, 2022; "No Longer Majority Black, Harlem Is in Transition," *New York Times*, January 5, 2010, www.nytimes.com/2010/01/06/nyregion/06harlem.html.
21. "No Longer Majority Black, Harlem Is in Transition."
22. "Is Gentrification Really a Problem?," *New Yorker*, July 11, 2016, www.newyorker.com/magazine/2016/07/11/is-gentrification-really-a-problem; see also Lance Freeman, Tyler Haupert, Jackely Hwang, and Iris Zhang, "Where Do They Go? The Destinations of Residents Moving from Gentrifying Neighborhoods," *Urban Affairs Review* 60, no. 1 (2024): 304–48, https://journals.sagepub.com/doi/10.1177/10780874231169921.
23. Lance Freeman, *There Goes the 'Hood: Views of Gentrification from the Ground Up* (Philadelphia: Temple University Press, 2006), 160–61.
24. "Denver city, Colorado," State and County QuickFacts, US Census Bureau, October 2, 2024, www.census.gov/quickfacts/fact/table/denvercitycolorado,atlantacitygeorgia/PST120223.
25. "Boston, MA," Data USA, accessed October 2, 2024, https://datausa.io/profile/geo/boston-ma/; "Massachusetts—Race and Hispanic Origin for Selected Large Cities and Other Places: Earliest Census to 1990" (table), US Census Bureau, archived from the original on August 12, 2012, https://mcdc.missouri.edu/population-estimates/historical/POP-twps0076.pdf; US Census Bureau, 1950–2000 Decennial Censuses, 2006–10 and 2011–15 American Community Surveys, Boston Planning and Development Agency Research Division Analysis, www.boston.gov/sites/default/files/embed/file/2018-06/boston-by-the-numbers-population-past-and-future_roxbury_presentation.pdf; "Race and Ethnicity in South Boston, Boston, Massachusetts (Neighborhood)," Statistical Atlas, October 2, 2024, https://statisticalatlas.com/neighborhood/Massachusetts/Boston/South-Boston/Race-and-Ethnicity; "Boston Gentrification Since '00: Some Parts More Than Others," Boston Curbed, February 1, 2016, https://boston.curbed.com/2016/2/1/10871802/boston-gentrification.

26. "Boston Housing Project Is Peacefully Integrated," *New York Times*, March 18, 1984.
27. James Jennings, "The State of Black Boston," Tufts University, 2010, https://sites.tufts.edu/jamesjennings/files/2018/06/reportsStateOfBlackBoston2010.pdf.
28. Zebulon Miletsky and Tomas Gonzalez, "How Gentrification and Displacement Are Remaking Boston," *Black Perspectives*, November 28, 2017. See also Ana Patricia Muñoz et al., *Color of Wealth in Boston*, Federal Reserve Bank of Boston, March 25, 2015, www.bostonfed.org/publications/one-time-pubs/color-of-wealth.aspx.
29. John Herbers, "Census Data Reveal 70's Legacy Poorer and Rich Suburbs," *New York Times*, February 27, 1983, www.nytimes.com/1983/02/27/us/census-data-reveal-70-s-legacy-poorer-cities-and-richer-suburbs.html.
30. John R. Logan and Mark Schneider, "Racial Segregation and Racial Change in American Suburbs, 1970-1980," *American Journal of Sociology* 89, no. 4 (1984): 874–88, www.jstor.org/stable/2779255; Susanna McBee, "Area Led U.S. in '70s Increase of Blacks in Suburbs," *Washington Post*, April 16, 1978; Douglas S. Massey and Jonathan Tannen, "Suburbanization and Segregation in the United States: 1970–2010," *Ethnic and Racial Studies* 41, no. 9 (2017): 1594–1611, doi:10.1080/01419870.2017.1312010; Quinton MacDonald, "A Brief History of African American Suburbanization," Black Past, March 10, 2022, www.blackpast.org/african-american-history/concepts-african-american-history/a-brief-history-of-african-american-suburbanization/.
31. "Where Black Home Ownership Is the Norm," *Stateline*, August 15, 2018, https://stateline.org/2018/08/15/where-black-homeownership-is-the-norm/; "Olympia Fields village, Illinois," US Census Bureau, accessed October 2, 2024, https://data.census.gov/profile/Olympia_Fields_village,_Illinois?g=160XX00US1755938; "Hispanic or Latino, and Not Hispanic or Latino by Race," US Census Bureau, accessed October 2, 2024, https://data.census.gov/cedsci/table?q=p2&g=1600000US1726571&tid=DECENNIALPL2020.P2; "Chicago, IL," Data USA, accessed October 2, 2024, https://datausa.io/profile/geo/chicago-il.
32. "New Deloitte Report Establishes Metro Atlanta Number Two City for Digital Supply Chain," PR Newswire, September 25, 2017, www.prnewswire.com/news-releases/new-deloitte-report-establishes-metro-atlanta-number-two-city-for-digital-supply-chain-300524983.html.
33. Andrew Van Dam, "Is Prince George's Still the Richest Majority-Black County in America?," *Washington Post*, June 29, 2022, www.washingtonpost.com/business/2022/06/29/dept-of-data-prince-georges-richest-black-county/.
34. Em Shrider, "Poverty Rate for the Black Population Fell below Pre-pandemic Levels," US Census Bureau, September 12, 2023, www.census.gov/library/stories/2023/09/black-poverty-rate.html.
35. Like many cities, boundaries of communities within a city are sometimes nebulous and imprecise. The *Los Angeles Times*' Mapping L.A. project defines South LA as "51.08 square miles divided into 28 neighborhoods." Its 2000 population, according to the US Census, was 749,453, larger than all but thirteen cities in the United States. "Historic South Central" is a smaller community inside South Central measured at 2.5 square miles; while another, including Watts, is 8.6 square miles. Yet, some journalists have measured the area as 40 square miles. I have used the measurement included in the US Census. See "South L.A.," Mapping L.A., accessed October 2, 2024, https://maps.latimes.com/neighborhoods/region/south-la/; and Mike Sonksen, "The

History of South Central Los Angeles and Its Struggle with Gentrification," PBS SoCal, September 13, 2017, www.pbssocal.org/shows/city-rising/the-history-of-south-central-los-angeles-and-its-struggle-with-gentrification.

36. In the early 1990s, it was found that the Black populations had been declining in poorer parts of South Central, while immigrants from Mexico and Central America were moving into those areas. Simultaneously, middle-class, historically white Inglewood, a suburb adjacent to South Central, saw a sharp drop of its white population and a commensurate increase of Black families. The community generally grew more affluent with Black people, with poverty rates dropping with Black influx. Homeownership and education levels increased, as the community transitioned into majority-Black—classic metrics used for gentrification, as noted earlier in this introduction. In 1990, while the recession-era poverty rate of 6.3 percent was higher than it had been in 1960, it was nearly half the national poverty rate of 12.8 percent, as well as lower than the national white poverty rate. See "After the Riots: Census Reveals a City of Displacement," *New York Times*, May 15, 1992. See also "View Park–Windsor Hills CDP, California; Compton city, California; Ladera Heights CDP, California," QuickFacts, US Census Bureau, accessed August 3, 2023, www.census.gov/quickfacts/fact/table/viewparkwindsorhillscdpcalifornia,comptoncitycalifornia/PST045223.

37. These communities include everything from unincorporated areas, districts in the City of Los Angeles, and independent municipalities. *LA Times*, accessed March 6, 2023, https://maps.latimes.com/about/index.html https://maps.latimes.corn/about/index.html.

38. "View Park–Windsor Hills CDP, California"; see also Beatrice Maina, "The 8 Best Affluent Black Neighborhoods in America," Spotcovery, June 26, 2023, https://spotcovery.com/the-best-affluent-black-neighborhoods-in-america.

39. The average household income in Ladera Heights was higher than in Beverly Hills ($117,925 vs. $96,312) and comparable to that in Brentwood ($112,927) in 2008 dollars (or $171,887, $140,384 and $164,602, respectively adjusted for inflation). Both communities have since surpassed Ladera Heights nearly a decade later. See "Ladera Heights," Mapping L.A., accessed October 2, 2024, https://maps.latimes.com/neighborhoods/neighborhood/ladera-heights/index.html; "Beverly Hills," Mapping L.A., accessed October 2, 2024, https://maps.latimes.com/neighborhoods/neighborhood/beverly-hills/index.html; "Ladera Heights, California Population 2024," World Population Review, accessed October 2, 2024, https://worldpopulationreview.com/us-cities/ladera-heights-ca-population; "View Park–Windsor Hills, CA," Livability, accessed October 2, 2024, https://livability.com/ca/view-park-windsor-hills/; and "Ladera Heights, CA Housing Market," Zillow, accessed August 1, 2023, www.zillow.com/home-values/116042/ladera-heights-ca/.

40. "Black," Mapping L.A., accessed October 2, 2024, https://maps.latimes.com/neighborhoods/ethnicity/black/neighborhood/list/index.html.

41. "Returning to the South: What Can 'Reverse Migration' Do for Black Americans?," *The Guardian*, November 27, 2023, www.theguardian.com/film/2023/nov/27/south-to-black-power-hbo-documentary-charles-blow.

PART I

TOM ADAM DAVIES

A Piece of the Action

Black Mayors, the Black Business Class, and Black Progress in Urban America, 1965–1995

In August 1995, *Black Enterprise* marked its twenty-fifth anniversary with a special issue reflecting on African American economic progress since the magazine's creation in 1970. Founded amid surging interest in so-called Black capitalist strategies being championed by many in the Black Power movement and facilitated by the federal government, the publication had long tracked and celebrated the successes of Black entrepreneurs in the world of US business and the growing presence of Black executives in the once lily-white boardrooms of corporate America. The issue's cover story brought together a cross section of twenty-five "ambitious, determined, and prepared" African Americans (fourteen men and eleven women) who, born in the 1940s and coming of age during the civil rights and Black Power era, were now "classically middle-to-upper class" forty-five- to fifty-year-olds busy juggling family lives alongside "demanding careers." Their ranks included "a journalist, three physicians, several corporate managers and executives, a Colorado state Supreme Court Justice, a college president, a handful of successful entrepreneurs ... and one of only six black Admirals in the US Navy." All but four "held graduate degrees (some more than one)," and "their salaries ranged from $45,000 to $600,000 a year," with fourteen of the twenty-five "earning over $100,000 annually." What, according to *Black Enterprise*, explained the success of its "Class of '70"? In both their college education and subsequent employment, members of this "Class" had all been "first-line beneficiaries of a new program dubbed affirmative action."[1]

The period 1965–95 witnessed the high point for affirmative action's positive impact on Black economic mobility, and, as this essay explains, this was intimately tied to the remarkable expansion of Black political power in the United States (almost all of it within the ranks of the Democratic Party) that unfolded over the same period. In November 1967, Carl Stokes in Cleveland, Ohio, and

Richard Hatcher in Gary, Indiana, broke new ground when they were elected as the first Black mayors of major American cities in the twentieth century. By 1974, there were 101 Black mayors across the United States, and a decade later that number had soared to 252. By 1990, it had risen again to 316. This seismic shift in American urban politics also included multi-term Black political control evolving in most of the nation's largest and most populous cities, including Los Angeles, Detroit, Atlanta, Chicago, Philadelphia, New Orleans, and Washington, DC.[2] Grasping the initiative from federal policymakers, Black elected officials at the local level made a reality of the rhetoric of Black economic advancement—principally through affirmative action city hiring and minority business development policies—in their cities. The gains these programs delivered, however, were not evenly shared across the Black community.

After first outlining the development of the key relevant policies, this essay surveys the role that Black elected officials played in giving them meaning at the local level. It shows how events in Atlanta were particularly significant in pushing affirmative action and minority business enterprise programs forward nationwide, at both the federal level and the local level. It then finishes by outlining the impact of Black political power on Black progress during the first three decades following the 1965 Voting Rights Act and considers how it in some respects magnified and exacerbated intra-racial inequality in cities across the United States. In doing so, it shows how a story of Black upward mobility for some was entwined with the story of decline for the Black poor and working-class that unfolded alongside it.

The Roots of Affirmative Action and Minority Business Development Policies

Although it would principally be African American politicians at the local level who wielded affirmative action and minority business development policies to greatest effect (particularly during the 1970s and 1980s), these policies had their roots in the earlier efforts of white national policymakers to address racial injustice and economic inequality.

Affirmative action evolved out of fair employment legislation of the early 1940s and in response to Black civil rights activism and resistance to widespread and endemic racial discrimination in the American workplace. The term "affirmative action" entered the political lexicon thanks to Democratic president John Kennedy's May 1961 Executive Order 10925, which required federal contractors to not discriminate in their hiring and treatment of staff with regard to "race, creed, color, or national origin." This strategy became a more substantial part of federal civil rights policy under President Lyndon Johnson, whose September 1965 Executive Order 11246 established the Office of Federal Contract Compliance and directed the Equal Employment Opportunity Commission (EEOC) to challenge discrimination in private employment.[3] It was, however, Johnson's Republican successor, Richard Nixon, who made affirmative action central to the federal government's approach to advancing Black interests—albeit, as historian Manning Marable has argued, with a conservative purpose: to expand the Black middle class in the hope that its members might vote Republican.[4]

In July 1969, the Nixon administration's updated Philadelphia Plan took existing efforts to deal with hiring discrimination in the construction industry to a new level by introducing hiring ratios and goals (attacked as "quotas" by its opponents) for federal contractors and set timetables for meeting them. The Supreme Court subsequently endorsed results-oriented targets as constitutional, and the federal government's commitment in this area saw race and gender-based hiring goals extended to other areas of employment and universities. An important factor in progress made here was Nixon's appointment in May 1969 of African American lawyer William H. Brown III as EEOC chairman. A strong affirmative action advocate, Brown made the EEOC an increasingly active and effective player in the fight against employment discrimination in the private sector over the course of Nixon's tenure.[5]

Just as affirmative action was becoming more established on the national policy landscape, so too were policies concerned with Black economic development. Although African Americans had been debating the value of and importance of business ownership and capitalist development in their fight for racial advancement for most of the preceding century, these strategies were meaningfully supported by public policymakers only from the mid- to late 1960s.[6] Here again, Nixon was a key figure. Impelled by the Black Power movement's vociferous demand for Black economic empowerment—and inspired by existing strategies to remedy inner-city poverty and drive urban regeneration—Nixon began touting "Black capitalism" on the campaign trail in 1968 and promising to help militants and their disillusioned fellow African Americans become "owners [and] entrepreneurs" and "have a share of the wealth, a piece of the action."[7] Here again, his purpose was conservative, with Black capitalism essentially an effort to co-opt and moderate the Black Power impulse and reframe it as the pursuit of fuller Black inclusion in the middle-class comforts of mainstream American life. Once in office, Nixon established the Office of Minority Business Enterprise to lead his administration's effort to support Black and other minority businesses and entrepreneurs.

In late December 1969, economist and Federal Reserve Board governor Andrew Brimmer (the first African American appointed to such a role) delivered his report, "The Economic Potential of Black Capitalism," to the annual meeting of the American Economic Association in New York. His deep skepticism soon became apparent. At the time Brimmer spoke, there were only 163,000 African American business owners (from a national Black population of 22,500,000), and their businesses, he explained, tended to be "small in terms of sales, employment, and profits, and heavily concentrated in personal services and retailing." The general low income and high unemployment of Black inner-city populations and the scarcity of skilled and experienced labor, along with other significant challenges, he explained, all worked to make urban Black communities (where Black capitalism's proponents and policymakers imagined a Black business revolution unfolding) particularly unpromising and risky environments for new business investment. Even if Black business ownership did expand significantly, he argued, it was still very unlikely to make a substantial impact on the biggest problem: Black unemployment. Ultimately, he concluded, "Black Capitalism . . . offers a very limited potential for economic advancement for the majority of the Negro population."[8]

Just over two decades later, however, Brimmer would play a key role defending what was in effect the nation's most successful Black capitalism program. In June 1990, Brimmer visited Atlanta City Hall to formally present the Brimmer-Marshall Disparity Study to the city council. There he was flanked by his coauthor and former secretary of labor in the Carter administration, Ray Marshall, and—most notably—by Mayor Maynard H. Jackson Jr., the man principally responsible for the "Atlanta Plan," the nation's most aggressive and impactful minority business enterprise (MBE) program. Established in 1975, the Atlanta Plan embodied Jackson's commitment to using city government spending to support minority businesses, and it helped transform the public policy landscape not only in Atlanta but—as we will later see—nationwide too.[9]

What Brimmer could not have known as he spoke on Black capitalism in December 1969 was that minority business development (as it soon came to be called) would, in the following years, not only evolve away from a concern with urban regeneration (which for Nixon had always been limited at best) but also become fused with affirmative action through the Nixon administration's efforts to dedicate a greater share of federal spending to minority-owned businesses. This saw federal procurement from such firms rise from $9 million in 1969 to $250 million in 1974, and annual federal purchasing from minority businesses increased to $475 million, rising 234 percent between 1970 and 1975. This practice of reserving a portion of government spending for minority-owned businesses brought affirmative action principles and minority business development goals together and evolved into a policy known as minority contract set-asides.

While the Nixon administration had got the ball rolling, it was Black elected officials who gave greatest meaning and impetus to these policies in the decades that followed. Along with affirmative action city hiring, minority set-aside programs in city contracts would become central to the efforts of many Black mayors to advance the interests of their Black and other minority constituents.[10]

Black Political Power and the Expansion of Affirmative Action, 1965–1995

In surveying the relationship between Black mayors and affirmative action and minority business development initiatives across the period 1965–95, this section necessarily talks in broad terms. While no two Black mayors had exactly the same political outlook or the exact same experiences in office, there are, as political scientist J. Phillip Thompson III suggests, some broad patterns that can be observed in Black-led urban politics in the post-civil rights and Black Power era. Thompson identifies three distinct "waves" of Black mayors, the first two of which are helpful for our purpose here.

The "first-wave" mayors—elected between 1967 and the mid-1970s and including the likes of Carl Stokes in Cleveland, Richard Hatcher in Gary (both elected in 1967), Kenneth Gibson in Newark (1970), Tom Bradley in Los Angeles and Maynard Jackson in Atlanta (both 1973), and Walter Washington in Washington, DC (1974)—typically governed in a race-conscious fashion amid very difficult and racially polarized circumstances. For many of them, winning political control of a US city in the late 1960s–early 1970s was something of a poisoned chalice. Sustained deindustrialization and white flight to the suburbs had by then seen many of those cities lose significant jobs, capital, and tax revenue but retain sizable poor and unemployed (often majority-Black) inner-city populations who brought with them spiraling welfare costs. All of these problems were exacerbated by the economic problems of the 1970s (rampant inflation, high unemployment, oil crises, numerous recessions) that beset the nation.[11]

With city finances generally heavily reliant on the tax revenue of downtown businesses, Black mayors—many of whom were desperate to confound the dire predictions of many white commentators that Black political power was bound to bring with it economic chaos and decline—faced strong pressure to align their agendas with the interests of local white business elites who were not above threatening to abandon central cities unless their needs were prioritized. Long accustomed to working hand-in-glove with local politicians, white downtown business interests had in cities nationwide since the New Deal era been part of local "pro-growth" coalitions that ensured that city hall advanced the interests of local business elites in a range of sectors (for example, law, banking, insurance, real estate, construction). To many white elites, Black mayors were interlopers in these existing power arrangements, and they treated them as such. Generally speaking, those Black elected officials who did try to implement more redistributive models of city spending and resource allocation—or to address the needs of historically underserved poor Black inner-city communities (for example, by tackling police brutality or improving city services and social welfare provisions)—met with such vehement opposition that they either curtailed those efforts and began instead deferring to local white business interests, or they left city hall altogether.[12]

The late 1980s and early to mid-1990s brought a "second wave" of younger, technocratic Black mayors who generally de-emphasized race in their campaigns, venerated government efficiency, and pursued aggressively pro-business agendas that did little to enhance the fortunes of their poor and working-class constituents. This second wave (to which we will return briefly at the end) included officials such as Mike White in Cleveland (1990–2002), Norman Rice in Seattle (1990–98), Dennis Archer in Detroit (1994–2002), Bill Campbell in Atlanta (1994–2002), and Wilson Goode in Philadelphia (1984–92), among many others.[13]

Black urban politics of the post–civil rights and Black Power era, then—like all kinds of politics—was at its core the "art of the possible." As such, there were real constraints over the scope of Black political power in many places to deliver tangible social and economic improvement for poor and working-class African American communities—particularly in a nation in which broader political support for welfare state liberalism and social spending was rapidly dwindling. Black elected officials, however, generally proved far more able to advance the interests of the Black middle class and economic elite. Here, two broad policy areas were of greatest significance: affirmative action city hiring and city contract set-asides for minority-owned businesses. In both of these areas, Black elected officials were pushing with the political current and working on the established terrain of federal policy.

Although it was the object of considerable conservative hostility, affirmative action nevertheless emerged as a key federal civil rights policy from 1969 onward, and its potency for Black mayors was enhanced by the Equal Employment Opportunity Act of 1972, which widened the scope of Title VII of the 1964 Civil Rights Act to include jobs in state and local government.[14] As studies have shown, the number of African Americans in city jobs and public sector employment increased steadily from the late 1960s through the rest of the century, with some of the biggest increases coming during the 1970s and 1980s. Here, Black elected officials—and particularly those in cities with large Black populations—played an especially significant role.[15]

Indeed, a commitment to affirmative action city hiring was, broadly speaking, a strong characteristic of Black political power in the United States during these decades. This often included the appointment of greater numbers of minority candidates to leadership roles in local government and other high-status administration jobs. Good examples here, among many others, include Mayors Maynard Jackson in Atlanta, Tom Bradley in Los Angeles (serving 1973–93), Coleman Young in Detroit (1974–94), Ernest Morial in New Orleans (1978–86), Kenneth Gibson in Newark (1970–86), and Marion Barry in Washington, DC (1979–91, 1995–99), all of whom increased Black representation in the ranks of local government in their cities, and especially its higher echelons. At the same time, many Black mayors (including some of those listed above) helped challenge long-standing patterns of discrimination in private sector employment by requiring companies who sought access to city resources and contracts to commit to equal employment and minority hiring goals.[16]

Support for minority businesses became, alongside affirmative action employment policies, a key signature trait of Black political power during this period. Here again, Black officials were able to pursue minority business development programs with real conviction because those programs had political legitimacy. Resting on certain core principles such as support for the free-market system and belief in the private sector's capacity to increase social equality and valorizing traditional values around hard work, individual initiative, and self-reliance—and requiring no significant expansion of government or tax increases to implement—minority business development policies were tailored to the nation's ongoing conservative realignment. As such, Black mayors generally found that their MBE programs proved more palatable to entrenched white local interests than did any attempt to shift to a redistributive model of city politics and spending. Nixon's Office of Minority Business Enterprise, though poorly funded, may have established the policy realm and set an important example by significantly increasing federal spending with minority-owned businesses, but it was Black mayors as a broad group who gave these policies greatest weight and meaning. That said, no individual politician—Black or white—did more for the advancement of minority business in the United States during this period than three-term Atlanta mayor Maynard Jackson (1974–82, 1990–94).

Elected as vice mayor in 1969 at just thirty-one years old alongside the white liberal mayor Samuel Massell, Jackson was a highly ambitious young politician who reflected the increasingly confident mindset of Black Atlanta's political elite. Having been the junior partners in local biracial governing arrangements that had reigned for most of the twentieth century, Atlanta's Black leadership sought the senior partner role once the city became majority-Black in 1970. Jackson won the 1973 mayoral race comfortably, unseating Massell thanks to a solid Black vote and significant white liberal support, and became the first Black mayor in the South since Reconstruction. He entered office determined to advance the interests of the whole Black community, and his strong racial advocacy met with implacable white hostility. As he recounts, "For the first two years I was mayor, the [local white] press was almost hysterical." In the face of this opposition (and particularly the resistance of local white business leaders), Jackson abandoned his efforts to redirect city resources to improving the lot of poor and working-class Black Atlantans by the end of his first term and started to work more closely with local white power brokers. Where Jackson's success in advancing Black interests was most obvious and significant—and his commitment unshakable—was in ensuring Black businesses shared in the spoils of city contracts and spending.[17]

Jackson firmly believed that economic power was the key to "Black survival" and, having criticized Nixon for not backing Black capitalism strongly enough, pledged to deliver on the promise of minority business development policies.[18] When he took office in 1974, less than 1 percent of city contract spending went to Black-owned businesses. By the end of his first term, that figure had leaped to 19 percent, and by the end of his second term in 1982, it had reached 34 percent. These remarkable increases stemmed from what has been called "the grandaddy of set-aside programs." Upon entering office, Jackson drew up a minority business enterprise program—known as the Atlanta Plan—that required 25 percent of city contracts go to minority-owned firms as either prime contractors or subcontractors or to joint ventures between white and minority businesses. Finalized in 1975, it was, as economist Thomas Boston has explained, "the first local program with a significant minority goal that was not tied to a federal mandate." Jackson's pioneering plan made waves when it was applied to his administration's ambitious airport redevelopment plans, which would turn Atlanta's Hartsfield airport from a national to an international hub.[19]

The minority business involvement stipulated in Jackson's $750 million airport scheme—one of the largest capital construction projects ever undertaken in the South at that point—dismayed local white business leaders who unsuccessfully petitioned then governor (and next US president) Jimmy Carter and the state legislature to take control of the project away from city hall. Although their agitation continued for nearly two years, Jackson ultimately prevailed. His terms met, construction on the project finally got underway in 1977.[20] Even before the project was completed in 1980—both on time and under budget—

it was being widely celebrated as an unqualified success and proof "that minority participation goals can be reached in a business-like manner."[21] While Mayor Jackson's airport project—as will be argued in due course—gave greater impetus and legitimacy to minority business affirmative action initiatives in cities across the country, it also helped shape a positive climate for minority business development policymaking at the national level that endured into the mid-1990s.

It was no coincidence that President Carter spoke at the airport's opening ceremony in mid-September 1980. Based between 1971 and 1975 in the Georgia Governor's Mansion in Buckhead, a northern suburb of Atlanta, Carter was already well familiar with Jackson and the project, and he continued to track its progress from the White House following his victory in the 1976 presidential election. At the ceremony, Carter lauded Jackson's "tremendous leadership" and celebrated significant minority contractor involvement as a "notable example of progress and faith and cooperation and decency and social progress and pride."[22] Both leading Georgia Democrats, Carter and Jackson had over time became political allies, and Jackson's commitment to supporting minority businesses inspired President Carter to build on the efforts of his predecessors Nixon and Gerald Ford and further increase federal government support for minority businesses.[23] Just under four months into his tenure, Carter sent an economic stimulus proposal to Congress that resulted in the passage of the Public Works Employment Act (1977)—an act that provided $4 billion in federal funding for state and local government public works projects and required, Carter explained, "10 percent of the total funds to be spent through minority businesses."[24] This act (along with the Omnibus Small Business Act of the following year) established percentage goals for minority business procurement for the first time—and in doing so wrote minority contract set-asides into federal law.[25] At the same time, the Carter administration reorganized and rebranded the Office of Minority Business Enterprise, creating the Minority Business Development Agency, and in only four years nearly tripled the amount of federal procurement from minority-owned firms (and more than doubled federal deposits in minority-owned banks). Furthermore, Carter also extended minority set-aside programs to NASA and the Departments of Energy and Transportation. He had succeeded, he declared in his final State of the Union address in January 1981, in making support for minority businesses "a matter of major importance" on the national policy agenda and believed it to be "one of the most successful developments of my Administration."[26]

Although the archconservative Ronald Reagan, Carter's successor, would prove to be deeply hostile to affirmative action, this did not mean the end of federal minority business development initiatives on his watch. Indeed, as historian

Robert Weems explains, "because of Reagan's belief in the free-enterprise system, pre-existing programs to assist black entrepreneurs remained intact" throughout his administration. With federal minority set-asides already written into law under Carter and subsequently declared constitutional by the Supreme Court in its July 1980 decision in *Fullilove v. Klutznick*, the percentage of federal procurement expenditures going to minority businesses—which stood at 3.4 percent when Carter left office—increased steadily through the 1980s, climbing to 8.3 percent by 1994 (equivalent to $14.4 billion annually).[27]

The positive impact of events in Atlanta could also be seen in other ways in the Black business world. Again, the Atlanta airport project was particularly transformative, as economist Thomas Boston's study of affirmative action and Black entrepreneurship in Atlanta explains, because it "changed the character of the city's black-owned businesses" by enabling them for the first time to diversify and move out of the traditional realms of Black entrepreneurship (such as personal service and retail activities) and into nontraditional industries. This, he argues, was "the most important legacy of minority business affirmative action plans," because "new market opportunities meant faster growth possibilities, greater profitability, and increased employment capacity" for those businesses.[28]

The impact of Jackson's approach went far beyond economic measures too and had, according to Boston, "an enormous psychological impact on the black business sector" in the United States. Black-owned firms from across the country bid for work on Atlanta city projects, and Black entrepreneurs began migrating to Atlanta to try to take advantage of the opportunities on offer.[29] In many respects, Atlanta offered a tantalizing vision of the potential of Black political power to help African Americans realize their dreams of a better future. As Jackson's speechwriter Michael Lomax has remembered, "When Maynard got elected and started a revolution at City Hall, that's what gave black people a piece of the pie and put that city on the map for every young black person in America who had ambitions of doing something spectacular with his or her life."[30]

As the example set by Maynard Jackson in Atlanta reverberated far beyond the city, it helped widen economic opportunity for Black entrepreneurs nationwide. Herman Russell, head of what became the nation's largest Black-owned construction company, described Jackson as "like Dr. Martin Luther King Jr., when it came to ensuring African Americans got a chance to participate in the nation's economic marketplace," because his administration's MBE program "got the attention of black mayors, and some white mayors, in other major cities like Detroit, Los Angeles, Boston, and Chicago." Jackson, he continued, "helped put us on another plateau in terms of our dollar volume, the larger jobs, and getting joint ventures with major contractors that would not look at us before. He opened the doors where we otherwise would have been shut out."[31]

Russell was right. In light of the Atlanta airport project's success (and in the wake of the 1980 Supreme Court's *Fullilove* decision), city and state governments across the country established their own MBE programs. Nationwide, by 1988 there were 190 local government agency programs and thirty-six state agency programs, and many of them were directly modeled on the Atlanta Plan.[32] Here again, Black elected officials were at the forefront of driving the proliferation and implementation of MBE programs to advance the interests of their Black and other minority constituents.

In 1983 in Detroit, Mayor Coleman Young's administration created the "Sheltered Markets Program," which stipulated a 20 percent target for minority business involvement in city contracts for goods and services. It also required major city contractors to subcontract out at least 10 percent of their work to minority firms. This highly effective program saw annual city spending with minority-owned businesses increase from $20 million to $132 million by 1987–88—a national record for local government spending with minority contractors in one year.[33] As the Coleman A. Young Foundation still celebrates today, over the course of his five terms in office, Mayor Young "increased the awarding of minority contracts an astounding seven thousand-fold, spurring an African-American entrepreneurialism that continues to transform the city."[34]

In 1983, Illinois state senator Harold Washington, a long-standing proponent of affirmative action, was elected mayor of Chicago and made support for minority businesses a key policy of his administration. Washington championed set-asides because, he explained, they "create jobs for minority businessmen, who in turn hire mostly their own people" and in the process give "hope to a whole class of young men and women who never had it before." When Washington took office, less than 5 percent of the city's $400 million worth of annual purchases and contracts went to minority firms. Within two years that number had jumped to nearly 15 percent, approaching the informal 25 percent minority business participation rate target, equivalent to around $64 million per year. In April 1985, he issued an executive order establishing a 30 percent MBE goal for city spending.[35] Here again, the influence of Atlanta could be seen. Harold Washington was close to both Andrew Young and especially Maynard Jackson, with both of them campaigning for him in 1983. Some of his critics argued that it was no coincidence that his administration awarded major city contracts to Atlanta-based Black-owned businesses, including (perhaps unsurprisingly) work on the $1 billion expansion of Chicago O'Hare International Airport. Reelected in 1987, Washington died less than a year into his second term before he could build on his record in this area.[36]

In June 1986, *Black Enterprise* ran a special report on Washington, DC, celebrating mayor Marion Barry. Elected in 1978, he had over his first two terms turned the US capital from "a city of politicians to a hub of enterprise." Barry was similar to Maynard Jackson in his commitment to including Black-owned businesses in city spending. "Blacks in politics," he declared, "should see to it that more economic power is distributed to the black community. As one of those with political power, I feel that it is my job to see to it that this power is achieved. That's what these programs are all about." He was more than good to his word. Striving to ensure the District's Minority Business Opportunity Commission's target of 35 percent minority contractor involvement in District business was always met, Barry delivered impressive results. During his first two terms in office, *Black Enterprise* explained, Barry's administration ensured that "more than $856 million in city procurement contracts" went to minority businesses.[37]

In New Orleans, Ernest Morial dramatically increased the dollar amount of city contracts going to minority firms during his first term ($79 million across the four years).[38] His successor, Sidney Barthelemy (in office 1986–94), carried this on, directing a total of $116 million to over 350 minority-owned firms during his first term in office.[39] In Newark, Mayor Kenneth Gibson had by the early 1980s established an MBE program for Newark that stipulated that "at least 25 percent of the construction costs of a project must go to a minority contractor."[40] This was later extended to cover all city spending on goods and services and survived for most of the five consecutive terms served by his African American successor, Mayor Sharpe James, until in 2003 it was abolished in response to further legal decisions undermining government set-aside programs.[41] In Birmingham, Alabama, the city's first Black mayor, Richard Arrington (who served for five terms between 1979 and 1999) declared in 1983 that his administration had in his first term "given more work to minority businesses" than the city had done "in all the other years of its 112-year history."[42] In 1989, as the city began a period of large-scale downtown development, his administration set up the "Birmingham Plan," which targeted 30 percent involvement of minority-owned businesses in the estimated $800 million worth of city construction works completed over the following half decade.[43]

Back in Atlanta, Maynard Jackson's successor—former civil rights leader Andrew Young—kept Atlanta at the forefront of local MBE policymaking by taking Jackson's efforts to the next level. As political scientist Clarence Stone has suggested, Young (who served two terms between 1982 and 1990) ran on an explicit promise to heal "the rift with the white business elite" that Jackson's aggressive approach had created. Young—a man with a "strong personal inclination to work with monied interests"—excelled in this effort and in the process was able to raise the target for minority business participation in city contracts and spending from 25 percent to 35 percent, continuing to boost the fortunes of minority-owned businesses in the Atlanta area and beyond.[44]

The period 1965–95, broadly speaking, witnessed the high point of the effectiveness of affirmative action hiring and MBE initiatives for African Americans. As has been shown, Black American mayors—and particularly those in Atlanta—played a key role in delivering those results by developing the political credibility and pushing the momentum of those policies during that period. However, the gains those policies delivered were far from evenly shared among their Black constituents.

Two Nations . . . Both Black: Black Political Power and Black Progress in the Post–Black Power Era

On February 10, 1998, an episode of the PBS investigative documentary series *Frontline* titled "The Two Nations of Black America" aired for the first time. Presented by leading Black public intellectual Henry Louis Gates, the episode explored African American progress over the nearly three decades since the assassination of Martin Luther King Jr. and asked why America now had "both the largest black middle class and the largest black underclass in our history."[45] The statistical picture of intra-racial inequality that Gates painted was stark. Whereas between 1968 and 1995 the richest quintile of Black American households had seen their average income, adjusted for inflation, rise from $60,782 up to $84,744, the poorest quintile had actually seen theirs decline (from $10,624 down to $10,200). Across the same period, the percentage of Black children born into poverty increased from 43 percent to 45 percent. The show also quoted an Urban Institute report asserting the so-called Black urban underclass—defined as those in single-mother-headed households who didn't finish high school, who were dependent on welfare, who were chronically underemployed, or who were criminal recidivists—had tripled in size between 1980 and 1995, rising from 900,000 to 2.7 million.[46]

The growth of socioeconomic inequality among African Americans during these decades was undoubtedly driven in part by the affirmative action policies and minority business development initiatives at the national and local level to which so many Black mayors had given strong emphasis. The impact of these policies was amplified by broader parallel economic trends—particularly the decline of blue-collar industrial employment and the growth of white-collar employment in an expanding office-based information economy—that reshaped the American jobs sector. In this environment, by the mid-1970s it became clear that affirmative action in college admissions and private and public employment, along with minority business development programs, disproportionately benefited upwardly mobile, middle-class, college-educated, and elite African Americans who were generally far better positioned to take up the opportunities such programs predominantly offered in a changing US economy.[47]

Although Black gains in public and private employment during these decades cannot be attributed solely to Black mayors, they certainly played an important role in facilitating them. In terms of public employment, as discussed in the previous section, Black mayors made a real impact through their control of city hiring. Overall, as scholars have noted, "public and publicly funded employment" during this period proved to be "a powerful vehicle for African American economic mobility."[48] Similarly, real headway was made in the private sector too. Between 1966 and 1996, the percentage of the nation's senior and midlevel officials and managers who were Black increased from 0.87 percent to 5.8 percent, and the percentage of African American professionals increased from 1.32 percent to 5.9 percent.[49] The efforts of Black mayors to foster a minority hiring commitment in private businesses that worked on and competed for city business—alongside the success of their own city programs—certainly played a part here. As Boston explains, the success of local city affirmative action and MBE programs "hastened the decline of racial stereotypes . . . and encouraged private companies to emulate public sector affirmative action initiatives."[50]

The period 1965–95 also witnessed substantial progress for many Black-owned businesses, as their collective revenues skyrocketed. That progress, *Black Enterprise* magazine argued in late 1994, rested on a fundamental transformation: "Once African American companies were limited to the black consumer. Now black-owned businesses have progressed in national and international markets, while doing business with the nation's largest customers—corporate America and the federal government." What had made such an important transformation possible? For *Black Enterprise*, the answer was clear: "Using public policy as a tool to break down the barriers of racism and economic injustice has been key to the growth of black-owned businesses." The incidence of Black economic empowerment, the magazine concluded, "can be measured in direct proportion to the degree that black capitalism is expressed through initiative, and not rhetoric."[51] Here again, it was Black elected officials who gave minority business enterprise policies greatest clout for African Americans.

But who in the Black community benefited from MBE initiatives? Ultimately, to an even greater degree than affirmative action city hiring, minority business development initiatives tended to funnel money into the hands of a relatively small number of people—and in some cases was further concentrated in the hands of the owners of the largest and most successful Black businesses, many of whom had connections to Black elected officials. For example, Herman Russell—a key contractor on Atlanta's airport project who received around $100 million across the three years it took—was a close political ally of Mayor Jackson and had helped to get him elected.[52] But Russell was far from alone in benefiting from city contract spending in Atlanta. As a 2018 *Black Enterprise* article naming Jackson's election in 1973 as number six in its list of forty-five "Great Moments in Black Business" explained, Jackson's MBE program created "legions of black millionaires" and helped many of the nation's biggest Black-owned businesses expand rapidly.[53] Mayor Andrew Young continued where Jackson had left off, and between 1976 and 1986 nearly a quarter of a billion dollars of Atlanta city spending went into the hands of minority-owned firms.[54] A similar effect was seen in Washington, DC, under Mayor Barry, as a recent commemorative article recounts: "Barry both expanded the black middle class and created dozens of black millionaires. Indeed, billionaire Bob Johnson [who became the first African American billionaire in 2001] got his start when Barry not only granted him the contract for wiring District Cable, but also selling him the land for the BET [Black Entertainment Television] building for just one dollar!"[55] As a 1993 study concluded, "Black-owned firms in cities with black mayors have higher total revenues, greater average sales revenues, and lower rates of failure" compared with their counterparts in cities without a Black mayor. The evidence, the authors concluded, was clear: "The presence of black mayors benefits the black business community."[56]

Established in 1970 by African American publisher Earl Graves Sr. to advise Black Americans how to "build wealth through business ownership, career advancement, and money management," *Black Enterprise* magazine illuminates the expansion of the Black business class during these decades.[57] An organ of Black capitalist thought, the magazine championed Black business acumen and offered practical guidance for Black entrepreneurs on how to access capital and how to break into emerging and growth industries, alongside tracking and celebrating the economic gains made by African Americans in the realms of business ownership and corporate management across this period. In 1973, *Black Enterprise* created the *BE* 100—an index of the 100 largest Black-owned businesses and the first of its kind. When the first *BE* 100 was announced, the businesses included had collective sales of $473.4 million. The 1995 *BE* 100 listed companies that had annual combined sales of $11.71 billion.[58] In a similar vein, *Black Enterprise* profiled successful Black corporate executives from its inception but gave them greater focus and attention from the late 1980s onward when it established a recurring series of reports that venerated "heavy hitters [in] the nation's largest corporations." These reports included "The 25 Hottest Black Managers in Corporate America" (February 1988); "21 Women of Power and Influence in Corporate America" (August 1991); and later the "Power 40" (February 1993), which listed forty "high-flying executives" receiving minimum annual compensation packages of $250,000.[59] The magazine not only reflected but also catered to this growing Black elite. Described by Robert Weems as the "premier gateway to the African American well-to-do," *Black Enterprise* was replete with targeted advertising, from wealth management companies advising readers on how to manage their investments and stocks and shares portfolios, to commercials for high-end family holidays, expensive cars, and a wide range of luxury goods and consumables.[60]

The combination of economic gains in these three areas—public and private employment and business ownership—drove the widening class divide in Black America between the mid-1960s and mid-1990s. As a 1995 statistical analysis of trends in Black socioeconomic mobility explained, the previous three decades had witnessed less of an explosion of the Black middle class—as was popularly claimed—and more of a significant expansion of the Black economic elite. Between 1970 and 1994, the number of Black families earning between $50,000 and $74,999 increased by 3.9 percent, while the number earning $75,000 and above increased by 5.7 percent. As the report concluded, the "true winners" during this period were "those classified (even as far back as 1970) as the upper class."[61] This growing African American prosperity found expression in mainstream American popular culture from the mid- to late 1970s onward. Family sitcoms such as *The Jeffersons* (1975–85) and particularly *The Cosby Show* (1984–92) and *The Fresh Prince of Bel Air* (1990–96) all in their own ways dealt with issues of Black economic progress and upward social (and residential) mobility, as well as intra-racial class politics, during these decades. However, while the popular impression of African American socioeconomic advancement during this period seemed to grow stronger—whether on the nation's television sets or in the world of US politics and government, in corporate management, or in the ranks of business ownership—the fact that that progress was so closely tied to public policy meant it was always vulnerable to shifting political priorities.

Although the Reagan administration did not roll back federal minority business development initiatives, its broader effort to curtail affirmative action—expressed in part through Reagan's three Supreme Court justice appointees, all of whom were hostile to the program—did eventually severely undermine them, first at the local level and then later at the national level.[62] In January 1989, the Supreme Court's ruling in *J. Croson v. Richmond* applied, for the first time, the highest standard of review—"strict scrutiny"—to local and state agency MBE programs with racial mandates. From that point forward, any program unable to produce specific evidence—rather than generalized findings—of past discrimination would now be deemed unconstitutional. The Brimmer-Marshall Disparity Study, commissioned by Atlanta mayor Andrew Young soon after, was the city's response to *Croson*. Although it ultimately worked to preserve Atlanta's MBE program, it was very costly to produce (at over $500,000) and set a bar that few other municipalities could match. In the following months and years, local and state governments collectively spent tens of millions of dollars on disparity studies (the appropriate evidential bases for which were left ill-defined by the Supreme Court) and still had to contend with persistent legal challenges to their MBE programs.[63] The result, Boston explains, was that within two years of the *Croson* decision, of the more than 200 programs nationally, "sixty-six had been challenged legally, thirty-three had been voluntarily terminated, and sixty-five were under re-evaluation." In June 1995, in *Adarand Constructors v. Peña and the U.S. Department of Transport*, the Supreme Court overturned *Fullilove* and extended strict scrutiny to federal minority set-asides, and they soon began to disappear at the federal level under President Bill Clinton. At the same time, congressional funding for the Minority Business Development Agency began to fall precipitously, hitting an all-time low in 1998, where it would hover for most of the next two decades.[64] As Boston suggests, strict scrutiny was essentially "a bed of quicksand for affirmative action programs."[65] African American progress in private employment was threatened by the federal government's retreat from antidiscrimination law enforcement during the 1980s, after President Reagan appointed African American conservative (and future Supreme Court justice) Clarence Thomas as EEOC chair. This did not, however, lead to a commensurate decline in equal employment opportunities and affirmative action compliance at US corporations because, as scholarship has shown, these management practices had by then—thanks in part to the efforts of many Black mayors nationwide—gained a significant enough institutional foothold within American corporations that they persisted despite the reduction in government enforcement. As broader national political and legal support for affirmative action began to wane significantly in the late 1980s and early 1990s, many US corporations (albeit to varying degrees) began instead articulating a commitment to workforce "diversity" that they framed as a competitive business advantage in an increasingly multicultural US society. Ultimately, though, "diversity management practices" in effect constituted "a weakened version of affirmative action" and, as such, were a step back in the fight for equal employment opportunities for American minorities and women.[66]

If the African American gains that public policy had helped make possible during these decades were precarious, they also had limits that must be acknowledged. For example, the headway that Black Americans made in private sector employment was relative. Not only did African Americans remain underrepresented in most professions by the mid-1990s, but EEOC data show that other minority groups (particularly Asian Americans) had made greater progress in some higher-status job categories during the same period too. Moreover, African Americans made more substantial progress in lower-level status and lower-income jobs (for example, office and clerical work, technicians, sales workers, and service workers) across the whole period (1966–96), maintaining, or in some cases expanding, their over-representation in such job categories.[67] And advances in Black employment—at whatever level—did not mean that racial discrimination in the workplace diminished. Nor did income gains narrow the nation's vast racial wealth gap. As sociologists Melvin Oliver and Thomas Shapiro argued in *Black Wealth/White Wealth*, still by the mid-1990s, "materially, black and white Americans constitute[d] two nations."[68] Finally, African Americans were, of course, not the nation's only minority group, which meant there were limits to how much they could benefit from affirmative action hiring policies or minority business development initiatives. With post-1965 immigration bringing greater numbers of Asian and Latinx newcomers to the United States, African Americans faced increasing competition from other minorities and women for both jobs and business contracts throughout these decades and were not, overall, the biggest winners from these policies (who were white women).[69]

For many poor or low-income African American communities, however, the post–civil rights and Black Power era—far from bringing tangible gains, precarious or otherwise—was a period of decline. Many inner cities further deteriorated as white flight continued and city tax bases shrank smaller still. With the welfare state under attack from the Right, federal support for the nation's cities declined precipitously under Reagan, compounding the ongoing decline of US industry and the disappearance of blue-collar jobs from urban centers. For many working-class Americans, of all colors, the 1980s brought a fall in real wages, especially for those in lower-income employment.[70] Worse still, the Reagan administration's War on Drugs—most aggressively prosecuted in poor urban Black communities—swept hundreds of thousands of African Americans (particularly young men) into the criminal justice system, with devastating consequences for them and their wider communities.[71] As historian Rhonda Williams, writing in the aftermath of the 1992 Los Angeles riots, suggested, for "African American males with twelve or fewer years of education, the 1980s were catastrophic."[72] Just as family sitcoms like *The Cosby Show* showcased the socioeconomic advances made by some Africans Americans during this period, the emergence of gangsta rap in the 1980s gave voice to the bitter realities of urban life for many in America's poor and working-class Black communities, particularly Black youth.[73]

If, as has been shown here, Black mayors played an important role in advancing the interests of local middle-class and elite African Americans through affirmative action city hiring and minority business enterprise programs, what responsibility did they bear for the plight of poor and working-class Black neighborhoods, which worsened as much in cities under Black political control (particularly big cities) as it did elsewhere? After all, as Thompson explains, "by 1990, Detroit, New Orleans, and Atlanta, which had continuous black mayoral administrations for more than a decade, were three of the five cities with the highest poverty rates in the nation."[74] In some respects, the ongoing decline of poor inner-city communities in cities under Black political control stemmed from political and economic shifts over which Black elected officials had little control. In other respects, though, it flowed from choices they made. Although many desired to improve the lives of all their African American constituents, they generally faced constant pressures to maintain pro-growth policies, and a commitment to affirmative action city hiring and minority economic development policies usually met less sustained opposition than did any attempt to implement redistributive spending policies designed to help poor and working-class communities (which were usually fiercely resisted by local power brokers). As such, most Black mayors spent their energy doing what they felt they legitimately could get done, and at its core, this often meant advancing the interests of their local middle-class and elite constituents—Black and white—at the expense of local poor and working-class people, Black or otherwise.

It is perhaps unsurprising that, generally speaking, Black politicians—drawn largely from the ranks of the Black middle class and elites themselves—delivered the most substantial gains to those African Americans in their own socioeconomic class, but here the bent of the policies themselves played a key role. This was especially true of minority business policies that, although many Black politicians believed they would benefit the masses, ultimately did very little to improve the lives of the majority. As one local advocate of Atlanta's poor Black residents commented as he chastised Mayor Andrew Young for his pro-business agenda, "Working under Reagan's 'trickle-down' theory . . . doesn't work for [poor] black people."[75] The disillusionment of poor and working-class urban African Americans with Black elected officials was in many places intensified by the fact that nearly all Black Democrats (like virtually all other Democratic politicians at the time) supported Reagan's War on Drugs, despite the deeply negative impact that racially targeted drug law enforcement had on their communities.[76] That disillusionment reached significant proportions in many places and often led to the political demobilization of low-income Black voters over time. A prime example can be found in Los Angeles, where five consecutive terms of a Mayor Bradley administration were punctuated by the devastating riots of April 1992 and brought a nearly 40 percent decline in Black voter turnout across his twenty years in office.[77]

By the late 1980s and early 1990s, "second-wave" Black mayors were entering office in a political landscape shaped by the neoliberal orthodoxies of Reaganite social and economic policies, when the conservative assault on "big government" and affirmative action and other race-conscious policies was reaching a crescendo, and in which color-blind thinking and policymaking were increasingly influential. In this environment, technocratic "second-wave" Black mayors routinely de-emphasized race and—as had become common practice among most "first-wave" mayors—aligned themselves with pro-business, pro-growth agendas that typically worked counter to the interests of those in poor and working-class Black neighborhoods. By the mid-1990s, then, after three decades of growing Black political power, it was clear that Black elected officials—although not wholly responsible for it—had, broadly speaking, done more to widen inequality among African Americans than they had to narrow it, and there seemed little reason to expect that trend to change in the years to come.

Conclusion

The tremendous growth in Black political power in the United States between 1965 and 1995 was, according to Thompson, "one of the most dramatic and abrupt changes" in twentieth-century urban American politics. However, as he explains, "scholars and activists alike are [still] divided as to whether it represented a giant step toward racial equality or blacks' political cooptation in exchange for a hollow prize."[78] Ultimately, the answer to this question is a matter of perspective.

As Henry Louis Gates wrote in a 1992 essay, "Today many black Americans enjoy a measure of economic security beyond any we have known in the history of black America." That prosperity, he suggested, was "a legacy of the post–civil rights era and just the sort of corporate and governmental programs of intervention that have fallen into such disfavor of late." What Gates did not explicitly acknowledge was the extent to which the "creation of an Afro-American elite . . . larger than it has ever been" was also intimately connected to the rise and expansion of Black political power in cities nationwide since the late 1960s.[79] As this essay has shown, broadly speaking, Black mayors during the intervening decades were at the forefront of legitimizing and advancing both affirmative action and minority business enterprise initiatives at the local level. Some individuals played especially important roles (for example, Maynard Jackson during his first two terms in Atlanta), but this was in general a strong characteristic of Black political power during this period, and these policies did make a positive difference, facilitating upward socioeconomic mobility for hundreds of thousands of African Americans. For those people, Black political power would much more likely have felt like a "step toward racial equality." However, for most poor and working-class African Americans during this period, the story was very different. In most cases, Black mayors' control of public policy delivered far fewer tangible gains for them than it had their more fortunate counterparts—and in many places Black urban mayors oversaw the hyper-decline of their poorest neighborhoods, particularly during the 1980s. For this section of African American society, Black political power might seem much more like a "hollow prize."

Overall, then, Black political power played an important role in complex transformations that took place during the first few decades of the post–civil rights and Black Power era, as the meaning of race and class in America's cities and suburbs changed fundamentally. Indeed, by the early 1990s, Gates could claim that "the 'black' community, as we knew it before 1965, simply does not exist any longer." There were now, he continued—more clearly than ever before—"two nations" within Black America: "the haves and the have nots." With the Black elite "isolated from the black underclass," an economic chasm between these two nations had also become a cultural one. The harsh realities of urban life, he argued, were completely alien to a whole "new crop of black youth, whose only experience has been of our affluent suburbs." In the decades that followed, commentators such as Michael Eric Dyson would lament the continued and growing estrangement of these "two nations."[80]

However, as Gates wrote, given how reliant the "astonishing" progress African Americans had made since the mid-1960s was on public policy, it was always vulnerable to its opponents. By the late 1980s, conservatives had severely undermined both affirmative action and minority business initiatives, and by the mid-1990s the future for race-conscious policymaking looked very bleak. As *Black Enterprise* asked in 1995, as the magazine reflected on the successes of its "Class of '70"—all prime beneficiaries of affirmative action—over the intervening quarter century: "They've achieved the dream. But can they secure it for their children?" There was, they feared, little reason for optimism.[81]

In retrospect, the period 1965–95 represented the high-water mark for public policy's positive impact on Black economic mobility, even if the gains were concentrated in the hands of relatively few. At the same time, however, public policies aimed at improving the lives of poor and working-class urban communities were greatly discredited and diminished. As this essay has demonstrated, Black city mayors over these decades were an integral part of this story—for better and for worse.

Notes

1. Caroline V. Clark, "Moment of Truth for the Class of '70," *Black Enterprise*, August 1995, 24–40 (here 24, 26).
2. David Colburn, "Running for Office: African-American Mayors from 1967 to 1996," in *African-American Mayors: Race, Politics, and the American City*, ed. David R. Colburn and Jeffrey S. Adler (Urbana: University of Illinois Press, 2001), 23–56 (here 24, 23).
3. Terry Anderson, *The Pursuit of Fairness: A History of Affirmative Action* (New York: Oxford University Press, 2004), 22–23, 60, 92.
4. Manning Marable, *Beyond Black and White: Transforming African American Politics* (London: Verso, 1995), 83.
5. Dean Kotlowski, *Nixon's Civil Rights: Politics, Principle, and Policy* (Cambridge, MA: Harvard University Press, 2001), 103–6, 117–18, 120.
6. On debates over capitalist development within the twentieth-century Black freedom struggle, see Laura Warren Hill and Julia Rabig, "Towards a History of the Business of Black Power," in *The Business of Black Power: Community Development, Capitalism, and Corporate Responsibility in Postwar America*, ed. Laura Warren Hill and Julia Rabig (Rochester: University of Rochester Press, 2012), 15–42. On the earliest federal government efforts to encourage African American entrepreneurship, see Robert Weems and Lewis Randolph, "'The Right Man': James A. Jackson and the Origins of U.S. Government Interest in Black Business," *Enterprise and Society* 6, no. 2 (Spring 2005): 254–77.
7. Nixon quoted in "Nixon Urges Aid for 'Black Capitalism,'" *Washington Post*, April 28, 1968, A1. On the most immediate precursors to Richard Nixon's "Black capitalism" policies, see Kotlowski, *Nixon's Civil Rights*, 129–30; and Tom Adam Davies, *Mainstreaming Black Power* (Oakland: University of California Press, 2017), 69–74, 80–84.
8. Andrew F. Brimmer and Henry S. Terrell, "The Economic Potential of Black Capitalism: A Paper Presented before the 82nd Annual Meeting of the American Economic Association," December 29, 1969, 1–32 (here 8–10, 15, 31–32), https://fraser.stlouisfed.org/title/statements-speeches-andrew-f-brimmer-463/economic-potential-black-capitalism-10372.
9. Marcus K. Garner, "Disparity Studies Provide Evidence to Confirm Contractual Inequality: Remembering the Impact of Atlanta's First Disparity Study on Policies to Support Minority Business," *American DBE Magazine*, Summer 2020, 28–30; Thomas Boston, *Affirmative Action and Black Entrepreneurship* (London: Routledge, 1999), 40.

10. Anderson, *Pursuit of Fairness*, 200; Kotlowski, *Nixon's Civil Rights*, 144.
11. J. Phillip Thompson III, *Double Trouble: Black Mayors, Black Communities, and the Call for a Deep Democracy* (New York: Oxford University Press, 2006), 3–6. As I have argued elsewhere, Tom Bradley is a notable exception here and was in many respects a forerunner of the race-neutral technocratic second wave of mayors. See Davies, *Mainstreaming Black Power*, 181–87, 205, 232.
12. Thompson, *Double Trouble*, 39–41.
13. Thompson, *Double Trouble*, 5–15. Thompson's "third wave" consists of a rare breed: those Black mayors who, despite opposition, offered a more enduring commitment to redistributive politics that prioritized the needs of their poor and working-class Black majorities (and who in some cases were also committed to affirmative action programs, too). This wave included Harold Washington in Chicago (1983–87), David Dinkins in New York (1990–93), and Kurt Schmoke in Baltimore (1987–99).
14. Anderson, *Pursuit of Fairness*, 134–35.
15. Michael Katz, Mark Stern, and Jamie Fader, "The New African American Inequality," *Journal of American History* 95, no. 1 (June 2005): 75–108 (here, 87–88); Peter Eisinger, "Black Employment in Municipal Jobs: The Impact of Black Political Power," *American Political Science Review* 76, no. 2 (June 1982): 380–92.
16. On Jackson, see Ronald Bayor, "African American Mayors and Governance in Atlanta," in Colburn and Adler, *African-American Mayors*, 178–99 (here 181); on Bradley, see Heather Parker, "Tom Bradley and the Politics of Race," in Colburn and Adler, *African-American Mayors*, 153–77 (here 161–63). On Young, see Heather Ann Thompson, "Rethinking the Collapse of Postwar Liberalism: The Rise of Mayor Coleman Young and the Politics of Race in Detroit," in Colburn and Adler, *African-American Mayors*, 223–48 (here 238–39); on Morial, see Monte Piliawsky, "The Impact of Black Mayors on the Black Community: The Case of New Orleans' Ernest Morial," *Review of Black Political Economy* 13, no. 4 (Spring 1985): 5–23 (here 15–16); on Gibson, see "Gibson Proposing Minority-Hiring Plan," *New York Times*, November 4, 1973, 121; and on Barry, see Howard Gillette Jr., "Power and Protest in Washington D.C.: The Troubled Legacy of Marion Barry," in Colburn and Adler, *African-American Mayors*, 200–222 (here 204).
17. Bayor, "African American Mayors and Governance in Atlanta," 179–80, 183–88; Maynard Jackson interview, *Eyes on the Prize II*, October 24, 1988, 7, 9–10, Washington University Digital Gateway Texts, http://repository.wustl.edu/downloads/qz20sx258.
18. "Jackson Calls for Survival; Rips Kennedy and Wallace," *Jet*, May 9, 1974, 19.
19. Boston, *Affirmative Action and Black Entrepreneurship*, 4, 14.
20. Derek T. Dingle, "Maynard Jackson: The Ultimate Champion for Black Business," *Black Enterprise*, February 10, 2009, www.blackenterprise.com/maynard-jackson-the-ultimate-champion-for-black-business/.
21. Dave Miller and Gordon Kenna, "Minority Participation in Construction of Atlanta Airport," *Southern Changes* 1, no. 2 (1978): 24–25.
22. Jimmy Carter, "Remarks at Dedication Ceremonies for the Hartsfield Atlanta International Airport in Atlanta, Georgia," The American Presidency Project, September 16, 1980, https://www.presidency.ucsb.edu/documents/remarks-dedication-ceremonies-for-the-hartsfield-atlanta-international-airport-atlanta.

23. For a detailed discussion of the Carter administration's minority business development policies and their impact, see Robert Weems, *Business in Black and White: American Presidents and Black Entrepreneurs in the Twentieth Century* (New York: New York University Press, 2009), 190–218.
24. President Carter, "Remarks on Signing Public Works Employment and Economic Stimulus Appropriations Bills," May 13, 1977, https://www.presidency.ucsb.edu/documents/remarks-signing-public-works-employment-and-economic-stimulus-appropriations-bills.
25. Boston, *Affirmative Action and Black Entrepreneurship*, 11–12.
26. Jimmy Carter, "State of the Union Address 1981," Jimmy Carter Presidential Library and Museum, January 16, 1981, www.jimmycarterlibrary.gov/assets/documents/speeches/su81jec.phtml.
27. Boston, *Affirmative Action and Black Entrepreneurship*, 12; Weems, *Business in Black and White*, 219–20.
28. Boston, *Affirmative Action and Black Entrepreneurship*, 14.
29. Boston, *Affirmative Action and Black Entrepreneurship*, 14.
30. Quoted in "Maynard H. Jackson Jr., First Black Mayor of Atlanta and a Political Force, Dies at 65," *New York Times*, June 24, 2003, A29.
31. Russell quoted in Dingle, "Maynard Jackson."
32. Anderson, *Pursuit of Fairness*, 156–57; Boston, *Affirmative Action and Black Entrepreneurship*, 34, 17.
33. Emily C. Palacios, "Detroit's Public Contracting Policies: Is It Time for a Change?," *Journal of Affordable Housing and Community Development Law* 9, no. 3 (Spring 2000): 244–46; "Coleman Young, 1918–1997," *Detroit Free Press*, December 5, 1997, 5C.
34. "Accomplishments," Coleman A. Young Foundation, accessed May 20, 2024, www.cayf.org/coleman-a-young.html.
35. "Mayor Defends Minority Contracts," *Chicago Tribune*, March 24, 1985, 1, 18.
36. "Chicago Mayor's Critics Warn of an 'Atlanta Mafia,'" *Atlanta Journal-Constitution*, April 7, 1985, A1. On Jackson's close relationship with Mayor Washington, see "Maynard Jackson: In Atlanta and Chicago, Former Mayor Wields Power in City Hall," *Chicago Reporter*, May 1, 1985, 4.
37. Patricia A. Jones, "Washington: District of Commerce," *Black Enterprise*, June 1986, 253–63 (here, 262, 263, 256).
38. Piliawsky, "Impact of Black Mayors on the Black Community," 15.
39. "Give and Take Part of Politics Says Barthelemy," *New Orleans Times-Picayune*, July 28, 1990, B4.
40. "Newark Issues Affirmative Action Report on Construction Projects," Newark Public Information Office Press Release, November 30, 1982, Mayor Kenneth A. Gibson Collection, Newark Public Library, https://archive.org/details/GibsonBox3_044.
41. "UMDNJ Set-Aside Program Dismantled—Women and Minorities Seeking Contracts Are Affected," *Newark Star-Ledger*, July 24, 2003, 1.
42. Arrington quoted in Piliawsky, "Impact of Black Mayors on the Black Community," 15.
43. "Amid Birmingham's $1 Billion Construction Boom, will Minority- and Women-Owned Firms Finally Prosper?," AL.com, February 2, 2020, www.al.com/news/2020/02/amid-birminghams-1-billion-construction-boom-will-minority-and-women-owned-firms-finally-prosper.html.

44. Clarence Stone, *Regime Politics: Governing Atlanta, 1946–1988* (Lawrence: University Press of Kansas, 1989), 144.
45. "The Two Nations of Black America," PBS/*Frontline*, February 10, 1998, www.pbs.org/wgbh/pages/frontline/shows/race/etc/synopsis.html.
46. "Viewing the Class Divide," PBS/*Frontline*, accessed May 20, 2024, www.pbs.org/wgbh/pages/frontline/shows/race/economics/sam.html.
47. See, for example, William J. Wilson, *The Declining Significance of Race: Blacks and Changing American Institutions* (Chicago: University of Chicago Press, 1978), 151–53.
48. Katz, Stern, and Fader, "New African American Inequality," 87–88 (quote from 88).
49. *American Experiences versus American Expectations*, United States Equal Employment Opportunity Commission 50th Anniversary Report, July 2015, 7–9, www.eeoc.gov/special-report/american-experiences-versus-american-expectations.
50. Boston, *Affirmative Action and Black Entrepreneurship*, 14.
51. Alfred Edmond Jr. and Cassandra Hayes, "25 Years of Black Capitalism Initiatives," *Black Enterprise*, November 1994, 155–57.
52. Dingle, "Maynard Jackson"; Stone, *Regime Politics*, 97.
53. Jeffrey McKinney, "45 Great Moments in Black Business—No. 6: Maynard Jackson Becomes Atlanta's First Black Mayor," *Black Enterprise*, August 10, 2018, www.blackenterprise.com/maynard-jackson-atlantas-first-black-mayor/.
54. "Atlanta Contractors Host 'Thank You' Banquet for Ex-Mayor Maynard Jackson," *Jet*, November 25, 1986, 27.
55. Julianne Malveaux, "A Statue for Marion Barry, and for Us Too," *Mississippi Link*, February 22, 2018, 12.
56. Timothy Bates and Darrell Williams, "Racial Politics: Does It Pay?," *Social Science Quarterly* 74, no. 3 (September 1993): 507–22 (here, 521).
57. "Black Enterprise 50th Anniversary," *Black Enterprise*, December 23, 2020, www.blackenterprise.com/blackenterprise-com-50th-anniversary-hub-earl-graves-sr/.
58. "The Nation's 100 Top Black Businesses," *Black Enterprise*, June 1973, 29–48; Alfred Edmond Jr., "23rd Annual Report on Black Business," *Black Enterprise*, June 1995, 83–110 (here 86).
59. Shelley Branch, "America's Most Powerful Black Executives," *Black Enterprise*, February 1993, 78–135 (here 78–79).
60. Robert E. Weems, *Desegregating the Dollar: African American Consumerism in the Twentieth Century* (New York: New York University Press, 1998), 107.
61. The statistics cited here are taken from a report created for Henry Louis Gates's 1998 *Frontline* documentary. See A. J. Robinson, "An Analysis: Percentage of Blacks and Income Group 1970–1994," PBS/*Frontline*, February 1997, www.pbs.org/wgbh/pages/frontline/shows/race/economics/analysis.html.
62. Weems, *Business in Black and White*, 219–20.
63. On the challenges that disparity study authors faced in proving past discrimination and satisfying the requirements imposed by the *Croson* decision, see Mitchell Rice, "Justifying State and Local Government Set-Aside Programs through Disparity Studies in the Post-Croson Era," *Public Administration Review* 52, no. 5 (September–October 1992): 482–90.
64. For details on Minority Business Development Agency funding levels, see Congressional Research Service Report, *The Minority Business Development Agency: An*

Overview of Its History and Programs, November 30, 2021, updated June 6, 2024, 1–36 (here 27–28), https://sgp.fas.org/crs/misc/R46816.pdf.
65. Garner, "Disparity Studies Provide Evidence to Confirm Contractual Inequality," 29; Boston, *Affirmative Action and Black Entrepreneurship*, 38, 40–41, 44, 47, 4.
66. Erin Kelly and Frank Dobbin, "How Affirmative Action Became Diversity Management: Employer Response to Antidiscrimination Law, 1961–1996," *American Behavioral Scientist* 41, no.7 (April 1998): 960–84 (here 966–67, 972, quote from 981).
67. *American Experiences versus American Expectations*, 35–36, 11–20.
68. Melvin Oliver and Thomas Shapiro, *Black Wealth/White Wealth: A New Perspective on Racial Inequality* (New York: Routledge, 1995), 8.
69. Marable, *Beyond Black and White*, 85; Weems, *Business in Black and White*, 220.
70. For a statistical analysis of growing wage inequality from the 1970s through the 1980s, see Rhonda M. Williams, "Accumulation as Evisceration: Urban Rebellion and the New Growth Dynamics," in *Reading Rodney King/Reading Urban Uprising*, ed. Robert Gooding-Williams (New York: Routledge, 1993), 82–96 (esp. 83–90).
71. For an insightful overview of the war on drugs and its impact on Black Americans, see Michelle Alexander, *The New Jim Crow: Mass Incarceration in the Age of Colorblindness* (New York: New Press, 2010).
72. Williams, "Accumulation as Evisceration," 82.
73. See, for example Robin D. G. Kelley, *Race Rebels: Culture, Politics, and the Black Working Class* (New York: Free Press, 1996), chap. 8.
74. Thompson, *Double Trouble*, 6.
75. Stone, *Regime Politics*, 166.
76. For a discussion of Black political support for the War on Drugs, see, for example, James Forman Jr., *Locking Up Our Own: Crime and Punishment in Black America* (New York: Farrar, Straus and Giroux, 2017); and Donna Murch, "Crack in Los Angeles: Crisis, Militarization, and Black Response to the Late Twentieth-Century War on Drugs," *Journal of American History* 102, no. 1 (June 2015): 162–73.
77. Thompson, *Double Trouble*, 54–62, 47.
78. Thompson, *Double Trouble*, 3.
79. Henry Louis Gates, "Two Nations . . . Both Black," *Forbes*, September 14, 1992, reprinted in *Reading Rodney King/Reading Urban Uprising*, ed. Robert Gooding-Williams (New York: Routledge, 1993), 249–54 (here 249–50, 251).
80. Gates, "Two Nations . . . Both Black," 251, 252. For a compelling analysis of class divisions within Black America, see Michael Eric Dyson, *Is Bill Cosby Right? Or Has the Black Middle Class Lost Its Mind?* (New York: Basic Civitas Books, 2005).
81. Gates, "Two Nations . . . Both Black," 251; Clark, "Moment of Truth for the Class of '70," 24.

JEFFREY O. G. OGBAR

Black Mecca or Black Dystopia?

Race, Class, and Power in Atlanta

Two days before Christmas in 1930, in the midst of the Great Depression, Maggie Googson and Rogers Russell gave birth to their eighth child. Herman Jerome Russell was the last born to this hardworking but poor family that etched out a living in one of the most destitute sections of Atlanta, Summerhill. It was a poor, all-Black section rife with dilapidated homes, outside sewage, primitive infrastructure, and an all-white hostile police presence. At the time, William B. Hartsfield was a typical southern mayor who openly used racist language, expressed antipathy toward the Black community, and resisted efforts to hire Black people in any skilled capacity within municipal government. Black people were taxpayers but not allowed to attend any high school except the underfunded, overcrowded, understaffed Booker T. Washington High School in the southwest section of the city. In fact, until Washington High had opened only six years prior, no Black public high school was available to any Black person in the entire state of Georgia.[1] Although Black citizens' taxes supported all city services, the local government refused to hire African Americans as police officers, firefighters, or city managers. They were not allowed to access the main library downtown. They were not represented in the city council, which was shaped by the statewide white supremacist Democratic Party, which barred Black citizens from voting in its white primary. Less than a decade earlier, it had been the national headquarters to the country's oldest terrorist group, the Ku Klux Klan. The mayor, Walter Sims, and many other local and statewide officials were open Klansmen. According to a former police chief, Herbert Jenkins, over half of the Atlanta Police Department's officers were dues-paying Klansmen. The Gate City was nearly sacred for the Klan, which called it the group's "Imperial City."

Atlanta was, as were all other southern cities, a hostile, anti-Black space, where its city government not only expressed apathy toward Black misery but crafted policies and practices that were openly antipathetic to the Black community. City contracts with Black firms were, like meritocratic hiring in municipal government, dismissed. Fewer than thirty years later, in 1959, during the civil rights movement, when many southern cities garnered national infamy for violent suppression of civil rights activists, the city adopted a new sobriquet, the "City Too Busy to Hate." Another fifteen years later, its new moniker, the "Black Mecca," evinced its latest iteration, complete with a Black mayor and majority-Black populace. In the mid-1970s, the city opened opportunities to African Americans in hiring, promotion, and public contracts. It also developed programs to highlight and promote diverse cultural and intellectual work. In this latest incarnation, few people had financially benefited more than Herman J. Russell, whose company grew to be the largest Black construction firm in the United States. Despite the neo-Confederate sensibilities of the state and local government, the arc of Herman Russell's life would lay bare an astounding transformation of the Gate City by the time of his passing in 2014.

The story of Herman Russell highlights the extraordinary opportunities afforded African Americans in Atlanta in the years since the election of the city's first Black mayor. By the second decade of the twenty-first century, the city would be widely heralded for its remarkable achievements in Black municipal control. It had the highest concentration of Black-owned businesses, the highest concentration of Black millionaires, and an overrepresentation of African Americans among municipal and county jobs—at every stratum of skill. Most police officers, public school teachers, and firefighters were Black. These visible strides attracted Black people seeking employment opportunities, better and more affordable housing, and (more nebulously measurable) "Black excellence." Between 1980 and 2020, more African Americans relocated to Atlanta and its surrounding suburbs than to any other city in the United States. For many people, Atlanta, as the Black Mecca, approximated the goals of the Black Power movement more than any other city. In every arena—political, economic, cultural, and educational—Atlanta appeared to do what few, if any, cities had achieved. It outpaced cities (those majority-Black or not) in so many metrics, and no single person was more instrumental to setting this course than the city's first Black mayor.

The story of Maynard H. Jackson Jr. is widely documented.[2] In 1974, he became the first Black mayor of a major southern city and implemented aggressive policies to open the municipal structure—at every level—to African Americans. No facet of the political economy was unaffected by Jackson's efforts, from public safety to municipal business contracts. When Jackson entered office, less than 1 percent of city contracts went to minority business enterprises (MBEs). One year after taking office, city contracts to MBEs increased to 5 percent. The next year, the percentage increased to 25 percent. By 1978 almost 40 percent of city contracts went to minority-owned businesses, almost all which were Black-owned. City economic policies, known as the Atlanta Plan, created dozens of new Black millionaires, most from airport development opportunities.[3] Despite these achievements, the city was not unburdened by various challenges and crises.

Atlanta in the years after the election of its first Black mayor would achieve a range of inglorious distinctions: murder capital, second-highest rate of child poverty, highest rate of residents in public housing, yawning wealth gaps, and lowest rate of social mobility. Inasmuch as the "City Too Busy to Hate" proved more aspirational than actual, the popular refrain that Atlanta had become a veritable Black "city on a hill" or "Black Mecca" similarly trafficked in mythical proclamations that obfuscated complexities of class, race, and the limits of municipal power in the political economy.

There was no inevitable outcome to Jackson's consequential terms as mayor. It was a result of many variables, chief among them the country's highest concentration of Black colleges and universities in the city. The Atlanta University Center, home to Atlanta University, Clark College, the Interdenominational Theological Center, Morehouse College, Morris Brown College, and Spelman College, created a broad pool of Black professionals with resources and institutional management experience.[4] Moreover, Atlanta had cultivated a long tradition of what I call Afro-self-determinism, the belief that the advancement of Black people is best ensured by the creation of black-controlled institutions—economic, religious, social, cultural, educational, etc.—that presaged the Black Power movement by generations. It endorsed the creation of Black institutional development in conspicuous ways. By the ascension of Black municipal control, Jackson exploited the broad appeal of the Black Power movement that resonated among African Americans. In the process, he forged an exceptional landscape for Black opportunity and stories like that of Herman Russell.

Beyond Black-dominated municipal affairs, or even a Black-majority city, Atlanta had emerged as a city sui generis. It was not a deindustrialized city hollowed out by white flight, loss of manufacturing jobs left with a professional class of Black people who operated as managers of a crumbling, stressed municipal structure that was overextended, underfunded, and overburdened by poverty, crime, and diminished tax dollars. The city was more than this cliché. It was not Detroit, Gary, or Newark, although it shared many demographic indices with them. In fact, at times, it measured worse than those cities in some arenas, even as it outperformed most cities in others. Atlanta was more than a tale of two cities but rather a tale of multiple cities—large enough to contain various running narratives of success and failure, of Black power and white power, of

Black political exceptionalism and Black political impuissance. Through it all, the political economy and the role of affirmative action proved essential for carving out Black access to what had been closed spaces reserved for whites only.

This chapter explores the history of Atlanta in the half century since the election of the first Black mayor of a major southern city. It gives attention to the adversaries of the Atlanta Plan and to the rise of Black capitalist power in the nation's Black Mecca. Despite its remarkable ability to attract transplants, is the Gate City, after fifty years of Black administration, quantifiably improved? Is it, as some have argued, a failed, but well-intentioned, example of Black governance? Or, as the most hostile critics have contended, has Atlanta become an example of malfeasance and proof that Black administrators cannot govern any better than their white predecessors? Is it a veritable "Wakanda"—a nearly idyllic locus of Black self-determination, remarkable achievement, and excellence? What do the data say? The narrative is not simple, but one thing is certain: in the two generations after the Great Migration, Black movement has focused on Atlanta more than on any other city in the country. Its appeal is undisputed.

· · · · · · ·

During the civil rights movement, Atlanta proved remarkably agile and creative in forging a myth of being racially progressive. Millions of Americans and others around the world were appalled and shocked at the savagery of racist resistance to school desegregation in cities like Little Rock and New Orleans. The bombings and violence directed at peaceful activists in Montgomery and Birmingham laid bare the cruelty of Jim Crow and the vulgarity of city leaders. When Atlanta avoided these public displays of racist rancor, Mayor Hartsfield in 1959 quipped that Atlanta was the "City Too Busy to Hate." The slogan stuck, even as the city experienced more terrorist bombings than Birmingham, integrated its buses only after scores of cities—including Montgomery—did, and desegregated its schools after and at a slower rate than all but one southern city.[5] Atlanta, despite its effective marketing, was measurably *less progressive* than most southern cities. In 1971, *Ebony* magazine anointed Atlanta the country's "Black Mecca" and drew attention to the president of the Atlanta Public School Board, Dr. Benjamin E. Mays, former president of Morehouse College and mentor to Martin Luther King Jr., who had been assassinated three years earlier. The article also highlighted the "big and bold" thirty-three-year-old vice mayor, Maynard H. Jackson Jr., who also served as president of the city council. After his election as mayor in 1973, Jackson created an aggressive affirmative action policy, known as the Atlanta Plan, which opened city contracts beyond the racially exclusive practices of the city since slavery. Additionally, he appointed more Blacks and women to managerial and commissioner positions than had all prior mayors combined.

Class, Ideology, and City Hall

In the midst of the Black Power movement, Atlanta was swept up in white flight, constant reports of police brutality against Black people, and simmering tensions as Black youth endured high rates of unemployment and poverty. With a white mayor, white police chief, white president of the Atlanta Public School Board, and majority-white city administrators, Atlanta was an unlikely site for the moniker "Black Mecca." There were, however, some prominent Black businesses—including insurance companies and a Black bank—that amplified Black economic power. Additionally, the leadership of the Black colleges proved important to how Black power played out in intellectual and academic arenas. These leaders often worked with white counterparts for coordinated campaigns in times of crisis.

In the spring of 1971, the Atlanta Action Forum, which had been recently formed as "an informal biracial group of business leaders," utilized its considerable resources and influence to initiate a hiring campaign of Atlanta youth, following fears that there might be a summer of urban unrest. Jesse Hill, a prominent Black businessman who headed Atlanta Life Insurance Company, joined Russell in calling other businesses. "I need you to create eight summer jobs and hire eight black interns," Hill asked of various business colleagues. The effort resulted in a commitment to hire 6,500 people, almost all of whom were Black, in summer jobs.[6] The forum also played an important role in the controversial "Second Atlanta Compromise," concerning public school desegregation, which foreshadowed the degree to which racial integration, as a strategic goal, had lost appeal (if it was ever the dominant ambition) among the city's Black and white leadership. By 1970, Atlanta's school system was three-quarters Black, but among its 153 public schools, 106 remained mostly segregated. Additionally, most administrators were white. Although Atlanta had a long, storied history of extraordinary Black achievement in various professions, especially education, the white superintendent, John W. Letson, argued that the overwhelmingly white administration was a consequence of being unable to find qualified Black people.[7]

Simultaneously, under court order, the Atlanta Public School system was in negotiations to bus nearly 30,000 of its Black students into white schools. Aware of the deep white opposition, Black leadership, including the Atlanta chapter of the NAACP and its chapter president, Lonnie King, endorsed a compromise with the white leadership: only 10 percent of the original number of Black students would be bused into white schools in exchange for a Black superintendent of the Atlanta Board of Education and more Black administrative control. King believed that "administrative desegregation" and a Black superintendent of the 77 percent Black school system was a more substantive policy to advance Black educational equity than sending Black children to schools with mostly white students, teachers, and administrators.[8]

On February 20, 1973, with an 8–2 vote, the Atlanta Board of Education approved an out-of-court settlement of a desegregation lawsuit. The agreement resulted in administrative desegregation at a higher ratio than student desegregation, creating increased Black control of the school system.[9] This was aligned with the central thrust of the Black Power movement. Many African American leaders and communities in general (across the country) prioritized equal application of justice, protection, access to resources, and employment as essential. This meant, of course, desegregation of hospitals, schools, and all public accommodations. Integration, or the notion that real justice or equality could exist only in integrated spaces (schools, churches, or other public accommodations), was not necessarily an ambition. A Black college, for example, could outperform most white colleges in a range of metrics—selectivity, graduation rates, rates at which graduates eventually earn MDs, PhDs, MBAs, or JDs. A white presence, therefore, was not essential for Black achievement. Resources, however, were. Many people had come to embrace the notion that Black people could control an apparatus that primarily served Black people—like a public school system. Black teachers, principals, and other administrators, if properly resourced, could deliver excellent educational services that would affirm and develop healthy, academic spaces. There was nothing incongruent with wanting desegregation and opportunities to secure Black control over institutions primarily serving Black people. The Atlanta Action Forum leadership essentially agreed.

Many people viewed these forum efforts as an important advancement of racial cooperation in the interest of the Black poor, as well as a demonstration of the growing influence of Black leadership in the city. There was, however, a community of Black critics who viewed the forum and the city's new Black power brokers with deep suspicion. Some dismissed the Atlanta Action Forum and programs like it as tepid attempts to address the root causes of Black poverty. Revolutionaries had long argued that capitalism could not be reformed to free the mass of exploited workers. Anything short of its destruction would offer compromises with the oppressors—regardless of their skin color. Capitalism, after all, they insisted, used racism to grease the machinery of exploitation and oppression. White conservatives, however, protested the forum because they thought that it pandered to Black militants, or to Black people in general, who deserved no "handouts" or special treatment. There was a deep irony in this argument against "handouts" and "special treatment," given the aggregation of wealth and power the white community had accrued over centuries of exclusive and discriminatory access to resources. Any attempt to provide opportunities and widen pathways to theretofore restricted whites-only spaces were viewed as discriminatory against whites.

In many ways, the Atlanta Action Forum was a predictable model of what was to come under the administration of the city's first Black mayor. In the view of some recalcitrant whites, the forum itself pandered to the most volatile segments of the Black community. By systematically targeting jobs for them, it was a capitulation to veiled threats and intimations of violence from radical leftists. For poor and working-class whites in the city, particularly those in communities like Cabbage Town, this was a sign of the rise of Black Power and the degree to which Black people would be the "first hired and last fired," or a fundamental reversal of how racial politics had theretofore operated in the city—and the country. In many respects, huge swaths of white Americans considered shifts in the racial politics and landscape in the country to be a zero-sum game. Any progress that Black people made would be at the expense of white people, some reasoned. This sentiment, though measurably untrue, was not constricted to working-class whites who might compete with working-class Blacks for municipal jobs or temporary summer employment. The hostility to Black access to wealth of the region was more virulently expressed in legal cases—not burned crosses or Molotov cocktails—in courtrooms in the judicial system. A series of lawsuits were filed in the first term of Jackson's administration, reflecting the deep-seated unease that many white business leaders had with democratizing access to the city's wealth.

In the early 1970s, before Jackson's election, there was considerable concern about the degree to which urban unrest would undermine the economic vitality of the city for the business elite. But, for many Black people, there was speculation that such incidents destabilized an already economically fragile ecosystem of concentrated Black poverty and limited investment in quality services and infrastructure. In fact, there is evidence to suggest that urban unrest did push the most vulnerable elements of the Black community further to the margins. Research from William Collins and Robert Margo found that between 1960 and 1980, cities that experienced major cases of urban unrest had relative decreases in male employment rates of 4–7 percent. The researchers also found that the violent unrest "significantly depressed the median value of black-owned property between 1960 and 1970, with little or no rebound in the 1970s." They concluded that "household-level data for the 1970s indicate that the racial gap in property values widened substantially in riot-afflicted cities relative to others."[10]

For business leaders like Jesse Hill, who headed an insurance company, or Herman Russell, who sat on the board of a bank, any trepidation that investors had with working in poor Black communities was made more acute with the threat of urban rebellion. Risks related to property would precipitate higher insurance premiums; and violence would likely encourage those with the means—Black and white middle-class people—to leave those communities, which would lead to decreases in the tax base and a decrease of resources for city services, from education and infrastructure to the police and fire departments. And, finally, securing municipal bonds could be more difficult. In the end, there were sundry reasons for the Black leadership and grassroots members of the Black community to mobilize against violent rebellion in the form of what were generally called "race riots."

For the Black radicals and revolutionaries, there was a strong admonishment against these sporadic cases of violent unrest as well, but for different ideological reasons. Revolutionaries like Huey P. Newton and Bobby Seale, cofounders of the Black Panther Party, and integrationists like Dr. Martin Luther King Jr. understood that urban rebellions were a direct consequence of the poorest, most powerless, most marginalized elements of society demanding justice and pushing back against oppression, hunger, and exploitation. There were, however, deep philosophical and ideological reasons why groups like the Southern Christian Leadership Conference and the Black Panthers opposed violent urban rebellions. The SCLC's commitment to nonviolent social change saw violent unrest as anathema. The Black Panthers argued that, ultimately, any unorganized, sporadic fit of violence—even that of the oppressed against the oppressor—could not be an effective method of struggle. Such violence invited opportunities from the state to, in turn, violently repress the people through targeted arrests and police sweeps of activists and subversives who destabilized organizations. Meaningful resistance meant a systematic and organized mobilization of the people. The people also, the Panthers argued, must be properly informed and educated on the principles of revolution. Otherwise, chaotic purges and fits of rage would fail to achieve the radical transformation that the people needed.

In addition to how various Black people across ideological lines viewed urban rebellion as a net negative impact in Black communities, there was also the realization that on a macro level, the pervasive fear of Black violence—in any form—had helped invite the rise of the rhetoric of "law and order" and an increasingly punitive state apparatus in the administration of Richard M.

Nixon. In no uncertain terms, Nixon ran a presidential campaign that pandered to fears of radicalism and a decline in "order." After the assassination of King in April 1968, the country witnessed the most expansive case of domestic unrest since the Civil War when rebellions erupted in over 100 cities. Immediately, and for weeks, national polls placed concerns around "riots" as important an issue as the Vietnam War. It was after these rebellions that Nixon, who had mostly avoiding discussing civil rights, adopted a new rhetoric around "law and order."[11] Political scientist Omar Wasow argues that an analysis of polls following the spate of rebellions in April 1968 pushed many white voters to Nixon. He writes, "These findings suggest that the 'transformative egalitarian' coalition identified by Rustin (1965), King and Smith (2005) and others was fragile but, in the absence of violent protests, would likely have won the presidential election of 1968. In this counterfactual scenario, the United States would have elected Hubert Humphrey rather than Richard Nixon and, in the absence of white antipathy to black uprisings, the ethnocratic coalition would not have carried the day."[12] Clearly, the opposition to urban unrest transcended ideology, but some Black groups did look askance at, if not direct outright contempt at, the Atlanta Action Forum and its mission.

Some criticism of the forum was a predictable response from the radical elements of the Black Power movement, but criticisms from Black circles were not identical. For the Nation of Islam, for example, the notion that Black and white businessmen would come together to make appeals to Black youth was indicative of a mendacious and disingenuous effort to lure Black militancy away from "nation building." "Nation building" was the term popularized by various Black nationalists to refer to the efforts and ambitions to create self-sufficient institutions in the Black community to meet the community's social, economic, spiritual, educational, and cultural needs independent from whites. It was a critically important component to the long-term goal of territorial separatism and the establishment of a Black nation-state. Black nationalists had long argued that Black people must "do something for themselves." This fundamental philosophy of self-determination is a critical component of the African American community, as historian V. P. Franklin explains: "Within the urban black communities black churches, separate schools, fraternal institutions, voluntary associations, and advancement groups sprouted up to meet the social and cultural needs of expanding populations."[13]

For more leftist, revolutionary elements of the Black community, the Atlanta Action Forum was a classic example of the co-option of militancy by elites—Black and white—who were allied by class to serve their mutual interests to protect capital. Such elites were loath to consider the spread of truly radical politics and cultivated a facade of empathy for the poor through passive reformist programs like summer jobs that did little to address the fundamental causes of poverty, gross inequality, war, and imperialism. In the end, according to the leftists, there would be wars to expand the wealth of the rich (of any race), while poor people (of any race) largely would be forced to fight those wars. Race, revolutionary nationalists explained, was used as a tool of division to undermine the possibilities of coalition building among oppressed people. The Panthers, for example, insisted that all poor and oppressed people had been on the losing end of the very idea of racism. The notion that the marginalized poor of all races could unite and organize for social, economic, and political transformation was a fundamental threat to the ruling class, which exploited poor whites and Blacks alike. "We say All Power to the People—Black power to Black people, and Brown power to Brown people, Red power to Red people and Yellow power to Yellow people. We say White power to White people."[14]

The notion that Atlanta needed substantive economic reform had been an enduring component of Black politics—radical and mainstream—since the 1960s. The Atlanta Project, created by members of SNCC in 1966, had systematically addressed pronounced class cleavages in the Black community, especially in urban spaces. The radical critiques from the Institute for the Black World similarly addressed the need for public policies that addressed both class and race. Even the SCLC, cofounded and led by Dr. Martin Luther King Jr., had come to see class as an essential pivot for social justice organization in the Black community. Ralph D. Abernathy Jr., who succeeded King following his assassination in 1968, expressed deep concerns over the limits of success in the city. In 1972 he explained that "during Dr. King's lifetime we dealt with the obvious, overt forms of segregation. Now we are faced with more subtle forms. Sure, we have the right to eat downtown and stay in a hotel. But do we have the right to hold the job to earn the money to pay the hotel bill? We earned the right to schools, but do we have quality education? There once was a time when we could expose evil through mass demonstrations. But demonstrations alone will not solve our problems. We have to have jobs, income, control of our communities."[15] The city was majority-Black, but its wealth remained acutely concentrated in the hands of white people. Providing Black access to schools, hospitals, jobs, and electoral politics did not instantly provide Black access to the wealth that white America had accumulated over centuries from legally codified racial subjugation. A Black major municipal government had done little to alter that fact. But Black political control of Atlanta municipal governance did result in efforts to increase access to economic development in the Black community. The process was, of course, an inexorable challenge.

There had been, by the early 1970s, increased dialogue between more radical expressions of Black political control and the more moderate representatives of reformist liberal politics. In the 1971 Gary, Indiana, National Black Political Convention, a rich cross-section of Black activists, from revolutionaries to capitalist-oriented Black nationalists, liberals and moderates, attended. By the second such convention in Little Rock in 1974, the ideological divide between more left-leaning Black radicals and the mainstream Black liberals had become more rigid. Major Black elected officials did not attend. Los Angeles mayor Tom Bradley, Detroit mayor Coleman Young, and Congressman Charles Diggs were some of the most visible ones not to attend. One major political player with national name recognition, the newly elected mayor Maynard Jackson, did, however, attend.[16]

Of course, as the Democratic Party leadership endorsed civil rights, millions of white southerners departed the party, transforming the region into a Republican stronghold. Many Black elected officials insisted that a third party was not viable and would, in fact, undermine the successes achieved in the Democratic Party. Maynard Jackson, who embraced the utility of the Democratic Party to advance the political agenda of the wider Black community, showcased the advances that his administration had been able to accomplish in Atlanta. In addition to the appointment of African Americans to a wide range of powerful positions in the city, the mayor had opened the city to Black firms as no city had. In order to aggressively push for widening these efforts, Jackson recruited African Americans from across the country. From Shirley Franklin and Michael Lomax to Rodney Strong and Walter Huntley, young people—mostly in their twenties—relocated to Atlanta to work in the mayor's office.

Aaron Trupeau Sr., who migrated to Atlanta in the early 1970s, worked with Mayor Jackson as a policy advisor and a commissioner. While the administration made remarkable strides in public contracts, the private sector was another matter. The effort to crack the all-white space of large-scale private contracts was formidable. The obstinate resistance is legendary. While white business leadership opposed Jackson's attempt to expand opportunities beyond white firms, his successor, Andrew Young, developed a different strategy. Young, a chief lieutenant of Dr. King, had cultivated a rich international network of contacts as former US ambassador to the United Nations under President Jimmy Carter. Young developed a new tactic: global prestige. Mayor Young invited business leaders to join him on international trips to meet heads of state, including kings and princes. Business leaders adored these opportunities. "They loved Andy," Trupeau explained. Foreign investment and trade were important; consequently, with Young's advocacy, many Black companies were positioned to penetrate what had been a closed spaced. The efforts paid off in Young's first term with the construction of the forty-seven-story high-rise BellSouth Tower, completed in 1982. One Black developer, Oscar Harris, secured a major contract for the parking garage to accompany the skyscraper. At the ceremonial groundbreaking, various city officials gathered, including Aaron Trupeau. "We had been fighting [to break through the private sector] for so long" that "I wept" at the ribbon cutting.[17] Ultimately, Trupeau served multiple administrations over seventeen years with Jackson and Young. The doors were slowly being pried open.

The efforts produced powerful success stories. No one was as visible as Herman J. Russell, who secured contracts at a scale wholly denied Black businesses before. Through "joint venture" contracts between larger white firms and smaller MBEs, access to major projects widened. Russell's construction company scaled up to bid on a range of building projects across Atlanta and beyond.

From the 1970s to the twenty-first century, Russell's indelible imprint on the city of Atlanta is palpable. From middle-income apartment complexes to higher-end ones, from academic buildings on college campuses to skyscrapers, the H. J. Russell Company—largely as a result of the Atlanta Plan—has thrived. The Atlanta Plan attracted increasing numbers of Black firms from across industries, but the development of Black construction companies was especially notable. Other Black-owned firms emerged, like C. D. Moody Construction and Bryson Constructors, becoming some of the largest construction companies in the city. These two companies alone have handled projects that have netted billions in revenue since the 1980s. Black-owned firms, providing everything from banking and insurance to extermination and custodial services, brought about a stunning transformation of what had been the putative capital of the neo-Confederate South.

By the early twenty-first century, popular media had produced numerous articles, videos, and other coverage on Atlanta as a veritable capital of Black America. In 1997, *Ebony* magazine revisited Atlanta's status as Black Mecca, even calling it the "land of milk and honey" for Black people. According to a poll of the magazine's 100 most influential African Americans, Atlanta was rated as the overall best city for Blacks and "possessed the most employment opportunities for blacks." Although many cities have a higher percentage of Black people or percentages that more closely reflect the national rates of Latinx and Asians (both underrepresented in Atlanta per the 1990 census), the Gate City was also called America's "most diverse city." Surprisingly, it was lauded for being the city with the best schools and most affordable housing for Blacks. In line with the historical accolades directed at the city, these modern hagiographic claims were rarely accompanied by actual metrics. Did the city have the best schools for Black children? What were the graduation rates? Test scores? Rates of college attendance after graduation? What about poverty rates or homeownership rates? These and other metrics were omitted. At the start of the next century, the boosterish stories proliferated, whether evidence proved them or not. Some of the praise, especially regarding businesses, were not without merit. They were often tied to the highly successful affirmative action efforts of city hall.

The impact of the construction projects in and around Atlanta has shaped the iconic skyline. The Mercedes-Benz Stadium (home to Atlanta Falcons professional football), State Farm Arena (home to Atlanta Hawks professional basketball), Coca-Cola's global headquarters, college and university buildings, and terminals at Hartsfield-Jackson Atlanta International Airport are some of the notable landmarks built jointly or solely by Black developers in the Black Mecca. When the city hosted the world for the 1996 Summer Olympic Games, 80,000 cheering fans witnessed the former Olympian Muhammad Ali light the flame in the Olympic Stadium (later Turner Field, home of the Atlanta Braves baseball team, 1997–2016) that was built, in part, by Black construction companies. A Black firm even emerged as one of the official apparel makers of the Summer Games. Throughout the Summer Olympics, hundreds of thousands of spectators, athletes, government officials, and tourists arrived at the Atlanta airport, which itself showcased Afro-Selfdeterminism to the world. In addition to being the busiest airport in the world, it was under Black executive control and had mostly Black employees. Its contracts with Black firms exceeded all other US airports *combined*. No other city in America comes close to boasting a skyline, three professional sports stadiums, and a major airport fully or partly constructed by Black firms on any comparable scale.

Among many firsts, Russell became the first Black member (and president) of the Atlanta Chamber of Commerce and the Capital City Club. He also served as chairman of the board of Citizens Trust Bank, one of the oldest Black banks in the country. Michael H. Ross, CEO of MHR International, a construction management company, argues that Russell became a national titan of Black business who elevated the visibility of Black economic power and potential. Ross, who has worked with cities across the country as a consultant to procurement policies and is an alumnus of Morehouse, insists that many municipalities want to achieve the metrics established in Atlanta. The reputation to widen economic access has been so significant that he was the only US consultant on a South African procurement task force established by President Nelson Mandela. Ultimately, South African president Thabo Mbeki developed a "Black Economic Empowerment Program" that was partially inspired from the Atlanta Plan.[18] Through it all, the political economy and the role of affirmative action proved essential for carving out Black access to what had been closed spaces reserved for whites only, and mainstream media continued to take notice of the city's conspicuous Black success stories.

In 2003, a CBS *60 Minutes* segment, "Going Home to the South," explored the extraordinary appeal of the Gate City. It showed marvelous visuals of well-manicured lawns and large homes in suburban subdivisions with pools, tennis courts, and basketball courts. From afar, these communities looked similar to affluent, mostly white suburbs outside most American cities. These, however—located in the suburbs to the south, east, and west of Atlanta—were almost completely Black. According to the *60 Minutes* feature, "Black suburban Atlanta may look like Beverly Hills, but it's Mecca for many new migrants who are buying homes worth from $200,000 to more than $2 million [$320,000 and $3.2 million adjusted for inflation today]. And new subdivisions keep sprouting, marketed especially to blacks." Featuring several Black families, the *60 Minutes* report was clear that many, if not most, were transplants from other cities, especially from the North. "I blazed a trail to get out of New York," explained one transplant. "I just wanted a better way for my kids."[19]

The rise of upscale Black subdivisions had resulted from systematic efforts that Black developers had initiated in the 1980s. Like many other features of the city's landscape, an explicit Afro-self-determinist politics played a role in the proliferation of these neighborhoods. Upscale Black residential areas or suburbs are not unique to Atlanta. From Los Angeles's Baldwin Hills, Ladera Heights, and Windsor Hills enclaves to Chicago's Pill Hill or Chatham through Harlem's Sugar Hill, high socioeconomic status Black neighborhoods have existed for generations. In every case of those listed above, however, they transitioned from white to Black. Areas like Guilford Forest, Camp Creek Parkway, Beazer Homes, Cascade Place, and Wolf Creek Chase in Atlanta were Black since inception. "We were intentional about that," explains Rodney Strong, former Director of Contract Compliance for the City of Atlanta.[20] In the late 1980s, Atlanta's high socioeconomic status Black areas included sections of the neighborhood Southwest like Ben Hill, Collier Heights, and Cascade Heights. These neighborhoods became home to old-guard African American leaders in business, education, electoral politics, and even professional sports. Everyone from Herman J. Russell, Martin L. King Sr., Benjamin Elijah Mays, and baseball Hall of Famer Hank Aaron called these sections home. But the expanding demand for new housing from the growing Black middle class required new construction. In the mid-1980s, Greg Baranco, an African American owner of a local car dealership, became one of the lead developers of a sixty-six-home residential subdivision, Sandstone Shores, in Decatur. Around the same time, Guilford Forest, in Southwest, was built. These became the largest upscale Black subdivisions created in the area since Collier Heights in the 1950s, which had also been built by Black developers. These immediate successes demonstrated to banks, realtors, and developers the potential for upscale Black subdivisions in the region.

Since the late 1980s, over twenty middle- to luxury-level Black housing developments have been established throughout the metro area. From Stonecrest Estates in DeKalb County, with sprawling mansions on impressive lots in an overwhelming Black area of the county, to the more modest new subdivision of Le Grande in Fulton County, the rise of these stretches of Black residential comfort has been heralded as proof of the city's claim to exceptionalism. In many ways, the swaths of Black suburban affluence feed the narrative of Black opportunity, which draws more migration, particularly highly skilled African Americans seeking to optimize their resources.

Some people have attempted to focus more on the persistence of Black poverty in a Black politically dominated city rather than on the rise of Black affluence. The poor have been overlooked in the grand narrative of Black success, they argue. Larry Keating, a professor of city planning and a specialist on Atlanta, argues, "Even after African Americans gained control of the city government black elected officials largely ignored the problem of black poverty."[21] Despite the "higher than" rates that Black Atlantans have relative to African Americans elsewhere, Black Atlantans trail their white counterparts in nearly every positive index and lead them in nearly every negative one, from infant mortality, poverty rates, and homeownership to life expectancy. In fact, most Atlantans—across racial lines—perceive the racial wealth gap as significantly lower that what it is in the Atlanta metro area. While they believe Black household wealth to be between 40 and 63 percent of white wealth, it is actually only 10 percent of white household wealth. While Black affluence has grown under Black municipal control, whites in the region, under Black public administrative dominance, have gotten wealthier and achieved higher standards of living across the board.[22] In short, whites have thrived in the Black Mecca more than ever. For African Americans, the advancements are undeniable but less remarkable. These strides have been complicated by the persistence of poverty, which itself is not unique to the Gate City as it is a common problem anywhere in America. Still, so many Black success stories must be measured against the vexing presence of Black poverty.

One Black Atlantan, nearly fifty years after the election of Mayor Jackson, reflected on her city, arguing that attention to Black achievement in various public displays, such as museums and murals, "evoke feelings of pride in what once was." Her city was fundamentally different from what it was in her childhood.

"But if you look closer," she writes, these celebrations of Black Atlanta "smack of hagiography verging on self-regard, a monument to what remains frustratingly incomplete. So, yes, Atlanta is, in many ways, the 'Black Mecca,' the historical center of a movement. But today, outside its bourgie Black bubble, with its McMansions and Beamers, deep inequities persist."[23] This attention to class differences in the city is not novel, of course. The city, like any, has always had Black class diversity, but few cities have such conspicuous displays of Black wealth. Moreover, fewer wider metro areas have been transformed by Black movement into the suburbs, as African Americans have relocated to newer and larger homes and more space.

Of course, the city alone could not cure all social ills. Scores of grassroots organizations and local branches of national nonprofits have attempted to address the exigencies faced in Atlanta. Some of the wealthiest Black Atlantans have been at the forefront of these efforts. Founded by the Herman J. Russell Foundation, the Russell Innovation Center for Entrepreneurs (or RICE) seeks to replicate the extraordinary businesses successes for which Atlanta is known. Importantly, it provides resources and training, connects investors, and offers grants to create Black business development among communities most isolated from traditional methods of investment. Jay Bailey, president and CEO of RICE, notes that these disturbing data on Black poverty and social immobility demand creative solutions. The city, with its deep wells of talent, has, Bailey explains, the "greatest potential to get it right."[24]

Indeed, the narrative of Atlanta has always been complicated, variegated by class and race in incredibly complex ways. Julian Bond, a veteran of the civil rights movement, explained that "for poor Black people without resources, circumstances are no different" than in any other city. Rodney Strong, who has played an important role in shaping the city's aggressive and effective affirmative action policies, differed with his friend and mentor: "I think that it is not entirely that dismal for African Americans with less training. Many of the jobs created [through municipal and county government efforts traced back to Maynard Jackson's model] have benefited working-class Black people without college degrees."[25] To illustrate his point, Strong points to the Atlanta airport, renamed Hartsfield-Jackson Atlanta International Airport in 2003, which has been the busiest airport in the world each year since 1998.[26] In 2002, *Ebony* praised the successes of the airport, noting that around "90 percent of the contracts that go to minority-owned firms that do business with American airports are at Hartsfield." Decades later, it continues to be an industry leader with MBE contracts, exceeding almost all major airports. Atlanta's Hartsfield-Jackson International Airport set its 2017 MBE concession goal at 41 percent, compared with goals of 23.2 percent and 32 percent at Los Angeles International Airport and Chicago O'Hare International Airport, respectively. This compares to New York's JFK International's 17 percent and San Francisco International's 8 percent MBE goals.[27]

With over 63,000 employees, Hartsfield-Jackson Atlanta International Airport is the largest employer in the state and generates over $82 billion to the Atlanta metro economy. It has been under an unbroken line of executive Black leadership since the mid-1980s and holds the notable achievement of scores of honors and awards for its management and innovation over decades. In 2021, for the eighteenth consecutive year, the Air Transport Research Society celebrated Hartsfield-Jackson as "the most efficient airport in the world." In 2023, it was ranked the world's "most profitable" airport. In a metro region that is 34 percent Black, about 75 percent of the airport's employees are Black. Far from being relegated to menial jobs, African Americans are pervasive at every level of the airport's administration—even in its contracts with outside firms. In fact, the number of contracts with firms owned by women and people of color exceeds all other airports in the country *combined*.[28] The airport, Strong explains, as well as dozens of occupations connected to the political economy, provides access to the middle class without college degrees. Numerous studies continue to affirm Strong's argument.

Across multiple years, *Forbes* magazine has listed Atlanta as the city where "African Americans are doing the best economically." By 2015, Atlanta led all cities with the ratio of Black-owned businesses and ranked as the city with the highest concentration of Black millionaires. Only New York State has more Black-owned businesses than Georgia. And during the movement of thousands of people to the city and (mostly) its suburbs, the city witnessed plummeting homicide rates. In 1994, two years before the city hosted the world in the Summer Olympic Games, it was ranked as the "most dangerous city" in the country. By 2018, under the administration of the city's sixtieth (and second Black woman) mayor, Keisha Lance Bottoms, the Gate City had witnessed a dramatic decline of homicides and other violent crimes. In Mayor Bottoms's first year in office, the city's homicide rate dropped lower than in any year since 1963. For context, the same list that ranked the city as the most dangerous in 1994 would declare Atlanta the thirteenth safest city spot—between Mesa, Arizona, and Colorado Springs—with the same data from 1994. In 2018, the violent crime rate was lower than the national average, significantly lower than rates in New York, Los Angeles, and Chicago years earlier.[29] These data helped strengthen the appeal of the Black Mecca, marking an increase in the city's population for the first time in fifty years, as detailed in the last chapter of this book. Its sixty-first (and seventh consecutive Black) mayor, Andre Dickens, was elected in 2021. A graduate of Benjamin E. Mays High School, Dickens was born in Atlanta the same year that Maynard Jackson first took office. He is the city's first mayor to have always lived under a Black mayor. Today, Atlanta remains one of only three cities over 250,000 (along with Washington, DC, and Newark) to share the distinction of having only Black mayors for over fifty years.

Not to be constricted to municipal power only within the city limits of Atlanta, the suburbs have been transformed with the influx of African Americans and other people of color. In 1993, a former student of Martin Luther King Jr., Charles Burris, won a seat on the Stone Mountain City Council. Former Imperial Wizard of the Klan James Venable, who served as Stone Mountain mayor (1946–49), was among the many residents whom Burris convinced to host a campaign sign in the yard. An attorney and former analyst for Mayor Maynard Jackson, Burris was elected mayor in the former Klan stronghold in 1997. His election marked the rise of Black municipal control in suburbs throughout the metro area. "There's a new Klan in Stone Mountain," Burris told the *New York Times*. "Only it's spelled with a C: c-l-a-n, citizens living as neighbors. And I guess I'm the Black dragon."[30]

In 2021, Stone Mountain elected its second Black mayor in its over 180-year history, Beverly Jones, a graduate of Morris Brown College. Its chief of police, superintendent of schools, and heads of many other municipal departments are African American. Over a century ago, James Venable was a schoolmate with Nathan Bedford Forrest III at Lithonia High School during the heyday of the Second Klan.[31] By 2022, the previous whites-only school was mostly Black with a Black principal. Much of these changes would have been unimaginable when Burris first sat in a class to listen to Dr. King teach or when he cast his first vote for Maynard Jackson. "This area is rich in history. Some of it is painful to many people. I want to deal with those facts in a way that people can [benefit] from. This should be a place where everyone can come to the table, not just black and white residents but also Hispanic and Asian." Burris reflected a bit and added, "The place has a tricky history."[32]

The election of Maynard Jackson was consequential not only as a historical first but as a powerful example of the potential to disrupt hardened traditions and codified forms of racial exclusion extending across centuries. Though he was not a leftist revolutionary or a Black nationalist, the ideological thrust of Jackson's administration largely aligned with most African Americans. He and his administration opened corridors of power in ways that no mayor of any major city had. The visibility of these strides changed Atlanta and its surrounding communities in remarkable ways in the process. While his administration could not remedy all social ills, it was fundamentally transformative across a range of metrics—even as the city continues to struggle with poverty and chasms in wealth. Hundreds of years of legally sanctioned racist wealth accumulation could not be corrected by any city over two generations. The achievements, nevertheless, cannot be ignored, even as measured against their structural limitations as part of the wider American enterprise.

For well over a decade, when all travelers exited the busiest airport on Earth, through 2020, they rose on the escalator and were greeted by an expansive, colorful wall depicting a beautiful, smiling Black girl with open arms welcoming everyone to Atlanta. While visitors to smaller airports, like JFK in New York or LAX in Los Angeles, could see a similar warm welcome from a Black child, its meaning in Hartsfield-Jackson strikes a special chord. Just like the airport's name, the image invites visitors familiar with the city's history to recognize a particular past meeting the present—wrapped with triumph, defeat, destruction, and resurgence. More than anything, however, there has always been the optimistic Atlanta spirit, rife with hope, promise, contradiction, tension, and drive. And though the city has always promoted itself as modern, it has never, at any point, ignored the power of history in shaping its present or future.

Notes

1. In 1880, African Americans in Augusta established Ware High School, which was the first public high school for Black people in Georgia. The county, however, closed it in 1897 despite Black protest. Jay Winston Driskell Jr., *Schooling Jim Crow: The Fight for Atlanta's Booker T. Washington High School and the Roots of Black Protest Politics* (Charlottesville: University of Virginia Press, 2014); "Marker Monday: Ware High School: Civil Rights Milestone," Georgia Historical Society, February 4, 2019, https://georgiahistory.com/marker-monday-ware-high-school-civil-rights-milestone/. See also "Booker T. Washington High School," City of Atlanta, accessed September 15, 2024, https://www.atlantaga.gov/government/departments/city-planning/historic-preservation/property-district-information/booker-t-washington-high-school.
2. Maurice Hobson, *The Legend of the Black Mecca* (Chapel Hill: University of North Carolina Press, 2017); Gary M. Pomerantz, *Where Peachtree Meets Sweet Auburn: The Saga of Two Families and the Making of Atlanta* (New York: Scribner, 1996).
3. Pomerantz, *Where Peachtree Meets Sweet Auburn*, 447, 460.
4. In 1981, the Morehouse School of Medical was founded as a separate and distinct school from Morehouse College. In 1988, Atlanta University and Clark College merged, forming Clark Atlanta University.
5. Ronald H. Bayor, *Race and the Shaping of Twentieth-Century Atlanta* (Chapel Hill: University of North Carolina Press, 2000), 229; Stephen Meyer, *As Long as They Don't Move Next Door: Segregation and Racial Conflict in American Neighborhoods*

(Lanham, MD: Rowman and Littlefield, 1999), 104. See also Karcheik Sims-Alvarado, *Atlanta and the Civil Rights Movement, 1944–1968* (Charleston: Arcadia, 2017); Frederick Allen, *Atlanta Rising: The Invention of an International City* (Greenville: Taylor Trade Publishing, 1996); Kevin Kruse, *White Flight: Atlanta and the Making of Modern Conservatism* (Princeton: Princeton University Press, 2005); Winston A. Grady-Willis, *Challenging U.S. Apartheid: Atlanta and Black Struggles for Human Rights, 1960–1977* (Durham, NC: Duke University Press, 2006); Tamiko Brown-Nagin, *Courage to Dissent: Atlanta and the Long History of the Civil Rights Movement* (New York: Oxford University Press, 2011).

6. Herman J. Russell, *Building Atlanta: How I Broke through Segregation to Launch a Business Empire* (Chicago: Chicago Review Press, 2014), 135–36.
7. Susan M. McGrath, "From Tokenism to Community Control: Political Symbolism in the Desegregation of Atlanta's Public Schools, 1961–1973," *Georgia Historical Quarterly* 79, no. 4 (1995): 864–70.
8. Allen, *Atlanta Rising*, 176.
9. Paul West et al., "School Desegregation in Metro Atlanta, 1954–1973," *Research Atlanta*, February 1973; McGrath, "From Tokenism to Community Control," 865.
10. Quoted in David R. Francis, "How the 1960s' Riots Hurt African-Americans," The Digest, September 1, 2004, National Bureau of Economic Research, www.nber.org/digest/sep04/w10243.html.
11. Jonathan Chait, "Riots and Social Change," *Popular Resistance*, June 13, 2015, https://popularresistance.org/riots-and-social-change/.
12. Omar Wasow, "Do Protests Matter? Evidence from the 1960s Insurgency," February 12, 2017, 31, accessed March 24, 2017, https://web.stanford.edu/group/peace justice/Wasow_Protests_on_Voting10_19.pdf.
13. V. P. Franklin, *Black Self-Determination: A Cultural History of African American Resistance* (New York: Lawrence Hill, 1992), 143.
14. Fred Hampton, "You Can Murder a Liberator, but You Can't Murder Liberation," in *The Black Panthers Speak*, ed. Philip S. Foner, 1st Da Capo Press ed. (Boston: Da Capo Press, 1995), 72.
15. Peter Range, "S.C.L.C. What Happened to the Dream?," *Atlanta Magazine*, April 1, 1972, www.atlantamagazine.com/civilrights/sclc-whats-happened-to-the-dream/.
16. Derrick White, *The Challenge of Blackness*, (Gainesville: University of Florida Press, 2011), 138.
17. Aaron Trupeau Sr., interview by author, July 13, 2018.
18. Michael H. Ross, "How Cities Create Systems to Support the Growth of Black-Owned Businesses," *The Empowerment Zone with Ramona Houston* (podcast), October 29, 2022, https://ramonahouston.com/podcast/how-cities-create-systems-to-support-the-growth-of-black-owned-businesses/?utm_term=jeffreyogbar@yahoo.com&utm_campaign=podcast%20update%20220628&utm_medium=email&utm_source=mail_from_10/29/2022.
19. "Going Home to the South," *60 Minutes*, June 12, 2003, www.cbsnews.com/news/going-home-to-the-south.
20. A similar pattern has emerged in the wealthiest Black-majority counties in the country, Prince Charles County and Prince George's County in Maryland. The latter has more Black people than all but three cities: New York, Chicago, and Philadelphia.

21. Larry Keating, *Atlanta: Race, Class, and Urban Expansion* (Philadelphia: Temple University Press, 2001), 76. See similar concerns expressed more recently in Michael Kruse, Brittany Gibson, and Delece Smith-Barrow's article on the secession of South Fulton from Atlanta, "What Will Become of 'America's Blackest City'?," Politico, September 16, 2022, www.politico.com/news/magazine/2022/09/16/americas-blackest-city-political-power-00054676.
22. Note that African Americans are more likely to live in non-married households than any other ethnic group. The wealth gap between married Black households and married white households, while still wide, is narrower than without controlling for marriage. Per capita income, similarly, finds even narrower gaps between whites and Blacks. Jim Skinner, "Income Inequality and Black Wealth: Opinions from Metro Atlanta Speaks," 33°N: Finding Meaning at 33.7°N, February 25, 2022, https://33n.atlantaregional.com/friday-factday/income-inequality-and-black-wealth-opinions-from-metro-atlanta-speaks.
23. Teresa Wiltz, "How Atlanta Became a City I Barely Recognize," Politico, September 16, 2022, www.politico.com/news/magazine/2022/09/16/atlanta-black-mecca-inequality-00055390.
24. Neima Abdulahi, "Is Atlanta Really Wakanda?," 11Alive (Atlanta), August 26, 2020; Russell Innovation Center for Entrepreneurs, accessed June 15, 2022, https://russellcenter.org/about-us/.
25. Julian Bond, interview by author, New Orleans, spring 2007; Rodney Strong, interview by author, Atlanta, May 31, 2022.
26. It briefly lost its title as busiest airport in 2020 during the global coronavirus pandemic but regained the rank in 2021. Marnie Hunter, "This US Airport Has Reclaimed Its Title as the World's Busiest," CNN, updated April 11, 2022, awww.cnn.com/travel/article/worlds-busiest-airports-2021/index.html.
27. "Hartsfield-Jackson Wins 2021 Airport Service Quality Award," AviationPros.com, March 10, 2022, www.aviationpros.com/airports/press-release/21259906/hartsfield jackson-atlanta-international-airport-atl-hartsfieldjackson-wins-2021-airport-service-quality-award; "Atlanta's Hartsfield-Jackson Named Most Efficient Airport in the World," WSBTV.com, September 6, 2021; "Is Atlanta the New Black Mecca?," *Ebony*, March 2002; "Hartsfield-Jackson Hikes Disadvantaged Business Contracting Goal," *Atlanta Journal-Constitution*, December 8, 2015, www.ajc.com/blog/airport/hartsfield-jackson-hikes-disadvantaged-business-contracting-goal/LHUayFtzPzCPWReowJiICK/.
28. "Hartsfield-Jackson Receives Multiple Awards," AviationPros.com, July 15, 2021, www.aviationpros.com/airports/press-release/21230612/hartsfieldjackson-atlanta-international-airport-atl-hartsfieldjackson-receives-multiple-awards; "Hartsfield-Jackson Generates Billions in Economic Activity in Region," *Atlanta Journal-Constitution*, February 10, 2020, www.ajc.com/business/hartsfield-jackson-generates-billions-economic-activity-region/1yb862FcDLyUjmLk0a1gjP/; Afifa Mushtaque, "5 Most Profitable Airports in the World," Insider Monkey, June 21, 2023, www.insidermonkey.com/blog/5-most-profitable-airports-in-the-world-1161364/?singlepage=1.
29. The raw number of homicides in 2018, eighty-eight, matched the number of 2013, when the population was smaller; therefore, the rate was lower. "Atlanta Police

Department, Cobra Report, Year-End 2018," Atlanta Police Department, accessed June 15, 2022, www.atlantapd.org/home/showpubliksheddocument/5571/638260 504379200000; "The Cities Where African-Americans Are Doing the Best Economically," *Forbes*, January 15, 2015, www.forbes.com/sites/joelkotkin/2015/01/15/the-cities-where-african-americans-are-doing-the-best-economically/; "What Are The Most Educated Cities In The U.S.? Top 100 Cities Ranked," *Forbes*, August 28, 2024, https://www.forbes.com/advisor/education/student-resources/most-educated-cities/. www.atlantapd.org/home/showpublisheddocument/5571/63826 0504379200000; "Atlanta Homicides 2nd Lowest in 50 Years," *Atlanta Journal-Constitution*, January 10, 2013; "Atlanta, GA, Crime Rate and Safety," *US News and World Report*, https://realestate.usnews.com/places/georgia/atlanta/crime. In 1994, Mesa, Arizona, and Colorado Springs, Colorado, had homicide rates of 18.83 and 20.17 (per 100,000 people) respectively. Atlanta's 2018 rate was 19.53 per 100,000 people. "The First Safest/Most Dangerous City Listing," Morgan Quitno Press, State and City Ranking Publications, (1995), accessed June 18, 2022, www.morganquitno.com/1st_safest.htm.

30. D. L. Chandler, "Chuck Burris Becomes 1st Black Mayor of Stone Mountain on This Day in 1997," News One, https://newsone.com/2755472/charles-chuck-burris-stone-mountain.

31. Nathan Bedford Forrest III was the grandson and namesake of the infamous Confederate general accused of war crimes against Black and white Union soldiers at the Fort Pillow Massacre in 1864. The Confederate was also the first Grand Wizard of the Ku Klux Klan. The Atlanta chapter of the Klan was named for Forrest, as was a street in the city of Atlanta.

32. *Smithsonian*, January 1999, 56–67; *New York Times*, November 22, 1997, A1; *Ebony*, October 1998, 128–31; *AC*, March 25, 1993, XA3, and November 5, 1997, C5. Chuck Burris died in 2009.

PART II

MAURICE J. HOBSON

Greetings, Earthlings, Take Me to Your Leader

A Post-1968 History of Black Atlanta through the Prism of Black Sci-Fi

Over the past thirty years and with constant allure, a shining example of Black science fiction in popular culture has come through OutKast, an Atlanta based hip-hop duo. Emerging from the shadows of the "Black Mecca" and Olympic City, OutKast and its LaFace Records labelmate Goodie Mob chronicled Atlanta's Black experience through their music, art, and symbolism. Rife with soul and funk, OutKast and Goodie Mob's music presented the meanings and significance of a self-defined southern style of rap and hip-hop culture called the Dirty South, creating the Atlanta "sound" and the imagery of the Black southern experience in urban spaces in a post-1968 context.

Influenced by Atlanta's unique experience of winning the bid to host the Centennial Olympiad (1996), the roots of the Dirty South were a combination of several factors, including a vibrant community-based Black arts scene, one developed and fostered at the Atlanta University Consortium's fine art programs, and the Black Arts movement—the cultural arm of the Black Power movement. Moreover, when Atlanta's first Black mayor, Maynard Jackson, created the City of Atlanta's Bureau of Cultural Affairs—the first institution within city government dedicated to the support of artists, their creative expression, and arts organization—it furthered efforts to make Atlanta attractive to Black artists worldwide. Through this snapshot of Atlanta's experience and with the implementation of the Georgia Entertainment Industry Investment Act's tax breaks, Atlanta attracted music moguls, writers, artists, and musicians from across the Black world, making Atlanta's Black expressive culture one of the city's greatest exports.[1]

While onlookers welcomed the Dirty South's sound, which "blended the feel of blues, the togetherness of funk, the conviction of gospel, the energy of rock, and the improvisation of jazz," OutKast and Goodie Mob's debut presented a much more nuanced idea of Atlanta as a "Black Mecca."[2] While their early music explicitly detailed the social cost paid by Atlanta's Black working and poor communities on behalf of the city's elite as witnessed through the "Olympification" of the city, it gave audiences glimpses of Black life in the urban South—including notions of religion and spirituality outside the norms of Bible Belt southern Christianity.[3] But there is more to the story than meets the eye.

Between 1865 and 1965, millions of Blacks left the South for the Midwest, North, and West to pursue jobs and a better quality of life. This movement is known as the Great Migration.[4] Yet, a series of civil rights victories called for Black migrants to reconsider the South as a new frontier. Shaped by their experiences in the Midwest, North, and West, Black folk joined a return, or reverse, migration. Over either multiple generations or just a decade, these Black migrants gave new meanings to an amalgamation of Black cultures, arriving with multitudes of new Blackness honed in the inner cities of the urban North, Midwest, and West. Journalist Isabel Wilkerson asserts that the "warmth of other suns" spewed new Black Americans who had thrived in every aspect of life outside of the South.[5]

In some ways, Black southerners who had never left the American South accused returning Blacks as being "generations who knew not Pharaoh," a term suggesting that these newer generations had not come up through a Black culture dragged in Louisiana swamp water, Mississippi mud, an Alabama summer breeze, or Georgia red clay. Conversely, Black migrants accused these same Black southerners of being "generations who knew not Joseph"[6]—or the possibility of what life could be minus the sordid racial history of the South. Most notably, Black religions and spiritualities of all persuasions were central and gave the experiences of African people a paradigm, combining the metaphysics of spirituality and community activism—a particular form of Black liberation theology that emerged out of necessity.[7] One aspect of religion and spirituality that flourished during this transition was the teachings of the Moorish Science Temple, which presented a spiritual awakening that birthed a series of religious factions, including the Nation of Islam, the Black Hebrews, and the Mystic Order of Melchizedek. Here, notions of Kemetic, Islamic, and Judeo-Christian cultures melded under the auspices of Black liberation. While the Nation of Islam, the Mystic Order of Melchizedek, and the Five Percenters had impact on Black life in cities such as New York, Chicago, Detroit, and Philadelphia, they had quasi-southern roots. Yet, the United Nuwaubian Nation of Moors had the most input in terms of Atlanta's Black popular culture.

Oftentimes, the American mainstream considered these groups to be cults, rife with kooks and crazies. But one must also consider the eccentricity of those who believe in Jesus Christ. Christians believe that Jesus rose from the dead on the third day after being crucified and ascended into the heavens on a cloud. When the ritual of Communion is practiced, they believe bread is converted to Christ's flesh and wine is converted to his blood (whether literally or symbolically). Despite how one sees the spiritual world, the beauty of this demonstrates the power of faith, defined as "the substance of things hoped for, the evidence of things not seen."[8] Since the beginning of time, human beings have looked to the heavens to make sense of this world. Black folk are no different.

The literature around Black phenomena in Africanizing cosmology, whether it be through indigenous African spirituality, Judeo-Christian traditions, or others, is growing and remains fascinating, to say the least, and a revived interest in Black concepts of religion and spirituality has reached new heights. Some credit this renewed interest to Beyoncé's 2016 studio album, *Lemonade*, which included themes and tropes that embodied African American folklore such as Zora Neal Hurston's *Their Eyes Were Watching God* and Black speculative fiction such as Octavia Butler's *Kindred*. The album also referenced African indigenous religion and spirituality, such as body paint and initiation into Santeria.[9] And while Beyoncé's *Lemonade* is one of the greatest albums of all time, these concepts are not new. Black folk have always drawn from the African ethos—where time travelers, super-humans, imaginary worlds, and other worldly characters are commonplace. From Sun Ra and the Arkestra to Octavia Butler and Ishmael Reed to Minister Fard Muhammad, Black creatives have forged elaborate fantasy worlds for generations. When Black people dare to dream of a world free of oppression and hatred, they create new worlds—which serve as refuge from the hostility of this world. With freedom as a theme, the lore of Black imagination is all-encompassing and necessary. It is in this vein that we must understand the necessity for Black cosmology and the fruits thereof.

An example of this thinking is the United Nuwaubian Nation of Moors, also known as the Nuwaubian Moors. According to Africana studies scholar Yusuf Nuruddin, the Nuwaubian Moors branched off from the Nation of Islam and the Moorish Science Temple, creating a contemporary urban mythology through Black religious "cults" expanded during the second and third phases of the Great Migration. As Black culture adapted due to Blacks migrating from the South to the Midwest, Northeast, and West Coast, these "myths" became a feature of this expanding culture.[10] Nuruddin states, "Part of the resistance to ascribing mythological status to urban narratives might be the notion that these narratives are after all merely political metaphors rather than expressions of universal truths."[11]

Nuruddin further asserts that science fiction motifs are present throughout Black urban landscapes both past and present, drawing from the scholarship produced by Alexei Panshin and Cory Panshin. In their book *The World beyond the Hill: Science Fiction and the Quest for Transcendence*, the Panshins maintain that science fiction is the mythology of the contemporary world—filling a "human need for imaginative transcendence—a need to transcend boundaries of the normal world by entering imaginative worlds of wonder, amazement and astonishment. Yet ancient myths of 'gods and ghosts, witches and wizards, brownies and elves, ogres and angels, cyclopses and centaurs, giants and jinns' were based on an idealistic worldview which affirmed magical causation."[12] Nuruddin further explains that these myths lost their influence due to the scientific revolution, when human consciousness subscribed to materialism rather than idealism.[13] While he provides an in-depth understanding of the Nation of Gods and Earths and the United Nuwaubian Nation of Moors, his analysis, steeped in the demographic shifts of the Great Migration, is dated. New scholarship trends and tensions focus on Blacks returning to the American South in what I call the Black New South and are critical to a better understanding of Black culture in the late twentieth and early twenty-first centuries.[14]

Much of my earlier research has investigated the role that the modern civil rights movement and larger Black freedom struggle played in establishing Atlanta's image as the "Black Mecca." In this essay, the global contexts as seen through the by-products of the political economies of race and the whitewashing of Dr. Martin Luther King Jr.'s dream; urban renewal and gentrification; and the expansion and annexation that rebranded and sanitized the city while criminalizing, demonizing, disenfranchising, and displacing Atlanta's Black, poor, and homeless populations created a moment where all aspects of the Black Atlanta experience were called into question. Thus, the rise of Dirty Southern hip-hop in the early 1990s has remained true to hip-hop's social justice orientation while advancing the total arc of hip-hop culture. But, because the experiences of Black southerners, both urban and rural, have often been misrepresented and dismissed by northern, midwestern, and western Blacks, a new analysis is needed to understand this culture through this southern Black urban mythology. Atlanta's development, over the last thirty years, presents the best conditions for how Black sci-fi serves as a lens to understand southern Black urban life in the city. Using OutKast as a focal point, this essay will demonstrate how the duo's music utilized the teachings of the United Nuwaubian Nation of Moors and Black sci-fi motifs as a prism to detail a counternarrative to the "Olympification" of Atlanta. Through an analysis of their artwork and symbolism as seen in their video "Elevators (Me & You)" from their sophomore album *ATLiens*, this essay will engage the trends and tensions surrounding the Sunbelt boom and the shift from the industrial age to the information age, the rise of crack cocaine, the HIV/AIDS epidemic, the War on Drugs and the rise of the prison industrial complex and the school-to-prison nexus, and the militarization of the police in the midst of Atlanta's unique process of urban renewal and gentrification that has been termed the "Olympification" process. Moreover, a unique feature of this scholarship shows how Black sci-fi coalesced Black liberation theology and convened an alternative world for Black Atlantans through the Moorish Science teachings of Dwight "Malachi" York and the United Nuwaubian Nation of Moors (formerly known as the Ansaru Allah community). This alternative form of Black spirituality influenced early forms of OutKast's music, connecting African cosmology, time traveling, and the extraterrestrial sensibilities of Black sci-fi to the experiences of Black Atlantans and the city's development.

Presently and problematically, many of the Black folk who converted to or subscribe to these religious factions are fashioned as "Hoteps" in the Black urban lexicon. According to journalist Damon Young, the term is Egyptian in origin, meaning "'at peace' or 'what's good?'" However, a misrepresentation of the term gained traction through Black cancel culture and is correlated with "woke left-wing" political views, whose adherents, while framing themselves as activists, also personify what is believed to be a thoughtless self-righteousness. In this, Black mainstreams present "Hotep" as "an all-encompassing term describing a person who's either a clueless parody of Afrocentricity . . . or someone who's loudly, conspicuously and obnoxiously pro-black but anti-progress."[15] Again, I pass no judgment, nor would I question how one comes to understand the universe—as scripture indicates that a talking serpent beguiled Eve to eat fruit from the tree of life.

The Black New South: A Homecoming

The factors that caused Atlanta to boom as a Black Mecca, attracting Blacks of all types, came about after 1965. A demographic shift spawned the Black New South, and the Black return or reverse migration forged new Black experiences. According to the 1971 US Census projection, 108,000 Blacks left other parts of the country and settled in the South, up from 97,000 in 1970. Studies show that between 1970 and 1973, 247,000 Blacks moved to the South, whereas 166,000 moved out of the South simultaneously. Many returners were either born or reared in the South, yet one-third of them had never lived in the South before.

While Black populations were concentrated in the South and millions of Blacks left the region from the 1860s to the 1960s, the majority of Black people stayed, connecting those who migrated through their remaining kith and kin.[16]

The catalyst that spawned the return of Black urban northerners, midwesterners, and westerners was civil rights victories in Birmingham and Selma and the subsequent legislation—the Civil Rights Act of 1964 and the Voting Rights Act of 1965. Most of the Blacks returning to the South were young professionals relocating to larger urban areas such as Birmingham, Nashville, and Memphis. The potential gained from citizenship and voting inexorably led to this shift, and by 1971 Atlanta was known as a "Black Mecca of the South" where entrepreneurship and political ambition thrived.[17]

Returning Blacks did not perceive the South as a perfect promised land free of racism, crime, and other social ills. Yet, there were two considerations why the American South became so attractive. First, there was growing discontent with the North, Midwest, and West's discrimination. Second, Blacks noticed shifts in the South's social climate as civil rights legislation stymied anti-Black racist policies that marked the Old South. As proof of this, there were 2,000 Black elected officials across the South, including several Black big city mayors. The Civil Rights Act and the Voting Rights Act galvanized Black politics and gave hope that the South was changing.[18]

Perhaps the most shining example of this trend was in 1973 when a unique coalition of white progressives and Black voters elected Maynard Jackson as Atlanta's first Black mayor, a watershed moment in southern Black political empowerment and electoral politics. Jackson's rise to power personified the city's Black educational and economic systems, giving Atlanta, as the Black Mecca, a new meaning. After waiting in the wings and biding their time, Black benefactors of civil rights legislation ruled the city.[19]

While many saw Jackson's election as pure symbolism, his affirmative action policies became the gold standard for American industry, producing an overabundance of Black millionaires buttressed by the expansion of Atlanta's airport and public transportation system—the Metropolitan Atlanta Rapid Transit Authority—and presenting economic inclusion as his significant contribution to modern civil rights. Crime and police brutality subsided under Jackson, and his creation of the Neighborhood Planning Unit allowed for Black communities to have a say in their development, which prevented displacement through gentrification.[20]

However, Atlanta's status with *international* implications, was inspired by Andrew Young, a lieutenant of Dr. King turned congressman, ambassador to the United Nations, and eventually the second Black mayor of Atlanta. Young inherited several social ills and an impending financial crisis due to President Ronald Reagan cutting federal funding to American cities. Moreover, the ability of Young, a shrewd statesman, to reach people—honed by his time as a foot soldier in the modern civil rights movement, his time in Congress, and his tenure as ambassador to the United Nations—catapulted Atlanta to a rebranding as the nation's newest world-class and international city. The Convention and Visitors Bureau deemed the city "Hotlanta" and welcomed business partners with Africa, the Arab world, Asia, the Caribbean, and Europe, promoting a global Black nationalism and citizenship that called the American South home. To do this, Young found it necessary to expand the city through international investments and neoliberal forms of urban renewal and gentrification. He used his Rolodex and political influence to modernize a city worthy of hosting the Democratic National Convention of 1988, a dress rehearsal for the Centennial Olympiad in 1996.[21]

When Atlanta hosted the Democratic National Convention, the international press marveled at the city's new facelift. The *Times* of London called the convention "the most spectacular event to hit the city since General Sherman—a republican—burnt it down in 1864"; Israeli state television said Atlanta "was trying to showcase itself to the world"; a French reporter stated, "It is appropriate that the convention is here because this year, for the first time, blacks feel they are really participating in the system"; the *Daily Telegraph* in London noted, "This is not politics. This is show time"; the *Frankfurter Allgemeine* asserted, "Mayor Andrew Young rules a city where political power is black and economic power is white"; and Bonn's daily newspaper, the *General Anzeiger*, announced, "This boomtown in the South looks like an energetic combination of Washington and Hollywood."[22]

With Atlanta having achieved world-class recognition, its people, history, and culture became of interest to the world, and because Atlanta was a majority-Black city at the time, Black expressive culture represented the city on the world's stage. However, Atlanta's ability to do this successfully started in 1974 with Maynard Jackson's creation of the City of Atlanta's Bureau of Cultural Affairs, the first institution within city government dedicated to the support of artists, their creative expressions, and arts organizations. The goal of the bureau was to make all forms of art—established and experimental—more accessible to Atlanta's citizens. The bureau empowered a multitude of artists and arts organizations through city-funded grants and broke new ground in fostering a niche for Black musical genres such as jazz and classical music as well as for alternative films. This set the stage for Atlanta to boom in terms of Black popular culture, as Jackson's notion of Black political power yielded an expressive arm, a Black

Arts movement unique to Atlanta and the larger Black New South, making the city ripe for popular culture to be spewed and accessed critically.[23]

It is in this vein that OutKast and Goodie Mob gained traction not only in Atlanta but throughout the world. Atlanta was bursting at the seams with talent, and its world-class international airport and revamping of its downtown area made the city worthy of receiving the world. With Atlanta rising, the city enjoyed worldwide praise but endured local blame. Also, the benefits of the city's public relations victory were not, and have never been, distributed impartially. As Black communities had suffered at the hands of anti-Black racism, they, as any group of humans, imagined themselves in better worlds to cope with the harsh reality of Black life. They sought worlds that fostered Black pride—whether bogus or genuine—and the United Nuwaubian Nation of Moors offered the space to imagine. Controversial and crucial, some Black folks saw the Nuwaubians as the aforementioned "evidence of things unseen." For many, nearly 500 years of the oppressors' religion had not delivered Black folk to the "promised land," and it is here that the United Nuwaubian Nation of Moors found its niche. This was not the first time a Black religious-nationalist organization set its sights on the Atlanta metro area. Several other groups had asserted their presence in the city, including the Pan-African Orthodox Christian Church, known to Atlantans as the Shrine of the Black Madonna, located in Atlanta's West End; the African Hebrew Israelites congregation known as House Yisrael of Atlanta, located in southwest Atlanta; the Nation of Alkebulan; the Nation of Islam; and the Moorish Science Temple of America.

The United Nuwaubian Nation of Moors

Out of Atlanta's notable Black experience and with Black reverse or return migrations, a vehicle of Black spirituality steeped in the politics of liberation emerged, eventually designated as the United Nuwaubian Nation of Moors, whose "factology" reflected the rules by which members governed themselves.[24] The Nuwaubians mixed ideas of Black power and reverence for Egypt and its pyramids and lent credence to UFOs and numerous conspiracies related to the Illuminati and the Bilderbergers.[25]

According to the Southern Poverty Law Center, the Nuwaubians state, "We are the Indigenous people of these shores, before the settlers from Europe came to these shores spreading their way of life, their filth and religion," refuting the idea that the majority of African people arrived in the Western world as enslaved bondmen. In an undated lecture given by the group's leader (who styles himself as "Dr."), Dwight "Malachi" York argued that "Christianity is merely a tool used by the Devil (Paleman) to keep you, the Nubian (Black) man, woman, and child blind to your true self heritage and perfect way of life (Islam). It is another means of slavery."²⁶ York's most scathing critique:

> The Caucasian has not been chosen to lead the world. They lack true emotions in their creation. We never intended them to be peaceful. They were bred to be killers, with low production levels and a short life span. What you call Negroid was to live 1,000 years each and the other humans 120 years. But the warrior seed of Caucasians is only 60 years old. They were only created to fight other invading races, to protect the God race Negroids. But they went insane, lost control when they were left unattended. They were never to taste blood. They did, and their true nature came out. . . . Because their reproductive levels were cut short, their sexual organs were made the smallest so that the female of their race will want to breed with Negroids to breed themselves out of existence after 6,000 years. It took 600 years to breed them, part man and part beast.²⁷

While these words are credited to a November 10, 2004, letter written by York, the sources providing this information, which include the organization's website, a counterintelligence investigation conducted by the Federal Bureau of Investigation, and the Southern Poverty Law Center, should be considered compromised in their perspective. On the organization's website, readers cannot validate this information as truth, while the FBI and the Southern Poverty Law Center's intent was to indict the organization as a Black supremacist group. The rhetoric of the Nuwaubians, when called in question, was a quasi-response to anti-Black racism, which cannot be denied.

Selling his people on the fact that "a land of milk and honey" awaited them in Georgia, Dwight "Malachi" York bought a 476-acre parcel of land just outside of Eatonton in Putnam County, Georgia, in 1993. The cost of the property was $975,000, and the United Nuwaubian Nation of Moors quickly moved its headquarters there from Brooklyn, New York. The settlement took the name of Tama-Re.²⁸ As expected, the Nuwaubian invasion was met with resistance from local authorities—both Black and white. Using zoning regulations, local authorities attempted to restrict movement and growth of the community. Conversely, the Nuwaubians arrived in Georgia seeking widespread acknowledgment and acceptance of their "sacred knowledge." While all races were taken aback, the group's secrecy raised concerns with the white residents of Eatonton in particular, concerns that were exacerbated when the Nuwaubians in 1997 erected a forty-foot-high black pyramid, eight-foot-high statues of ancient Egyptian gods and goddesses, columns with hieroglyphics, a sphinx, and smaller twenty-four-foot pyramids made of wood and stucco.[29]

Many Black and white Americans in the mainstream saw this settlement as the next iteration of doomsday cults such as Jim Jones's Jonestown in Guyana or David Koresh's Branch Davidians in Waco, Texas. While Jonestown ended with mass suicide in 1978, the Branch Davidians made headlines in February 1993 when the group came under attack by the US Bureau of Alcohol, Tobacco, Firearms and Explosives (ATF). But the Nuwaubians presented a different context. Dwight York was born in New York in 1935, and his understanding of Black religion and spirituality was impacted by other Black movements that emphasized Black Power, self-determination, and Pan-Africanism, including the Nation of Islam, Black Hebrews such as the Commandment Keepers, the Five Percenters, and Marcus Garvey's Universal Negro Improvement Association. In 1969, York commanded his disciples to embrace their "true Jewish identity, creating the Nubian Islamic Hebrews, Ancient Holy Tabernacle of the Most High, the Children of Abraham, and the Mystic Order of Melchizedek, all of which blended elements of Judaism and Christianity," and he told them to believe they were a "chosen people."[30] Demonstrating that human behavior is often governed by unconfirmed beliefs and other unforeseen forces, this community's faith and "factology" are how members governed their lives.

York convinced his disciples that he could build "a real nation, our own nation . . . with our own passports, with our own tax system, where no one tells us what to do but us." Upon moving to Georgia, he distanced the Nuwaubians from Islam, and the group went through several changes in terms of names and affiliation, which included York declaring himself "Chief Black Eagle" of the "Yamassee Native American Moors of the Creek Nation."[31] In attempting to self-identify as having Indigenous status, his goal was to apply for a casino operating license, to no avail. Conveniently, the group took the name of the United Nation of the Nuwaubian Moors. He then identified as a god from outer space.[32]

In Georgia, York lived in a mansion while his disciples lived in "cheap trailers." In June 1998, he grossed about $500,000 by charging Nuwaubians $25 a year for their "passports," which allowed them to enter and exit the compound. He also created organized chapters and bookstores called "All Eyes on Egipt [sic]" and illegally operated a nightclub called "Club Ramses."[33] In a 1999 interview, Nuwaubian leader Minister Marshall Chance, head of the Nuwaubian's Holy Tabernacle Ministries, was asked if the nation expected the return of a spaceship. His answer, "Some of us do, and some of us don't." Julius H. Bailey asserts that Chance's measured response "exemplifies the ideological mixed message the group has promulgated throughout its existence, in part, to safeguard their complicated evolving self-identity."[34]

Turning to OutKast: Kevin Sipp—the fine artist, independent scholar, curator, and arts administrator for the City of Atlanta's Gallery 72 Cultural Affairs—stated in an interview, "I used to attend the Ansaru Allah community on Edgewood [downtown Atlanta in the Sweet Auburn District] and would see all of Organized Noize in the center. We became cool and I would work with them on helping them understand some of the teachings. This allowed for me to serve as the poet featured on an album track by Organized Noize artist Da Witchdoctor. A lot of what they put in their music comes from these teachings."[35] Dalithian Hibbler, also known as Peaches the Queen and business manager of Organized Noize, stated that OutKast and Goodie Mob bought books, magazines, and newspapers for group members' consumption and had them write their rhymes around current affairs.[36] Hibbler later disclosed that the materials came from the All Eyes on Egipt bookstore.

By the end of OutKast's debut album, André Benjamin (André 3000) and Antwan Patton (Big Boi) signaled that they had been either influenced by Dwight "Malachi" York or under his teachings. Case in point, their lyrics on the sixteenth track of *Southernplayalisticadillacmuzik*, titled "D.E.E.P.," start with a voiceover of an alien life form stating, "Greetings, Earthlings, take me to your leader,"[37] manipulated by either an Electro-Harmonix "Golden Throat" or a Yamaha DX100 FM synthesizer known as a talk box made popular by Roger Troutman and Zapp, a late twentieth-century funk band hailing from Dayton, Ohio. The two members of OutKast began to present their otherworldliness. Later on the track, André Benjamin goes even deeper by referring to the alleged mad scientist Dr. Yakub (Jacob) when he states, "No, I ain't never been pimped by the system, that's because I ain't no slave. / Don't be tryna sunbathe, never lived off in no cave. / Bloody old chap and in this head of mine is full of naps."[38] While the teachings of the Moorish sciences believe Yakub (Jacob) to be a mad scientist, the teachings of the Nation of Islam believe Yakub to be a geneticist who believed he could bring out a new people from the original Black man. The new people were white. Often referred to as Dr. Yakub, the personification of this character is centered on the biblical character Jacob, the grandson of Abraham, son of Isaac, and younger twin brother of Esau. After finagling Esau's birthright in exchange for some stew, Jacob was forced to flee Palestine. While on the lam, he arrived at his uncle Laban's home and there fell in love with his cousin Rachel. To earn her hand in marriage, he worked for Laban for seven years, only to receive the hand of Laban's other daughter, Leah. Feeling disrespected, Jacob worked for Laban for another seven years and was granted marriage to Rachel. As a shepherd and animal husbandry practitioner, he was promised not only land but all of the bred sheep that were snow white—or, as it is referred to in the Holy Bible, without a spot or blemish. Jacob's breeding program punished the deceitful Laban; he took not only his daughters and his land but most of his flock of sheep as well. These white sheep are believed to be a product of his scientific acumen and the birth of eugenics, with the creation of cave-dwelling white men.[39]

Furthermore, a more direct correlation with York's teachings are the visuals seen in the music video for OutKast's track "Elevators (Me & You)" from the duo's sophomore album, *ATLiens*. After *Southernplayalisticadillacmuzik* was met with positive reviews, moving up to #20 on the US *Billboard* 200 chart,[40] #3 on the US Top R&B/Hip-Hop Albums chart,[41] and going certified platinum in 1995 after being on the charts for nearly a year,[42] onlookers waited for *ATLiens* with bated breath. During this time, André Benjamin had stopped smoking marijuana, became vegan, locked his hair, got into books of spiritualism, became celibate, and earned his GED. Antwan Patton had his first child and lost his aunt.[43] When the single premiered, it detailed their experience of being from Atlanta, their growth, and how they were making a way for the South to be taken seriously in hip-hop culture. In an interview with hip-hop scholar Regina Bradley, she noted that the song discussed "the price and consequences of the come up[pance] and who gets to come with you . . . what they did to make it and how they were dealing with success in their own unique ways."[44]

Moreover, the symbolism found in the "Elevators (Me & You)" video presented more of a Nuwaubian experience than the mainstream realized. The video opens with a view of an earthlike planet from space and zeroes in on a jungle where a group of nomadic people dressed in white and black are led by André 3000 and Big Boi. The scene then cuts to a comic book version of the nomadic group and spins out to 1996, where a young boy, with his skateboard at his side, is reading a comic titled *LaFace Records Presents . . . ATLiens: The OutKast Encounter*, with a green alien donning its cover. In the video, André wears his signature turban and graduates with his GED. When the scene cuts back to the wilderness, André, Big Boi, and the nomadic group are seen sitting around what seems to be a giant hookah or some kind of incense-burning cipher circle and are meditating. While they meditate, a group of white scientists dressed in hazmat suits are searching the area with an infrared detector device and infrared spectacles. It is believed that these scientists are the aliens because they must wear a suit to survive. They are in search of the nomadic group or original people. When the hook is sung, a bouncing lyric ball in the likeness of an alien head appears to hover over the words "Me and you / Your mama and your cousin too / Rollin' down the strip on vogues,[45] / Comin' up, slammin' Cadillac doors."[46]

After the chorus, the scene goes back to the scientists, who, looking through their infrared spectacles, see the infrared alien footprints of nomadic people. When André starts his verse, he is being accommodated by a woman dressed in a galabiya, or djelleba, a loose-fitting traditional garment from the Nile Valley, and, realizing that they are being hunted by the mad scientists, they move clandestinely through the jungle seeking refuge. Maneuvering through the woods, André puts his hand on a tree, unknowingly leaving a mark able to be seen only by the mad scientists wearing the infrared goggles. When the scientists lay eyes on André, Big Boi, and the nomads, they realize that the nomadic group are aliens—original men. But moving closer to refuge, André, Big Boi, and the nomads come to an open grassland full of pyramids—the city of Atlantis. When the lost children run toward the pyramids, they are seen in their true form, as aliens—Black and swarthy. When the scene cuts back to André and Big Boi, they are beginning to convert to their alien selves, with big green eyes.[47]

Putting OutKast's "Elevator (Me & You)" in context, it becomes clear that the video is influenced by the teachings of Dwight "Malachi" York and the United Nuwaubian Nation of Moors. According to intel gathered by a counterintelligence sting operation that brought down the Nuwaubian nation, the group's mythology was a mystifying myriad of UFO theories, affinity for Egypt and the pyramids, references to Atlantis, and a recasting of biblical and other Abrahamic scriptures with a new racialized context. While these ideas may be far-fetched, consider this experience through the lens of Atlanta's Black communities that witnessed the city's "Olympification." The 1970s and '80s were plagued with a series of murders where the city's most vulnerable yet vibrant citizens—Black children—were being hunted by a serial killer or killers. This episode is known to the public as the Atlanta child murders.

When President Ronald Reagan slashed federal funds to American inner cities, Mayor Andrew Young, a lieutenant of the late Martin Luther King Jr., found a workaround, the expansion of the city through foreign investments in conjunction with neoliberal forms of urban renewal and gentrification. While Young did all he could to survive a right-wing president and an often schizophrenic set of Democratic Georgia governors, he had no plan to deal with the issue felt by the most marginalized in Atlanta—the Black poor, homeless, and working-class communities. Subsequently, the demise of industrialization and the rise of the information age left Atlanta's Black working classes and poor drowning in unemployment. Reaganomics eviscerated Atlanta's Black communities on issues of education and fair housing, while the emergence of crack cocaine produced the War on Drugs—a war on Black people—and diverted funds from education to this cause. Thus, the prison industrial complex and the militarization of the police reached new heights. Examples of this include turf wars between the "Miami Boys" and "Atlanta Hustlers" over crack cocaine and the subsequent creation of the Red Dog police.[48] The arrival of AIDS crippled Black communities in Atlanta, where Black populations suffered some of the highest rates of HIV/AIDS in the world. When a manifold crowd of private financiers produced the capital to give Atlanta a viable shot at winning the Olympic Games, the United States Olympic Committee and the Atlanta Committee on the Olympic Games worked to ready the city for hosting, waging war against poverty and poor people. Thus, Atlanta's Olympic movement—disguised as progress and steeped in King's dream on steroids—was seen as a movement to further criminalize, demonize, disenfranchise, and displace Atlanta's Black indigenous people at record levels.[49] Atlanta's overwhelmingly poor and Black citizens did not share in the vision of Atlanta as an international city.[50] While those in Atlanta's Black city government did the best they could in these circumstances, the limited powers of city government, in a claret-red state, reared its ugly head. Urban renewal, gentrification, displacement, disenfranchisement, and criminalization, along with the passage of a state-sanctioned "two strikes" law, which overwhelmingly incarcerated Black men, weaponized the Olympics to wreak havoc on Black Atlantans.

The fall of Dwight "Malachi" York started when he came under fire after his son Jacob York, who broke away from the group in 1990, went to Georgia to confront the Nuwaubian leader. The younger York helped law enforcement build a case against his father. Putnam County officials schemed to raid Tama-Re but wanted to avoid a standoff that would have rivaled David Koresh and the Branch Davidians' 1993 siege and bloodbath brought on by the ATF. The compound was eventually raided on May 8, 2002, by 300 law enforcement agents, including the FBI, ATF, and local sheriff's departments after York and his most trusted "wife," Kathy Johnson, were arrested. Agents found guns and other contraband. York was indicted on seventy-four counts of child molestation, twenty-nine counts of aggravated child molestation, and one count of rape. After these violations were made public, more accusations came forth, which led York to be charged with racketeering and transporting children across state lines for the purpose of sexual intercourse. York was eventually sentenced to 135 years in prison on the state charges.[51]

OutKast and Goodie Mob's music eventually broke away from the teachings of the United Nuwaubian Nation of Moors around 2002, when the group came under fire. But their intrigue with the Nuwaubians was understandable, because much like the genre of hip-hop, which borrowed, sampled, and manipulated sounds from other genres, the urban myth adapted by the Nuwaubians borrowed from all kinds of spiritual systems—including Judaism, Islam, Hinduism, and African and American Indigenous spiritual practices. After 2002, OutKast's André Benjamin referenced comets, spaceships, and Atlantis but not as frequently as he had earlier.

OutKast is now recognized as one of the most acclaimed duos in music history, boasting forty-one awards, including seven Grammys, four World Music Awards, three BET Awards, and the title of Band of the Year at the GQ Men of the Year Awards. However, many overlook their modest beginnings and their pivotal role in shaping Atlanta, Georgia, into what some would consider the hip-hop capital of the world. By embracing Black southern elements like dialect, sensual appeal, and older musical genres rooted in southern Black traditions, OutKast created a unique identity that helped them carve out space in a rapidly growing music industry. Alongside this, they incorporated Black sci-fi themes to craft a counternarrative to the "Olympification" of Atlanta, best exemplified by their track "Elevators (Me & You)."

Through their music, OutKast presents Black cosmological insights that explained the Sunbelt economic boom, the transition from the industrial to the information age, the crack epidemic, the HIV/AIDS crisis, the War on Drugs, the rise of the prison-industrial complex, and the school-to-prison pipeline. They also address the militarization of the police that occurred during Atlanta's unique urban renewal and gentrification process, often referred to as "Olympification."

In Atlanta, where music and spirituality intertwine, Black sci-fi merged with Black liberation theology, offering an alternative reality for Black Atlantans, influenced by the Moorish Science teachings of Dwight "Malachi" York and the United Nuwaubian Nation of Moors. This alternative spirituality shaped OutKast's early aesthetic, connecting African cosmology, time travel, and extraterrestrial ideas in Black sci-fi to the lived experiences of Black Atlantans and the city's evolution.

Notes

1. Maurice J. Hobson, *The Legend of the Black Mecca: Politics and Class in the Making of Modern Atlanta* (Chapel Hill: University of North Carolina Press, 2017), 203–4.
2. Alona Wartofsky, "Dirty South Rides High in Hip-Hop World: Rap Heading in a New Direction," *Florida Times-Union*, March 15, 2000, C/1; Sonia Murray, "Welcome Noize: Local Producing Trio behind Big TLC Hit Puts Positive Spin on Its Brand of Rap That Revisits the Spirit of '60s Soul Sound," *Atlanta Journal-Constitution*, November 14, 1995, D/1.

3. Hobson, *Legend of the Black Mecca*, 2, 10. The "Olympification" of a city is an umbrella term where gentrification, neoliberalism, racial uplift, urban renewal, and urban regime theory all work together to present a process for which cities are franchised for world consumption due to big sporting events—the Olympics, World Cup, Pan Am Games, Super Bowl—yet criminalizes, demonizes, disfranchises, displaces, and destroys the poor communities. The context of how this works is important.
4. The Great Migration began as early as the 1860s and spanned through the 1970s. The movement of Black people from the American South to the Midwest, Northeast, and West operated in waves, the first period being from 1860 to 1875; the second from 1890 to 1925; the third, 1945 to 1960; and the fourth, 1965 to 1975.
5. Isabel Wilkerson, *The Warmth of Other Suns: The Epic Story of America's Great Migration* (New York: Vintage Press), 2011.
6. Both terms—generations who knew not Pharaoh and generations who knew not Joseph—are references to the biblical character Joseph. Of course, the reference to Pharaoh connotes Egypt's enslavement of Israel and the Israelites' forty-year journey through the wilderness. The reference to Joseph is to the story of Joseph, the son of Jacob and Leah, who was hated by his half-brothers and sold into slavery to Egypt. His gift of interpreting dreams landed him as second in command over all of Egypt. The generation who knew not Joseph indicates that some are able to grow and thrive in new locations.
7. James H. Cone, *Black Theology and Black Power*, anniversary ed. (Maryknoll, NY: Orbis Books, 2019); *A Black Theology of Liberation*, 40th anniversary ed. (Maryknoll, NY: Orbis Books, 2010); and *God of the Oppressed* (Maryknoll, NY: Orbis Books, 1997).
8. Hebrews 11:1.
9. Zeffie Gaines, "A Black Girl's Song Misogynoir, Love, and Beyonce's Lemonade," *Taboo: The Journal of Culture and Education* 16, no. 2 (2017): 97–114; Jamie Moore, "Beyonce's *Lemonade* Is Made for Readers," review of Beyonce's *Lemonade*, *Book Riot*, May 5, 2016, https://bookriot.com/beyonces-lemonade-is-made-for-readers/#:~:text=Beyonc%C3%A9's%20Lemonade%20was%20made%20for,specific%20book%20list%20ohere!.
10. Yusuf Nuruddin, "Ancient Black Astronauts and Extraterrestrial Jihads: Islamic Science Fiction as Urban Mythology," *Socialism and Democracy* 20, no. 3 (2006): 131.
11. See Nuruddin, "Ancient Black Astronauts," 131.
12. Nuruddin, "Ancient Black Astronauts," 132–33.
13. See Nuruddin, "Ancient Black Astronauts," 132–33.
14. In the Black New South theoretical framing presented here, I assert that the Black New South focuses on the experiences of Black Americans in the post-1965 contexts, challenging tensions and trends often overlooked by scholars studying the Black experience, and analyzes and explicates national and international implications centered on history, urban and rural experiences, Black popular culture, education, electoral politics, landownership, health disparities, and the social, mental, spiritual, and economic health of the Black world.
15. Damon Young, "Hotep, Explained," *The Root: Black News and Black Views with a Whole Lotta Attitude*, March 5, 2016, www.theroot.com/hotep-explained-1790854506.

16. Hobson, *Legend of the Black Mecca*, 61, 219; US Census Data from 1970 to 2000, WAGDA, accessed May 20, 2024, http://wagda.lib.washington.edu/data/type/census/; Virginia H. Hein, "The Image of 'A City Too Busy to Hate': Atlanta in the 1960's," *Phylon* 33 (Fall 1972): 211.
17. Phyl Garland, "Atlanta: Black Mecca of the South," *Ebony*, August 1971, 151–57; Hobson, *Legend of the Black Mecca*, 61–62.
18. David A. Bositis, *Black Elected Officials: A Statistical Summary 2000* (Washington, DC: Joint Center for Political and Economic Studies, 2002).
19. Hobson, *Legend of the Black Mecca*, 3.
20. See Hobson, *Legend of the Black Mecca*, 161.
21. Hobson, *Legend of the Black Mecca*, 140.
22. See Hobson, *Legend of the Black Mecca*, 140; Matthew Vita, "Decision '88—a View from Foreign Press: This Is Not Politics: This Is Show Time," *Atlanta Journal-Constitution*, July 21, 1998, C/1.
23. Maurice J. Hobson, "All That Jazz: Forty Years of Influence through the Atlanta Jazz Festival, a Brief and Concise History," in the official publication commemorating forty years of the Atlanta Jazz Festival titled *Atlanta Jazz Festival: Forty Years* (Atlanta: Two Paths Press, 2017); Maynard Jackson Mayoral Administration Records, box 45, folder 3, Robert W. Woodruff Library at the Atlanta University Center, Atlanta, GA; City of Atlanta News Release, July 21, 1978, Maynard Jackson Mayoral Administration Records; *30 Years of the Atlanta Jazz Festival in Pictures* (Atlanta: Office of Cultural Affairs, 2007); Francine Earl, "Sun Ra Sends Jazz Lovers Soaring into Outer Space," *Atlanta Daily World*, September 24, 1978.
24. "Nuwaubian Nation of Moors," Southern Poverty Law Center, accessed April 30, 2023, www.splcenter.org/fighting-hate/extremist-files/group/nuwaubian-nation-moors?gclid=CjwKCAjwo7iiBhAEEiwAsIxQEWX7zkxBxTdx_1J_IEkJVBE9vQYbBBDYFtZyw_QVJcxxtbr8M7g-AhoCoIIQAvD_BwE.
25. According to *Britannica* Online, members of the Illuminati see themselves as a source of light because of their "direct communication" from a higher source or due to their exalted condition of human intelligence. The Illuminati's origins were in Spain at the end of Muslim Spain (711–1492), and it has spawned several movements that have circled the globe. It is believed to be a form of white supremacy. In a similar fashion as the Illuminati, the Bilderbergers are elite leaders of governments and experts in finance, media, and academia from Europe and North America. According to *Britannica* Online, their meetings are held in a different European or North American country each year and provide a private, informal environment in which those who influence national policies and international affairs in the West can get to know each other and discuss without adhering to national interests. It is widely believed that these members are all white, and this group is perceived to be a higher-level form of white supremacy.
26. See "Nuwaubian Nation of Moors."
27. See "Nuwaubian Nation of Moors."
28. See "Nuwaubian Nation of Moors."
29. See "Nuwaubian Nation of Moors."
30. Julius H. Bailey, "The Final Frontier: Secrecy, Identity, and the Media in the Rise and Fall of the United Nuwaubian Nation of Moors," *Journal of the American Academy of Religion* 74, no. 2 (2006): 304.

31. "Nuwaubian Nation of Moors."
32. Bob Moser, "United Nuwaubian Nation of Moors Meets Its Match in Georgia," Southern Poverty Law Center, September 20, 2002, www.splcenter.org/fighting-hate/intelligence-report/2002/united-nuwaubian-nation-moors-meets-its-match-georgia.
33. "Nuwaubian Nation of Moors."
34. Bailey, "Final Frontier," 302–23; Sylvester Monroe, "Space Invaders: Strangers from the North Send a Southern Town into a Tizzy," *Time*, July 12, 1999.
35. Kevin Sipp, interview by Maurice J. Hobson, October 21, 2015.
36. Dalithian Hibbler, interview by Maurice J. Hobson, February 6, 2016.
37. OutKast, "D.E.E.P.," track 16 on *Southernplayalisticadillacmuzik*, LaFace Records, 1994.
38. See OutKast, "D.E.E.P."
39. For more context, please read Genesis 25:19–34. Jacob later wrestled with an angel, and his named changed to Israel. Among Jewish groups, he is considered the patriarch of Israel, having thirteen children, twelve of whom are considered founders of the tribes of Israel.
40. "Billboard 20, Week of May 14, 1994," *Billboard*, www.billboard.com/charts/billboard-200/1994-05-14/.
41. "Top R&B/Hip-Hop Albums," *Billboard*, May 14, 1994, www.billboard.com/charts/r-b-hip-hop-albums/1994-05-14/.
42. "The Recording Industry Association of America," Gold & Platinum, April 5, 1995, www.riaa.com/gold-platinum/?tab_active=default-award&ar=Outkast&ti=Southernplayalisticadillacmuzik&format=Album&type=#search_section.
43. Andres Tardio, "11 Things You Might Not Know about OutKast's 'ATLiens,'" *Billboard*, August 27, 2016, www.billboard.com/music/rb-hip-hop/things-you-might-not-know-outkast-atliens-big-boi-andre-300-7487857.
44. Regina Bradley, interview by Maurice Hobson, April 21, 2023.
45. Tire Agent Staff, "What Are Trues and Vogues?," *Tire Agent*, January 17, 2022, www.tireagent.com/blog/what-are-trues-and-vogues-wheels-and-tires. Trues and Vogues reference a combination of luxury tires and cool wire wheels on classic cars such as the Cadillac, Oldsmobile Cutlass, and Box Chevy. More specifically, wheels made by Truespoke are referred to as "Trues," and luxury tires made by Vogue Tyre and Rubber Co. are referred to as "Vogues."
46. OutKast, "Elevators (Me & You)," track 3 on *ATLiens*, LaFace Records, 1996.
47. OutKast, "Elevators (Me & You)," official HD video on YouTube, accessed April 30, 2023, https://youtu.be/uqB_UVlhlPA.
48. Hobson, *Legend of the Black Mecca*, 150–51.
49. Anita Beaty, *Atlanta's Olympic Legacy: Background Paper* (Geneva, Switz.: Center on Housing Rights and Evictions, 2007), 20, 25, 27, 31; Atlanta Olympic Conscience Coalition, "A Displacement Analysis of the OCDA Master Olympic Development Program for the City of Atlanta" (Atlanta: Metro Atlanta Task Force for the Homeless, 1993).
50. Dorothy Bolden oral history interview, March 16, 1994, Atlanta Interfaith Broadcasters Oral History Interviews, Auburn Avenue Research Library, Atlanta-Fulton Library System, Atlanta, GA.
51. "Nuwaubian Nation of Moors."

SCOT BROWN

Bands to Make You Dance

Dayton, Ohio, Black Bands, and Popular Music

When I was making "I Can Make You Dance," all I could think about was evangelists, you know, how all evangelists would always say, they would touch somebody and heal them and make them feel better or ease their pain, and they wouldn't need crutches or they wouldn't need a doctor and that's what I was thinking about with this record—I was trying to reach out and touch everybody so they could forget about their problems by just dancing.—**Roger Troutman**

Songs boasting of a group's onstage prowess were hallmarks of the golden age of Black bands and the funk era of the 1970s. In the mid- to late 1960s, an undercurrent of self-contained bands began to carve out a space in Black popular music during a time when the Motown model of vocal groups and solo vocalists dominated the airwaves. Groups such as Sly and the Family Stone, the Ohio Players, Funkadelic, Charles Wright and the Watts 103rd Street Rhythm Band, the Bar-Kays, the Jimmy Castor Bunch, Mandrill, Kool & the Gang, the Meters, the J.B.'s, Jimi Hendrix (Band of Gypsys), the Isley Brothers, and Earth, Wind & Fire represented a vanguard force in what music historian Rickey Vincent described as a "rhythm revolution." Groups of musicians within a single unit applied the musical formula set forth by James Brown whereby the instrumentation and vocal tracks were arranged and layered polyrhythmically to form a river of sound known colloquially as the "groove."[1]

By the late 1970s, the earlier cohort of bands inspired an avalanche of charting groups, moving the presence of Black bands from the margins to the center of popular music: Graham Central Station, Commodores, Heatwave, Brothers Johnson, Rufus featuring Chaka Khan, Parliament, Bootsy's Rubber Band, Slave, the S.O.S. Band, Brick, Cameo, Con Funk Shun, L.T.D., Pleasure, Lakeside, Rick James and the Stone City Band. In 1976, when describing the dominant music industry trends in Black music, Henry Allen, the president of

Cotillion Records and senior vice president of Atlantic Records, observed, "The self-contained group now has an unbelievable hold on the market, and this is the type of group I am seeking."[2] Allen, from Springfield, Ohio, would have to venture only about twenty-five miles southwest of his hometown to neighboring Dayton, where the largest per capita number of Black bands signed to major record labels in the latter 1970s to the early '80s.[3] African Americans made up over one-third of a population of roughly 243,601 in 1970, down to 203,371 by 1980.[4] Dayton's contribution to the cultivation of Black bands is a history that raises questions beyond beats, sounds, and notes.

The standing of certain cities noted for having made exceptional contributions to Black music has more to do with commerce than the quantity of talent. Cities such as Chicago, Detroit, Memphis, Philadelphia, and Minneapolis (in the 1980s) were coronated by record labels—as in Chess, Motown, Stax, Philadelphia International, and Paisley Park, correspondingly. The impact of the music industry on the urban map of African American music has implications for the study of artists not only from Dayton but also from other cities that don't have an apparatus capable of branding and selling local style in the national/global music marketplace. The history behind the Dayton bands who became recording artists (roughly from 1976 through 1979) reveals the Black urban public sphere foundations in the training and cultivation of Black self-contained bands. Furthermore, the experience of these bands underscores the complicated two-way exchange between music as a part of a local cultural economy and its widened commodified form in the popular music marketplace.

It didn't take the Wright Brothers but a band comprising the right brothers, the Ohio Players, to inspire a slew of younger Black musical groups from Dayton, Ohio, onto the stratospheric flight path of commercial success in the late 1970s. Without a major record label, the Players opened a door of possibility for Black bands in Dayton's local Black music scene. From 1972 through 1977, the band had an incredible five-year run of top-charting albums and singles, big arena tours, multiple television appearances, a Grammy award, and even a film score—*Pain* (1972) on Westbound Records had the hit single "Pain"; *Pleasure* (1972) yielded the smash "Funky Worm"; *Ecstasy* had a deep-grooving title track; the debut album on Mercury Records, *Skin Tight* (1974), gave listeners "Jive Turkey" and "Skin Tight"; *Fire* (1974) burned up the charts with "I Want to Be Free" and "Fire"; *Honey* (1975) pushed the flame further with "Love Rollercoaster" and "Sweet Sticky Thang"; *Contradiction* (1976) pushed out the hit "Who She'd Coo"; and *Angel* (1977) contained the group's last single to reach the top ten *Billboard* R&B chart, "OH-I-O." As the Players faded from the spotlight of "megastardom," an outpouring of their protégés, younger Dayton artists and bands, scored contracts with major record labels: Junie (Westbound), Heatwave (Epic), Sun (Capitol), Lakeside (SOLAR), Slave (Cotillion/Atlantic), Faze-O (SHE/Atlantic), Platypus (Casablanca), Shadow (Elektra), Dayton (United Artists), Zapp (Warner Bros.), Steve Arrington's Hall of Fame (Atlantic), and New Horizons (Columbia). This essay will explore Dayton's Black public sphere and social conditions responsible for the rise of Black bands in popular music from the Gem City.

Dayton's Black Public Sphere and Cultural Economy

More than a century and a half before the sounds of Dayton bands hit the *Billboard* charts, Dayton emerged as one of the many towns in northern states where a significant number of African Americans escaping the terror of enslavement, had settled. In the aftermath of the Civil War, their numbers swelled into the state of Ohio. Nevertheless, laws enacted at the turn of the nineteenth century in Ohio (known as the Black Laws) relegated African Americans to second-class citizenship, denying them the right to vote, serve on a jury, hold office, or even receive a public education. Even though the mainstays of the Black Laws had been repealed by the late nineteenth century, due to decades of upheavals, protests, and court challenges, the ever-growing African American populace in Dayton still faced harsh de facto discrimination, limiting access to quality jobs, decent pay, adequate housing, and equitable access to retail outlets. Twentieth-century Black life in Dayton was, furthermore, shaped by a segregated residential geography whereby the Great Miami River was a boundary delineating an east-west racial divide in the city.[5] Unlike most southern states but in keeping with most northern ones, segregation in Ohio was not etched in legal stone. Nevertheless, the machinery of custom, federal housing policies, white flight, neighborhood schooling, racist police practices, and racialized representational politics proved to be solid enforcer of Dayton's color line. For most of the twentieth century, West Dayton was synonymous with Black Dayton—a community that saw substantial growth due to a strong economic tug from 1940 to 1960. Dayton's Black working class found abundant and relatively high-wage employment at manufacturing industries, such as McCall's Printing, Frigidaire, General Motors, Chrysler, Wright-Patterson Air Force Base, and National Cash Register, and in the service sector, as well as at small businesses located in West Dayton.

The damage done by the system of American apartheid (through law and custom) and the consequent holding of Black people in ill-repute has been well documented. Beyond the harm of segregation, recent studies in Black urban history have highlighted the transformative impact of African American migration and settlement. Urban culture, cuisine, politics, social institutions, music, and language were dramatically refashioned by African Americans whose daily lives and choices were shaped as much by a collective will to be together as by the coercive hand of segregation.[6] Earl Lewis's concept of "home sphere" captures the interrelated nature of Black public spaces and social circles in segregated urban settings. Home in this space is synonymous with household, leisure activity, socialization, and community.[7] West Dayton joined the ranks of the South Side of Chicago, the "Black Bottom" in Detroit, Cincinnati's West End, the Ville in St. Louis, Pittsburgh's Hill District, Minneapolis's Northside, and numerous Black urban enclaves, specifically in the Midwest and, more broadly, throughout the United States.

Just as a "political economy" lens zeroes in on the relationship between government and governance (for example, institutions, public policy, and law) to the interests of concentrated wealth or capital in society, a "cultural economy" frame of reference emphasizes the critical links between culture and the local economy. The local soul and funk band as an expressive artistic unit in Dayton and other industrial cities was sustained by the availability of jobs and an operative economic base with employment opportunities for Black workers. Revenues generated by manufacturing and service sector jobs were also central to additional activities in which audiences participated in music-related activities and consumed musical products made by bands: nightclub performances, shows and competitions funded by municipal parks and recreation, public school performances, and the sale of locally manufactured records and promotional goods.[8]

Access to jobs also presented opportunities and challenges for career decisions that musicians had to make for themselves. For brief intervals, some local artists used job opportunities to earn good money after high school "on the line" in manufacturing and generated supplemental revenue to handle expenses that came with building a career as a music professional. One bandleader, for example, worked at Delco Products in neighboring Kettering in a job that paid more than enough to rent a house where other members could stay and practice in the evenings. Over the course of several months, the band was able to pay its bills from performances in the club and college circuits, and the bandleader then promptly resigned from Delco to work as a full-time musician.[9] In other instances, the guarantee of a stable income, with benefits, inspired artists to reroute away from music as a main career aspiration altogether. The deep-rooted investment in industrial jobs led some parents to shun their children's plans for making a career in music. Tim Dozier, who eventually played drums for Slave, one of Dayton's top recording groups, said that he "didn't get any family support" for his determination to become a musician. "At that time," he shared, "they didn't want you to do anything but work in a factory."[10]

Though many of the jobs were located outside of the Black residential community in Dayton, the income earned by Black workers supported an entertainment district with numerous service sector businesses, theaters, clubs, taverns, banquet halls, and restaurants. Working peoples' money and music worked together, circulating both through and inside diverse Black home sphere institutions. The availability of jobs was a decisive factor in the cultural infrastructure and social fabric out of which young people received musical training and found places to perform.

Community Music Education

At the most basic level, household income had everything to do with introducing young people to instruments and sometimes music lessons. Most of the members of Dayton bands, including those who eventually made their way to national and international airwaves, were introduced to instruments and sometimes private lessons from monies spent by their parents, as well as through the cultural resources of sharing and mentoring networks in the Black community. Steve Shockley, the famed guitarist for Lakeside, grew up in a household in which his father, Alfred Shockley, earned the lion's share of income for a family of five, working as a bricklayer. His mother, Laura Shockley, worked primarily as a homemaker and occasionally as a comanager of a jazz lounge and independent seamstress. At twelve, Steve had grown past the early stages of imitating Little Stevie Wonder, playing harmonica, beating on bongos made of Folgers coffee cans, and strumming on ad hoc stringed instruments. His mother purchased his first Silverstone electric guitar from Sears Roebuck. Steve remembered the national chain as a department store with plans in place for customers who "couldn't afford Barney's [music store] then." He added that Sears was where his mother "could put it [the guitar] on layaway.... I think it was only fifty-nine dollars or sixty-nine dollars."[11]

Paying for private lessons was another expense that working families had to consider when evaluating their capacity to support their children's musical passions. Alfred and Laura Shockley, like many other Black parents in Dayton, were able to lean on communal ties and traditions of sharing and mentoring young people. Mrs. Shockley was friends with the mother of an up-and-coming guitarist, William "Boots" Vaughn, who began teaching Steve fundamental guitar chords and scales. Vaughn at the time, roughly 1966, was already playing with the highest-earning Black group in Dayton, Big Jay Bush and the House Rockers, and eventually went on to record and tour with Isaac Hayes for many years. The resources of his parents, the Black community culture of knowledge sharing, and a layaway option at Sears helped to nurture one of the great rhythm guitarists among the group of Black bands of the late 1970s heard on the radio and in nightclubs. The story of Vaughn's outreach in teaching Steve also reveals an informal network of artistic mentoring with a lineage of knowledge sharing among guitar players. Boots himself had learned to play from other musicians, including noted blues guitarist and vocalist Bobby Warren. "I would go down there, over to [Bobby Warren's] house, and he would give his lessons," Vaughn said, and "he would teach [me] how to chord, and how to play different things."[12] In turn, Warren traced his early inspiration from lessons given by Robert Ward, leader of the Ohio Untouchables. One afternoon the singer-guitarist drove down the street in a convertible Chevy and noticed Warren sitting on the porch holding a guitar. Ward stopped, came over, and showed Warren some of the first chords that launched his passion for playing the blues. Though not as structured or consistent as music lessons for pay, organic networks were a vital resource that significantly increased the acquisition of music knowledge and instruction for Black musicians in West Dayton and Black neighborhoods throughout the United States.

Informal arts education, though, was not the only avenue available to young people in West Dayton. Conventional music education was also accessible and affordable to many Black working-class families. Gwen Allman was one of the few women who worked as an instrumentalist (keyboardist) in Dayton bands during their professional years, both Platypus and Heatwave. Her two sisters and brother received musical training in the church and formal lessons. Gwen's parents, Arthur and Georgia Allman, settled in the Westwood/Residence Park neighborhood in the early 1950s, roughly the same period in which husband and wife James and Olga Gates moved to West Dayton. Olga Gates was a master musician and instructor at the Miami Conservatory of Music in Dayton. In 1953, a class of hers played their first recital, held at the Dayton Art Institute, performing classical pieces by Handel, Schubert, and Rachmaninoff.[13] Steadfastly dedicated to exposing West Dayton to formal music training, Mrs. Gates also taught classes independently. Gwen Allman was only four years old when she began taking classes in the Gateses' home in 1956, also located in the Westwood/Residence Park neighborhood. "It was basically like a little piano school," Allman recalled, "because I wasn't the only student—she had a lot of students enrolled."[14] Gates's piano lessons were organized around the *John W. Schaum Piano Course: Leading to Mastery of the Instrument*, a nine-unit course that begins with the rudiments of the piano and continues progressively to a level of proficiency. Sharing how she thrived under Mrs. Gates's tutelage, Gwen said, "I was the only student that completed all nine grades in that book, and that took me into a classical piano mode."[15] Gwen's younger sisters, Valeria and Teresa, also studied music with Mrs. Gates, focusing primarily on singing, and the three of them would later form the group the Allman Sisters, releasing the singles "Goin' Back" and "Afro Child." All three of them went on to work with Dayton major recording artists Heatwave and Junie. Her brother, guitarist Derrick Allman, however, leaned more on the informal network of music instruction from older musicians and peers. In any case, formal music training was also available in the public schools. Roosevelt, Dunbar, Roth, and Jefferson High Schools, for instance, all had extensive music programs and in certain cases required courses in music theory as prerequisites for participation in intramural choirs and marching bands. Most musicians in Dayton bands were able to read music during their high school years.

Bands and the Performance Aesthetic

The public schools provided young people with performance opportunities and training. Teachers and staff at Roosevelt, Roth, Dunbar, and Jefferson High Schools raised money with events featuring a performance by a professional group and a competition among various student bands. As Black student-formed musical and vocal groups proliferated in the late 1960s, talent shows and "battle of the bands" competitions became a source of funding for school marching bands and choirs. During the 1960s to the late 1970s, school talent shows and dances were among the most popular social gatherings for Black young people in Dayton—filling up school auditoriums and cabaret halls just as major Black recording artists did when they came to town. While still teenagers in the 1960s and early 1970s, the would-be members of Lakeside (as was the case with Slave, Sun, Faze-O, Roger and Zapp, Platypus, Dayton, Heatwave, Junie, and other artists from Dayton) had already learned how to assemble the building blocks necessary for mastering the art of live onstage performance. Beyond schools, this "battle of the bands" ethic had tentacles throughout the city—in parks, nightclubs, backyards, or any place folks could gather. Even older Dayton bands—such as the Ohio Players, the Morroccos, and Big Jay Bush and the House Rockers—sharpened their performance edge on local stages in Dayton. Sometimes bands were competing for prizes, while in other cases, they participated in events with an unspoken knowledge that their mission was to leave the stage so hot that the bar for audience satisfaction jumped to an even higher expectation for the act to follow. Good playing and singing were not enough. Costumes, choreography, and charismatic stage presence were essential requirements for the victors in these battles.

Talent shows were among the most popular social gatherings for Black youth in Dayton. Audiences regularly filled school auditoriums, cabaret halls, mobile stages, and recreation centers to see local groups perform and compete. Crowd excitement for these shows compared to the hype and anticipation for a major recording artist coming to town. Young people sat and watched, danced, and sometimes even roller-skated to the sounds and sights of Huncie and the Entertainers, Big Jay Bush and the House Rockers, Nate and the Typicals, the Apollos, the Young Mods, the Citations, the Imperials, the Overnight Low Show Band (the Majestics), the Four Corners, the Bad Bunch, Dayton Sidewinders, Phase III, Soul Ages, the Fabulous Originals, and many others.

Talent shows of the late 1960s and early 1970s had the effect of pushing artists to high levels of professionalism, musicality, and showmanship. Audiences also had high expectations and turned out for these shows knowing that the bands were performing at levels associated with top recording artists. Guitarist Harry McLoud noted that talent shows "came to be bigger than the prom or anything. . . . If you were in high school from September to June, you might have had fifty dances. . . . Most of the time, you had bands [performing]."[16] More than 1,300 people, for instance, packed into Dunbar High School's main auditorium for a talent show in early 1966. Nine of the thirty-five contestants were bands. The others were vocalists, dancers, and solo musicians. After four hours of tight competition, the Apollos emerged as winners of the prize for "best band," overtaking the Majestics and the Fabulous Originals.[17]

Playing on high school stages produced a homegrown brand of celebrity. An events column called the "Falcon Flyer" in the *Dayton Express* newspaper promoted a talent show in 1965 as an "all-star" event at Roth High School. Fittingly, the all-stars listed on the bill were bands that were already well-established as top acts in the area: the Imperials, Jaguars, and Apollos.[18] These were the groups that did not have to audition in order to participate, whereas newly minted or up-and-coming talent was summoned for a trial performance: "For all that have talent here is your chance, tryouts will be March 4 and 11 from 3:00 to 6:00 pm."[19] Some musicians idolized the stage in Dayton. Byron Byrd led the group Sun (Capitol Records), whose first LP, *Wanna Make Love*, appeared in 1976. More than a decade earlier, he had watched one band's performance at a talent show in total awe. Though comprising musicians close to Byrd's age at the time, the group called the Imperials had a very mature and professional presence with an entire horn section, tailored uniforms, and a tight stage show. Still gaining confidence in his horn chops, Byrd said that he "idolized" Imperial's saxophonist, Virgil Smith, for his "tone" and "the way he played."[20]

The "battle of the bands" was not restricted to school auditorium stages. The nightclub called Tahiti Club set aside special nights for teenagers that featured live band competitions. Local roller-skating rinks similarly featured multiple bands on designated evenings. Talent show competitions were also held in businesses and municipal areas.[21] The Montgomery County Recreation Department began holding an annual ten-week series of summer activities at playgrounds and parks throughout the county in the mid-1950s. In 1967 the department allotted roughly $180,000 to support sporting events, arts and crafts, and dramatic and musical performances held in neighborhoods throughout Dayton and surrounding areas.[22] The county set up mobile stage units at parks and playgrounds for youth bands to perform and compete for prizes. These "Show Wagons" became ripe terrain for bands to throw down, compete, and perform in different neighborhoods. An announcement in the *Dayton Express* summoned "singers, dancers, comediennes and musicians" to come and try out. The "purpose of the auditions," it continued, "is to select acts and entertainment for the shows to be presented on the traveling 'Show Wagon.'"[23] Keyboardist Keith Harrison, leader of Faze-O, who scored the smash "Riding High" in 1977, just ten years prior played with a band called the Medallions while at Jefferson High School. The band won an early battle at the Show Wagon competition. The trophy earned, though, was no shield against the culture of sports-like competition and rivalry that constantly pushed another band forward to show and prove itself onstage.[24]

As the 1960s were closing, younger musicians gradually shifted away from the Temptations-styled positioning of the singers out front. Many began moving toward self-contained bands like Sly and the Family Stone and Dayton's own Ohio Players. These changes overlapped with the remainder of singing groups in the Gem City that were still holding on to the Motown format. Representatives of both sensibilities (vocal groups and self-contained bands) competed on the same stage at talent shows. No style, setup, age group, or neighborhood or school affiliation was assured victory from the audience packed in the seats and aisles—not even before a crowd of people mainly from one school. Some older and more experienced groups appeared as special guest performers rather than as competitors at these contests. Singer Arthur "Hakim" Stokes still remembers a poignant lesson on the merits of professionalism and experience at a Roth High School talent show in 1967. The eleventh grader and his musical comrades, in a group called the Emeralds, calmed their jitters by using nearly every moment of preshow time rehearsing choreography and going over singing parts while backstage. Stokes and company couldn't avoid noticing a different demeanor on the part of the more experienced guests, Nate and the Typicals. Nate, the silky-voiced crooner, and the others in his group were seen laughing and cavorting with fans just before the start of their set. "They didn't have to do what we were doing," Stokes noted. Nate and the Typicals coolly mounted the stage and launched into a perfectly executed routine with steps and vocal arrangements that had the natural flow of a well-oiled machine.[25]

Some groups sought to win over the audience quickly with a grand entrance with elements of surprise and elaborate theatrics. In some cases, a local band's opening routine at a talent show could also induce audience cheer by replicating the well-known show moves of top-selling artists. A string of singers and musicians in Dayton won thrills onstage by putting on their very best imitation of James Brown's dance moves.[26] Black teen idols the Jackson 5 were also influential. The Jackson 5 performed live as a self-contained band. Jackie, Marlon, and Michael were in the center as vocalists. They were flanked on either side by Jermaine and Tito on bass, guitar, and vocals; other accompaniment came from Johnny Jackson on drums and Ronnie Rancifer on keyboards. Together the seven dazzled crowds in concert with a tight rhythm section, magician-like choreography, layered harmonies, and the sensational lead voice of boy wonder Michael Jackson. If Jackson 5 fans could not make it to a concert, they had opportunities to see the group perform on several televised appearances. The teenage members of Dayton's own Hawthorne Express watched the ABC show *Goin' Back to Indiana*, which starred the Jackson 5, in 1971. Concert highlights in the TV show persuaded Hawthorne Express to emulate the Jackson 5's rendition of Isaac Hayes's "Walk On" in a talent show held shortly after the TV program aired. Band members practiced the Jackson 5 routine—especially the percussive choreography led by Michael, Marlon, and Jackie, which made for the perfect onstage intro. Hawthorne Express put together a tight set for a slot limited to five minutes. Weeks of rehearsal and the song selection produced the desired effect. The front four singers (Milton and Tony Baskins, Audrey Hayes, and Keith Wilder, bordered by Billy, Pedro, and Doug Jones on guitar, bass, and drums) summoned crowd cheers as they opened up with the "Walk On" vamp. They stepped precisely to a hypnotic groove punctuated by a minimalist bass line, eerie guitar riffs, dancing snare pops, and a forceful kick drum. Equally captivating was the group's seamless cut into the latest hit on the R&B charts at the time, "You're a Big Girl Now" by the Stylistics.[27] After seducing the crowd with a current hit, Hawthorne Express flaunted its versatility as the guitar player and bassist quickly switched instruments and closed the show with a funky musical bow of gratitude with Sly and the Family Stone's "Thank You (Falettinme Be Mice Elf Agin)." Roaring applause greeted the finale, but radio station WDAO didn't plan to announce the winner of the Friday night contest until the following day. The band members had piled into a car on their way to rehearsal on Saturday afternoon when a WDAO radio announcer declared Hawthorne Express the winner of the grand prize of fifty dollars.

Women off the Stage

It took numerous women to work alongside men to handle aspects of a band's affairs. Women often led the management or were part of the management team of these bands. Thirteen-year-old drummer Bobby Allen formed a band with his Weaver Elementary School buddies—two brothers, guitarist Lester Marbury and bassist Raymond Marbury. The trio found ways to sound much fuller than their numbers portended. Lester Marbury's style of playing chords and rhythm parts matched his brother's sustained low notes, and Bobby Allen's steady pocket and space-taking drum rolls gave this small unit a full sound.[28] Their lean size and hot sounds made the trio an attractive choice as the backup band for vocal groups, such as the Four Corners and Nate and the Typicals. Bobby's great-aunt Mary Jeter, who regularly drove the group to and from different venues, made an impactful observation: "You guys are fabulous," she said, "and you are originals, you should be [named] the 'Fabulous Originals.'" The name stuck. Determined that their look needed an upgrade to match their name, Jeter promptly carted them off to Price Stores in downtown Dayton and got them fitted for tuxedos—which became their new onstage uniforms.

Bobby Allen's grandmother Margaret Harris (known as "Angel") began managing the Fabulous Originals once the demands for performances extended to nightclubs and adult establishments in Dayton and venues throughout the tristate area (Ohio, Indiana, and Kentucky). The Fabulous Originals grew as a self-contained band, acquiring two sensational lead singers, Daria Dillard and Edmond Early. The rhythm section also sprouted to include Reggie Harmon on saxophone, Delbert Taylor on trumpet, and Tony Foster on keyboards. Angel earned a reputation for a high level of professionalism in running the affairs of the group. One of her crown accomplishments was producing the 45-inch single "It Ain't Fair but It's Fun," released by the Fabulous Originals in 1971 on the Cincinnati-based Jewel Records. Her style was the antithesis of the stereotypical slick-talking manager. When auditioning as a singer, Daria Dillard was "shocked" upon first meeting Angel, who was in her fifties when she joined the group: "She's such an older lady.... I'm trying to figure out how [does] she keep up with these young boys?"[29] Indeed, Angel made parents and young people in the group feel safe in a family-like environment while holding potentially shady characters in the local entertainment scene to a high standard. Summing up the range of her manager's work, Daria Dillard explained that Angel "would get us gigs, she was our publicist, our PR, our agent . . . the whole nine yards . . . Angel did it all"—an assemblage of jobs that would require three or four individual staff members in the music business today.[30]

Managers, concerned parents, educators, and civically invested adults in the community contributed to spaces for women in an urban music scene, which tended to exclude or constrain the involvement of women artists. Women instrumentalists struggled to create pathways in a difficult social and cultural playing field. Stratified gender norms limited women's involvement in bands. Official school bands, municipal orchestras, and churches were far more inclusive than groups that performed in nightclubs and after-hours establishments. Male teenage musicians could more easily negotiate parental acceptance of late-night hours. Some of the fellows from specific neighborhoods or associations had fostered gendered camaraderie that predated working together in a band, thanks to participating on sports teams, in clubs, and in church groups. Several members of recording groups Slave, Lakeside, and Platypus, for instance, previously lived in the Westwood/Residence Park area. There was only one all-women's band in the local Dayton music scene.

The future in Dayton, however, was not what it used to be. By the 1970s, unemployment soared, as did a myriad of social ills, due to the loss of manufacturing jobs. Most of the bands that ascended to stardom in the late 1970s did not survive the 1980s. Paradoxically, through the mid- to late 1970s, the very period in which numerous groups from Dayton acquired initial contracts with major record labels, an essential pillar of the city's local funk music culture—West Dayton's Black schools—was being dismantled. Dayton's public schools in the 1970s continued to mirror the racially separated residential demographic in the city and became an arena in the national debate over the scope of the 1954 *Brown v. Board of Education* ruling. After several years of litigation at the lower court level, the US Supreme Court ultimately granted, in what is known as the Dayton II decision, federal judges the power to order vast desegregation plans and busing for an entire school system, as opposed to restricting them to areas designated as racially imbalanced.[31]

Contrary to the integration ideal, which envisioned a two-way exchange and sharing of social and residential space with the goal of narrowing the power differential between Black and white communities, the court-ordered desegregation plan and busing had unintended negative consequences for Dayton's African American community. In 1975 Roosevelt High School, known for its renowned music program, was abruptly closed, while two others in the city were "integrated" with large portions of Black students and faculty reassigned to predominantly white schools farther east. White families overwhelmingly chose to relocate outside of the jurisdiction of the desegregation plan rather than participate. Keyboardist Frank Renfrow was twelve in 1966 when his family moved to the Dayton View neighborhood in the city, which he described as "all white" when they arrived. One year later the first Black family moved into the area, and, as he stated, "all the White folks (except us) were alarmed and subsequently within two or three years the whole neighborhood was predominantly Black."[32]

While white flight persisted, African American students and teachers were bused to schools outside of their home neighborhoods. African American music teachers who mentored student musicians contend that this turn of events was disruptive to the school- and community-based music education tradition in Dayton. Ironically, during the latter 1970s, when Dayton bands received recording contracts and had begun to impact Black popular music nationally and internationally, the social structure that supported Black bands at the local level was rapidly unraveling. The onslaught of deindustrialization and incumbent downsizing and the decline of manufacturing jobs upended socioeconomic conditions in Dayton—as was frequently the case with many other industrial cities. The unemployment rate in Montgomery County, Ohio, was 7.59 percent in 1970 and leaped to 17.51 percent in 1980.[33] The economic downturn in Dayton brought on high unemployment and increased poverty in the ranks of Dayton's Black working class. The cultural capital of Dayton's Black home sphere, which had been supported by income from workers in the industrial sector, faced turmoil. An ominous 1975 article in *Jet Stone News* by Cyndi Floyd notified Black residents in Dayton of the opening of Unemployment Inc., a nonprofit corporation that provided relief and employment to the jobless. "In the 1930s," Floyd declared, "our country went through a phase of perpetual unemployment, which in turn, triggered off a host of economic malfunctions within our basic structure.... The specific period was given the name 'depression,'" but she noted also that "today we are faced with a similar problem ... the only difference being its name, for top American officials have chosen to label it 'recession.'" "But whatever the name given it," Floyd concluded, "the effect is another high and rising unemployment rate, coupled with a sagging economy that seemingly allows no way out!"[34] From 1970 to 1980, the Black unemployment rate in Dayton jumped catastrophically from 7.8 percent to 19.3 percent.[35] Ironically, through the mid- to-late 1970s, the very period in which numerous groups from the Gem City received recording contracts from major record labels, essential pillars of the city's

Black music culture were crumbling or had already fallen. In this period, major economic players in the region either closed their doors, relocated, or significantly shrunk their labor force: Dayton Steel, Dayton Tire, Defense Electronics Supply Center, Frigidaire, General Motors, McCall's Printing, National Cash Register, and a host of smaller businesses. This economic downturn accelerated rapidly in the 1970s, undermining the Black working class and the community-based networks that sustained Dayton's Black cultural economy.

The interconnectedness between the availability of jobs and community culture come through explicitly in a 1977 statement by the Dayton chapter of the National Association for the Advancement of Colored People (NAACP). In light of the Defense Electronics Supply Center depot's plan to scale down its workforce and relocate, the statement alerted readers that 51 percent of the employees set to lose jobs were Black. In so doing, not only did the NAACP recognize the disproportionately high unemployment rate in the Black community (at 18.3 percent in 1977), but the NAACP chapter noted the downwardly spiraling interconnection between job loss and community cohesion. "It is these jobs [and] wage earners who support the barbers, druggists, and other black business" and also "support the churches and are active in many civic and social endeavors."[36] As cultural and artistic entities within Dayton's civic and social life, Black self-contained bands at the local level were sustained by an empowered Black working class. Ironically, as an avalanche of younger Dayton groups signed recording deals with major labels in the latter 1970s and early 1980s, the local conditions that enabled the cultivation of Black bands were deteriorating. Dayton's Black musicians who were reaching the charts had initially developed their craft in an urban community and public sphere anchored in a working-class social and cultural context. The sounds of these bands trekked to popular music from basement rehearsals to performances at school talent shows and into local nightclubs and multiple spaces in Black public spheres. In any case, the connection between music and urban sociologies of local culture is not limited to any one city or region, as the patterns highlighted in the Dayton story occurred in industrial cities throughout the United States. The role of community institutions is an under-recognized but consistent theme in the artistic journeys of Black musicians—for example, James Brown and networks of local Black clubs and performance venues (the "chitlin circuit"); Sly and the Family Stone and Black Pentecostal church and Bay-area countercultural movements; Parliament/Funkadelic and Black barbershops in Plainfield and Newark, New Jersey; War and youth low-rider car culture in Los Angeles; and Rick James and Prince and music education in public schools in Buffalo and Minneapolis, respectively.[37]

Transformation

There was a lag between the on-the-ground social conditions in Dayton and the experience of bands in the world of commercial music. The two comprised countervailing or even contradictory tendencies. On the one hand, the bands from Dayton who were given record deals earned the lion's share of those contracts from 1976 through 1980. Ironically, this was the same period in which bands plummeted in status and numbers at the local level. However, a coming new decade narrowed the gap between how bands fared at the local and national levels. Even during the best of times, bands are difficult to keep together, and the 1980s were especially perilous to group unity and the tight relationships that made these artistic outfits such a powerful force in the making of funky music. Yet, a simple story of the 1980s decline does not tell the entire story. Some artists displayed creative resilience and experimented with new music technologies in their recordings.

In the 1980s, sounds in R&B and funk were largely, though not exclusively, supplanted by grooves driven by synthesizers and drum machines. By mid-decade, these newer technologies had staked out a central place in the rapid, earth-shattering rise of hip-hop. Groups like Earth, Wind & Fire, L.T.D., Commodores, Mass Production, Parliament, Graham Central Station, Funkadelic, B. T. Express, Bootsy's Rubber Band, Tower of Power, Rick James and the Stone City Band, Fatback Band, Rose Royce, War, the J.B.'s, Raydio, the Bar-Kays, Switch, GQ, and Faze-O were either pushed to the margins, dropped from their label, splintered, or broke up entirely. Solo acts and vocal groups, rather than bands, became the configuration of choice in this new era: Michael Jackson, New Edition, Lionel Richie, Janet Jackson, Luther Vandross, the Mary Jane Girls, DeBarge, En Vogue, Boyz II Men, Patrice Rushen, Whitney Houston, Keith Sweat, Jody Watley, Jeffrey Osborne, Sade, Al B. Sure, Ray Parker Jr., and so on. Though nudged off the dominant position in popular music, many bands managed to thrive nonetheless: Prince and the Revolution, the Gap Band, Mtume, Atlantic Starr, the Time, the S.O.S. Band, Kool & the Gang, Con Funk Shun, Midnight Star, Skyy, and Cameo.

While the Ohio Players were going through internal dissension throughout most of the 1980s, several groups and artists who had come out of (or had close ties to) the Dayton scene adjusted to the changing tenor of the times—some of whom even scored hit singles: Slave, Aurra, Steve Arrington's Hall of Fame, Heatwave, Dayton, New Horizons, Sun, Shadow, Junie, Lakeside, and Zapp. Roger Troutman and his band Zapp put a special stamp on 1980s electro-funk with fat, bottomed-out synth bass lines, choppy rhythm guitars, and a device known as the talk box, which blends with other electronic instruments to produce a hybrid fusion of singing with the electronic signal of the instrument. "Be Alright," "More Bounce to the Ounce," "Playin' Kinda Ruff," "I Can Make You Dance," "Do-Wa-Diddy," "Computer Love," and "I Want to Be Your Man" were noteworthy classic singles from Zapp and Troutman. Beyond music, Zapp and Troutman sought to address urban problems in Dayton through entrepreneurial activism. Troutman Enterprises consisted of recording studios, a construction firm, and a limousine service—situated on Salem and Catalpa Avenues—and the compound was the largest musical establishment to come out of the era when bands ruled Dayton and the charts.[38]

Paradoxically, the kinds of electronic technology that had contributed to the downsizing and diminished status of Black bands in popular music, effectively reintroduced their sounds to the music marketplace of a new era. During the 1980s, hip-hop producers used electronic instruments (such as the Akai MPC) to efficiently capture and replay music from other recordings. A sample from a segment of a previously recorded song enabled hip-hop producers to mimic the elongated instrumental breakbeats, which DJs had accomplished at live parties with two turntables, in the earlier stages of what became known as hip-hop in the 1970s. This instrumental space and repetition opened up more sonic room, more complex rap styles, and experimentation. Many of the samples extracted and used on hip-hop megahits were from songs that were from popular hits and B-sides from the 1970s. By the mid-1980s and 1990s, sampling had become a serious art form. The music industry eventually sorted out rules for clearances and payment procedures for the original creators of the music. Many old-school musicians and songwriters unexpectedly received revenue from artists who had sampled their music. As the costs for clearances increased, hip-hop producers frequently hired musicians to "interpolate" or play songs by old-school artists rather than use a sample from a recording. This production technique proved less expensive. Through sampling and interpolation, Dayton bands found their way back into popular music.

In 1982, Roger Troutman produced a song by Ronnie Hudson and the Street People called "West Coast Poplock," in which Troutman used the music from his single "So Ruff, So Tuff" off the *Many Facets of Roger* LP, released a year earlier. From "West Coast Poplock," he would later use the same hook "California knows how to party" in the anthemic West Coast hip-hop song "California Love" (1995) featuring 2Pac (Tupac Shakur). This link between California and Ohio sounds grew closer as artists and producers who came of age in the late 1980s and 1990s displayed their strong affinity for the music of Parliament/

Funkadelic and many Dayton bands (especially Roger Troutman and Zapp) in samples and interpolations—Ohio Player's "Funky Worm" (1972) in N.W.A.'s "Gangsta Gangsta" (1988); Sun's "Conscience" (1977) in DJ Quik's "Get at Me" (1995); Faze-O's "Ridin' High" (1977) in Daz Dillinger's "Ridin' High" (1998); Lakeside's "Fantastic Voyage" (1980) in Coolio's "Fantastic Voyage" (1994); Steve Arrington's Hall of Fame's "Weak at the Knees" (1983) in Ice Cube's "The Nigga Ya Love to Hate" (1990); and Slave's "Watching You" (1980) in Snoop Dogg's "Gin and Juice" (1993), among many, many others.[39] East Coast and southern producers and artists also reached into the fountain of funky music by Dayton funky bands—Zapp's "More Bounce to the Ounce" (1980); EPMD's "You Gots to Chill" (1988); Ohio Players' "Pride and Vanity" (1972) in Mary J. Blige's "What's the 411" (1992); Ohio Players' "Ecstacy" (1973) in Jay-Z's "Brooklyn's Finest" (2000); Faze-O's "Ridin' High" (1977) in Kris Kross's "Tonite's tha Night" (1997); and Heatwave's "Boogie Nights" (1976) in Timbaland's "Up Jump the Boogie" (1997). The late 1980s through the early 2000s was a period that solidified the standing of the 1970s bands by designating the music of the era as part of the old-school canon, thereby situating Black bands in old-school radio programming and special events aimed at their listening demographic. Dayton bands like the Ohio Players, Zapp, Lakeside, Heatwave, and Steve Arrington to this day have opportunities to reach fans and audiences at urban festivals, theme cruises, televised performances, television series, and film documentaries. Even though bands are no longer the main artistic unit in Black popular music, this creativity—emanating from industrial spaces of a bygone era—speaks to the soul in a musical language that still . . . makes you dance.

Notes

1. Rickey Vincent, *Funk: The Music, The People, and The Rhythm of The One* (New York: St. Martin's Griffin, 1996), 60–62.
2. "MCA's Black Invasion Seen as Aid, Impetus," *Billboard*, November 20, 1976, 3, 16.
3. Portia Maultsby, "Funk Music: An Expression of Black Life in Dayton, Ohio and the American Metropolis," in *The American Metropolis: Image and Inspiration*, ed. Marja Roholl and Tity de Vries Hans Krabbendam (Amsterdam: Vu University Press, 2001), 198–213.
4. "Dayton, Ohio Population History 1840–2021," "Dayton Population 40 Percent Black," *Jet Stone News*, December 29, 1976.
5. Margaret E. Peters, *Dayton's African American Heritage: A Pictorial History*, 2nd ed. (Donning Company Publishers, 2005), 14, 85.
6. Virginia and Bruce Ronald, *School Days: An Informal History of Education in Montgomery County, Ohio, from 1926 to 1990* (Dayton: Landfall Press, 1991), 64; Peters, *Dayton's African American Heritage*, 146; Earl Lewis, *In Their Own Interests: Race,*

Class, and Power in Twentieth-Century Norfolk, Virginia (Berkeley: University of California Press, 1991), 3, 5, 90–92; Waldo E. Martin, *No Coward Soldiers: Black Cultural Politics and Postwar America* (Cambridge, MA: Harvard University Press, 2005), 14, 23. For a kindred discussion of the Black public sphere in Birmingham, Alabama, see John F. Szwed, *Space Is the Place: The Lives and Times of Sun Ra* (New York: Pantheon Books, 1997), 13–15.

7. Lewis, *In Their Own Interests*, 5.
8. Rosanne Currarino, "Toward a History of Cultural Economy," *Journal of the Civil War Era* 2, no. 4 (2012): 564–85.
9. Kym Yancey, interview by Scot Brown, 2009, author's possession.
10. Tim "Tiny" Dozier, interview by Stan "The Man" Brooks, 2016, YouTube video, accessed September 15, 2024, www.youtube.com/watch?v=bEf16SONm0Y.
11. Steve Shockley, interview by Scot Brown, 2011, author's possession; Dozier interview.
12. William "Boots" Vaughn, interview by Scot Brown, 2015, author's possession.
13. "Social Notes," *Dayton Daily News*, June 7, 1953, 18.
14. Gwen Richardson, interview by Scot Brown, 2011, author's possession.
15. Richardson interview.
16. Harry McLoud, interview by Scot Brown, 2005, author's possession.
17. "1300 View Dunbar Talent Show," *Dayton Express*, January 20, 1966, 5.
18. "Falcon Flyer," *Dayton Express*, February 13, 1965, 5.
19. "1300 View Dunbar Talent Show," 5; "Falcon Flyer," 5.
20. Byron Byrd, interview by Scot Brown, author's possession, 2010.
21. Charlie White, "Interview: Something in the Water: The Sweet Sound of Dayton Street Funk," 1997, Archives of African American Music and Culture, Indiana University, 3–4.
22. "Recreation Program Closes," *Dayton Express*, August 24, 1967, 10.
23. "Auditions for Summer Shows," *Dayton Express*, June 8, 1967, 3.
24. Keith Harrison, "Interview: Something in the Water: The Sweet Sound of Dayton Street Funk," 1997, Archives of African American Music and Culture, Indiana University, 7; "Jefferson Township Day—Big Success," *Jet Stone News*, July 22–29, 1974, 9.
25. Harrison, "Interview: Something in the Water," 9.
26. Cynthia Sloan Hummons, interview by Scot Brown, 2007, Dayton, author's possession; Arthur "Hakim" Stokes, interview by Scot Brown, 2011, Dayton, author's possession.
27. Billy Jones, interview by Scot Brown, 2013, Dayton, author's possession; J. Randy Taraborrelli, *Michael Jackson: The Magic, the Madness, the Whole Story, 1958–2009* (New York: Grand Central, 2009), 85; Clarence "Chet" Willis, "Interview by the Author. Transcript" (Atlanta, 2010), 4–6; Colleen Matthews, "Interview by the Author. Transcript" (phone interview, 2015), 5; Greg Webster, *The True Story of the Ohio Players* (Dayton: Daysville Publishing, 2001), 44–45; Richardson interview, 7.
28. Bobby Allen, interview by Scot Brown, 2012, 17, author's possession.
29. Daria Dillard Stone, interview by Scot Brown, 2011, author's possession.
30. Stone interview.
31. "System-Wide Busing Orders Reaffirmed by High Court," *Washington Post*, July 3, 1979, A8; "Impending Desegregation Brings Some Uneasiness to Ohio Cities," *New*

York Times, August 30, 1977, 10; "High Court Agrees to Hear Dayton's Challenge of Busing Order," *New York Times*, January 18, 1900, 8; William Gordan, "Implementation of Desegregation Plans since Brown," *Journal of Negro Education* 63, no. 3 (1994): 310–22.

32. Frank Renfrow to Scot Brown, 2014, author's possession.
33. "Unemployed, 1970" and "Unemployed, 1980," accessed via Social Explorer (based on data collected by the US Census Bureau) on September 15, 2025, www.socialexplorer.com.
34. Cyndi Floyd, "There's Help for the Unemployed," *Jet Stone News*, May 7, 1975, 11.
35. "Production Jobs Vanish," *Dayton Daily News*, March 13, 1983, 11; "Unemployed, 1970"; "Unemployed, 1980."
36. "NAACP Acts to Halt Desc Move," *Pride: Ohio's Leading Black Publication*, July 1977.
37. James Brown, *The Godfather of Soul: An Autobiography* (New York: Thunder's Mouth, 1986); R. J. Smith, *The One: The Life and Music of James Brown* (New York: Gotham, 2012); Jeff Kaliss, *I Want to Take You Higher: The Life and Times of Sly and the Family Stone* (New York: Backbeat Books, 2008); Mark Anthony Neal, "Sly Stone and the Sanctified Church," in *The Funk Era and Beyond: New Perspectives on Black Popular Culture*, ed. Tony Bolden (New York: Palgrave Macmillan, 2008), 3–12; George Clinton and Ben Greenman, *Brothas Be, Yo Like George, Ain't That Funkin' Kinda Hard on You?: A Memoir* (New York: Atria, 2014); Dave Marsh, ed., *George Clinton and P-Funk: An Oral History* (New York: Avon, 1998); Kris Needs, *George Clinton and the Cosmic Odyssey of the P-Funk Empire* (London: Omnibus, 2014); Denise Sandoval, "The Politics of Low N Slow/Bajito Y Suavecito: Black and Chicano Lowriders in Los Angeles, 1960's to 1970's," in *Black and Brown: Beyond Conflict and Coalition*, ed. Josh Kun and Laura Pulido (Los Angeles: University of California Press, 2014), 176–200; Rick James, *The Confessions of Rick James: "Memoirs of a Super Freak"* (New York: Colossus Books, 2007); *Glow: The Autobiography of Rick James* (New York: Atria, 2014).
38. "For Troutmans, Success Comes When You Provide People with Something Good," *Dayton Daily News*, May 1, 1983, F2.
39. Ben Westhoff, "Backstabbing, Moogs and the Funky Work: How Gangsta Rap Was Born," *The Guardian*, September 13, 2016, www.theguardian.com/music/2016/sep/13/gangsta-rap-historynwa-ice-cube-dr-dre; Who Sampled website, www.whosampled.com; Dave Tompkins, "Golden Throat: Roger Troutman's Talk Box Sings the Human Body Electric," *Wax Poetics*, no. 35 (2009): 93–94; Clinton and Greenman, *Brothas Be, Yo Like George, Ain't That Funkin' Kinda Hard on You?*, 291–95.

PART III

TATIANA M. F. CRUZ

We Are All in the Same Boat Now

Mel King and the Origins of Boston's Rainbow Coalition

On October 11, 1983, community activist Mel King proclaimed, "Somebody said last night that a number of myths were going to die and one myth said that people of color wouldn't vote and stay together. That myth has died." King, a tall, dark-skinned, "brawny, bald, bearded" fifty-four-year-old man, always had a larger-than-life presence that the local press seemed fixated on.[1] He sported his signature hand-knotted bowtie, which had recently become his political trademark and supposedly spoke to his new "seriousness," a marked difference from the more radical Afrocentric dashikis of just a few years prior that raised some eyebrows.[2] He continued on, passionately addressing his supporters, "We started off by saying that we may have come on different ships but we are all in the same boat now. We're here to say that the boat is changing its course. Welcome to the rainbow coalition!"[3] "Rainbow!" the crowd roared. "Rainbow! Rainbow!" While King spoke to a packed ballroom on the fourteenth floor of the Parker House, over 1,000 supporters could not fit into the Election Night party and took over the hotel lobby until it became so crowded and rowdy that the Boston Fire Department ordered people to evacuate. The jubilee spilled out onto the streets of downtown Boston as the crowds chanted, "Mel King! Mel King!" King then led the group down Tremont Street to City Hall Plaza, where he paused and spoke to the crowd and sea of reporters: "There ought not to be any doubt in anybody's mind that we have changed Boston."[4]

Mel King made history that night by becoming the first African American to ever advance beyond the preliminary and become a mayoral finalist in the city of Boston. This was his second run for mayor, as he had suffered a disappointing loss four years prior in a challenge to Mayor Kevin White. King not only redeemed himself that night, but his triumphant speech was a testament to his decades of grassroots organizing and his growing coalition of supporters in the city. He positioned his candidacy as part of a larger electoral movement that would bring together a "rainbow coalition" of diverse, marginalized groups in the city including African Americans, Latinx, Asians, women, queer people, people with disabilities, working-class laborers, the youth, and the elderly. A smiling King told the cheering crowd in his victory speech that night that the "rainbow coalition" was for all people, made up of those who were "interested in bringing the city together" and making a "city that works for all people."[5] Though King's coalition reflected national trends, as marginalized groups joined forces with white liberals and leftists to challenge Reaganism in the early 1980s, the local origins of the coalition remain obscured. This is especially true since the literature on Boston's racial history remains limited, most of which centers the so-called busing crisis of court-ordered school desegregation in the 1970s and often that furthers a simplistic Black-white binary framework of the city.

In this essay, I locate the origins of King's coalition politics in Boston and offer a succinct examination of his use of it in his 1983 mayoral campaign. I begin by briefly mapping the city's changing racial and economic landscape in the postwar era and emergence of "urban crisis." I pay particular attention to the growth of the African American and Latinx communities and to the central role of autonomous social service organizations in cultivating activist leadership in the 1960s and 1970s. I examine how African American and Latinx social worker–activists forged overlapping racial and political identities, engaged with one another, and organized strategic multiracial/multiethnic coalitions in the city. I also thread an analysis of Mel King's own racial and political identities and lived experiences growing up in the city that mirrored the experiences of other African American and Latinx activists, collectively shaping their organizing philosophies.

Building off the successes of these early coalitions and increasing political power in the city, radical activists of color like King recognized the role that electoral politics could play in the long freedom movement. As they entered this new political realm in the 1980s, they built a broad voter base premised on the shared identities and experiences they built while community organizing in the 1960s and 1970s. Though King ultimately lost to city councilor Raymond Flynn in a landslide in the general election, I argue that his mayoral campaign proved transformative as it represented a decades-long struggle of coalition building across racial and ethnic lines at the intersection of antipoverty organizing, the long struggle for educational equity, and mobilizations for fair housing, which collectively formed the broader civil rights movement in Boston. King's Rainbow Coalition emerged as a powerful, optimistic symbol for the future of Boston's African American and Latinx communities in the 1980s and decades that followed.

Boston's Urban Crisis

Though the African American and Latinx population in Boston never reached the heights of other major urban centers in the North such as New York or Chicago, a look at the city's shifting demographic patterns from 1950 to 1980 reveals the rapid growth of these groups and their increasing influence on the city's politics. This provides critical context for understanding the emergence of King's Rainbow Coalition. From 1950 to 1980, the city's overall population declined by over 200,000, reaching its lowest point of just over 560,000, where it stabilized for some time.[6] Boston's "white flight" was driven by the booming technology, research, and development industry in the newly prosperous and thriving suburbs. As the city's overall population declined in these thirty years, the population of African American and Latinx residents continued to grow. In certain neighborhoods such as Roxbury and Dorchester, these groups became the clear majority, in large part due to patterns of housing discrimination and residential segregation, as well as to the city's urban renewal programs. This demographic data coupled with an examination of the persistent poverty sheds light upon the emerging "urban crisis" that propelled the establishment of social service organizations centered on combating poverty in the city's ghettos. These organizations became breeding grounds for activists of color such as Mel King and for early experiments in multiracial/multiethnic coalition building.

Boston's African American population grew quickly in the postwar era as part of the long Great Migration. These southerners were joined by migrants from across the African diaspora, particularly Caribbean and West Indian nations. Mel King's West Indian family reflected the earliest waves of migration. He was born in Boston in 1928 as one of eleven children to parents from Guyana and Barbados.[7] In the fifty years or so between King's family's arrival to the city and his decision to run for mayor, the population of African American and African diasporic peoples grew drastically. By the time he was preparing to run for the second time in 1980, the Black population in Boston had grown to over 100,000 people, constituting 22 percent of the city's total population.[8] The Latinx population in the city was smaller than that of African Americans yet grew quicker during the postwar era. Though most were Puerto Rican, other Latinx people, including Cubans, Dominicans, and Central Americans, began arriving in the late 1960s and early 1970s seeking refuge from the political struggles in their home countries. In 1970, the first year that the census started asking about Hispanic origin, close to 18,000 Latinx people labeled as "Hispanics" were counted in Boston, over 40 percent of whom were Puerto Rican. According to that census, the Latinx community made up only 3 percent of the city's total population.⁹ The Latinx community officially constituted 6 percent of the city's population in the 1980 census, but many estimated the actual numbers were close to double that.¹⁰

Latinx migrants settled alongside African Americans in neighborhoods such as the South End, Roxbury, and Dorchester, which were undergoing demographic shifts due to patterns of white flight. By 1960, 97 percent of African Americans and similarly high numbers of Latinx in Boston lived in these three neighborhoods, known as the "Black Boomerang."¹¹ Federal, state, and local housing and banking officials played a critical role in creating and maintaining the racially segregated neighborhoods through restrictive covenants, redlining, discriminatory lending practices, and public housing policies. The city's urban renewal plan contributed to racial segregation as well. The South End was one of the first neighborhoods targeted to help revitalize the city, boost the economy, and encourage white Bostonians to stay and settle (or even return had they already left for the suburbs). Mel King grew up in the diverse "New York Streets" area of the South End, which was eventually destroyed by urban renewal. He later reflected, "By the late 1950s, the Master Plan for Boston had begun its job of forcing black people out of the South End and into Roxbury and Dorchester in order to accommodate the commercial and residential needs of Boston's banks, insurance companies, and, of course, MIT and Harvard."¹² African Americans and Latinx faced high rates of unemployment and poverty, inadequate housing, and underperforming schools in Boston's "Black Boomerang." Despite the programs established in the 1960s by President Lyndon B. Johnson's War on Poverty, the "Black Boomerang" of Boston contained pockets of poverty that rivaled parts of the rural South. Mel King summarized, "This systemic denial of jobs, housing, education, and political representation by the Boston power structure came to full development in the creation of the 'ghetto.'" King continued, asserting that "the image of the ghetto allowed the ruling elite to blame the Black [and Latinx] community for what they had systematically imposed upon us."¹³ Boston city officials repeatedly placed blame on communities of color for their own poverty and lack of upward mobility.

Early Multiracial/Multiethnic Ideologies and Coalitions

Mel King's organizing philosophy and commitment to multiracial/multiethnic coalition building was forged early in his life. His diverse South End neighborhood was known as a little "Ellis Island," Boston's port for newly arrived immigrants. King's experience growing up in a multiracial/multiethnic working-class neighborhood shaped his racial and political formation and was nurtured by his grassroots organizing, long before he conceived of the 1983 Rainbow Coalition at the center of his mayoral platform.[14] King's racial and political formation mirrored that of fellow social workers of color who emerged as local leaders, developing their own solutions to the urban crisis as the city of Boston chronically failed to meet the growing needs of African American and Latinx communities.

African American social workers Muriel and Otto Snowden established the first African American social service organization in Boston in 1949, Freedom House, which quickly became a center for community activism and the city's leading organization committed to racial uplift. As an integral part of the civil rights movement, it earned a local moniker as Boston's "Black Pentagon" since it served as an anchor for the Black community during the city's greatest racial conflicts, such as urban riots and the desegregation of schools.[15] As a grassroots organization that emerged from the concerns of self-determined Black residents who collaborated with white residents, Freedom House provided an early model of multiracial coalition building with Black leadership in the city. Like the Snowdens, Mel King also became a leader in the city's social service organizations. He worked as the youth director at the United South End Settlements, which provided essential resources to the South End community, particularly recently arrived migrants. There he established educational enrichment and tutoring programs for children of color and provided resources for street gangs.[16]

King joined several other African American and Latinx educators and social workers such as Hubert "Hubie" Jones and Frieda Garcia to provide essential resources and services that would empower and "upbuild" Boston's communities of color. Jones, an African American social worker, and Garcia, a Black Dominican social worker, both grew up in diverse working-class neighborhoods in New York City and developed organizing philosophies centered on coalition building. As social worker–activists in Boston, they recognized the critical role of social service organizations and the fight for economic justice in the long civil rights movement. King and Jones began collaborating in 1963, when they organized a "Stop Day," a one-day general strike on the city of Boston and mass march to protest all forms of racial discrimination in the city. Then in 1965, Jones became the founding assistant director of a new social service organization, the Roxbury Multi-Service Center (RMSC), which was originally modeled after settlement houses similar to those where King worked.[17] Shortly afterward, Frieda Garcia was hired as the RMSC's first coordinator of Spanish programs.[18] The new position reflected the changing demographics of the city, since the RMSC needed staff members to respond to the needs of the rapidly growing Latinx community. Like Freedom House before it, the RMSC quickly emerged as a base for cultivating activist leadership and early multiracial and multiethnic coalition building.

The shared vision for this collaborative work was most evident in the establishment of a new Latinx multiservice center. By 1970, Garcia argued that the RMSC could no longer meet the needs of the rapidly growing Latinx community in Boston and pushed to establish an autonomous Latinx organization. She was inspired by Ana Maria Rodriguez and Betsy Tregar, two ESL teachers in Boston schools who had formed a group called the Spanish Alliance to support Latinx students and their families. Garcia and Jones thought strategically about how establishing a separate social service center for the Latinx community would provide additional funding opportunities through the city's Model Cities Administration. With Rodriguez and Tregar, Garcia founded La Alianza Hispana (LAH), or the Hispanic Alliance, in 1970. Unlike other groups that were exclusively Puerto Rican, the new agency's name served as a testament to the city's diverse, pan-Latinx community. It also demonstrated the increasing solidarity between African Americans and Latinx, as Jones loaned Garcia out to act as the LAH's first director. In 1971, she sought out funds to set up a storefront office, and, using the RMSC as a conduit, she secured a $33,000 grant from Boston's Model Cities Administration following a small sit-in at the Model Cities office. Though struggling financially, the RMSC also raised an additional $8,000 for the new multiservice center, which illustrated Jones's commitment to the Latinx community in Boston and to the success of the LAH; this allowed the agency to expand its operations and services.[19]

Even as La Alianza Hispana began to gain administrative and fiscal autonomy from the Roxbury Multi-Service Center, both boards remained committed to maintaining a meaningful relationship and supporting one another. Rodriguez, the LAH president, explained in a letter in 1971, "Our interest now is in maintaining and cultivating the relationship in order that the Black and Hispanic communities may move together on common concerns and interests."[20] The organizations not only supported each other symbolically but did so literally; the RMSC loaned offices to the LAH's bookkeeping department, and the two groups physically shared space and worked with one another. The RMSC also aided the organizational development of the LAH in numerous ways, such as providing staff training. Staff members of both organizations even attended each other's board meetings. Together, the RMSC and the LAH worked to up-build the African American and Latinx communities of Roxbury and the city of Boston more broadly.

One notable example of the early multiracial/multiethnic coalition building that came out of the cooperative African American–Latinx relationships of the RMSC was the establishment of the Task Force on Children out of School, an urban coalition chaired by Hubie Jones that investigated the performance of

Boston schools. The interracial coalition reflected the intersection of the local antipoverty and education movements and was composed of approximately fifty social workers, academics, lawyers, clergymen, and support staff. In 1971, the task force published the report *The Way We Go to School: The Exclusion of Children in Boston*, which revealed that 10,000 or more children were systematically excluded from Boston Public Schools or were warehoused in classrooms or schools that provided inferior or merely custodial care. The bulk of these children were "Spanish-speaking," mainly Puerto Rican. The report also stressed how exclusion from school led to unemployment, poverty, and juvenile delinquency among Latinx youth. To address this population in particular, the task force advocated for the hiring of Spanish-speaking teachers and assistants and the expansion of the city's bilingual education programs.[21] The report had a profound effect on the Boston Public Schools and on local and national laws. In 1971, Massachusetts passed the nation's first bilingual education law and then the first special education law in 1972, which served as the model for the first federal special education law that passed in 1975.[22] The efficacy of the task force and the impact of its groundbreaking report exemplifies the increasing power of solidarities and coalitions built between African American and Latinx communities in Boston in the decade or so prior to King's mayoral run.

Another social worker of color who played a critical role in the local intersecting antipoverty and education movements was Alex Rodriguez, a member of the Task Force on Children out of School. As a Black Puerto Rican, he felt racial solidarity with African Americans and saw their fates linked. Like Hubie Jones and Frieda Garcia, Rodriguez's racial identity and early experiences growing up in a diverse multiracial New York City neighborhood informed his political organizing. He began his career in Boston in 1965 as a social worker in the United South End Settlements, where he met Mel King, and at the Hattie B. Cooper Community Center.[23] He also emerged as a leader in one of Boston's first Latinx organizations, APCROSS, the Association Promoting Constitutional Rights of the Spanish-Speaking, which was established in the South End in 1967 and worked to create a more powerful political presence for the city's Puerto Rican community.[24]

King, Jones, Garcia, and Rodriguez were at the forefront of the antipoverty movement, promoting an inclusive organizing philosophy centered on coalition building. While this movement intersected with the local education movement, it also overlapped with the movement for fair housing. As these social workers continued to forge shared racial and political identities as activists in social service and civil rights organizations, they pressured Boston mayor John Collins and other city officials to provide immediate relief to the substandard housing crisis in the "Black Boomerang," often leading tours throughout the city's "slums" and staging small protests throughout the 1960s. The struggle for decent, affordable housing in Boston demonstrates how early African American and Latinx coalition building shaped Mel King's political philosophy and had a major influence on his future voter base in the 1983 mayoral election.

King's South End neighborhood became a fertile ground for coalition building across ethno-racial lines around the issue of housing. In 1967, King founded Community Assembly for a United South End (CAUSE), a multiethnic/multiracial organization that sought to give residents a voice in their neighborhood. A *Harvard Crimson* article described CAUSE's main goal as to "bring Negroes and Puerto Ricans together for more grass-roots power."[25] King led CAUSE organizers in a series of direct-action mobilizations to protest the city's urban renewal plan. In 1968, over 100 families were displaced when the corner of Dartmouth and Columbus Streets was leveled for a new parking lot. At first the organizers staged sit-ins at the Boston Redevelopment Authority offices, arguing that the community would be better served by the building of affordable housing instead of a parking lot, but then shifted strategies. CAUSE demonstrators blocked the site, occupied the lot, pitched tents, and camped there for three days. They erected a group of shanties and tents with a sign welcoming all to "Tent City." Community support grew for the "Tent City" protest, especially after activists were arrested. The movement gained additional media attention as Boston Celtics player-coach Bill Russell provided food for the protesters from his local restaurant and especially when Martin Luther King Jr.'s father arrived to give encouragement to the protesters, just two weeks after his son's assassination.[26] CAUSE was eventually awarded a grant from the Episcopal Diocese of Massachusetts, and Tent City dissolved, yet CAUSE organizers eventually triumphed twenty years later. After decades of battles with the city, a mixed-income development was finally built on the site in 1988, with two-thirds of its units made affordable for low-income tenants. Boston named the building Tent City to honor the movement.

CAUSE continued to organize after Tent City, serving as an umbrella organization that brought various South End tenants' groups into one coalition against the Boston Redevelopment Authority and urban renewal. Other multiracial/multiethnic groups in the fair housing movement coalition included the South End Tenants Council) and Inquilinos Boricuas en Acción (Puerto Rican Tenants in Action, or IBA). The South End Tenants Council picketed outside slumlords' homes and offices, brokered agreements with the Rabbinical Court of Justice, and initiated mass rent strikes, eventually setting up its own community development corporation, the Tenants Development Corporation. The Tenants

Development Corporation persuaded the Boston Redevelopment Authority to turn over fifty properties formerly owned by a slumlord family to the community corporation. The Tenants Development Corporation, in turn, renovated the properties into affordable housing for low-income families. Inquilinos Boricuas en Acción also cooperated with the Boston Redevelopment Authority to save Parcel 19 of the South End, which was slated to displace thousands of residents, most of whom were Puerto Rican. In 1968, Inquilinos Boricuas en Acción incorporated under the name Emergency Tenants Council of Parcel 19, Inc. Seeking community control of the land, the Emergency Tenants Council earned the right to become Parcel 19's developers. With the help of young architects, Emergency Tenants Council tenant-organizers helped design a new 844-unit housing complex for low- and middle-income residents. Naming the community "Villa Victoria" (or "Victory Village") this project became an award-winning complex of three-story houses and included stores, a residential tower, and public spaces such as community gardens, features designed to build a tight-knit community. The Emergency Tenants Council eventually reclaimed its original name as the Inquilinos Boricuas en Acción in 1974 and evolved into an organization focused on managing Villa Victoria and organizing community services and events. Mel King greatly admired the community, arguing it was one of the best developments in the country. "The whole complex is managed by the people," he explained.[27] He held it up as a model that should be replicated across the city as he continued to fight for fair housing into the 1980s, arguing, "It's probably one of the best pulled together housing developments run by Latino folks in the country."[28] The lasting impact of CAUSE, the South End Tenants Council, and Inquilinos Boricuas en Acción, like the social service organizations they emerged out of, proved not only that multiethnic/multiracial cooperation was possible but that they were incredibly effective in movements addressing poverty, education, and housing. King's experience organizing multiethnic/multiracial movements also proved useful later as he sought to garner the Latinx vote and forge broader diverse coalitions in his 1983 mayoral run.

King's 1983 Mayoral Campaign

Mel King's local reputation was propelled drastically by his organizing for fair housing and his leading role in the Tent City protest, which remained one of the defining moments in his long activist career. He and other radical organizers of color gained increasing political power in Boston in the 1960s and 1970s, and many recognized the role that electoral politics could play in the long freedom movement, but getting elected was a lengthy, difficult process. After failing to win a seat on the Boston School Committee three times throughout the 1960s, King eventually left the United South End Settlements and became director of the New Urban League of Greater Boston in 1967. In 1970, he created the Community Fellows Program at the Massachusetts Institute of Technology, which he directed, and taught as adjunct professor of urban studies and planning at MIT for the next several decades. King finally won his first seat in public office in 1973 as state representative for the Ninth Suffolk District and served for five terms in the Massachusetts legislature, until 1982.[29] In 1981, he also authored his first book, *Chain of Change: Struggles for Black Community Development*, which documented the development of the Black community and the struggles for racial justice in Boston.

King's growing interest in electoral politics mirrored that of other African American and Latinx activists in the city. Housing rights activist Doris Bunte made history as the first African American woman in the Massachusetts legislature when she was elected as state representative for the Seventh Suffolk District in 1972, one year prior to King. Then, in 1982, Byron Rushing, an African American organizer for the Congress on Racial Equality and the Northern Student Movement as well as Frieda Garcia's partner, was elected as state representative serving the Ninth Suffolk District, where he took over for King and served for more than thirty years. On the city level, John O'Bryant ran unsuccessfully for the Boston School Committee in 1975 but then then finally won a seat in 1977, becoming the first African American to ever serve on the committee.

Latinx candidates, however, struggled to get elected compared with their African American counterparts. On the state level, Alex Rodriguez ran for state representative in 1968 but was defeated in the primary. In 1980, Black Puerto Rican housing and education activist Carmen Pola became the first Latina to run for statewide office but also failed to get elected as state representative. Similarly, on the local level, Puerto Rican activist Felix Arroyo made failed bids in his run for the Boston School Committee in 1981 and 1983, though he became the first Latinx person to ever run citywide as well as the first to move on from the primary election to the runoff stage. As African American and Latinx organizers attempted to get elected in the city and across the state, both groups built off their earlier experiences in grassroots coalition building to develop multiracial/multiethnic voter bases that blossomed in the 1980s.

In 1983, Mel King announced his intentions to run for Boston mayor again when Kevin White decided not to seek reelection after sixteen years in office. Despite finishing third in a disappointing loss in the 1979 mayoral election, King was enthusiastic about his chances this time around, especially amid the broader developments on the national Black political scene. While the major cities of Cleveland, Los Angeles, and Detroit all saw the election of their first Black mayors in the 1960s and 1970s, it was the election of Harold Washington in Chicago in April 1983 that provided a major boost to King's campaign and lent confidence to Boston's Black residents in the possibility of finally electing their own Black mayor. As the lone Black candidate, King was confident he could win the African American vote in the city. While the numbers of African Americans had grown to almost one-quarter of the city's population by 1980, he knew that would not be enough to swing the election. In fact, King dismissed the idea that he or any candidate should be expected to receive 100 percent of any particular racial community's vote, arguing that the Black community was not a monolith and that he would need to build a larger multiethnic/multiracial coalition of supporters to beat Irish Catholic populist and city councilor Ray Flynn.[30]

The 1970s marked a particularly hostile time in Boston's history, exemplified by the racial violence that arose from court-ordered desegregation of public schools, or what some have called the "busing crisis" of 1974. In response, King centered his 1983 mayoral campaign on unifying Boston's segregated and politically divided neighborhoods and promoted broader racial healing. His opponent Ray Flynn, on the other hand, had been staunchly opposed to "busing" and served as state representative representing South Boston, the center of the city's Irish community and white resistance to desegregation. Thus, the press pitted the two Democratic candidates against one another and depicted the mayoral race as one that needed to win over each ethno-racial group, neighborhood by neighborhood. For example, the *Boston Observer* commented, "The Boston campaign is really seven distinct campaigns waged in seven ethnically and ideologically homogenous sections of the city."[31] King, however, took this challenge head-on and decided to "take the campaign everywhere." He was sure to campaign in every neighborhood, particularly South Boston, the area considered most unwelcoming to residents of color. He later reflected, "I walked South Boston. I went to the beaches in South Boston. I walked Charlestown. I went through public housing developments in Charlestown. People would say you're crazy for doing that. I said—and why are you here? I said if I'm gonna be the mayor, I'm gonna be mayor of the whole city and not just part of it."[32] King argued that his broad campaigning across the city revealed a common desire: "People tell me they are tired of tension. Hostility tears away at our city." He continued, "People want to feel proud of Boston again, instead of ashamed of the racist, narrow-minded image it has throughout the United States."[33] King held tight to this ambitious goal, framing his election as a critical moment for the city to move past its racist history and come together in healing. Slogans such as "We can save our neighborhoods" and "We can save this city" reflected this commitment to uniting the city across racial and ethnic lines.

King's vision manifested into the Rainbow Coalition, a coalition of diverse, marginalized groups in the city including African Americans, Latinx, Asians, women, queer people, people with disabilities, working-class laborers, the youth, and the elderly. On the campaign trail, he explained, "We have all kinds of people, all colors, all ages, from all parts of the city, involved in the campaign ... you name it, we can claim it."[34] King recognized the potential of the Rainbow Coalition as a symbol of "togetherness" and unity. He later reflected, "I tried to come up with something which was kind of an umbrella of the different groups so that people could see that they were interrelated, interwoven, and that it should be that way because we shouldn't be playing one against ... the other."[35] King called for a "politics of inclusion." Critical to the success of his campaign was support beyond the Black community, particularly winning the Latinx vote.

King sought to build off of his success coalition building with Latinx activists in the 1960s and 1970s to secure the Latinx vote. The "Latinos for Mel King" arm of his campaign led the charge, playing a very active role fundraising, organizing events, and distributing campaign materials in both English and Spanish to the Latinx communities across the city. The campaign's Spanish language leaflets centered on King's long track record supporting the Latinx community:

> If you want a mayor with an unparalleled record of working with Latinos in Boston, vote for what you want. You want to vote for Mel King. Back in the 1950's when the center of the Latino community in this city was a fairly small group of Puerto Rican families in the South End, everyone knew Mel King as someone who fought against injustice and was willing to help in any circumstance. Many considered him family. In the thirty years that have elapsed since then, it is hard to think of a single major effort or struggle of Latinos in this city in which this man has not been involved as a friend in some way.[36]

The campaign organizers strategically reminded voters that King was considered a "friend" or "family" to the Latinx community. King was incredibly popular among Latinx for his activist work in housing, having walked the picket lines in support of the creation of Villa Victoria in the South End, been arrested alongside Puerto Rican organizers in the Tent City protest, and advocated for tenants' rights across the city. He was also active in the community by supporting Latinx organizations, helping to establish the "Borinquen Stars," the city's first Latinx baseball team, as well as negotiating Boston's first Puerto Rican festival. He supported Latinx people in their runs for public office and employed them in his own campaign and offices. For all of these reasons, he easily won the endorsement of many Latinx community organizers and political figures, such as his friend and fellow South End resident Alex Rodriguez. Another key endorsement came from Felix Arroyo, a Puerto Rican community leader, who was running his own campaign for the Boston School Committee at the same time as King's run for mayor. In Arroyo's endorsement, he addressed the crowds, arguing that "there is no doubt that Mel King is the best candidate to serve the Latino community in Boston."[37] However, despite the support he garnered, the Latinx community constituted only around 6 percent of the city's total population, and even fewer participated in the election. In fact, only 5,000 Latinx people were registered to vote in the city by the time of the election, while three times as many Latinx were unregistered. Still, an African American–Latinx coalition could not carry King to victory, and the only way he had any hope of winning was to rally across Boston's diverse white communities.[38]

Overall, Mel King was very optimistic about his potential to make it far in the 1983 mayoral election. In a nightly news interview in September 1983, King argued, "I am running for mayor of Boston because I know that I can win. I know that we can affect the kind of positive changes in the city and that we can bring people together in a way that will impact them very positively." Decades later, he reflected a similar sentiment: "I knew I could be in the final because we had done our work. I knew that they had underestimated the voting potential of folks of color."[39] Despite these high hopes and his hard work trying to unify the city throughout his campaign, King did, in fact, only make it to the final round.

In October 1983, Mel King finished second in the mayoral primary, a tight race against Ray Flynn. In fact, King and Flynn had both garnered 28.7 percent of the vote, with King losing by just one vote—47,432 to 47,431. The *New York Times* wrote that the "virtual tie" in the primary between King and Flynn reflected "the emergence of a more liberal electorate in Boston after a century of domination by conservative and Irish politicians."[40] King's success in the mayoral primary was largely due to his ability to register new African American and Latinx voters. King's campaign team successfully registered 51,000 new voters, of whom more than 40,000 were Black, Latinx, or "other minorities."[41]

Despite amassing a coalition of supporters across the city of Boston, Mel King lost the mayoral election on November 15, 1983, to Ray Flynn. In a "landslide victory," according to the *Globe*, Flynn led King 66 percent to 34 percent. Flynn's win was largely due to his success in the white neighborhoods of Boston, since King received only about 20 percent of the white vote.[42] Some argued that King was too radical and made too many political "mistakes" that turned off many white moderates and were impossible to overcome, such as his interest in and support of controversial revolutionaries like Fidel Castro of Cuba and Yasser Arafat of Palestine. Yet King's campaign and supporters continued to hail the mayoral bid as a victory for the city despite the loss. "It will be said that the 'rainbow coalition' did not win, but it never can be said that the 'rainbow coalition' was defeated," King declared in his concession speech.[43] He continued, "You have given me the privilege to be able to guide us through what historians will recognize as the turning point in the social, cultural, and political history of Boston."[44] Indeed, King had the foresight to recognize the impact his mayoral run would have on the city in the decades that followed.

Conclusion

After a lifetime of community activism in Boston, Mel King passed away on March 28, 2023, at the age of ninety-four. Hailed as Boston's Martin Luther King Jr. or Nelson Mandela, the city's most well-known civil rights icon was praised in countless media outlets specifically for the impact of his 1983 mayoral campaign, which was said to have "ushered in a new era in Boston race relations."[45] Focused on the positive tone and surprising civility of the election, the *Globe* argued that King's run "helped close a dark chapter in Boston history while opening a notable new one in national politics."[46] Ray Flynn would echo this statement, reflecting forty years later that "the city was racially divided, but the campaign wasn't divisive." He continued, "It was the first sign of wounds beginning to heal."[47] While Boston's communities of color might argue that the wounds of racial inequality and trauma of the school desegregation era have never fully healed in the city to this day, King's Rainbow Coalition did emerge as a powerful, optimistic symbol for the future of Boston's African American and Latinx communities in the 1980s and decades that followed.

King's 1983 mayoral run proved transformative, providing an inclusive political model that centered on multiracial and multiethnic coalition building. As his campaign buttons declared, "We can save this city," King never swayed from his vision to unite Boston and promote racial healing. His rallying cry that "we are all in the same boat now" from his early victory speech in the preliminary election resonated across his voter base, particularly with those like Alex Rodriguez, who had worked alongside him for decades building a movement for racial justice. After the loss, Rodriguez wrote to King, calling him a "moral giant among us, pushing and leading, forcing people to confront themselves and each other." He thanked King not only for running for mayor but for his "twenty years of example and coalition building." He encouraged King to "hang in there," writing that they had "more work to do."⁴⁸ This certainly resonated with King, as he continued to advocate for Boston's most marginalized people. Jesse Jackson adopted the "Rainbow Coalition" as part of his national effort in his 1984 presidential run, with King cochairing his Massachusetts campaign. King remained active in politics, launching the Rainbow Coalition Party in 1997, which merged with the Massachusetts Green Party in 2002 to form the Green-Rainbow Party.

Forty years after Mel King's historic mayoral run, the city of Boston has still not elected a Black mayor. It remains one of only a few major cities to have never done so. While Kim Janey served as acting mayor for several months in 2021 when Marty Walsh departed the role to serve as secretary of labor for the Biden administration, Janey, like King, also came up short. She was one of three Black candidates in the 2021 mayoral election and had received King's endorsement, but none of them made it to the final runoff. Many felt the five-person race was too divided with three competing Black candidates, who inevitably split the vote in communities of color, resulting in none of them winning. Regardless, the election proved to be historic in its own right, as Boston elected its first mayor who was not a white man: Michelle Wu, who is Asian American, is the first woman and first person of color elected to lead the city. While many have celebrated this victory, others have questioned what this means about the current state of racial politics in Boston and whether perhaps, after all these decades, the city is still not ready or willing to have a Black person lead it. Wu herself was very aware of what her election meant to many Black Bostonians. She explained, "I have heard and want to continue acknowledging the disappointment of many in our community who wish to see a representative from the Black community. And we will continue working to meet this moment to take on systemic racism and the barriers that have been perpetuated for far too long."⁴⁹ Boston's voters will be watching her closely to see if she remains committed to this racial justice work, as Congressman Ayanna Pressley pointed out after Wu's election: "I expect that the Black community will hold her accountable."⁵⁰ Though Mel King was an unwavering advocate for multiracial and multiethnic solidarity and coalition building, he also encouraged Bostonians to remain vigilant and skeptical of the city's political system. In his 1981 book, he explained, "If, on the other hand, we find that the system is incapable of responding to our changes and that the needs of people cannot be met even when we have reorganized local political structures, then we will be prepared and skilled to go on to the final work."⁵¹

The future of Boston's politics is unclear, but one thing is not: Mel King's leadership and long career as a grassroots activist and coalition builder has left a permanent mark on the city. This is evident in Mayor Wu's political platform, which reflects King's vision of uniting the city in a movement toward racial justice. Following King's death, Wu aptly summarized his impact and legacy, explaining that he "taught us all how to serve, how to build, and how to love."[52] King's Rainbow Coalition did indeed center love, one that thankfully has not been lost on younger generations. His inclusive political philosophy was, in many ways, ahead of its time, and his vision is just as inspiring and relevant today as it was in the 1980s: "If we share the vision about what is possible and what we want to see in our country and our community, we can work in unity as a community, resisting the isolation and separation that makes us vulnerable."[53]

Notes

1. James Green, "The Making of Mel King's Rainbow Coalition: Political Changes in Boston, 1963–1983," *Radical America* 17, no. 6 (November 1983), 9–34., and 8, no. 1 (February 1984): 9; "Mel King Interview," *Ten O'Clock News*, WGBH, September 19, 1983, Boston TV News Digital Library: 1960–2000, https://bostonlocaltv.org.
2. Larry Goldsmith, "Flynn and King: Not Lookalike Candidates—the Real Issue in the Boston Mayoral Election," *Gay Community News*, December 3, 1983, 3, box 1, folder "1983 Mayoral Campaign: Correspondence/ 1983 A–L /1," Melvin King Papers, 1983 Mayoral Campaign, Roxbury Community College Archives and Special Collections, Boston.
3. Mel King quoted in "KING: '... The Boat Is Changing Its Course," *Boston Globe*, October 12, 1983, 59.
4. Charles Kenney, "Incredibly Warm, Positive Responses Buoyed King," *Boston Globe*, October 12, 1983, 1.
5. King quoted in "KING: '... The Boat Is Changing Its Course."
6. US Census Bureau, "Characteristics of the Population, By Census Tracts: 1950," https://www2.census.gov/library/publications/decennial/1950/population-volume-3/41557421v3p1ch3.pdf; US Census Bureau, "General Characteristics of the Population, By Census Tracts: 1960," https://www2.census.gov/library/publications/decennial/1960/population-and-housing-phc-1/41953654v1ch7.pdf; US Census Bureau, "General Characteristics of the Population: 1970," https://www2.census.gov/library/publications/decennial/1970/phc-1/39204513p3ch05.pdf; US Census Bureau, "Detailed Population Characteristics: 1980," https://www2.census.gov/library/publications/decennial/1980/volume-1/massachusetts/1980a_mad-01.pdf.
7. Mel King, interview by Robert Hayden, December 8, 2005, HistoryMakers Digital Archive, www.thehistorymakers.org/biography/honorable-melvin-king.
8. US Census Bureau, 1980.
9. US Census Bureau, 1970.
10. The actual number of Latinx residents was hotly debated, though, since Puerto Ricans were American citizens and immigration officials did not count them, which skewed "official" numbers, while others did not participate in census surveys at all. The data also do not account for many undocumented immigrants from the Caribbean and Central America who lived discreetly in constant fear of deportation. Latinx social

workers, educators, and activists adamantly argued that the Latinx population in Boston was significantly higher than official census records indicated, estimating between 30,000 and 40,000 people in 1970, and grew rapidly in the decades afterward. See US Census Bureau, 1980; Task Force on Children out of School, *The Way We Go to School: The Exclusion of Children in Boston* (Boston: Beacon Press, 1971), 16–17; and Phyllis W. Coons, "Hub Programs Battle Giant Language Problem: New Doors Opening for Spanish-Speaking Children," *Boston Globe*, August 17, 1969, 67.

11. A 1963 state study on housing discrimination in Boston explained, "Within the city, almost the entire Negro population lives in a contiguous, geographically compact area, which has been very aptly described by the Urban League of Boston as a curved area resembling a 'black boomerang.' Fewer than 1,500 of the 63,165 Negroes in Boston live outside this belt. It appears that the real reason Boston doesn't have a Harlem or South Chicago ghetto yet is that we don't have enough Negroes to completely fill this belt." Massachusetts Advisory Committee to the United States Commission on Civil Rights, *Discrimination in Housing in the Boston Metropolitan Area: Report* (Washington, DC: United States Government Printing Office, 1963), 3, 7.

12. Mel King, *Chain of Change: Struggles for Black Community Development* (Boston: South End Press, 1981), 26.

13. King, *Chain of Change*, 26.

14. King, *Chain of Change*, 10, 21; King interview by Hayden, December 8, 2005.

15. "Historical Note," Freedom House, Inc. Records, Northeastern University Library Archives and Special Collections, Boston.

16. "Biographical Note," Melvin King Papers, 1983 Mayoral Campaign.

17. Hubert Jones, interview by author, Newton, MA, March 16, 2013; "Proposal for the Development of the Roxbury Multi-Service Center over the Next Five Years: 1969–1974," Roxbury Multi-Service Center Records, box 1, folder 68, Northeastern University Library Archives and Special Collections.

18. Frieda Garcia, interview by author, Boston, March 1, 2013.

19. Garcia interview.

20. Ana Maria Diamond (neé Rodriguez) to John D. O'Bryant, September 20, 1971, box 1, folder 21, La Alianza Hispana Records, Northeastern University Library Archives and Special Collections.

21. Task Force on Children out of School, *The Way We Go to School*.

22. Transitional Bilingual Education Act (M.G.L., c.71A, 1971); Massachusetts Special Education Law (M.G.L., c.766, 1972).

23. Alex Rodriguez, interview by author (Skype), October 8, 2015.

24. Rodriguez interview.

25. John Killilea, "The South End: 'Puerto Rican Power!,'" *Harvard Crimson*, November 16, 1967.

26. F. Taylor Jr., "South End Decision Left to Lot's Owner," *Boston Globe*, April 29, 1968, 1.

27. Mel King quoted in Marie Steffen, "Candidate King Speaks on Housing, Crime Rate, Racism and Education," *Mass Media* 18, no. 4 (August 1983): 3.

28. Mel King, interview by Robert Hayden, February 6, 2006, HistoryMakers Digital Archive, www.thehistorymakers.org/biography/honorable-melvin-king.

29. King, interview by Hayden, February 6, 2006.

30. "Mel King Interview," *Ten O'Clock News*.
31. Thomas Driscoll and Mark Zabierek, "Handicapping the Mayor's Race," *Boston Observer* 2, no. 8 (October 1983), in box 1, folder "1983 Mayoral Campaign/ Correspondence / 1983 A-L / 1," Melvin King Papers.
32. King interview by Hayden, December 8, 2005.
33. Mel King, "Statement Accepting Endorsements of Mayor Harold Washington and an Ecumenical Group of Clergy," August 7, 1983, 1, box 4, folder 1, Melvin King Papers.
34. "Mel King Interview," *Ten O'Clock News*.
35. King interview by Hayden, December 8, 2005.
36. Comite para Eligir a Mel King Alcalde, "Empleos para Boston," translation by author, 1983, box 2, folder 4, Melvin King Papers.
37. Felix Arroyo quoted in Viola Osgood, "Hispanics, Youth Rally for King," *Boston Globe*, October 30, 1983, 40.
38. Kenneth J. Cooper, "Denver and Boston: Why One City Elects Black Mayors and the Other Has Not," *Trotter Review* 20, no. 1, article 5 (2012): 72–73.
39. "Mel King Interview," *Ten O'Clock News*; King interview by Hayden, February 6, 2006.
40. Fox Butterfield, "Signs of Change Appearing in Boston's Electorate," *New York Times*, October 13, 1983, A1.
41. Dudley Clendinen, "Black's Mayoral Bid Brings Change to Boston," *New York Times*, October 7, 1983, A14.
42. Robert Jordan, "Flynn Wins in a Big Way, 66%–34%," *Boston Globe*, November 16, 1983, 1.
43. Mel King quoted in "After Boston's Decision," *Boston Globe*, November 17, 1983, 28.
44. Mel King quoted in Jordan, "Flynn Wins in a Big Way," 1.
45. See, for example Mark Feeney, "Mel King, Whose 1983 Mayoral Campaign Ushered in a New Era in Boston Race Relations, Dies at 94," *Boston Globe*, March 28, 2023; Max Larkin, "Boston Activist and Politician Mel King, 'Our Nelson Mandela,' Dies at 94," WBUR, March 28, 2003; Richard Sandomir, "Mel King, Whose Boston Mayoral Bid Eased Racial Tensions, Dies at 94," *New York Times*, April 9, 2023.
46. Feeney, "Mel King."
47. Raymond Flynn quoted in Feeney, "Mel King."
48. Alex Rodriguez, letter to Melvin King (November 22, 1983), box 1, folder 4, Melvin King Papers.
49. Michelle Wu quoted in "Why Boston Will Need to Wait Longer for Its 1st Elected Black Mayor," NPR, November 16, 2021, https://www.npr.org/2021/11/16/1055972179/boston-first-black-mayor.
50. Ayanna Pressley quoted in "Why Boston Will Need to Wait Longer for Its 1st Elected Black Mayor."
51. King, *Chain of Change*, 261.
52. Michelle Wu quoted in Lisa Creamer and Samantha Coetzee, "Local Elected Officials React to Mel King's Death: He Was the 'Generational Conscience' for Massachusetts," WBUR, March 29, 2023, https://www.wbur.org/news/2023/03/29/mel-king-death-reactions-boston-massachusetts-wu-markey.
53. King, *Chain of Change*, 249.

BRIAN PURNELL

Living and Working in a World of Overlapping Diasporas

Black New Yorkers' History in the Metropolis since the 1970s

To study African Americans requires us to historicize the process of racial formation and identity construction. Race in turn is viewed as historically contingent and relational, with full understanding of that process dependent on our abilities to see African Americans living and working in a world of overlapping diasporas [dispersed communities]. . . . If we are to take race seriously, we must begin in earnest to theorize and historicize how racial identity informs individual identity and how identity formation in turn informs racial construction—in a sense, we must take the process of community-building seriously.—**Earl Lewis**, "To Turn as on a Pivot"

Something else Ma wanted: for Black people in Brooklyn, in America, not to forever be effectively refugees—stateless, homeless, without rights, confined by borders that they did not create and by a penal system that killed them before they died, all while trying to rear children who went to schools that taught them not about themselves but about what they didn't have.—**Hilton Als**, "Homecoming"

Introduction

Black urban people live in a world of "overlapping diasporas": "interconnected worlds demarcated by race, class, color, and other factors."[1] Overlapping diasporas have shaped four centuries of Black lives in places now part of the New York City metropolis.[2] Most histories of Black people and communities in New York City focus on the city's five counties, or boroughs, with occasional reference to surrounding suburbs, but since the 1970s, Black people have been on the move in and around the Big Apple. Places where few, if any, Black people lived experienced noticeable Black population increases. Places long considered strongholds of Black life witnessed profound changes in their Black populations.

Sometimes Black metropolitan communities, which have had overwhelmingly large Black populations for over half a century, experienced historic reductions in their Black populations along with arrivals of significant, if not always large, populations of people who were not Black. Other times, Black communities underwent replenishments of their populations with new groups of Black people, oftentimes immigrants from various parts of the Caribbean and Africa. These trends of movement and community reconfiguration—and the political dynamics, economic structures, and cultural expressions they reflected and produced—have not been unique to Black people in New York City and its larger metropolitan region. They represent the predominant social characteristics of the past fifty years of Black urban life in the United States.[3]

Scholars have tended to examine these changes in Black urban life through three major historic themes and frameworks: gentrification, suburbanization, and immigration. Gentrification can be defined as the historic processes, economic causes, and political policies that reconfigure erstwhile industrial and manufacturing urban spaces, and the poor and working-class residential districts connected to those sites of production, to benefit economically mobile people with access to emerging forms of capital.[4] Gentrification has disrupted and disturbed—indeed, sometimes even destroyed—elements of Black communal life. Gentrification can uproot long-term residents, displace businesses, and attract entirely new populations of people from different cultures and class backgrounds. Gentrification also has brought investment dollars to urban Black communities, which has created new businesses and housing developments, among other kinds of experiential changes in policing, street life, schools, and recreation. Lance Freeman, a social scientist who has studied gentrification in New York City, shows how diverse groups of Black New Yorkers in Harlem (Manhattan) and Clinton Hill (Brooklyn) responded in multiple ways, including—sometimes—favorably, to neighborhood changes caused by gentrification. As Freeman writes, "Although negative reactions were certainly an important theme, many residents welcomed the changes taking place in their community due to gentrification." By focusing on the thoughts, interpretations, and experiences of local Black residents, Freeman's book, in part, uncovers "an often ignored facet of the gentrification process—the perceived benefits flowing to current residents." That said, Freeman's study also shows how the social ties and networks of gentrifiers and long-term residents rarely cross over. People share space, and long-term residents express appreciation for new economic developments, but "the social networks within these neighborhoods seem impervious to the changes taking place around them."[5]

Freeman's multiple published studies show how gentrification is a complex social and economic process. Transformations of urban neighborhoods produced by gentrification do not always have negative effects on long-term urban Black populations. Freeman examines data to uncover whether, and when, gentrification influences residential displacement of long-standing community members. He also reveals how some demographic changes, like levels of population movements in or out of gentrifying neighborhoods, correspond to social factors in a neighborhood other than race and class, such as the number of housing units in a community that are regulated by rent-control laws.[6] Scholars such as Freeman, Brian D. Goldstein, John L. Jackson, Monique M. Taylor, Amanda T. Boston, and others have shown how gentrification's social realties for Black people are much more nuanced than first appear in many analytical narratives that present gentrification as inevitably producing displacement of poor Black people. Displacement of Black residents and disruptions of long-standing Black urban communities is a fact, but it is not the *only* fact regarding how histories of gentrification play undeniable roles in the ways that Black urban communities have developed, changed, and evolved over the past fifty years.[7]

The second major analytical theme concerns suburbanization.[8] Scholars such as Andrew Wiese, Mary Pattillo, Todd Michney, Thomas Sugrue, and Orly Clerge, among others, have shown how Black suburbs, once considered a "dubious historical subject" by scholars, constitute a central aspect of twentieth-century urban and suburban history.[9] Summarizing the importance of Black suburbanization to the history of the first Great Migration, Wiese shows how, even though most southern Black migrants went to central cities, "suburbs accounted for approximately 15 percent of black population growth in metropolitan areas outside the South between 1910 and 1940, or about 285,000 people. By 1940, approximately 500,000 African Americans lived in suburbs north of the Mason-Dixon line, a number that represented almost one-fifth (19 percent) of the African Americans in metropolitan areas of the North and West."[10] Since the 1970s, suburban populations of Asians, Hispanics, and African Americans increased dramatically; some of the largest surges happened at the end of the twentieth century.[11] For decades, Black suburbanites have lived in overlapping diasporas defined by the social, cultural, and economic nuances of communities that are geographically sliced up along racial and class lines, as well as by the continued connections between Black suburban life and Black life and culture in center cities.[12]

The third theme, Black immigration, has dramatically shaped the evolution of the Black metropolis, especially since 1965.[13] The Lewis Mumford Center for Comparative Urban and Regional Research at the University at Albany concluded in its survey "Black Diversity in Metropolitan America" that the number of Black people in the United States originally from sub-Saharan African countries tripled during the 1990s. During that same time, the number of Black people with origins in the Caribbean increased by 60 percent. The 2000 US Census recorded over 1.5 million Afro-Caribbean people and over 600,000 people who came originally from the African continent. According to that report, "Nationally nearly 25% of the growth of the black population between 1990 and 2000 was due to people from Africa and the Caribbean." Afro-Caribbean immigrants and migrants concentrated on the East Coast, but African immigrants were spread throughout different parts of the United States. Interestingly, like Black Americans, Afro-Caribbeans and Africans lived separately from white people, but according to the Mumford Center report, Black immigrants also "overlap only partly with one another in neighborhoods where they live. Segregation among black ethnic groups reflects important social differences between them."[14] New waves of Black immigrants from Africa, the Caribbean, and South America required that academic studies focus anew, with more attention to intra-racial, intercultural dynamics, on a host of social and cultural questions that have been foundational to generations of urban studies on Black Americans—around Black identity formation and definitions; around class and cultural diversity within Black communities; around the composition of Black political coalitions; and around the effects that racism and discrimination have on Black people's quality of life. This scholarship has also broadened and deepened understandings of Black life in the New York metropolis.[15]

A fourth analytical lens through which to see how overlapping diasporas shape Black metropolitan life, which deserves more study and recognition by historians of Black urban communities, is mass incarceration. Over a decade ago, Heather Thompson reminded US historians of the dramatic influence the politics of mass incarceration had on electoral politics and American liberalism; on organized labor and the decline of the American labor movement; and on the "origins of the urban crisis"[16] and the demographic and political-economic transformations of urban and rural communities.[17] Ruth Wilson Gilmore uncovered spatially scattered gulag archipelagos that, since the 1960s, have irrevocably reshaped all aspects of American politics, society, economics, and the environment.[18] Michelle Alexander brought these trends to mainstream attention with her book on the existence of a caste system based on incarcerated, and previously incarcerated, Black Americans' almost permanent status as social, political, and economic outcasts—noncitizens unable to vote, rejected from jobs, and denied social services.[19] "Despite these realities," write historians Heather Thompson and Donna Murch, "scholars of urban history and the American metropole have, to date, asked remarkably few questions about the buildup of such a massive carceral system. And because we have not yet fully probed this major punitive turn in American policy and culture, we have not even begun to consider the ways in which our existing urban historiography might be limited having missed such an important elephant in the room."[20]

As urban historians and scholars uncover more evidence of the profound influences the age of mass incarceration has had on Black metropolitan life, new understandings will emerge about how the rise of a carceral state in America has shaped the past five decades of Black communal life, Black people's political power, and Black individuals' social mobility.[21] Specifically, the overlapping diasporas that connect incarcerated Black people to Black metropolitan communities is a subject deserving increased study. How do Black people living in prisons located in rural or suburban counties form and maintain social bonds—friendships, parental relationships, kinship ties, marriages, romances—with people living in metropolises that are sometimes hundreds of miles away? And what about inside the prison itself—what kinds of overlapping diasporas of race, class, religion, culture, and regional identity influence the types of communities that incarcerated Black people form among themselves and with others?[22]

The concept of overlapping diasporas and a metropolitan regional focus offers the best approach for historians who want to synthesize and narrate the broad, deep, complex evolution of Black history in the urban United States since the 1970s. Earl Lewis reminds historians that overlapping diasporas (among Black people and between Black people and others) have always influenced Black community and cultural formations in significant ways.[23] This has been especially true during the decades since 1965, when major changes in US national immigration policy occurred and when metropolitan populations shifted in ways that disrupted several decades of steady increases in total Black populations and seemingly fixed geographic concentrations of those populations. In the decades since the mid-1960s, the New York metropolis's population grew in its numbers of Black immigrants, increased in total Hispanic and Latino people, and witnessed significant demographic fluctuations in communities long considered Black strongholds. Overlapping diasporas do not only occur between and among people of different ethnicities or nationalities. Lewis's invitation to scholars to see histories of Black community and culture unfolding through processes of social interaction, political conflict, and economic and cultural exchange with other people who are, and are not, Black becomes particularly relevant to the history of Black urban people since 1970, a time when Black people were on the move into, around, and throughout urban America. A framework of overlapping diasporas, with its emphasis on *processes of* community formation and social identity reconfiguration, allows historians to see the key structural, political forces of gentrification, suburbanization, and immigration (as well as mass incarceration) as lived experiences that develop at individual and communal levels. Commercial and demographic transformations in historically Black communities, suburban and exurban spread of Black people, influxes of Black immigrants, and metropolitan-wide Black social networks between and within incarceration facilities are not merely external impingements placed upon Black life from outside forces but instead occur in time, space, and place—that is, in history. This history of overlapping diasporas within Black metropolises unfolds through the ways Black people make their individual lives and their communities within the broader places and spaces of the metropolis.

The metropolitan framework—rather than merely the city, county, or neighborhood—also emerges as significant to Black urban history since the 1970s. Zooming out to view an entire metropolis sacrifices the nuance and texture of the micro-level communal, or even citywide, view, but while a historian loses knowledge gained through granular, up-close, intimate views, much is gained through examining changes over time within broad, wide spaces. Since the 1970s, the significant movements and changes that define Black life at the metropolitan level have also called into question (once again) the usefulness of the "ghetto" as a site in which to locate Black urban history.[24]

Since the 1970s, overlapping diasporas within *the entire metropolitan region* have drastically reconfigured the nature of Black communal life in and around New York City. The ghetto has an important (albeit controversial) interpretive position within histories of post–World War II American metropolises, and within post–WWII African American urban histories specifically. Scholarship on racialized ghettos contributed to decades of rich historical analysis of a broad range of subjects: racial segregation in post–WWII cities and suburbs,[25] creation and maintenance of generational racial wealth disparities,[26] inequities of government services and economic development initiatives that adversely affected Black urban communities for decades[27] and the dynamic efforts to undo those unjust policies,[28] environmental racism in modern US cities,[29] the post-1960s history of mass incarceration,[30] white political resistance against civil rights and racial justice initiatives,[31] transformations of Black political power and shifting trends in Black electoral politics,[32] and deep analysis of the causes and effects of urban uprisings and rebellions, during and beyond the 1960s.[33] It is worth asking, however, if the ghetto, as a place and as an analytical framework of structural political and economic racial injustices, still holds the same, or equal, significance to the past fifty years (1970–2020) of metropolitan Black history as it held for understanding the fifty years of Black urban history that unfolded from 1920 to 1970.

Histories of overlapping diasporas in metropolitan regional contexts provide keys for unlocking broader understandings of how diverse forms of Black urban life have developed over time, within and beyond racialized ghettos. A cursory examination of the last fifty years of Black people's history in New York City reveals how historians' widening their analytical aperture to include the broader metropolitan region reveals important, perhaps surprising, sites where Black communal life has emerged and grown. Population changes throughout the metropolis recorded in five decennial censuses (1970–2010) tell a revealing story about Black people's dynamic movement and diverse community characteristics. Metropolitan-wide movement of Black people and the overlapping diasporic nature of Black community formation provide significant analytical frameworks through which historians can examine the past fifty years of social, economic, political, and cultural changes in urban Black life, in and beyond the New York City metropolitan region.[34]

Overlapping Diasporas in the Metropolitan Region

The concept of overlapping diasporas helps explain dynamic processes of creation, invention, and negotiation that Black people have used constantly, since the Atlantic slave trade began up to the present, to define themselves. For Earl Lewis, focusing on the types of communities that Black people made and joined provided the key to breaking away from a strictly "racial" understanding of Black history and moving toward seeing the Black past in the United States through the actions, ideas, institutions, cultures, and relationships that Black people created, formed, chose, and rejected. Black people, therefore, were more than the "race" that social-historical processes of slavery and segregation made. They always negotiated social processes of racial formation with and through the communities they formed (with other Black people and with people who were not Black), which took shape in institutions, social movements, cultural expressions, families, and class identities.[35]

Black people's overlapping diasporas that have defined the New York metropolis since the 1970s happened through multiple series of movements.[36] After the 1960s, immigration patterns brought people from around the world into the region. After gains made during the civil rights and Black Power movements, especially federal legislation outlawing racial discrimination in housing, Black people from the Greater City of New York dispersed into surrounding suburbs. During the post–WWII period, the violently transformative process of mass incarceration also unfolded. From the city into far-flung areas throughout the state, a Gotham gulag[37] connected Black communities in metropolitan New

York to Black individuals and communities in jails and prisons spread over hundreds of miles throughout the metropolitan region. Within center cities, increased housing costs, new forms of investment capital, and policy decisions that favored wealthy housing and business development over working-class and poor people's commercial and residential tastes and needs turned communities once dominated by Black people into gentrified zones. A metropolitan framework for examining Black people in New York City since the 1970s captures how Black New Yorkers' history does not end, or even begin, at the borders of the five boroughs but instead unfolds through the relationships and connections that, like a web, make Black people in different places and across wide spaces stick together.

Overlapping diasporas throughout the New York metropolis, caused by emigration from Latin America, Africa, and the Caribbean; migration from the city to various suburbs; and politics of mass incarceration created new forms of Black communities, full of internal tensions, class and cultural divisions, intergenerational divergences, and fluctuating African American identities. Overlapping diasporas involved play and pleasure, too. Black metropolises within New York City and the surrounding cities, towns, and suburbs took shape through Black people's cultural creativity, recreation, and joy making with others who were not Black and with each other.[38]

Today's Black communities in the Greater New York metropolitan region truly exist within overlapping diasporas that have come to define not only Black people's lives but the entire metropolis's political, economic, and social life. While still concentrated within certain areas of counties, the spatially fixed, seemingly unchanging, immobile nature of Black communal life (commonly referred to as the Black ghetto) in the New York metropolis has ended.[39] The Black ghetto, for the most part, has been unmade. Other types of communities and social-spatial experiences—some predicated upon Black people's vulnerability, exploitation, and susceptibility to racist policies and practices, others stemming from increased and improved economic and social conditions—have arisen. Whatever these new metropolitical communities are, they no longer emerge directly from the types of political-economic conditions and policies that made twentieth-century racial ghettos.

The polices that made ghettos in the US city still shape legacies of poverty, disorder, disinvestment, punitive policing, and social isolation that characterize much of Black life in the New York metropolis.[40] And ghettoized places and spaces, once the dominant context for understanding Black metropolitan lives, connect directly to *some* of the metropolitan Black communities that grew since the 1970s, like the pockets of Black populations in all-white counties where prisons are located, far from the metropolitan core.[41] Similarly, a link exists between the underdevelopment polices that turned Black communities into ghettos during the middle third of the twentieth century (the 1930s–60s) and the investment policies connected to gentrification, which have disrupted and broken up once solidly Black urban communities. But other metropolitan Black communities that arose outside central cities since the 1970s have reflected increased social and economic mobility and opportunity; increased immigration from abroad; and the aftershocks of gentrification, which has included displacement of some Black people from the metropolitan core and dramatically altered lives of urban Black people who remain in, or move to, gentrified neighborhoods. Thus, new spaces and places, and the communal and cultural relationships that define them and emerge from them, characterize Black metropolitan life in the Greater New York City metro area since the 1970s.

These are the histories that, for the foreseeable future, will shape what it means to be a Black individual, or living in a Black community, in the New York metropolis. These are also the histories that will define places within the New York metropolis itself as centers of overlapping diasporas of Black life in the late twentieth and early twenty-first centuries. Black metropolitan history since the 1970s also provides insight into the nature of the metropolis itself—how politics, culture, economics, and society in America's largest metropolitan core area have developed over the past fifty years and how that area might continue to evolve in the future with and through its diverse Black residents.

Black Population Changes in the Metropolis, 1970–2010

Population statistics and community data uncover important social evidence about changes in spaces and places of Black life in the New York metropolis from 1970 to 2010. Where Black New Yorkers lived, their concentrations within specific counties, and population changes in counties outside of urban cores revealed significant amounts of Black people's spatial mobility throughout the metropolis during this fifty-year period. Census tract–level data also uncover how Black communities throughout the metropolis differ from each other in terms of income, education levels, population density, and property ownership levels. The overall takeaway from this information for historians is that many Black people are on the move, socially, economically, and geographically, and that movement has significant implications for where Black communities and Black lives exist within the metropolis (see table 1).

The five counties with the largest numbers of Black people in 1970 (Kings, New York, Bronx, Essex, and Queens) remained on top numerically in 2010. Almost all of these counties experienced between modest and noticeable relative

Table 1. Total Black population (and as percentage of total county population) in New York metropolitan area counties, 1970–2010

State	1970	1980	1990	2000	2010	Percentage change of total Black population (+/-), 1970 to 2010
New York						
Kings	654,988 (25.17%)	722,812 (32.40%)	872,305 (37.92%)	898,350 (36.44%)	860,083 (34.34%)	31.31%
Queens	257,873 (12.98%)	354,129 (18.72%)	423,211 (21.69%)	446,189 (20.01%)	426,683 (19.13%)	65.46%
New York	379,731 (24.67%)	309,854 (21.69%)	326,967 (21.98%)	267,302 (17.39%)	246,687 (15.56%)	-35.03%
Bronx	357,099 (24.26%)	371,926 (31.82%)	449,399 (37.33%)	475,007 (35.64%)	505,200 (36.47%)	41.47%
Richmond	15,779 (5.34%)	25,616 (7.27%)	30,630 (8.08%)	42,914 (9.67%)	49,857 (10.64%)	215.97%
Westchester	84,272 (9.43%)	104,815 (12.09%)	120,195 (13.74%)	131,132 (14.20%)	138,118 (14.55%)	63.89%
Putnam	115 (0.20%)	417 (0.54%)	851 (1.01%)	1,562 (1.63%)	2,350 (2.36%)	1943.48%
Rockland	13,101 (5.70%)	18,016 (6.94%)	26,468 (9.97%)	31,472 (10.98%)	37,058 (11.89%)	183.86%
Suffolk	54,312 (4.83%)	71,741 (5.59%)	82,910 (6.27%)	98,553 (6.94%)	111,224 (7.45%)	104.79%
Nassau	65,693 (4.60%)	90,743 (6.87%)	111,057 (8.63%)	134,673 (10.09%)	149,049 (11.13%)	126.88%
Dutchess	14,489 (6.52%)	17,131 (6.99%)	21,788 (8.40%)	26,097 (9.32%)	29,518 (9.92%)	103.73%
Orange	14,361 (6.48%)	16,225 (6.25%)	22,223 (7.22%)	27,601 (8.09%)	37,946 (10.18%)	164.22%
Ulster	4,930 (3.49%)	6,474 (4.09%)	8,055 (4.87%)	9,646 (5.43%)	10,982 (6.02%)	122.75%

Table 1. (continued)

State	1970	1980	1990	2000	2010	Percentage change of total Black population (+/-), 1970 to 2010
New Jersey						
Bergen	25,049 (2.79%)	33,043 (3.91%)	40,031 (4.85%)	46,568 (5.27%)	52,473 (5.80%)	109.48%
Hudson	61,358 (10.07%)	70,050 (12.58%)	79,770 (14.42%)	82,098 (13.48%)	83,925 (13.23%)	36.77%
Passaic	49,998 (10.85%)	59,171 (13.22%)	66,077 (14.58%)	64,647 (13.22%)	64,295 (12.83%)	28.59%
Mercer	49,970 (16.44%)	55,545 (18.04%)	61,481 (18.87%)	69,502 (19.81%)	74,318 (20.28%)	48.72%
Middlesex	25,755 (4.41%)	35,768 (6.00%)	53,629 (7.98%)	68,467 (9.13%)	78,462 (9.69%)	204.64%
Monmouth	38,044 (8.28%)	42,985 (8.54%)	47,229 (8.54%)	49,609 (8.06%)	46,443 (7.37%)	22.07%
Ocean	6,323 (3.03%)	9,439 (2.73%)	12,035 (2.78%)	15,268 (2.99%)	18,164 (3.15%)	187.26%
Somerset	7,088 (3.57%)	10,123 (4.98%)	14,824 (6.17%)	22,396 (7.53%)	28,943 (8.95%)	308.33%
Essex	279,068 (30.01%)	316,440 (37.18%)	316,262 (40.64%)	327,324 (41.24%)	320,479 (40.88%)	14.83%
Union	60,786 (11.19%)	81,207 (16.11%)	92,807 (18.79%)	108,593 (20.78%)	118,313 (22.05%)	94.63%
Morris	8,415 (2.19%)	10,017 (2.46%)	12,491 (2.96%)	13,181 (2.80%)	15,360 (3.12%)	82.53%
Sussex	260 (0.34%)	680 (0.59%)	1,242 (0.95%)	1,502 (1.04%)	2,677 (1.79%)	929.61%
Hunterdon	1,223 (1.75%)	1,123 (1.29%)	2,217 (2.06%)	2,743 (2.25%)	3,451 (2.69%)	182.17%

Table 1. (*continued*)

State	1970	1980	1990	2000	2010	Percentage change of total Black population (+/-), 1970 to 2010
Pennsylvania						
Pike	44 (0.37%)	55 (0.30%)	256 (0.92%)	1,513 (3.27%)	3,322 (5.79%)	7450.00%
Monroe	568 (1.25%)	982 (1.41%)	1,727 (1.80%)	8,343 (6.02%)	22,348 (13.16%)	3834.51%
Connecticut						
Fairfield	56,326 (7.10%)	66,155 (8.20%)	81,519 (9.85%)	88,362 (10.01%)	99,317 (10.83%)	76.32%
New Haven	56,954 (7.65%)	67,488 (8.86%)	82,011 (10.20%)	93,239 (11.32%)	109,850 (12.74%)	92.87%
Litchfield	1,027 (0.71%)	1,233 (0.79%)	1,631 (0.94%)	1,998 (1.10%)	2,558 (1.35%)	149.07%

Source: Data from U.S. Census Bureau, U.S. Census, Total Population: Black only, 1970, 1980, 1990, 2000, 2010. Prepared by Social Explorer (socialexplorer.com), accessed September 15, 2024.

population increases between their 1970 and 2010 total Black populations. The Black population in Essex County in New Jersey grew by just under 15 percent between 1970 and 2010. Black populations in Kings and Bronx Counties in New York grew noticeably larger. Queens County had the most significant total Black population growth, with a 65 percent increase. Interestingly, despite these relative gains across five decades, three of these counties *lost* Black people between 2000 and 2010—Kings lost roughly 38,000; Queens lost about 19,500; Essex lost around 6,800—while Bronx County *gained* 30,000 Black people.

The most staggering total population change happened in Manhattan (New York County). The home of Harlem, which was once commonly considered a "Capital of Black America"[42] and the creative source for some of the most significant urban cultural and intellectual expressions in modern African diasporic history, *lost* 35 percent of its Black people from 1970 to 2010. Roughly 70,000 Black people left Manhattan from 1970 to 1980, and after modest gains from 1980 to 1990, roughly 60,000 Black people moved out of Manhattan from 1990 to 2000. Of the thirty-one counties that make up the Greater New York metropolitan area, Manhattan was the only place that experienced a net loss (just over 133,000 in total) of Black people from 1970 to 2010.

A closer look at Harlem reveals what Black population loss looked like in Manhattan. The Black population in forty-three census tracts that corresponded to Harlem's traditional boundaries[43] changed in seemingly small but significant ways from 1990 to 2000. During this ten-year period (after Manhattan's total Black population rebounded from the significant losses recorded in the 1980 census), Harlem lost a total of 10,064 people who identified as Black. In 1990 (out of a total population of 150,437), the 133,174 Black people in Harlem made up 88.52 percent of the community. In 2000, the total number of people in the community *grew* to 161,871, a roughly 7.60 percent increase, but the total number of Black or African American people (not including Hispanics) decreased to 123,110, or 76.05 percent of the 2000 total. Thus, African American Harlem experienced a drop in raw numbers *and* a drop in percentage of Harlem's total population. The total number of Hispanic or Latino people and their percentage of the area's population increased significantly, from 21,563 (14.33 percent of total population) in 1990 to 36,342 (22.45 percent of total population) in 2000. Harlem's Hispanic population grew at a rate of 68.53 percent from 1990 to 2000, or nine times the rate of the total population growth for the community, while the total population that identified as Black or African American alone and its percentage of the community both fell. Within Harlem's Hispanic or Latino population are people who identified as Black, which would add to the Black population, but would not change how Black populations that do not include

Latinos decreased significantly. The number of white (non-Hispanic or Latino) people living in Harlem grew from 6,261 in 1990 (4.16 percent of the total population) to 11,208 in 2000 (6.92 percent of the total population), a 79.01 percent increase, a rate ten times the rate of the total population growth for the community. Within Harlem's Hispanic or Latino population are also people who identified as white, which would only add to Harlem's white population growth during this decade.

Neither the total increases of white people in Harlem nor their relative percentages are large, numerically; but the *percentage increases* of Hispanic or Latino people and white people in Harlem from 1990 to 2000 juxtaposed with the *percentage decrease* of Black or African Americans in Harlem during the same period is noticeable. Black or African American total percentage decrease in Harlem from 1990 to 2000, relative to the area's total population increase, fell at a rate of 14.08 percent. When compared with the rest of Manhattan for that decade, which had a 18.24 percent decline in Black or African American people, Harlem's total percentage loss of Black or African American people was slightly less, but Harlem grew by 7.60 percent in that decade; and Black Harlem shrunk by 7.55 percent in that decade. Considered alongside sizable percentage increases of Latinos and whites, the decline of Harlem's population that identified as Black or African American alone raised some serious questions about the community's Black identity. *Would Harlem remain a Black community if its African American and Black population kept declining and if its white and Hispanic and Latino population kept increasing?*[44]

Furthermore, the cost of housing in these Harlem census tracts changed noticeably from 1990 to 2000. In 1990, the median value for specified owner-occupied housing units in this wide swath of northern Manhattan was $177,493, and the median gross rent for specified renter-occupied housing units paying cash rent was $334. In 2000, the owner-occupied housing value was $361,099, and the rent increased by almost $170 to $501 a month.[45]

While Manhattan lost Black people overall, and Kings, Queens, and Essex Counties saw dips in their Black populations from 2000 to 2010, the metropolitan regional context shows that Black populations were not diminishing everywhere. Equally fascinating as these trends of Black population loss were the places that experienced dramatic explosions in their Black populations. Seventeen counties saw at least a doubling of their Black populations. Seven others experienced increases in Black populations that ranged between 48 percent and 95 percent. In 1970, twenty-two counties had Black populations of 10 percent or less of the total population. By 2010, only fourteen of those twenty-two counties still had Black populations less than 10 percent of their total populations. When a county's Black population is negligible, any increase may seem significant. In 1970, 11,818 people lived in Pike County, Pennsylvania, and only 44 of them identified as Black. In 2010, Pike's population nearly quintupled to 57,369, and its Black population boomed to just over 3,300: a more than 7,000 percent increase! Right next door in Monroe County, Pennsylvania, the African American population grew more than thirty-nine times, from just under a total of 600 in 1970 to slightly over 22,000 in 2010.

The Black migration to eastern Pennsylvania represents a significant aspect of the overlapping diasporas remaking the Greater New York metropolis and unmaking spatial concentration and confinement of urban Black people as their default social experience. Drawn to the areas featuring the picturesque Pocono Mountains, affordable housing, and a less-than-two-hour commute by car to Manhattan, New York metropolitan residents settled in these counties by the thousands. Monroe County's total population had boomed from 1970 (45,422) to 2010 (169,842), and its Black population surged from just over 1 percent of the total in 1970 to around 13 percent in 2010.[46]

In 2010, Black people had settled in a handful of Monroe and Pike Counties' census tracts spread out into five clusters. Two tracts in Pike County that were about 18 percent and 23.5 percent Black both contained roughly 2,200 of that county's 3,300 Black people, and they abutted tracts in Monroe County that were also over 15 percent Black. Four other clusters of Black people living in census tracts where they made up between 15 percent and 35 percent of the communities' populations spread across the county. Between these groupings, contiguous tracts with 10–15 percent Black populations filled in the county's interior.

While it would be a stretch to say that Monroe County's census tracts are racially integrated, it is not far-fetched to conclude from the spatial distribution of Black populations throughout the county that Black residents are not racially segregated within it. The 2019 American Community Survey's 5-Year Survey data indicated that one census tract, 3003.05, while not definitively representative of the other tracts in the county with 10 percent or more Black populations, was racially and ethnically balanced: 32 percent white, 32 percent Black, 28 percent Hispanic. Moreover, the community comprised recent homeowners. Ninety-eight percent of the housing units in this community were single-unit homes. The median value of owner-occupied homes was $114,500, which was two-thirds the value of homes in Monroe County ($168,000). Roughly 38 percent of the single-family homes in the census tract were valued at below $100,000; 49 percent were valued between $100,000 and $200,000; and 10 percent were valued between $200,000 and $300,000. Ninety-six percent of the residents had lived in their home for at least one year. Roughly 11.5 percent of the residents had lived in the area before the 1990s, which made around 90 percent of the community members people who arrived since 2000. Thirty-five percent had moved to the census tract during the first decade of the twenty-first century.[47] The 2000 census for the entire county indicates 8,300 Black residents, a 383 percent increase from 1990 (see table 1). Inevitably, many of these Black newcomers to the county were property owners with homes worth slightly below the county medium value. They likely had white and Latino neighbors with comparable socioeconomic profiles. The dispersal of Black people from the areas in the New York metropolis where they had concentrated for decades and the settlement trends in places like Monroe County, Pennsylvania, indicate one of the important overlapping diasporas defining Black communal metropolitan life since the 1970s: economically mobile Black people becoming homeowners in parts of the metropolis where few if any Black people lived before 1970, or even 1990, living next to people who are not African American, or Black, and living comparable lifestyles as their neighbors.

The spatially restrictive and high concentration of Black people in a handful of "ghettos" is not and cannot be the social standard for thinking about the history of Black people in the post–Great Migration metropolis. One overlapping diaspora shaping Black life pulls mobile Black people to communities outside the center of the city. That movement layers upon the migration patterns drawing people of similar class backgrounds who are not Black to the same places. Black people may still have connections and community identity with places and relationships back in the central city neighborhoods where they once lived and where they still may have family members or business ties.[48]

But they are also creating new communities, spatially metropolitan, accompanied by significant demographic changes within the counties and census tracts where they are settling. Historians need to know more about these places: how the booms in Black populations overlapped onto the communities' ongoing social history; how Black newcomers in places where Black people had little historic presence shaped communities' civic institutions, like churches, town governing councils, businesses, athletic leagues, and neighborhood associations; how Black communities within the metropolis make and remake themselves through relationships with other Black newcomers and with neighbors who are *not* Black.

Monroe and Pike Counties in Pennsylvania are important for the trends they signal about property-owning suburban Black metropolitan communities that have grown in the last thirty years. Black suburban communities also stretch back to the middle of the twentieth century. Those places' histories changed in ways that mirrored urban Black neighborhoods. Segregation and discrimination shaped initial community formation and development. Black populations grew. In recent years, Black communities in these more traditional suburbs have either decreased in size or become smaller proportions of the total population as newcomers arrive. Sharing suburban space with new populations layers an overlapping diaspora onto traditional Black communities. Black history in the metropolis altered through these changes as Black people formed new political and social relationships.

Just outside New York City's five boroughs, in Nassau and Suffolk Counties on Long Island, the existence of sizable Black suburban communities stretches back to the 1950s, although Black communities' presence on Long Island extends back even further, to pockets of free-Black settlement that date as early as the post–Revolutionary War period and then grew during the decades after New York State fully abolished slavery in 1827. The post–World War II history of Black people on Long Island reveals how suburbs opened to Black residents through real estate practices that steered them toward a handful of areas, as well as through "blockbusting" tactics that sowed fear among whites, forcing sales of homes in once-white communities that realtors then turned over to Black buyers at inflated prices. Up through the 1980s and 1990s, these practices replicated the types of tight population concentrations and limited geographic settlement associated with the city core's racial ghettos.[49]

By the 1960 census, Black communities existed in and around the towns of North Amityville, Wyandanch, and Gordon Heights in Suffolk County, on Eastern Long Island; and in and around the towns of Roosevelt, Hempstead, New Cassel, and Lakeview in Nassau County, on the western part of Long Island that borders Queens, New York. Central Islip and North Bellport, in Suffolk County, showed emerging concentrations of Black people in 1970. (See tables 2 and 3.) In 2019, the newspaper *Newsday* published an extensive investigation into the history of racial segregation on Long Island that concluded, "The segregation of blacks and whites has been embedded on Long Island as firmly as the Meadowbrook Parkway.... The six-lane road divides overwhelmingly minority Freeport from overwhelmingly white Merrick; then overwhelmingly minority Roosevelt from overwhelmingly white North Merrick; then overwhelmingly minority Uniondale from East Meadow, where seven of 10 residents are white."[50]

From 1960 to 2000, Black populations grew in racially separate and segregated Long Island suburbs. By 1960 in the Suffolk County town of North Amityville and its borders with Southeast Farmingdale, Black people had made up roughly 75 percent of the population. Similarly, in a section of Hempstead, in Nassau County, Black people were 78 percent of the population in 1960. Many other Long Island towns where Black populations grew recorded much smaller

Table 2. Total Black population (and as percentage of total population) in Suffolk County (Long Island) sample towns, 1960–2010

Town/village/hamlet	Census tract	1960	1970	1980	1990	2000	2010
North Amityville	BA003300	3,345 (72.37%)	.	.	.	.	.
	1233	.	4,470 (61.00%)	.	.	.	.
	1233.1	.	.	3,797 (62.83%)	4,210 (64.61%)	4,624 (61.31%)	4,206 (56.72%)
	1233.2	.	.	1,459 (93.89%)	1,366 (88.99%)	1,327 (79.80%)	1,238 (63.10%)
N.Amityville/S-E Farmingdale border	BA003200	3,005 (80.20%)	.	.	.	.	.
	1232	.	3,901 (86.59%)	.	.	.	.
	1232.1	.	.	657 (57.53%)	660 (55.32%)	722 (46.70%)	575 (26.61%)
	1232.2	.	.	5,019 (89.85%)	5,233 (89.96%)	5,463 (73.59%)	5,076 (60.97%)
Wyandanch	BA002500	2,193 (51.19%)	.	.	.	.	.
	1225	.	6,371 (86.20%)	.	.	.	.
	1225.1	.	.	3,048 (93.24%)	3,095 (91.92%)	3,228 (83.87%)	3,009 (65.83%)
	1225.2	.	.	4,089 (93.36%)	3,756 (90.57%)	3,752 (83.58%)	3,478 (74.03%)

Table 2. (*continued*)

Town/village/hamlet	Census tract	1960	1970	1980	1990	2000	2010
Wyandanch/ Wheatly Heights	BA002400	792 (11.78%)	.	.	.	.	.
	1224.2	.	2,626 (42.67%)	.	.	.	.
	1224.6	.	.	3,029 (81.73%)	3,422 (80.23%)	3,932 (74.78%)	3,473 (64.84%)
	1224.5	.	.	1,158 (34.37%)	1,667 (47.86%)	1,826 (52.64%)	2,038 (57.15%)
Wheatly Heights	1224.3	.	.	776 (32.23%)	764 (33.10%)	1,307 (52.89%)	1,414 (56.27%)
Central Islip	1462.2	.	563 (31.66%)	2,248 (70.43%)	2,427 (65.51%)	2,319 (53.01%)	1,791 (36.71%)
Gordon Heights	BR008700	1,446 (24.26%)	.	.	.	.	.
	1587.1	.	607 (40.44%)	.	.	.	.
	1587.5	.	.	1,364 (85.79%)	1,586 (72.09%)	1,922 (62.12%)	2,139 (52.92%)
	1587.4	.	.	1,062 (22.39%)	1,307 (20.55%)	1,294 (17.87%)	1,561 (18.71%)
North Bellport	1591.3	.	2,186 (39.32%)	2,481 (49.59%)	2,352 (49.29%)	2,408 (46.92%)	2,292 (37.97%)

Source: Data from U.S. Census Bureau, U.S. Census, Total Population: Black only, 1960, 1970, 1980, 1990, 2000, 2010. Prepared by Social Explorer (socialexplorer.com), accessed September 15, 2024.

Table 3. Black populations (and as percentage of total population) of Nassau County (Long Island) sample towns, 1960–2010

Town/village/hamlet	Census tract	1960	1970	1980	1990	2000	2010
Hempstead	HV007000	5,020 (78.21%)	.	.	.	.	.
	4070	.	5,501 (87.58%)	5,234 (89.42%)	5,645 (88.95%)	5,047 (75.19%)	4,573 (63.83%)
Lakeview	HE006200	2,514 (33.45%)	.	.	.	.	.
	4062.02	.	4,478 (82.10%)	4,676 (88.63%)	4,948 (90.36%)	4,763 (84.95%)	4,568 (81.35%)
Roosevelt	HE014000	1,812 (26.50%)	.	.	.	.	.
	4140	.	6,833 (81.82%)	.	.	.	.
	4140.01	.	.	3,626 (91.40%)	3,827 (93.57%)	3,451 (85.25%)	2,922 (72.98%)
	4140.02	.	.	3,610 (95.00%)	3,498 (91.26%)	3,625 (81.94%)	2,833 (61.11%)
New Cassel	NH004200	2,693 (35.65%)	.	.	.	.	.
	3042.1	.	5,115 (84.39%)	6,248 (90.81%)	6,015 (79.65%)	5,485 (55.38%)	.
	3042.03	.	.	.	.	.	2,803 (50.42%)
	3042.04	.	.	.	.	.	1,790 (37.69%)

Source: Data from U.S. Census Bureau, U.S. Census, Total Population: Black only, 1960, 1970, 1980, 1990, 2000, 2010. Prepared by Social Explorer (socialexplorer.com), accessed September 15, 2024.

concentrations of Black people in the 1960 census. Wyandanch's population was roughly 50 percent Black in 1960; Gordon Heights' was 24 percent; Lakeview's, 33 percent; and Roosevelt's, 26.5 percent. In the span of two short decades, Black populations in these areas grew. Wyandanch did not remain racially integrated long. By 1980, Black people made up roughly 90 percent of Wyandanch communities. Sections of Gordon Heights were over 85 percent Black. A 1962 image (attributed to being in Lakeview) proved prescient. It showed two children staring at a sign on a lawn in front of a home that read: "Negroes! This community could become another ghetto. You owe it to your 'family' to buy in another community."[51] By the 1970 census, Lakeview had split into two tracts. The Southern State Parkway became the border between Black Lakeview, to the south, and white Lakeview, north of the Parkway. By 1990, South Lakeview had double the population and 1.6 times the population density of North Lakeview, and it was 90 percent Black. Eastern portions of town of Roosevelt, by 1980, were over 90 percent Black. (See tables 2 and 3).

Racial segregation and separation alone, however, tell us little about the types of Black communities that existed and that Black people created in the places where they moved and settled. The memory of one Black resident of Lakeview bears repeating. Gary McLendon grew up in Lakeview in the 1960s. Years later, he saw the 1962 image that warned Black people would turn Lakeview into a "ghetto" and remarked, "I don't know then that my parents had made a mistake . . . when they moved from Queens to Lakeview. . . . All I knew was Lakeview was a great place to grow up. Lakeview was, and for the most part still is, a stable place to raise a child of any color. It wasn't Disneyland, but it was far from the negative stereotypical 'ghetto' that people always seem to label black neighborhoods as."[52]

In the Black section of Lakeview, the median income in 1989 dollars ($50,279) was *higher* than the median income of the neighboring predominantly white section ($43,935) and on par with most surrounding census tracts. The same was true for the median family income ($54,186 for Black Lakeview and $49,507 for white Lakeview). Slight disparities between the two sections emerge when comparing the average family and individual incomes. White Lakeview edged out Black Lakeview in those categories, but barely. The average annual family income in the white section was $62,052 in 1989 dollars, versus $58,282 in Black Lakeview. The average nonfamily annual income reveals greater racial difference: $32,894 for the white section and $24,282 for the Black section.[53] Racial steering, discrimination, and segregation practices developed Lakeview into racially separate communities, but nothing about Black Lakeview conformed to the tropes and cultural assumptions tied to African Americans and ghettos.

Ninety-five percent of the total residents of Black Lakeview lived in family-based households. Fifty-five and a half percent of all 1,304 family households in Black Lakeview were married couples, slightly lower than white Lakeview's 62.9 percent but 300 households larger given the Black section's higher population density. Twenty-four percent of all households in Black Lakeview were headed by single females (5.6 percent by single males), compared to 10.7 percent of white Lakeview's family households headed by single females (and 3.2 percent headed by single males). These statistics about Black Lakeview's female-headed families and households, a subject that loomed large in mid- to late twentieth-century scholarship and journalism about Black urban communities and families, did not seem detrimental to the community's economic and population stability.

The most significant overlapping diasporas and movement trends that shaped Black communal life in the New York metropolis, including its suburbs, were the movements of Hispanic and Latino populations, as well as West Indian, Caribbean, and African populations, that occurred during the late twentieth and early twenty-first centuries. By 2010 the traditionally Black section of Lakeview had become 15 percent Hispanic or Latino. Eighty-one percent of the district remained Black, and 78 percent of those Black people were *not* Hispanic or Latino, but from its high point in 1990 the Black population's total numbers had decreased by close to 400 people. Similar trends happened in Roosevelt, Hempstead, Central Islip, New Cassel, and North Amityville. The 2000 and 2010 censuses in these Long Island towns and hamlets show decreases in both total Black population and in Blacks as percentages of total population in census tracts. Total populations in these census tracts often rose from influxes of Latino and Hispanic residents. (See tables 2 and 3.) Hispanic and Latino immigration and migration altered traditionally Black metropolitan communities and introduced overlapping diasporas of people and culture that affected population numbers, shaped communal identity, and potentially influenced cultural expressions in Black communities. Immigration and migration of newcomers into historically Black communities—some of which brought Black people from other countries; some of which brought Latinos and Hispanics who did not identify as Black or who identified as more than one race; and some of which brought people with access to money and capital—have had the most significant effects on Black metropolitan communities over the past fifty years.

The overwhelming numbers of Black people in the New York metropolis have constituted and reconstituted communal and individual identities over the last five decades within overlapping diasporas of dispersal and dislocation. Upwardly mobile urban Black people moved to suburbs. Underdeveloped suburbs also attracted poorer Black city dwellers. Gentrification patterns shaped Black urban communities in complicated, complex ways. Gentrification priced out and pushed out some poorer Black people from metropolitan communities where Black people had lived for decades and generations. Gentrification also made historic Black urban neighborhoods desirable and attractive for long-term residents who were not displaced. And gentrification became a magnet for people—some Black, most not—with access to capital and wealth, attracting them as property owners and investors in erstwhile Black ghettos. Black newcomers, especially immigrants, also contributed to the dramatic changes that shaped the history of the metropolis since the 1970s. Overlapping diasporas that remade Black metropolitan communities also stemmed from histories of migration and immigration that pushed and pulled people of African descent from beyond US borders and drew them into the New York metropolis. Emigration from parts of the West Indies and Caribbean, as well as the African continent, combined with a diffusion of African Americans from neighborhoods where they held long majorities, remade Black life in key areas of the metropolitan region.

The population histories of Black people in the New York metropolis's cities and urban counties reveal decreases and diffusions of once tightly concentrated, densely populated communities. Every major urban core community in Manhattan, Brooklyn, Queens, and Newark lost Black people from 2000 to 2010 (see table 1). Essex County in New Jersey, home to the largest number of Black people outside of boroughs in New York City, lost about 7,000 Black people, or 2 percent of its total Black population, during that decade. Kings and Queens Counties each lost about 4 percent. And New York County lost over 7.7 percent of its Black population, a total of 20,615 people. Brooklyn (Kings County) lost more Black people, with a total decrease of 38,267, but the total Black population was so high there that its percentage drop of 4.25 percent was less significant than Manhattan's. On the other side of the urban Black population fluctuation, Bronx County and Richmond County (Staten Island) saw *increases* from 2000 to 2010. Just under 30,200 Black people moved into the Bronx during that decade, increasing the total percentage of Black people by 6.4 percent. And from 2000 to 2010, slightly fewer than 7,000 Black people moved to Staten Island: a sharp 16.2 percent increase of the county's Black population.

As the *only* New York City counties to experience recent increases in their Black populations, Bronx and Richmond Counties deserve much more attention than they currently receive in scholarship on Black life in the New York metropolis.[54] Queens, Kings, Bronx, and Richmond Counties all experienced increases in their Black populations from 1970 to 2010, but during that time the number of Black people in Staten Island increased by over 200 percent. Sometimes derided as "the forgotten borough" and long known as a politically conservative, overwhelmingly white place, made up mostly of Irish American and Italian American suburban-styled homeowner communities, Black people will play increasingly stronger roles in the future of Staten Island's culture and politics.

Furthermore, Staten Island and the Bronx emerged in the late twentieth and early twenty-first centuries as places where social science researchers and historians can witness the important overlapping diasporas shaping Black metropolitan life. Staten Island, thanks to the global popularity of the hip-hop collective the Wu Tang Clan, emerged as a global center of innovative hip-hop culture in the 1990s and next several decades. Unsurprisingly, the stark rise of Black people into Staten Island communities produced tension and violence, most notably in 2014 when New York police officers killed a Black man, Eric Garner, during an arrest of Garner for selling loose cigarettes. The area's attraction of Black people during these decades to its public housing complexes and to its private homeowner communities makes Staten Island a unique place to study the overlapping diasporas of class, culture, and color that define the nature of Black social life in the contemporary metropolis.

The growth of Black immigrant communities to the New York metropolis also emerged in Staten Island, and especially in the Bronx, as well as in Orange and Putnam Counties in New York; Hunterdon County in New Jersey; Pike and Monroe Counties in Pennsylvania; and Litchfield County in Connecticut. Whereas counties farther away from the New York metropolis's urban core experienced noticeable percentage increases in foreign-born Black populations, larger numbers of foreign-born Black people live in more urban areas. (See tables 4 and 5.)

In 2000 and 2010, the Bronx had the largest population of African-born immigrants of any county in the metropolis. Manhattan receives sustained attention form journalists and social scientists interested in African immigrant populations, but the future of African communities in the metropolis will likely unfold in the Bronx. The largest numbers of West Indian– and Caribbean-born people still live in major urban areas, although traditional communal strongholds for Caribbean immigrants in Manhattan, Queens, and Brooklyn saw their Caribbean-born populations decrease during these ten years. New York City and parts of New Jersey (Hudson, Essex, and Passaic Counties) remain important places where Caribbean culture and community exist and develop; but since 2000, so too are areas in Nassau and Suffolk Counties on Long Island, Westchester County just north of the Bronx, Orange County farther upstate in New York, and Fairfield County in Connecticut. (See tables 4 and 5.)

The overlapping diasporas that define Black communal life in those places

Table 4. Total foreign-born population from the African continent (and as percentage of all foreign-born) in New York metropolitan area counties, 2000, 2010

	2000	2010	Percentage change
New York			
Kings	23,588 (2.53%)	27,654 (3.00%)	17.23%
Queens	20,148 (1.96%)	22,460 (2.12%)	11.47%
New York	15,838 (3.50%)	18,479 (4.09%)	16.67%
Bronx	25,747 (6.67%)	38,811 (8.74%)	50.73%
Richmond	7,114 (9.79%)	7,777 (8.08%)	9.31%
Westchester	5,381 (2.62%)	6,847 (3.00%)	27.24%
Putnam	89 (1.06%)	245 (2.24%)	175.28%
Rockland	1,221 (2.23%)	1,573 (2.33%)	28.82%
Suffolk	2,698 (1.70%)	4,147 (2.00%)	53.70%
Nassau	5,088 (2.13%)	5,460 (1.98%)	7.31%
Dutchess	667 (2.83%)	1,325 (4.03%)	98.65%
Orange	436 (1.52%)	977 (2.35%)	124.08%
Ulster	161 (1.54%)	246 (1.89%)	52.79%
New Jersey			
Bergen	4,874 (2.19%)	6,125 (2.41%)	25.66%
Hudson	11,961 (5.10%)	11,552 (4.57%)	-3.41%
Passaic	1,734 (1.33%)	2,044 (1.52%)	17.87%
Mercer	3,115 (6.40%)	4,944 (6.87%)	58.72%
Middlesex	10,256 (5.64%)	10,877 (4.64%)	6.05%
Monmouth	1,732 (2.71%)	2,246 (2.76%)	29.67%
Ocean	784 (2.36%)	1,160 (2.63%)	47.95%
Somerset	2,742 (5.08%)	3,185 (4.53%)	16.15%
Essex	11,543 (6.86%)	16,389 (8.89%)	41.98%
Union	4,395 (3.36%)	6,778 (4.44%)	54.22%
Morris	1,714 (2.36%)	2,318 (2.53%)	35.24%
Sussex	318 (3.89%)	423 (4.40%)	33.02%
Hunterdon	144 (1.87%)	403 (3.85%)	179.86%

Table 4. (*continued*)

	2000	2010	Percentage change
Pennsylvania			
Pike	29 (1.27%)	73 (2.03%)	151.72%
Monroe	340 (4.22%)	824 (5.28%)	142.35%
Connecticut			
Fairfield	3,145 (2.11%)	5,200 (2.85%)	65.34%
New Haven	2,560 (3.44%)	4,622 (4.73%)	80.54%

Source: 2000 data from Native/Foreign Born, Africa, 2000. Social Explorer (based on data from U.S. Census Bureau; accessed September 15, 2024); 2010 data from Native/Foreign Born, Africa, 2010. Social Explorer (based American Community Survey Data, 5-Year estimates; accessed September 14, 2024).

Table 5. Total foreign-born population from the Caribbean (and as percentage of all foreign-born) in New York metropolitan area counties, 2000, 2010

	2000	2010	Percentage change
New York			
Kings	312,075 (33.49%)	297,370 (32.27%)	-4.71%
Queens	182,004 (17.7%)	170,653 (16.14%)	-6.24%
New York	152,122 (33.62%)	130,155 (28.79%)	-14.44%
Bronx	204,104 (52.9%)	224,236 (50.51%)	9.86%
Richmond	5,924 (8.15%)	6,819 (7.08%)	15.11%
Westchester	37,522 (18.27%)	41,309 (18.09%)	10.09%
Putnam	434 (5.15%)	879 (8.04%)	103%
Rockland	14,931 (27.26%)	18,118 (26.8%)	21.34%
Suffolk	23,891 (15.07%)	31,440 (15.15%)	31.59%
Nassau	42,649 (17.89%)	50,914 (18.51%)	19.38%
Dutchess	3,818 (16.18%)	6,388 (19.43%)	67.31%
Orange	3,031 (10.56%)	6,056 (14.56%)	99.80%
Ulster	1,297 (12.39%)	1,496 (11.48%)	15.34%

Table 5. (*continued*)

	2000	2010	Percentage change
New Jersey			
Bergen	19,890 (8.95%)	24,649 (9.69%)	23.93%
Hudson	59,406 (25.32%)	54,343 (21.51%)	-8.52%
Passaic	33,140 (25.44%)	31,425 (23.35%)	-5.18%
Mercer	5,591 (11.49%)	7,996 (11.12%)	43.02%
Middlesex	20,392 (11.22%)	25,203 (10.75%)	23.59%
Monmouth	6,144 (9.63%)	6,916 (8.49%)	12.57%
Ocean	2,188 (6.6%)	2,711 (6.14%)	23.90%
Somerset	3,554 (6.59%)	4,536 (6.46%)	27.63%
Essex	45,677 (27.16%)	47,424 (25.73%)	3.82%
Union	25,472 (19.46%)	27,802 (18.22%)	9.15%
Morris	3,331 (4.59%)	4,357 (4.76%)	30.80%
Sussex	472 (5.78%)	750 (7.8%)	58.90%
Hunterdon	285 (3.7%)	549 (5.24%)	92.63%
Pennsylvania			
Pike	231 (10.08%)	307 (8.54%)	32.90%
Monroe	1,223 (15.16%)	3,189 (20.43%)	160.75%
Connecticut			
Fairfield	22,252 (14.93%)	27,637 (15.16%)	24.20%
New Haven	7,591 (10.2%)	11,469 (11.75%)	51.09%
Litchfield	563 (5.69%)	1,323 (10.97%)	134.99%

Source: 2000 data from Native/Foreign Born, Americas-Latin America-Caribbean, 2000. Social Explorer, (based on data from U.S. Census Bureau; accessed September 15, 2024); 2010 data from Native/Foreign Born, Americas-Latin America-Caribbean, 2010. Social Explorer (based American Community Survey Data, 5-Year estimates; accessed September 14, 2024).

increasingly will be influenced by foreign-born Black people. Black immigrants from different parts of Africa have increased the visibility of Islamic culture in traditionally African American neighborhoods, like Harlem. The mostly Black American Nation of Islam has had a long presence in Harlem, but with increased immigration from Mali, Côte d'Ivoire, Senegal, and other African countries, mosques, halal grocers, and Islamic cultural and education centers now line streets of upper Manhattan and the Bronx where immigrants from West African countries have settled. High concentrations of French-speaking immigrants from the Ivory Coast and Senegal have changed a strip along 116th Street of Harlem into "Le Petit Senegal," and fabric shops, restaurants, cab stands, currency exchanges, and cafés reminiscent of the streets of Dakar now proliferate in the area. In many parts of the Bronx, large numbers of immigrants and resettlement communities from all over the African continent have increased needs for translators and interpreters in civic institutions like public schools, hospitals, and courts. As much as Black metropolitan history will continue to take shape in the urban core, it will also unfold in places spread throughout the metropolis through the culture that Black newcomers bring and the communities they form. Not since the Great Migrations of the late nineteenth and early twentieth centuries has Black metropolitan history experienced the level of foreign-born Black influence that the years 1970–2010 have brought to the metropolitan region. For the foreseeable future, these overlapping diasporas of people and culture will transform Black community and culture in urban, suburban, and exurban areas.

Over the past fifty years, the metropolitan region also includes areas, often suburban, exurban, and rural communities, where populations of incarcerated people have increased. Since the 1960s and 1970s, the disproportionate racial effects of mass incarceration make metropolitan regional census tracts where prisons are located important places to examine Black history. Upstate New York counties (Dutchess, Ulster, and Orange) that experienced significant increases in Black populations indicate that pockets where Black people concentrated most were places with prisons. Even a county that, over the past few decades, has had sizable Black populations, like Fairfield, Connecticut, reveals the effects mass incarceration can have on Black people's concentrations in isolated parts of the metropolis.

Fairfield is one of the sixteen counties (out of thirty-one total) in metropolitan New York City that recorded over 50,000 Black people in the 2010 census. Its Black population has increased steadily since 1970. With just over 99,000 Black people in 2010, it had the eleventh largest Black population in the metropolis.

This happened, largely, through growth in the county's urban areas, Stamford, Norwalk, and Bridgeport, which experienced increases in Asian, Hispanic and Latino, and Black populations.[55]

A color-coded map showing concentrations of Black populations in Fairfield County in 2010 portrays vast swaths of cool zones with a few warm pockets around the county's urban centers. Those warm pockets indicate census tracts where at least 20 percent of the population identified as Black or African American on the US Census. Not many of them exist. There are two tracts near Stamford that are around 30 percent Black. Norwalk has one such tract. Bridgeport has the largest concentrations of Black people. In 2010, ten of its census tracts were over 40 percent Black or African American; just under 59,000 Black people lived in areas surrounding Bridgeport, making up around 22 percent of the area's population.[56]

The rest of the map showing Fairfield County's Black population appears practically void. Almost no census tract outside of these urban areas is more than 5 percent Black. Most are barely 1 percent Black or African American—until one's eyes fall upon the town of Danbury. There, census tracts vary between 5 and 10 percent Black, with one small, isolated census tract that is 29.53 percent Black. Its base population is less than 1,400 people, and 406 of them are Black. Zooming out one's view further, this small warm spot of Black population concentration surrounded by communities with practically no Black people appears odd and misplaced. But when one scans through the other far-flung counties of the New York metropolis, Danbury's small, concentrated pocket of Black people no longer appears anomalous or accidental. Because Danbury is home to a federal correctional institution that houses roughly 1,000 people, census tract 2111, which includes little else but the prison, burns bright on a demographic map showing Black population concentrations. Incarcerated Black people are the largest sources of racial diversity in far-flung rural counties of the New York metropolis.

The same is true for Ulster and Dutchess Counties in Upstate New York. Dutchess County has concentrations of Black populations in Poughkeepsie and along the border it shares with Orange County's population center of Newburgh. But two census tracts with Black populations over 50 percent, which are surrounded by communities practically devoid of Black people, light up the Black demography map. These tracts house at least three major prisons, Green Haven, Fishkill, and Downstate Correctional Facilities. The pattern is more subdued but still noticeable in Ulster County, which is more rural, with only one population center of roughly 20,0000 people in the town of Kingston. With just under 11,000 Black people in 2010, Ulster County's census tracts housing four prisons burned brightest on a Black demography map.

Mass incarceration alone did not account for the stark rise in Black populations in these rural and exurban metropolitan counties. Black populations in these scattered prisons are, relatively, small. But dramatic increases in Black populations in practically all-white rural counties raises important questions about the Black communities and experiences of Black life that happen in and through these places, to say nothing about the ways rural counties experience employment increases, tax improvements, and state investment benefits from prisons, which mass incarceration policies ensure house Black majorities. Incarcerated Black people living in rural towns maintain ties to family members and communities in faraway cities and suburbs. Loved ones, domestic partners, children, parents, and other relatives travel to visit rural prisons, creating communal and commercial links between Black incarcerated people housed in rural sections of metropolitan counties and Black communities in other parts of the metropolis. Black inmates may not be *direct* members of the rural communities that house prisons with sizable populations of incarcerated Black people, but their lives are connected to what happens in those rural places, and their struggles to maintain ties to homes, families, and friends hundreds of miles away create overlapping diasporas of social connections worthy of consideration when scholars think about how the histories of mass incarceration remake an American metropolis.

Since 1970, the politics of mass incarceration contributed to noticeable rises in Black populations in the New York metropolis's rural counties, as well as to continued concentrations of incarcerated Black people in counties, like Westchester, that also have large populations of Black people who are not imprisoned. Westchester's northern and suburban-rural census tracts that house Sing Sing, Bedford Hills, and Taconic prisons are hot spots of Black population concentration outside the county's major population centers in its south. Along with gentrification, suburbanization, and immigration, mass incarceration policies have shaped Black life in the metropolis. In the process, this aspect of Black metropolitan history since the 1970s has also dramatically remade the overwhelmingly white rural and suburban communities that rely on housing inmates, a majority of whom, since 1970, have been Black and African American.

Conclusion

Hilton Als's meditative 2020 *New Yorker* essay about the struggles that urban Black people had with community formation during the 1960s and 1970s highlights an important aspect of the past fifty years of Black metropolitan history in the New York City region specifically and the United States more generally.[57]

A major engine driving Black urban people's social history during this time was the desire of people like Als's mother to form stable, nurturing, safe homes for themselves, their families, and their children. In a broad sense, that is the motivational force behind much of Black history in the modern world, at least when concern for the overlapping diasporas that Black people make and that shape Black people's lives, along with focuses on racial ideology and racist oppression, animates the historian's inquiry.

Since the 1970s, Black urban people have made history by making communities in different places throughout the metropolis. Black urban people and their history are no longer confined to racially segregated ghettos, at least not in the ways that scholars have studied the history of ghettos in mid-twentieth-century cities. Racism continues to matter in metropolitan history: in the spatial segregation of suburbs; in the social inequality in gentrifying cities; in the politics of mass incarceration. Since 1970, those trends continued alongside widening class diversity in Black communities, which enabled some Black people to become prosperous in the suburbs or to remain in gentrifying urban neighborhoods.

Black people expanded throughout the metropolis. They found new places to live where few if any Black people ever lived. New Black people came from countries outside the United States and settled in American metropolises. Upwardly mobile Black people moved to suburbs. Black people ensnared in the historic policies of mass incarceration became inmates in prisons in rural counties within the metropolis. In all these scenarios, Black people created communities—with each other, with others. Processes of movement, migration, and immigration and the histories of community formation they produced have shaped the past fifty years of Black urban history. Diverse casts of Black people, varied by class, immigration status, and culture, are the central subjects of these histories, as are the people with whom they form relationships through processes of overlapping diasporas. These same processes of community formation within overlapping diasporas in metropolitan regional contexts will likely shape Black history in the US metropolis for the foreseeable future.

Notes

1. Earl Lewis, "To Turn as on a Pivot: Writing African Americans into a History of Overlapping Diasporas," *American Historical Review* 100, no. 3 (June 1995): 765–84, quote on 779.
2. Lewis's "To Turn as on a Pivot" is a landmark essay that reviews a broad sweep of African American history and historiography to place at the center of US history three key ideas: (1) African Americans played a major role in writing and researching the nation's past; (2) racial formation and identity creation is a historicized process;

and (3) race is part of history; it is determined through human relations. For African Americans, this means the histories of how they, as a diverse, broad group of people shaped by class, color, gender, region, and ethnicity, among other factors, have lived and worked with others in overlapping diasporas, or dispersed communities. Historical studies of people of African descent in New York City that examine their lives in and through "overlapping diasporas" of race, class, color, nationality, culture, gender, religion, and sexuality over the course of four centuries include Andrea C. Mosterman, *Spaces of Enslavement: A History of Slavery and Resistance in Dutch New York* (Ithaca: Cornell University Press, 2021); Graham Russell Hodges, *Root and Branch: African Americans in New York and East Jersey, 1613–1863* (Chapel Hill: University of North Carolina Press, 1999); Leslie M. Alexander, *African or American? Black Identity and Political Activism, 1784–1861* (Urbana: University of Illinois Press, 2012); Leslie H. Harris, *In the Shadow of Slavery: African Americans in New York City, 1626–1863* (Chicago: University of Chicago Press, 2003); Craig Steven Wilder, *In the Company of Black Men: The African Influence on African American Culture in New York City* (New York: New York University Press, 2001); Prithi Kanakamedala, *Brooklynites: The Remarkable Story of the Free Black Communities That Shaped a Borough* (New York: New York University Press, 2024); David Levering Lewis, *When Harlem Was in Vogue* (New York: Oxford University Press, 1981, 1989); Cheryl D. Hicks, *Talk with You Like a Woman: African American Women, Justice, and Reform in New York, 1890–1935* (Chapel Hill: University of North Carolina Press, 2010); Clare Corbould, *Becoming African Americans: Black Public Life in Harlem, 1919–1939* (Cambridge, MA: Harvard University Press, 2009); Marcy S. Sacks, *Before Harlem: The Black Experience in New York City before World War I* (Philadelphia: University of Pennsylvania Press, 2011); Irma Watkins-Owens, *Blood Relations: Caribbean Immigrants and the Harlem Community, 1900–1930* (Bloomington: Indiana University Press, 1996); Mark Naison, *Communists in Harlem during the Great Depression* (Urbana: University of Illinois Press, 1983); Cheryl Lynn Greenberg, *Or Does it Explode? Black Harlem in the Great Depression* (New York: Oxford University Press, 1991); LaShawn Harris, *Sex Workers, Psychics, and Numbers Runners: Black Women in New York City's Underground Economy* (Urbana: University of Illinois Press, 2016); Shannon King, *Whose Harlem Is This Anyway? Community Politics and Grassroots Activism during the New Negro Era* (New York: New York University Press, 2015); Farah Jasmine Griffin, *Harlem Nocturne: Women Artists and Progressive Politics during World War II* (New York: Basic Civitas, 2013); Martha Biondi, *To Stand and Fight: The Struggle for Civil Rights in Postwar New York City* (Cambridge, MA: Harvard University Press, 2003); Winston James, "Harlem's Difference," in *Race Capital? Harlem as Setting and Symbol*, ed. Andrew M. Fearnley and Daniel Matlin (New York: Columbia University Press, 2019), 111–42; and Christina Greer, *Black Ethnics: Race, Immigration, and the Pursuit of the American Dream* (New York: Oxford University Press, 2013). See also Walter D. Greason, *The Path to Freedom: The Black Families of New Jersey* (Charleston, SC: History Press, 2010).

3. Ira Berlin, *The Making of African America: The Four Great Migrations* (New York: Penguin Books, 2010), esp. 201–40. See also Kenneth L. Kusmer and Joe W. Trotter, eds., *African American Urban History since World War II* (Chicago: University of

Chicago Press, 2009); and Joe W. Trotter et al., *The African American Urban Experience: Perspectives from the Colonial Period to the Present* (New York: Palgrave, 2004). Key to my understanding of urban history within a metropolitan framework is the excellent essay by Andrew Needham and Allen Dieterich-Ward, "Beyond the Metropolis: Metropolitan Growth and Regional Transformation in Postwar America," *Journal of Urban History* 35, no. 7 (2009): 943–69.
4. This definition of gentrification comes from Amanda T. Boston, "Manufacturing Distress: Race, Redevelopment, and the EB-5 Program in Central Brooklyn," *Critical Sociology* 47, no. 6 (2021): 961, where Boston quotes from Shannon Zukin, "Gentrification: Culture and Capital in the Urban Core," *Annual Review of Sociology* 13 (1987): 129–47.
5. Lance Freeman, *There Goes the 'Hood: Views of Gentrification from the Ground Up* (Philadelphia: Temple University Press, 2006), quotes from 13–14. See also Tatsha Robertson, "Harlem on the Rise," *The Crisis*, May/June 2005, 22–26.
6. Lance Freeman and Frank Braconi, "Gentrification and Displacement: New York City in the 1990s," *Journal of the American Planning Association* 70, no. 1 (2004): 39–52. See also Lance Freeman, "Displacement or Succession? Residential Mobility in Gentrifying Neighborhoods," *Urban Affairs Review* 40, no. 4 (March 2005): 463–91.
7. The scholarship, journalism, and documentaries on gentrification in New York City are extensive. Key academic studies include Boston, "Manufacturing Distress"; Sueliman Osman, *The Invention of Brownstone Brooklyn: Gentrification and the Search for Authenticity in Postwar New York* (New York: Oxford University Press, 2011); Brian D. Goldstein, *The Roots of Urban Renaissance: Gentrification and the Struggle over Harlem* (Cambridge, MA: Harvard University Press, 2017); Monique M. Taylor, *Harlem: Between Heaven and Hell* (Minneapolis: University of Minnesota Press, 2002); Neil Smith, *The New Urban Frontier: Gentrification and the Revanchist City* (New York: Routledge, 1996); and Richard Schaffer and Neil Smith, "The Gentrification of Harlem?," *Annals of the Association of American Geographers* 76, no. 3 (September 1986): 347–65. One example of the kinds of documentaries that highlight how gentrification displaces businesses and residents is Kelly Anderson, dir., *My Brooklyn: Unmasking the Takeover of America's Hippest City* (New Day Films, 2012). A long journalistic personal essay on the negative effects of gentrification in New York City is Jeremiah Moss, *Vanishing New York: How a Great City Lost Its Soul* (New York: Dey St., 2017).
8. Andrew Wiese's scholarship investigates the history of twentieth-century Black suburbanization in the United States and extends the timeline back to the early decades of the century. Todd Michney built upon Wiese's scholarship and uncovered the dynamic growth and diversity of Black suburban life in midsize cities like Cleveland, Ohio. See Andrew Wiese, *Places of Their Own: African American Suburbanization in the Twentieth Century* (Chicago: University of Chicago Press, 2003); Wiese, "Places of Our Own: Suburban Black Towns before 1960," *Journal of Urban History* 19, no. 3 (1993): 30–54; and Todd Michney, *Surrogate Suburbs: Black Upward Mobility and Neighborhood Change in Cleveland, 1900–1980* (Chapel Hill: University of North Carolina Press, 2017). See also Kenneth T. Jackson, *Crabgrass Frontier: The Suburbanization of America* (New York: Oxford University Press, 1985); Kevin M. Kruse

and Thomas J. Sugrue, eds., *The New Suburban History* (Chicago: University of Chicago Press, 2006); and Paige Glotzer, *How the Suburbs Were Segregated: Developers and the Business of Exclusionary Housing, 1890–1960* (New York: Columbia University Press, 2020). Mary Pattillo's scholarship has examined Black middle-class urban communities outside the more impoverished and centralized Black urban cores and the continued social and familial networks and links between these two areas. See Mary Pattillo, *Black Picket Fences: Privilege and Peril among the Black Middle Class* (Chicago: University of Chicago Press, 1999); and Orly Clerge, *The New Noir: Race, Identity, and Diaspora in Black Suburbia* (Los Angeles: University of California Press, 2019).

9. Nicholas Dagen Bloom, review of *Places of their Own: African American Suburbanization in the Twentieth Century*, by Andrew Wiese, *Journal of American History* 91, no. 4 (2005): 1540.

10. Andrew Wiese, "The Other Suburbanites: African American Suburbanization before 1950," *Journal of American History* 85, no. 4 (1999): 1496.

11. According to the Brookings Institution Center on Urban and Metropolitan Policy, in a study by William H. Frey, "Among the nation's 102 largest metropolitan areas, with populations exceeding half a million, minorities comprised more than a quarter (27.3 percent) of the suburban populations in 2000, up from 19.3 percent in 1990. Almost half (47 percent) of the minorities in the large metropolitan areas in this study lived in the suburbs in 2000, compared to just over 40 percent a decade ago." See William H. Frey, "Melting Pot Suburbs: A Census 2000 Study of Suburban Diversity," Brookings Institution, Census 2000 Series, June 1, 2001, page 2, www.brookings.edu/research/melting-pot-suburbs-a-census-2000-study-of-suburban-diversity/.

12. See Pattillo, *Black Picket Fences*.

13. Berlin, *Making of African America*, 201–29. Regarding Black immigration to New York City, a leading scholar has been Nancy Foner. See works listed in note 15.

14. John R. Logan and Glenn Deane, "Black Diversity in Metropolitan America," Lewis Mumford Center for Comparative Urban and Regional Research, University at Albany, August 15, 2003, http://mumford.albany.edu/census/BlackWhite/BlackDiversityReport/black-diversity01.htm. See also April Gordon, "The New Diaspora: African Immigration to the United States," *Journal of Third World Studies* 15, no. 1 (1998): 79–103; and Violet Showers Johnson and Marilyn Halter, *African and American: West Africans in Post–Civil Rights America* (New York: New York University Press, 2014). Mary Waters wrote an important overview of West Indian immigrants' experiences in the United States: *Black Identities: West Indian Immigrant Dreams and American Realities* (Cambridge, MA: Harvard University Press, 1999).

15. Nancy Foner has been a leader in publishing research on immigration to New York City since 1965. See her edited volumes *One out of Three: Immigrant New York in the Twenty-First Century* (New York: Columbia University Press, 2013); *New Immigrants in New York* (New York: Columbia University Press, 2001); and *Islands in the City: West Indian Migration to New York* (Los Angeles: University of California Press, 2001). More focused scholarship on African and Caribbean immigration in general and specifically to New York City includes Bernadette Ludwig, "It Is Tough to Be a Liberian Refugee in Staten Island New York: The Importance of Context for Second Generation African Immigrant Youth," *African and Black Diaspora: An International*

Journal 12, no. 2 (2019): 189–210; Bernadette Ludwig and Holly Reed, "When You Are Here You Have High Blood Pressure: Liberian Refugees' Health and Access to Health Care in Staten Island, New York," *International Journal of Migration, Health, and Social Care* 12, no. 1 (2016): 26–37; Violet M. Showers Johnson, "'What Then Is the African American?' African and Afro-Caribbean Identities in Black America," *Journal of American Ethnic History* 28, no.1 (2008): 77–103; Violet M. Showers Johnson, "When Blackness Stings: African and Afro-Caribbean Immigrants, Race, and Racism in Late Twentieth-Century America," *Journal of American Ethnic History* 36, no. 1 (2016): 31–62; and Sue Halpern and Bill McKibben, "How a Tightknit Community of Ghanaians Has Spiced Up the Bronx," *Smithsonian Magazine*, June 2014, www.smithsonianmag.com/arts-culture/how-tightknit-community-ghanaians-spiced-up-bronx-180951434/. See also the important oral history interview database created by the Bronx African American History Project, which includes nearly three dozen interviews about immigration to the Bronx by people of African descent. See, for example, interviews with Ramatu Ahmed (March 10, 2010); Phil Black (May 3, 2012); Nana Yartell III (June 25, 2010); and Johnson Otibu (October 15, 2008), Bronx African American History Project, Oral Histories, Fordham University, transcripts and audio files available through www.fordham.edu/academics/research/libraries-and-collections/bronx-african-american-history-project/digital-collections/.

16. Thomas J. Sugrue, *The Origins of the Urban Crisis: Race and Inequality in Postwar Detroit* (Princeton: Princeton University Press, 1996).
17. Heather Ann Thompson, "Why Mass Incarceration Matters: Rethinking Crisis, Decline, and Transformation in Postwar American History," *Journal of American History* 97, no. 3 (December 2010): 703–34. See "Rethinking Urban America through the Lens of the Carceral State," ed. Heather Ann Thompson and Donna Murch, special issue, *Journal of Urban History* 41, no. 5 (2015). See also "Historians and the Carceral State," ed. Kelly Lytle Hernández, Khalil Gibran Muhammad, and Heather Ann Thompson, special issue, *Journal of American History* 102, no. 1 (June 2015).
18. Ruth Wilson Gilmore, *Golden Gulag: Prisons, Surplus, Crisis, and Opposition in Globalizing California* (Berkeley: University of California Press, 2007).
19. Michelle Alexander, *The New Jim Crow: Mass Incarceration in the Age of Colorblindness* (New York: New Press, 2010).
20. Thompson and Murch, "Rethinking Urban America through the Lens of the Carceral State," 751.
21. Donna Murch, "Who's to Blame for Mass Incarceration?," *Boston Review*, October 16, 2015, which is Murch's critical review of Michael Javen Fortner, *The Black Silent Majority: The Rockefeller Drug Laws and the Politics of Punishment* (Cambridge, MA: Harvard University Press, 2015); and reply by Michael Javen Fortner, "Historical Method and the Novel Lie," *Boston Review*, October 23, 2015, www.bostonreview.net/articles/donna-murch-michael-javen-fortner-black-silent-majority/.
22. The book *Imprisoning America: The Social Effects of Mass Incarceration* (New York: Russell Sage Foundation, 2004), edited by Mary Pattillo, David Weiman, and Bruce Western, contains excellent essays on how mass incarceration affects families, communities, and individuals.
23. Lewis consistently discusses how race is not a monolithic, ahistorical category of analysis that encompasses everything and anything having to do with Black people.

"Race is but one part of the self, and race is always relational," Lewis summarizes. "Equally important, black Americans have lived in variegated communities where class, color, religious and other differences mattered. Therefore, how do we understand the relational matrix of identity formation? Essentially, how do we begin to understand historical actors as multi-positional?" E. Lewis, "To Turn as On a Pivot," 783.

24. Scholarship on and about Black ghettos in the United States is extensive. A formative text on Black urban history and life during the twentieth century is St. Clare Drake and Horace R. Cayton, *Black Metropolis: A Study of Negro Life in a Northern City*, first published in 1945. See the 2015 edition published by the University of Chicago, with a new foreword by Mary Pattillo. See also various essays on the state of the field of African American urban history in Joe William Trotter Jr., *Black Milwaukee: The Making of an Industrial Proletariat, 1915–1945* (Urbana: University of Illinois Press, 2007), 264–345. For expansive histories of ghettos, see Wendy Z. Goldman and Joe W. Trotter Jr., *The Ghetto in Global History: 1500–Present* (New York: Routledge, 2018).

25. Douglas S. Massey and Nancy A. Denton, *American Apartheid: Segregation and the Making of the Underclass* (Cambridge, MA: Harvard University Press, 1998); Colin Gordon, *Mapping Decline: St. Louis and the Fate of the American City* (Philadelphia: University of Pennsylvania Press, 2008).

26. Keeanga-Yamahtta Taylor, *Race for Profit: How Banks and the Real Estate Industry Undermined Black Homeownership* (Chapel Hill: University of North Carolina Press, 2019).

27. Jessica Trounstine, *Segregation by Design: Local Politics and Inequality in American Cities* (New York: Cambridge University Press, 2018).

28. Scholarship on the post–World War II Black freedom movement in American cities and suburbs is extensive. See Jeanne Theoharis and Komozi Woodward, eds., *Freedom North: Black Freedom Struggles outside the South, 1940–1980* (New York: Palgrave, 2003); Thomas J. Sugrue, *Sweet Land of Liberty: The Forgotten Struggle for Civil Rights in the North* (New York: Random House, 2008); Jason Sokol, *All Eyes Are upon Us: Race and Politics from Boston to Brooklyn—the Conflicted Soul of the Northeast* (New York: Basic Books, 2014); and Brian Purnell and Jeanne Theoharis, eds., with Komozi Woodward, *The Strange Careers of the Jim Crow North: Segregation and Struggle outside the South* (New York: New York University Press, 2019).

29. David Stradling and Richard Stradling, *Where the River Burned: Carl Stokes and the Struggle to Save Cleveland* (New York: Cornell University Press, 2015).

30. See notes 17–22.

31. Jonathan Reider, *Canarsie: The Jews and Italians of Brooklyn against Liberalism* (Cambridge, MA: Harvard University Press, 1985).

32. Ismail K. White and Chryl N. Laird, *Steadfast Democrats: How Social Forces Shape Black Political Behavior* (Princeton: Princeton University Press, 2020).

33. Elizabeth Hinton, *America on Fire: The Untold History of Police Violence and Black Rebellion since the 1960s* (New York: W. W. Norton, 2021).

34. The definition of the New York metropolis I use in this chapter is defined by the Office of Management and Budget as the New York–Newark, NY-NJ-CT-PA Combined Statistical Area that encompasses the greater New York, New Jersey,

Connecticut, and Pennsylvania region. This includes the Office of Management and Budget's Metropolitan Statistical Area with additional surroundings creating a designation that reflects "broader social and economic interactions, such as wholesaling, commodity distribution, and weekend recreation activities, and are likely to be of considerable interest to regional authorities and the private sector." Using the Combined Statistical Area definition of the wider New York metropolis enables one to think about Black communities through a much wider aperture and to see dramatic changes in Black populations in places that one does not usually associate with the city, or even metropolis, as traditionally defined. Bringing these places less connected to Black community studies into historic examination of contemporary Black communities allows us to investigate new connections and links between metropolitan cores and peripheries, or invites us to think about Black community life in parts of the metropolis where we are not accustomed to look for it, and this approach also forces us to break free from looking at urban Black communal life in only the same handful of places. In short, when the focus is on diverse types of metropolitan Black communities, broadly defined, Sussex County, New Jersey, in 2010, where over 2,500 Blacks lived spread out across different census tracts, is important to examine in addition to more traditional places of study, like Essex County, New Jersey, which was home to over 320,000 Black people in 2010 and is the location of the well-studied Newark–East Orange–Irvington historic Black urban core. The definition of the NY-NJ-CT-PA Combined Statistical Area comes from "Revised Delineations of Metropolitan Statistical Areas, Micropolitan Statistical Areas, and Combined Statistical Areas, and Guidance on Uses of the Delineations of These Areas," *OMB BULLETIN No. 20–01*, March 6, 2020. See also "New York–Newark, NY-NJ-CT-PA Combined Statistical Area Map," US Department of Commerce Economics and Statistics Administration, US Census Bureau, 2012 Economic Census, accessed September 15, 2024, www2.census.gov/geo/maps/econ/ec2012/csa/EC2012_330M200 US408M.pdf.

35. E. Lewis, "To Turn as on a Pivot"; Berlin, *The Making of African America*. See also Nell I. Painter, *Creating Black Americans: African American History and Its Meanings, 1619 to the Present* (New York: Oxford University Press, 2007); and Michael A. Gomez, *Reversing Sail: A History of the African Diaspora*, 2nd ed. (New York: Cambridge University Press, 2020).

36. Sherri-Ann P. Butterfield, "'We're Just Black': The Racial and Ethnic Identities of Second Generation West Indians in New York," in *Becoming New Yorkers: Ethnographies of the New Second Generation*, ed. Philip Kasinitz et al. (New York: Russell Sage Foundation, 2004), 288–312.

37. Ruth Wilson Gilmore's *Golden Gulag* offers the strongest analysis of the spatial, political-economic dynamic of the politics of mass incarceration. See also Heather Ann Thompson, *Blood in the Water: The Attica Prison Uprising of 1971 and Its Legacies* (New York: Vintage Books, 2017).

38. This subject does not receive adequate attention in this essay, but there is tremendous opportunity for historians to expand this theme by building on foundational work that examines music, culture, art, and "placemaking." The history of music creation and expression offers an incredible subject through which to see the overlapping

diasporas working in time and space and across multiple places. See, for example, the history of reggaeton and its connection to New York City and parts of Puerto Rico, Panama, and Jamaica. See Raquel Z. Rivera et al., eds., *Reggaeton* (Durham, NC: Duke University Press, 2009). See also Marcus Anthony Hunter et al., "Black Placemaking: Celebration, Play, and Poetry," *Theory, Culture, and Society* 33, no. 7–8 (2016): 31–56; and Marcus Anthony Hunter and Zandria F. Robinson, *Chocolate Cities: The Black Map of American Life* (Oakland: University of California Press, 2018). On Black place-making in New York City through hip-hop and reggaeton culture and creation, see Brian Purnell, "No Place Like Home: Black Communities and Black Cultures in New York City since the 1970s," in *New York City since the 60s*, ed. Johanna Fernandez, Kimberly Phillips-Fein, and Mason Williams (volume under review).

39. Steven Gregory made this argument in *Black Corona: Race and the Politics of Place in an Urban Community* (Princeton: Princeton University Press, 1998).
40. Patrick Sharkey, *Stuck in Place: Urban Neighborhoods and the End of Progress toward Racial Equality* (Chicago: University of Chicago Press, 2013).
41. Loïc Wacquant, "From Slavery to Mass Incarceration: Rethinking the 'Race Question' in the United States," *New Left Review* 13 (January/February 2002): 41–60.
42. See Fearnley and Matlin, *Race Capital?*
43. Understandings of a neighborhood's boundaries change often and vary from one person or context to another. The forty-three census tracts surveyed here correspond to the predominantly Black sections of northern Manhattan and Harlem's boundaries as they developed into the mid- to late twentieth century. These tracts included the following borders: 110th Street and Central Park to the south; on the western border, Morningside Avenue, then going into Amsterdam Avenue at 123rd street; on the eastern border, Park Avenue and then following Harlem River Drive northward, stopping at roughly 165th Street and St. Nicholas Avenue at the neighborhood's northwest corner border. This brief survey of these same forty-three census tracts in this area were examined in 1990 and 2000. The tracts were numbers 174.02; 184; 186; 190; and 197.02; 198; 200; and 201.02; 204; 206; 207.02; 208; 209.01 and 209.02; 210; 212; 213.01 and 213.02; 214; 216; 217.01 and 217.02; 218; 220; 221.01 and 221.02; 222; 224; 226; 227.01 and 227.02; 228; 230; 231.01 and 231.02; 232; 234; 235.01 and 235.02; 236; 239; 243.01 and 243.02. The 1990 data is from Black [map], Census 1990, accessed via SocialExplorer.com on September 15, 2024; 2000 data is from Black or African American Alone [map], Census 2000, accessed via SocialExplorer.com on September 15, 2024.
44. See John L. Jackson, *Harlem World: Doing Race and Class in Contemporary Black America* (Chicago: University of Chicago Press, 2001). For journalistic takes on these questions, see Michael Henry Adams, "The End of Black Harlem," *New York Times*, May 27, 2016; and Sam Roberts, "No More Majority Black, Harlem Is in Transition," *New York Times*, January 5, 2010.
45. More comparative data would be needed to see how these changes contrasted with other predominantly Black areas of the city and with the city as a whole, but these numbers confirm a basic pattern of metropolitan gentrification during the end of the twentieth century and the start of the twenty-first century: some Black people are

leaving traditionally Black urban areas; housing prices in those areas are increasing; noticeable populations who are not Black, like white Americans, are moving into communities where, for decades, few if any white people lived; *and* some Black people with higher socioeconomic status are also moving into traditionally Black urban communities and becoming property owners. See Robertson, "Harlem on the Rise," 22–26. See also Troy Closson and Nicole Hong, "Why Black Families Are Leaving New York and What It Means for the City," *New York Times*, January 31, 2023. Data cited here are from census information cited in note 43.

46. Social Explorer Tables, Census 1970, 2010, U.S. Census Bureau and Social Explorer, accessed via SocialExplorer.com on September 15, 2024.
47. Comprehensive census data from the 2019 American Community Survey 5-Year Estimates for Monroe County, PA, available at NYDatabases.com, https://data.democrat andchronicle.com/american-community-survey/monroe-county-pennsylvania /population/total-population/yty/05000US42089/. Social Explorer comparative data also provides detailed information on population and housing statistics.
48. See M. Pattillo, *Black Picket Fences*.
49. Scholarship on Black communities on Long Island is sparse. See the essays and photos in Jerry Komia Domatob, *African Americans of Western Long Island (NY)* (Charleston, SC: Arcadia Publishing, 2002); and *African Americans of Eastern Long Island (NY)* (Charleston, SC: Arcadia Publishing, 2001). See also David Everitt, "Lost Histories: Stories of Blacks on Long Island," *New York Times*, January 26, 2003. On blockbusting in the community of North Bellport, see Neil P. Buffett, "Blockbusting on Long Island: The Case of Gerald Kutler and the 1962 Legal Battle against Real Estate Bias in North Bellport, New York," *Long Island History Journal* 26, no. 1 (2017), https://lihj.cc.stonybrook.edu/2017/volumes/2017-vol-26-1/. Hofstra University Library's special collections division has a brief write-up on the subject; see "Black History on Long Island," Hofstra University, accessed September 15, 2024, www .hofstra.edu/library/libspc/libspc_lisi_blackhistory.html.
50. Olivia Winslow, "Dividing Lines, Visible and Invisible," *Long Island Divided, Part 10*, Newsday, November 17, 2019, https://projects.newsday.com/long-island/segregation -real-estate-history/.
51. "Striking Photo from 1962 Discouraging Housing Integration in Lakeview, New York," *Black Mail Blog*, accessed September 15, 2024, https://blackmail4u.com/2015 /09/05/striking-photo-from-1962-discouraging-housing-integration-in-lakeview-ny/.
52. Gary McLendon, "Growing Up Ghetto," *Democrat and Chronicle*, May 17, 2013, www.democratandchronicle.com/story/news/local/blogs/race/2013/03/21/growing -up-ghetto/2196241/.
53. Census Tract 4062.01 and Tract 4062.02, Nassau County, NY, Social Explorer Dataset, Census 1990, Social Explorer; US Census Bureau, 1990, accessed via SocialExplorer.com on September 15, 2024.
54. The Bronx's history has recently received thorough treatment by a booster in Ian Frazier, *Paradise Bronx: The Life and Times of New York's Greatest Borough* (New York: Farrar, Straus & Giroux, 2024). Frazier's research included ample use of qualitative oral history data about of African Americans in the Bronx from the 1930s to the present, available in the Fordham University's Bronx African American History Project

archive, https://research.library.fordham.edu/baahp_oralhist, accessed September 15, 2024. Outside of some local histories by groups such as the Sandy Ground community (see Sandy Ground website, https://sandygroundny.com/about-us, accessed September 15, 2024). Staten Island's rich Black history awaits its historians, boosters, and documentarians to bring it into larger studies of Black life in New York City.

55. Daniela Altimari, "Census Shows Stamford Is Booming and Connecticut's Population Up Slightly over Last 10 Years," *Hartford Courant*, August 12, 2021, www.courant.com/2021/08/12/census-shows-stamford-is-booming-and-connecticuts-population-up-slightly-over-last-10-years/.

56. Census Tracts 601–615; 701–706; 709–714; 716; 719–740; 743–744; 801–802; 804–812; 903–906; 1051; 2572, Fairfield County, CT, Social Explorer Tables, Census 2010, accessed via SocialExplorer.com on September 15, 2024.

57. Hilton Als, "Homecoming," *New Yorker*, June 29, 2020.

FIONA VERNAL

Unmooring and Tethering African American, Puerto Rican, and West Indian Lives

New Conceptual Frameworks for Interrogating Three Great Migration Traditions in Hartford, Connecticut

Between 1940 and 2020, three waves of internal and transnational migrations of African Americans, Puerto Ricans, and West Indians transformed Hartford into a minority-majority city.[1] This demographic transition represents the two sequential eras of the Great Migration of African Americans and the overlapping movement of Puerto Ricans and West Indians from the Caribbean. Spurred by state-sponsored labor programs under the aegis of their governments, the availability of air and sea travel, and the pursuit of economic opportunities, Puerto Ricans and West Indians created nascent communities in the United States. Monumental shifts in immigration policy in 1965 (with the Hart-Celler Act) led to the removal of quotas and eased the movement of men, women, and families from the Caribbean. American and British imperial socioeconomic and political forces produced a hypermobile Caribbean labor pool that became the basis of post–World War II guest worker programs and of new tributary diasporas in the United States. These intersections have fashioned Greater Hartford into an African American and Caribbean enclave with many historic firsts: the election of the first African American man and woman as mayors of a New England city in the 1980s; a succession of two Puerto Rican mayors in the 1990s and following decade; and two African American and one West Indian mayor in the suburban-ring towns of Bloomfield and Windsor. The coalition politics and demographic shifts that produced these historic firsts had their roots in Connecticut's iconic shade tobacco industry. Connecticut farmers forged recruitment partnerships with Caribbean governments as well as with the National League on Urban Conditions among Negroes, forerunner of the National

Urban League. African Americans, Puerto Ricans, and West Indians encountered each other in the tobacco fields and sheds and again in Hartford, as the closest city where they could establish embryonic communities. In addition to high rents, they faced limited, aging, and deteriorating housing stocks, racial hostility, and discrimination. An intricate system of segregation and zoning enclosed Black and Latino communities in the North End of the city. Hartford thus served as a stage for a protracted struggle over the right of communities of color to live in certain sections of the city and, later, in suburban-ring towns. These challenges fostered Black and Latino solidarity yet generated fissures over tactics, leadership, and ethnic loyalties. The afterlives of African Americans who joined in the Great Migration to urban hubs like Hartford are therefore deeply intertwined with the history of transnational migration of Blacks and Latinos. These three Great Migrations resulted in the renegotiation of space, race, ethnicity, and belonging, shifting the terrain of municipal and state politics from the 1970s to the 2020s.

Hartford is a generative case study crucial in several ways for thinking about the legacies of these overlapping migration traditions. First, this chapter makes the case that interrogating Hartford's transition to a Caribbean and an African American city requires an integrated transnational framework that draws insights from a broader Caribbean historiography that already privileges analyses of mobility, labor, and diasporic Blackness. The Caribbean's own colonial heritage and resulting ethnolinguistic diversity refracted in the multiethnic makeup of post–World War II Hartford. Moreover, Hartford matters for understanding how the lineaments of British and American imperial experiments in the Caribbean shaped citizenship and racialization in the newest outposts of America's Caribbean diasporas. Far from incongruous in chronology and space, the global, regional, and national circuits of labor that produced unfreedom, immobility, and economic migration in one era were the antecedents of the dislocation and relocation of West Indians and Puerto Ricans in another.

Second, this chapter brings African American migrations into conversation with the movements of Puerto Ricans and West Indians to deepen our understanding of willful, fitful individual migration as well as formal, state-sponsored mass migrations. As the terminus of not one but three Great Migration traditions, therefore, an integrated transnational framework also means connecting three historiographies that often treat these movements as discrete histories.

Third, Hartford also demonstrates the case for examining smaller urban hubs of the Great Migration. Chicago, Philadelphia, and New York, for example, still occupy the lion's share of case studies, although the historiography has addressed other unsung and understudied places.[2] Moreover, the places that produced the largest proportion of migrants in Hartford—Georgia, Jamaica, and Puerto Rico—also underscore that it is not only smaller cities that have been overlooked but also the various geographical nodes that came to be intimately connected to and are now overrepresented in Hartford. With some of the densest concentrations of Puerto Ricans and Jamaicans in the Northeast, Hartford is now 85 percent minority, and these residents have reshaped municipal elections and the city's spatial and cultural landscape.

The fourth intervention this chapter makes is the integration of community archives and oral history as part of a methodological approach aimed at incorporating Black and Latino voices, experiences, and recordkeeping.[3] This is particularly important because the history of the city's shifting racial and demographic profile is often saturated in discourses of urban decline and pathology. Slum clearance, white flight, redlining, urban renewal, and gentrification feature so prominently in the narratives of Hartford's contemporary history that they often occlude other ways of thinking about the city. The social and scientific imagination emphasizing deprivation and poverty casts Hartford as an archetype of urban malaise. Communities of color engaged these narratives. They, too, were vocal about the challenges of the built environment and the unjust ways that residential segregation enclosed and foreclosed their opportunities. Blacks and Latinos critiqued their own communities and leaders while indicting the broader system of racism and urban divestment. They decried how the failure of regional economic cooperation saddled Hartford with disparate service and welfare burdens and a declining tax base.[4] Yet they also promoted different perspectives and experiences of the city that matter for writing new histories of urbanization and migration. Hartford's newest residents thought of their experiences in multivalent ways, refuting familiar declension narratives of postwar urban decline.[5] For example, in their oral histories and community archives, they affirmed that the city offered hope, opportunity, and refuge. The scrapbooks of the Mann family, archives of the West Indian Social Club, interviews and documentaries of the Hartford Studies Project at Trinity College, and my oral interviews with residents fill important gaps in the historical record and reveal powerful, nuanced counternarratives. In these archives, residents document how they socialized and created new fraternal, athletic, and social organizations; confronted the challenges of housing; built new communities; and advocated for education, economic opportunities, civic engagement, and political enfranchisement.[6] Drawing on these community archives and oral histories, the chapter weaves together the stories of Lovely Mann Sr., Maria Colón Sánchez, and Sydney Barnett, three migrants who are representative of internal and transnational migrations, and their afterlives in Hartford.

Collective Biographies of Lovely Mann Sr., Maria Colón Sánchez, and Sydney Barnett

The year 1947 was a good one for Lovely Mann Sr., an African American migrant who had come of age in Montezuma, Macon County, Georgia. Just nineteen years old, Mann set his sights on migrating north. His vast kinship network, stretching from Georgia to South Carolina, Florida, Ohio, New York, and Connecticut, helped kindle this desire to leave Macon County.[7] This network gestured toward earlier traditions and generations of mobility that had brought his maternal and paternal family members to the Midwest and Northeast. These traditions drew on yearnings for a better life and the desire to escape Jim Crow strictures. They were also motivated by a sense of adventure as well as unnamed desires, other inklings lost to history. "The inchoate, what you wanted but couldn't name," Saidiyah Hartman argued, "the resolute, stubborn desire for an elsewhere and an otherwise that had yet to emerge clearly, a notion of the possible whose outlines were fuzzy and amorphous, exerted a force no less powerful and tenacious."[8]

Employment opportunities in the Northeast and Midwest nurtured these longings and quickened the pace of migration. Mann eventually settled on Hartford as his final destination, buoyed by manufacturing opportunities in the capital region. Mann wrote to his siblings, cousins, and friends in other states, sharing news of marriages, births, and employment opportunities.[9] He established deep roots in the city, starting a business and raising a family. His unmooring from the South and his tethering to the North were protracted processes of mobility that involved his family in reconnaissance travel, circular migration, secondary migration, chain migration, and return migration. These patterns of mobility, what sociologist Mimi Sheller calls "intermittent, interrelated mobilities," are captured in the voluminous literature on the Great Migration.[10] This literature has deepened our understanding of the protean nature of migration as both exile and embrace, as both reckoning and recognition. Once Mann was tethered to Hartford, his life history opens another window into patterns of African American community formation and succession and the legacies of the Great Migration. Now, as a permanent resident, he had to navigate Hartford's perennial problems of limited housing supply. He dreamed of owning a barbershop and needed a strategy to pivot between his manufacturing job and his desire to own a business. He also needed to identify a business location that would attract robust foot traffic. Through his barber shop on Albany Avenue, a major thoroughfare in Hartford's North End, Mann sought to gain a foothold in barbering, one of the industries that has provided generations of African American men a measure of economic autonomy, if not independence.[11]

As Mann weighed his housing options, thirty-two-year-old Sydney Barnett was also in a ponderous mood about where his journeys would take him.[12] Born in Westmoreland, Jamaica, Barnett was accustomed to a different kind of unmooring, part of a very long tradition of what scholars term circum-Caribbean migration.[13] Many were goaded by economic opportunities. "Labor market disparities drove emigration," Lara Putnam noted, "yet, migrants' economic decision-making reflected an evolving social panorama shaped by those who went before."[14] Before they set their sights on hubs like England, America, and Canada, West Indians traversed other Caribbean islands as well as Central and South America. Barnett, for example, was part of the legion of West Indian workers recruited to build the Panama Canal. Barely had he finished a four-year stint from 1940 to 1944 in the Canal Zone when the US government recruited him and several thousand other West Indians to aid in the war effort. War-related manpower shortages had ushered in new immigration opportunities for men to work in the United States. These guest workers provided relief for farming and industrial outfits facing desperate labor shortages along the entire Eastern Seaboard, from Maine to Florida, and in places as far afield as California, Wisconsin, Michigan, and Ohio.[15] In Connecticut, they netted, planted, and harvested shade tobacco for cigar wrappers. They cut sugarcane in Florida and picked apples in midwestern states. Growers were hardly picky about how they used West Indian laborers, whom they deployed for celery, corn, cane, and peas alongside mainstay crops like oranges and apples. Local farmers in Connecticut "borrowed" workers for harvesting potatoes, while sugar companies requested that those in the North be transshipped to augment their labor force.[16]

Like Lovely Mann's own reconnaissance trips, this type of recruitment gave Barnett and his West Indian counterparts a taste of life in America. They experienced everything from the Jim Crow segregation that Mann had sought to escape to northern iterations of racial discrimination.[17] But this was only one part of their experiences. Barnett and his coworkers were welcomed, and sometimes feted, by farmers and the government representatives who hosted exhibition cricket matches for them at Hartford's Colt Park.[18] Social agencies and religious groups, concerned about recreation and general welfare, sponsored excursions as well as religious and educational opportunities for these recruits.[19] The local African American community, including many southern transplants, also embraced West Indian guest workers, recognizing that they, too, were outsiders. Like Mann, Barnett settled in Hartford and remained a lifelong resident.

He also opened a business on Albany Avenue, Barnett's Clothing Store, which catered to a local clientele.[20] Just a few blocks away from his business, he purchased the home where his minister, Reverend Robert Moody of Shiloh Baptist Church, had originally found a room for him to rent and where he had previously done some yard maintenance.[21]

As Barnett was settling into his home on Brook Street, Maria Colón Sánchez rearranged her plans for life in Puerto Rico, setting her sights on Hartford. An aunt had made the journey before her, one family member whose experience and perhaps direct assistance could help tether her to a new city. It was the 1950s, the decade in which 470,000 people, or approximately one-fifth of Puerto Rico's population, relocated to the United States.[22] New York attracted the vast majority of these sojourners and remained a primary destination. Many Puerto Ricans worked in manufacturing, service, maintenance, and domestic jobs. But they also pursued other opportunities beyond their cities of first entry, a process aided by both government-sponsored recruitment of Puerto Rican farmworkers and kinship networks.

Once in Hartford, Colón Sánchez pursued any opportunity that would help her find an economic footing, including working in the shade tobacco fields and, later, at a meatpacking plant in New Britain.[23] Like Mann and Barnett before her, she eventually established a business on Albany Avenue. Maria's News Stand became an important gathering place and site of information and organizing for Puerto Ricans in the city. From this perch as well as through Sacred Heart Catholic Church, Colón Sánchez expanded her activism to address the challenges of both migrant farmworkers and the embryonic residential community in Hartford's North End. As she became a seasoned resident herself, she and other early members of the Puerto Rican community worked on a range of issues, from employment, housing struggles, and police brutality to political engagement and access to equitable education. They advocated the hiring of Spanish-speaking teachers and priests to cater to the growing population. These early efforts would lead to a mandate for bilingual education in Hartford public schools in the 1970s. In 1973 Colón Sánchez campaigned for a seat on Hartford's board of education, a victory that made her the first Puerto Rican elected to public office in Hartford. She took her tireless political campaign to the Connecticut General Assembly in 1988 as the first Hispanic woman to be elected to that body.[24]

Colón Sánchez, Barnett, and Mann spent decades in Hartford stitching together lives deeply embedded in and committed to communities whose hopes and dreams reflected their own. Their experiences and their eponymous entrepreneurial endeavors—Maria's News Stand, Barnett's Clothing Store, and

Mann's Barbershop—represent the North End's transition from a Jewish enclave to an African American, Puerto Rican, and West Indian neighborhood.

Integrating Historiographies

The history of African American migration has generated a voluminous interdisciplinary literature drawing on sociology, history, geography, literature, economics, and urban studies. From Carter G. Woodson and W. E. B. Du Bois's classic contemporaneous studies to the works of Nell Painter, Joe Trotter, Stewart Tolnay, Kenneth Kusmer, Isabel Wilkerson, William Cohen, and Saidiya Hartman, the field has produced a diverse corpus that is pivotal for understanding the implications of African American mobility.[25] African Americans were always willing to test their chains to try new economic and political experiments, as the scholarship of Steve Hahn, Leon Litwack, Kendra Field, and many others have amply demonstrated. African American itineraries featured local, regional, national, and global destinations.[26] In the immediate post-emancipation landscape, it was the entire notion of freedom and mobility that became the grand, risky experiment, whether one ended up on another farm or in a city, out west, up north, or overseas.[27] Edited volumes surveying and synthesizing new directions in the study of the African American urbanization also include innovative explorations of the role of gender in shaping the experience of migration as well as the emergence of civic and social reformers working to mitigate the challenges newcomers faced.[28] Historian James Gregory has produced an important volume connecting both Black and white southern diasporas and reframing the role of migration in US history, including connections to Latino and Asian migration and migrations in the era of the Dust Bowl.[29] African American flight to the suburbs and the new spatial configuration of poverty are also fruitful areas of inquiry. Through this literature comes a deeper understanding of how poverty has crept into suburban areas, sparking debates about opportunity zones and the connection between micro-geographies, educational equity, and economic life chances.[30] African American exoduses from urban areas, recalculations in these former political strongholds, and the advocacy for return migration all provide an opportunity to revisit what the earlier periods of history suggest about these new upheavals.[31]

Methodologically, oral histories and the public and digital humanities have reinvigorated studies of post–World War II urbanization. Isabel Wilkerson's *The Warmth of Other Suns: The Epic Story of America's Great Migration* is just one example offering a magisterial chronicle based on oral histories. For the Caribbean historiography, Ismael García-Colón's *Colonial Migrants at the Heart of Empire: Puerto Rican Workers on U.S. Farms* provides an authoritative account drawing on oral history methodology to explore labor migration and community formation.[32] Analyses drawn from public data samples have fostered longitudinal and more fine-grained explorations of the outcomes and ramifications of the Great Migration and provided the underlying data for updated studies and new digital projects. Gregory's interactive project provides an important entry point for exploring these overarching narratives of mobility and diasporas.[33] The public and digital humanities have produced engaging scholarship that provides new ways to dig into data, sometimes resurrecting analog projects on digital platforms; to collate datasets for visualizing the movement of people across time and space; and to delve deeper on particular case studies.[34] Oral and public history and the digital humanities improve accessibility to old and new stories and their underlying data sources and foster creative visualizations of the historical experience of migration and place-making.

Caribbean migration has also generated a voluminous historiography, shaped by generations of scholars who have explored the proverbial push-and-pull factors influencing the transnational flow of people across local, regional, and national borders. Like the Great Migration of African Americans, the Caribbean historiography captures the protean nature of Caribbean mobility, both its fitful and experimental character and the more calculated ways in which gender, generation, life stage, violence, and economic immiseration delimited people's life chances.[35] While overseas migration was sometimes the first opportunity for West Indians and Puerto Ricans to travel to the seat of empire, people in the Caribbean were always mobile.[36] For some people, kin and friends brought them from one community to another, from rural areas to urban areas.[37] Circum-Caribbean migration brought Puerto Ricans to Cuba and the Dominican Republic. In addition to the mainland United States, Puerto Ricans could also be found as far afield as Hawaii to work in sugar.[38] These same currents brought West Indians to Cuba, Panama, Costa Rica, and Venezuela at various periods between the 1870s and 1940s as they pursued opportunities in the banana and sugar industries and during the construction of the Panama Canal.[39]

Periodization, destination, and ethnic and racial formations have also been important in understanding the global flow of migration with scholars like Lara Putnam, Irma Watkins-Owens, Violet Johnson, Velma Newton, Glenn Chambers, Kaysha Corinealdi, and Reena Goldthree, among others, undertaking case studies of Harlem, Colón, Costa Rica, or Honduras.[40] US agricultural interests, whether configured as multinational conglomerates, cabals, cooperatives, or individual farmers, played an outsize influence in the movements of people. Tobacco, sugar, citrus, and bananas helped to move Caribbean residents from English imperial domains to the outposts of Spain's own far-flung empire throughout the Caribbean and Latin America. The United Fruit Company and US tobacco companies shaped the experiences of huge swaths of people, carrying on the British tradition of being among the largest exporters of human labor around the globe. Everywhere colonial migrants went, they created what I earlier termed "tributary diasporas" whose labor, while often celebrated, was more valued for its deportability than for its quantity and quality, as historian Cindy Hahamovitch has shown. The post-emancipation world of labor built on earlier traditions of autonomy and mobility in Caribbean societies, dispersing people once again for the crucial work of agriculture as well as infrastructure projects. Labor shortages during World War I presaged some of these shifts, but another crucial turning point came in the 1940s that would have even more profound demographic ramifications. By then, the United States had developed a formal contract system to satisfy agricultural labor demands as well as the new manufacturing jobs that came online to meet the exigencies of a wartime economy.

These crucial decades provided new opportunities for West Indians and Puerto Ricans to work seasonally in the United States. Whether fitful or calculated, neither internal nor transnational migration left clear records of people's decision-making process to leave home. Their voices appear intermittently in the official records, such as those of the Puerto Rican Migration Division or the Shade Tobacco Growers Association's records, crucial archives for understanding Hartford's entanglement with global labor migration. Oral histories, therefore, play an important role in what we can learn about other migration traditions. In addition to García-Colón's work on Puerto Rico's farm labor program and the creation of new diasporic communities, Ruth Glasser's *Aquí Me Quedo* provides an entry point for oral histories of Puerto Rican migration to Connecticut. Elena Rosario's forthcoming University of Michigan dissertation on labor migration and community formation makes important contributions to this historiography, especially in its multimodal presentation of Hartford's Puerto Rican history. In *Soldiers of the Soil*, Fay Clarke Johnson employs oral histories to create a composite profile of West Indian men who came to work in the United States and eventually became members of the West Indian Social Club of Hartford.[41]

American itineraries offered an opportunity for reconnaissance in Hartford. This glimpse of life in America shaped whether migrants wanted to return for another season or concoct other plans to stay in the United States permanently. Hartford has another toehold in this voluminous literature, with the sociological and historical interventions of Kurt Schlicting, Peter Tuckel, Richard Maisel, and Stacey Close.[42] Close's forthcoming Routledge history of Hartford's African American community fills an important gap by centering the Great Migration as a radicalizing catalyst in the struggle to achieve civil and political rights.[43] This framework will be important in pinpointing when and how Caribbean migrants became a catalyzing force similar to their southern counterparts. In documenting how the national struggle for civil rights refracted in Hartford, Close reminds us that the city's African Americans residents always saw themselves as part of the fight for freedom, justice, and equality. How did their Caribbean counterparts assimilate US civil rights discourse to their struggles for freedom, justice, and equality? Various tributaries of the African diaspora converged in Hartford, creating new roots and routes that are important for understanding the diversity of the Black experience and that have always featured prominently in the scholarship on Caribbean migration.[44]

Unmooring and Tethering

This essay's vocabulary of unmooring and tethering is intentional, an attempt to consider the emotional freight and agency involved in the decisions that African Americans, Puerto Ricans, and West Indians made to leave their homes. People did more than just move. They uprooted themselves. Finding the language to capture the trauma, alienation, and isolation as well as the sense of hope and possibility, intimates how oral histories can capture the emotional and psychological impact of migration. "Affective mobilities," a new, useful framework that mobilities scholars have coined, is a promising area for conceptual cross-fertilization.[45] To tether, migrants had to be attuned to the Greater Hartford region with its combination of manufacturing, industrial opportunities, and agricultural jobs. For Mann and Colón Sánchez, family members who had settled in an earlier period smoothed their transition. Both eventually ended up working in New Britain, about ten miles from the city—Mann at a manufacturing plant, Colón Sánchez at a meatpacking plant.[46] For Barnett, reconnaissance began while he was in Jamaica through the clientele at his father's garage. As a mechanic, Barnett came into contact with people who had enough capital to own a car in the 1940s, including clients who worked with the United Fruit Company, then a recruiter for the US government.[47] This network was crucial not only in connecting Barnett to the opportunity but also in advising him about Jim Crow laws. "You will never make it in Florida," Barnett's client warned him. Despite the clamor for employment opportunities in the United States, West Indian workers were attuned to racial strictures there. Through this personal network and a stroke of luck, Barnett landed in Connecticut.[48] But Barnett wanted more from the outset and hoped to bypass field labor. He made it known that he could drive and spent his agricultural season driving the truck that fetched the tobacco rather than laboring arduously in the field.

Barnett's mooring in Hartford came through African American religious and fraternal circles—the Shiloh Baptist Church and the Elks Club. Shiloh was among the churches that brought workers to Hartford for services. Here, Barnett connected with the minister, Reverend Moody, and African American congregants. Gregarious and resourceful, Barnett joined both the church and the fraternal organization, which helped to tether him to Hartford's African American community. By the time he was an octogenarian, he was a member of at least nine civic and social organizations that focused on providing access to economic opportunities and health care in Hartford's North End. Barnett owned his own business and his home, ran a choral group that performed widely, and became a lifelong member of the West Indian Social Club.[49]

Other West Indians anchored themselves to the African American community through marriage. They met southern women who also worked in tobacco. Kenneth Bennett Sr., the oldest member of the West Indian Social Club, recounted what it was like during the 1940s. The centenarian, who celebrated this milestone in August 2022, noted, "At that period . . . you have a lot of girls coming from the South working in tobacco. They sew the tobacco. . . . A lot of girls from Alabama, Florida . . . college girls come up and work. But you have to show them. . . . You become the straw boss." Reflecting on the interactions between West Indian men and African American women, Bennett acknowledged, "You work with them every day and [with] some of them you make dates." Bennett married his great love, Eva Mae McDowell, a student at North Carolina Central University who had moved north to work seasonally like hundreds of other students. They settled in Hartford and collaborated on business ventures in kosher catering and real estate that made them one of the most well-known families in Hartford. African American women who married West Indian men became crucial community anchors. They brought their organizing skills to the Ladies Auxiliary of the West Indian Social Club of Hartford, which they founded in 1954, and became formidable fundraisers who helped buoyed the organization.[50]

Colón Sánchez's integration into Hartford's Puerto Rican community came in the broader context of Puerto Rican labor migration. For Puerto Rican workers, direct recruitment meant a plane ticket to the United States. While many workers returned home, their citizenship status in the United States gave them freedom of employment without the threat of deportation that West Indians faced. Like African Americans had learned, however, citizenship was no guarantor of housing, jobs, or even dignity for Puerto Ricans. Every right was treated as a concession rather than an entitlement. Accessing those rights required intermediaries who could navigate a world that catered exclusively to English speakers. Some of those intermediaries included Puerto Ricans connected to Hartford through other means, like Colón Sánchez, Olga Mele, and Edna Negron Rosario. Olga Mele, a Puerto Rican from Guayama, met and married her Italian American husband, John Mele, while he was on military service on the island. The couple relocated to Hartford in 1941. Edna Negron Rosario's family had come to New York for a critical surgery her sister needed. As an ordained minister, her father, Jose Negron Cruzado, had access to a larger religious network, which eventually brought him first to Bridgeport and then to Hartford. While battling his own second-class treatment by other ministers in the Greater Hartford Council of Churches, he became an important lifeline for Puerto Rican migrant farmers. He brought his family on some of these visits, giving them firsthand knowledge of the terrible conditions at the labor camps.[51]

Both migrant farmers who stayed at the camps and opted for day haul labor and those who left the agricultural workforce had crucial allies in these early advocates who cut their political teeth in their attempts to address the needs of Puerto Rican residents in Hartford. Colón Sánchez had eventually settled on Williams Street in the North End, with her store on Albany Avenue. Olga Mele initially lived in the North End of Hartford on Main Street near Sacred Heart Church, where she became part of the burgeoning community of activists. Other Puerto Rican women became active, including Ana Cotto Nuñez and Nilda Ortiz, who all helped to build an infrastructure that could address access to health, education, employment, legal, and social services for Hartford residents.[52] Living in the North End and in some of the oldest housing stock in the Clay Arsenal neighborhood thrust Puerto Ricans into the same cycle of trying to address neglectful landlords and deteriorating housing conditions that African Americans faced.

Potential employment and a kinship network smoothed Lovely Mann's reconnaissance trips, making Hartford an affirmative, deliberate decision for him.[53] A generation of African American migrants before him had either begun in manufacturing or transitioned to manufacturing after a stint in agriculture. Others had hoped to get a high-paying job in the defense industry in the Greater Hartford region. This was far from an easy task. Employment discrimination was rife. Whether African Americans came during World War I or World War II, a National Defense Migration report noted in 1941 that in Hartford, "holders of defense contracts not only refused to employ competent and available Negro workers, but also barred Negro Youth from defense training programs."[54] Positions remained unfilled, and employers preferred to raise the labor supply alarm to attract white youth from out of state.⁵⁵ Even with state oversight of African American employment through the Commission on Human Rights and the Fair Employment Practices Committee, established in 1941, employment discrimination remained rampant.

Mann settled in a six-unit apartment and began to raise a family. Work and family networks took him about ten miles away to New Britain, but he anchored his immediate family in Hartford.⁵⁶ While his children came of age in Hartford, frequent trips to Georgia connected them to the extended family. His son Willie Mann, now an elder and keeper of the family memory, maintains the family reunion tradition and continues to document his family's history through his massive collection of scrapbooks. The family eventually moved to the South End, but Willie frequented his father's barbershop, eventually learning his father's trade. In his oral history, Willie discusses what the area looked like when he was a young man coming of age in Hartford:

> We would get to the barber shop by way of . . . Sigourney Street . . . turn down Homestead Avenue and go up Burton Street. And then as we made the right turn onto Magnolia Street, on the corner there was a Thrifty Cleaners. There was a laundromat, my dad's barber shop . . . a beauty salon and a bookie place . . . a little convenience store on the corner. . . . Directly across the street . . . was Crown Supermarket. That was there for a while. And then of course they closed down the building and the first Black bank institution was actually founded there. . . . There was a Black doctor. Dr. Wilson's office was down the road at the corner . . . then further down, there was another Black-owned barber shop . . . then there was a mini store. . . . But back in my time, there were a lot of Jewish businesses. A lot of delicatessens, and there was a supermarket which was Stop and Shop. And . . . a Five and Ten Cents store there as well.⁵⁷

The world Willie describes gives a small glimpse of the sense of self-sufficiency that emerged in the North End. One could get a haircut from one's choice of barber, see a doctor, run into a convenience or grocery store, and go to the bank. While conventional narratives of loss in Hartford accentuate declension and white flight, African American nostalgia focuses on the loss of community, services, personal security, and a sense of possibility.

All along the Albany thoroughfare, barbershops and beauty parlors dot the landscape, each with its own clientele and aesthetic. Even these spaces became places of particular repute and cultural loyalties. Puerto Ricans, West Indians, and African Americans desperately needed these safe spaces, as Edna Negron Rosario recounted in her interview. Her father could not get a haircut anywhere in the 1950s. Because of her darker skin, she always had to go to the back of a beauty school to get her hair cut. Here, she encountered African American women who were relegated to straightening hair.[58] The life of Earlene Nelson, an African American migrant, offers a brief glimpse of how women addressed the lack of access to personal services. Nelson became an entrepreneur by filling in the gaps for an African American and West Indian clientele. Her early life spanned the gamut, from working cotton with her mother and grandmother to working as a laundress. Nelson rejected these horizons and experimented with new opportunities. Her journey took her from South Carolina to Virginia, following her employers. First, there was the movement within South Carolina, from York to Florence, and then came New York, New Haven, and Washington—all in a quest for economic security. Hartford was the terminus of these journeys. Here, she ran a beauty parlor and, for a time, a beauty school. She married a West Indian man, Carmel Nelson, and became one of the presidents of the Ladies Auxiliary and a formidable force for civic engagement in the African American and West Indian communities.[59]

Through a confluence of global, local, and family decisions, African Americans, Puerto Ricans, and West Indians grew from a small part of the city of Hartford to a majority of the population. The intersection of these three Great Migrations between 1940 and 2020 offers an opportunity to think about the conceptual possibilities of integrating transnational and local frameworks on migration. This aperture offers new perspectives for creating an alloy of three disparate historiographies that have much to offer each other. How people become unmoored from their places of birth and tied to new homes—the experience of this as a form of exile and as a form of embrace—can be generative for understanding affective mobilities. Freighted in histories of imperialism and global circuits of capital and labor and relegated to marginal roles, the people in these communities, nevertheless, exerted agency over their lives by leveraging their cultural heritage as part of their strategies to secure employment, housing, and autonomous social and business spaces. In this way, they embarked on new journeys where the concept of mobility could capture microgeographic and socioeconomic patterns of movement within the city, just as it reveals to us distinct patterns of movement from Georgia, Puerto Rico, and Jamaica. This framework also holds important methodological possibilities, especially with the narration of these experiences through oral histories and community archives. What is at stake—and the intervention this chapter makes—is a model for integrating ethnic, urban, and social history with African American and Caribbean histories through the lens of a case study. The result, which will later be explored in a book-length monograph, is a narrative that relies on the cocreation and contribution of the generations of people like Olga Mele, Willie Mann, Maria Colón Sánchez, Edna Negron Rosario, Lovely Mann, Earlene Nelson, and Sydney Barnett whose itineraries brought them to Hartford. Having transformed Hartford into an African and Caribbean city, West Indians, African Americans, and Puerto Ricans continue to shape the civic and political landscape, making it possible to write new histories of Hartford.

Notes

1. On minority-majority cities, see Albert M. Camarillo, "Blacks, Latinos, and the New Racial Frontier in American Cities of Color: California's Emerging Minority-Majority Cities," in *African American Urban History since World War II*, ed. Kenneth L. Kusmer and Joe William Trotter (Chicago: University of Chicago Press, 2009), 39–59.
2. Kimberley L. Phillips, *Alabama North: African-American Migrants, Community, and Working-Class Activism in Cleveland, 1915–45* (Urbana: University of Illinois Press, 1999); Karida L. Brown, *Gone Home: Race and Roots through Appalachia* (Chapel Hill: University of North Carolina Press, 2018); Alice Mah, "A Layover Stop in the African American Great Migration: Identity, Ruination, and Memory," *Ethnic and Racial Studies* 42, no. 13 (2019): 2326–32.
3. For recent reflections on creating African American archives, see Karida L. Brown, "On the Participatory Archive: The Formation of the Eastern Kentucky African American Migration Project," in "Documentary Arts," special issue, *Southern Cultures* 22, no. 1 (Spring 2016): 113–27; for similar reflections on community archives, see Michelle Caswell, "Seeing Yourself in History: Community Archives and the Fight against Symbolic Annihilation," *Public Historian* 36, no. 4 (2014): 26–37.
4. Karlynn Carrington, "Residents Show Love for Clay Hill despite Deterioration," *Hartford Courant*, May 16, 1982, 1.
5. Citizen's Assembly Minutes, 1975–76, Hartford History Center, Hartford Public Library.
6. Hartford Studies Project Collection, Watkinson Library, Trinity College, "Juan Fuentes Vizcarrondo Interview," #1B, 2B, 3B, 4B; Lew Brown, Juan Fuentes, Jack Dollard, March 17–18, 2001; Chatfield, O. Mele, Virg Lewis, Frank Barrows, roll #5A–8A; "City Residents Propose Their Bills," *Hartford Courant*, December 9, 1976, 54.
7. The following profile of Lovely Mann is drawn from interviews with his son, Willie Mann, as well as from materials from Willie Mann's scrapbook collection, itself part of the African American tradition of collecting and preserving family histories. "My Dear Brother," Willie Mann [Cincinnati, OH] to Willie Mann [Hartford, CT], January 13, 1958, Willie Mann, Private Scrapbook Collection, n.d, used with permission of the collector, Willie Mann; Fiona Vernal and Willie Mann, "Willie Mann Oral History" [Hartford Stage, *Detroit '67* Collaboration], January 31, 2019, Hartford, CT. The oral histories in this chapter are in different phases of cataloging and accessioning. Uncataloged sources are not yet paginated.

8. Saidiya Hartman, *Wayward Lives, Beautiful Experiments: Intimate Histories of Riotous Black Girls, Troublesome Women, and Queer Radicals* (New York: W.W. Norton, 2019), 46.
9. "My Dear Brother," January 13, 1958, Willie Mann, Private Scrapbook Collection; Vernal and Mann, "Wille Mann Oral History," January 31, 2019; Fiona Vernal, "Herbert Hoover Brown, and William Mann," June 20, 2020.
10. Mimi Sheller, "From Spatial Turn to Mobilities Turn," *Current Sociology* 65, no. 4 (2017): 623–39.
11. *Report, Fifth Annual Convention, National Negro Business League*, Records of the Negro Business League, 1900–1919, Tuskegee University Archives; J. M. Hazlewood, "How to Establish and Maintain the Barber Business" (Pensacola: M. M. Lewey, Florida Sentinel, 1904), 106; Vernal and Mann, "Wille Mann Oral History," January 31, 2019; Lovely J. Mann Sr., obituary, *Hartford Courant*, March 4, 1970; "Mann's Barbershop," Private Scrapbook Collection, n.d.; "Barbershops in Hartford," Hartford Public Library Panel Discussion, February 13, 2020.
12. Sydney Barnett is rendered as both Sydney and Sidney in official documentation. Sydney appears more frequently, and the chapter will use this designation for consistency.
13. For one of the best summaries of circum-Caribbean migration patterns paired with maps and demographic data, see Lara Putnam, *Radical Moves: Caribbean Migrants and the Politics of Race in the Jazz Age* (Chapel Hill: University of North Carolina Press, 2013), 23–32.
14. Putnam, *Radical Moves*, 22.
15. Fiona Vernal and Sydney Barnett, "Sydney Barnett Oral History," Connecticut Historical Society, October 15, 2000, 16–17.
16. Vernal and Barnett, "Sydney Barnett Oral History," 16; Cindy Hahamovitch, *No Man's Land: Jamaican Guestworkers in American and the Global History of Deportable Labor* (Princeton: Princeton University Press), 48.
17. Fay Clarke Johnson, *Soldiers of the Soil* (New York: Vantage Press, 1995), 62–65; Fiona Vernal and Alice Marie James, "Alice Marie James Oral History," July 21, 2022.
18. Keith Carr, *Caribbean Echo*, June 14, 1969, and "Cricket in Hartford Takes on New Look," in Ephemera, West Indian Social Club Archives, Hartford, CT; Hahamovitch, *No Man's Land*, 50; Johnson, *Soldiers of the Soil*, 62, 82.
19. "Jamaicans Leaving for Homeland," *Hartford Courant*, October 10, 1943, 10.
20. "SBDC Seeks Disadvantaged: Poor Can Enter Big World of Small Business," *Hartford Courant*, May 26, 1966, 33.
21. Vernal and Barnett, "Sydney Barnett Oral History."
22. Edna Acosta-Belén and Carlos E. Santiago, *Puerto Ricans in the United States: A Contemporary Portrait* (Boulder: Lynne Rienner Publishers, 2006), 28.
23. "Interview, Jose D. Cruz Vaszquez," Hartford Studies Project Collection; "Second half Sylvia Carrasquillo Vargas and Edwin, Jose Cruz Vazquez," July 2000, Hartford Studies Project Collection.
24. "Una Conversación, Los Puertorriqueños y el Corte; y uno mas, la Señora Núñez y Sus Vecinos, Comerienos Asuentes," Hartford Studies Project Collection.
25. Carter G. Woodson, *A Century of Negro Migration* (Washington, DC: Association for the Study of Negro Life and History, 1918); W. E. B. Du Bois and Isabel Eaton, *The*

Philadelphia Negro: A Social Study (Philadelphia: published for the university, 1899); Stewart E Tolnay, "The African American 'Great Migration' and Beyond," *Annual Review of Sociology* 29, no. 1 (2003): 209–32; Nell Irvin Painter, *Exodusters: Black Migration to Kansas after Reconstruction* (New York: Knopf, 1977); Kenneth Kusmer, *A Ghetto Takes Shape: Black Cleveland, 1870–1930* (Urbana: University of Illinois Press, 1982); Kendra Taira Field, *Growing Up with the Country: Family, Race, and Nation after the Civil War* (New Haven: Yale University Press, 2018); Saidiya V. Hartman, *Wayward Lives, Beautiful Experiments: Intimate Histories of Social Upheaval* (New York: W. W. Norton, 2019); James N. Gregory, *The Southern Diaspora: How the Great Migrations of Black and White Southerners Transformed America* (Chapel Hill: University of North Carolina Press, 2005); Stacey Close, "Southern Blacks Transform Connecticut," *Connecticut Explored*, Fall 2013.

26. Steven Hahn, *A Nation under Our Feet: Black Political Struggles in the Rural South from Slavery to the Great Migration* (Cambridge, MA: Harvard University Press, 2003), 361; Kendra T. Field, "'No Such Thing as Stand Still': Migration and Geopolitics in African American History," *Journal of American History* 102, no. 3 (December 2015): 693–718; William Cohen, *At Freedom's Edge: Black Mobility and the Southern White Quest for Racial Control, 1861–1915* (Baton Rouge: Louisiana State University Press, 1991).

27. Leon F. Litwack, *Trouble in Mind: Black Southerners in the Age of Jim Crow* (New York: Vintage Books, 1998), 34, 405–6, 436, 482–83; Sydney Nathans, *A Mind to Stay: White Plantation, Black Homeland* (Cambridge, MA: Harvard University Press, 2018).

28. Adam Lee Cilli, "'The Curing of Ills': African American Women Activists at the Intersections of Race, Class, and Gender during the Great Migration," *Journal of Women's History* 33, no. 1 (2021): 37–60.

29. Gregory, *Southern Diaspora*; "America's Great Migrations," The Great Depression in Washington State Project, accessed July 8, 2023, https://depts.washington.edu/moving1/.

30. See, for example, Andrew Wiese, *Places of Their Own: African American Suburbanization in the Twentieth Century* (Chicago: University of Chicago Press, 2003).

31. Charles Blow, *The Devil You Know: A Black Power Manifesto* (New York: Harper, 2021).

32. Isabel Wilkerson, *The Warmth of Other Suns: The Epic Story of America's Great Migration*, first Vintage Books ed. (New York: Vintage, 2011); Ismael García-Colón, *Colonial Migrants at the Heart of Empire: Puerto Rican Workers on U.S. Farms* (Oakland: University of California Press, 2020). See also Dona L. Irvin, *The Unsung Heart of Black America: A Middle Class Church at Midcentury* (Columbia: University of Missouri Press, 1992); and Timuel D. Black Jr., *Bridges of Memory: Chicago's Second Generation of Black Migration* (Evanston, IL: Northwestern University Press, 2007).

33. Gregory, *Southern Diaspora*; "America's Great Migrations," The Great Depression in Washington State Project.

34. "Tales from the First Great Migration to Philadelphia," Goin' North, accessed September 5, 2022, https://goinnorth.org; Fiona Vernal and James Kolb, Hartford Bound, 2023, Hartfordbound.com.

35. Hahn, *Nation under Our Feet*, 330–63; Susan O'Donovan, *Becoming Free in the Cotton South* (Cambridge, MA.: Harvard University Press, 2007), 175, 192, 162–207; Gregory, *Southern Diaspora*.
36. Alejandro Portes and Ramón Grosfoguel, "Caribbean Diasporas: Migration and Ethnic Communities," *Annals of the American Academy of Political and Social Science* 533, no. 1 (May 1994): 48–69; Jorge Duany, *Blurred Borders: Transnational Migration between the Hispanic Caribbean and the United States* (Chapel Hill: University of North Carolina Press, 2011).
37. Fiona Vernal and Stan Walker, "Stan Walker Oral History," July 7, 2016, and July 26, 2022; Fiona Vernal and Narciso Airey, "Narciso Airey Oral History," January 16, 2001.
38. Portes and Grosfoguel, "Caribbean Diasporas," 51.
39. Putnam, *Radical Moves*; Lara Putnam, "Citizenship from the Margins: Vernacular Theories of Rights and the State from the Interwar Caribbean," *Journal of British Studies* 53, no. 1 (2014): 162–91; Robert Whitney and Graciela Chailloux Laffita, *Subjects or Citizens: British Caribbean Workers in Cuba, 1900–1960* (Gainesville: University Press of Florida, 2013); Olive Senior, *Dying to Better Themselves: West Indians and the Building of the Panama Canal* (Kingston, Jam.: University of the West Indies Press, 2014).
40. Velma Newton, *The Silver Men: West Indian Labour Migration to Panama, 1850–1914*, rev. ed. (Kingston, Jam.: Ian Randle, 2004); Glenn A. Chambers, *Race, Nation, and West Indian Immigration to Honduras, 1890–1940* (Baton Rouge: Louisiana State University Press, 2010); Violet Johnson, *The Other Black Bostonians: West Indians in Boston, 1900–1950* (Bloomington: Indiana University Press, 2006); Kaysha Corinealdi, *Panama in Black: Afro-Caribbean World Making and the Promise of Diaspora* (Durham, NC: Duke University Press, 2002).
41. Ruth Glasser, *Aqui Me Quedo: Puerto Ricans in Connecticut* (Middletown: Connecticut Humanities Council, 1997); Johnson, *Soldiers of the Soil*.
42. Kurt Schlicting, Peter Tuckel, and Richard Maisel, "Residential Segregation and the Beginning of the Great Migration of African Americans to Hartford, Connecticut: A GIS-Based Analysis," *Historical Methods* 39, no. 3 (2006): 132–44; Kurt Schlicting, Peter Tuckel, and Richard Maisel, "Social, Economic, and Residential Diversity within Hartford's African American Community at the Beginning of the Great Migration," *Journal of Black Studies* 37, no. 5 (2007): 710–36; Kurt Schlicting, Peter Tuckel, and Richard Maisel, "Great Migration of African Americans to Hartford, Connecticut, 1910–1930: A GIS Analysis at the Neighborhood and Street Level," *Social Science History* 39, no. 2 (2015): 287–310; Elizabeth J, Normen, Katherine J. Harris, Stacey K. Close, Wm. Frank Mitchell, and Olivia White, *African American Connecticut Explored* (Middletown: Wesleyan University Press, 2014).
43. Barbara Beeching, *Hopes and Expectations: The Origins of the Black Middle Class in Hartford* (Albany: SUNY Press, 2017). This volume shows how the Primus family used a web of kinship, social networks, religious affiliation, employment, and affective ties to stabilize their economic positions and to navigate the atmosphere of racial hostility in the nineteenth century. *Hopes and Expectations* provides an important anchor for understanding nineteenth-century geographical and social mobility for

an African American family in Hartford. It holds great promise as a model for how family history, collective biographies, and prosopographical approaches remain fertile methodological ground for exploring Caribbean histories of Hartford.

44. Reuel Rogers, "Black Like Who: Afro-Caribbean Immigrants, African Americas and the Politics of Group Identity," in *Islands in the City: West Indian Migration in New York*, ed. Nancy Foner (Berkeley: University of California Press, 2001), 163–92.
45. Vlad P. Glaveanu and Gail Womersley, "Affective Mobilities: Migration, Emotion and (Im)possibility," *Mobilities* 16, no. 4 (2021): 628–42.
46. Carol Giacomo, Jon Sandberg, and C. L. Smith Muniz, "An Institution called Sanchez: Politician, Role Model, Refuge," *Hartford Courant*, January 15, 1981, 20.
47. Wayne D. Rasmussen, *A History of the Emergency Farm Labor Supply Program, 1943–47* (Washington, DC: US Dept. of Agriculture, Bureau of Agricultural Economics, 1951), 262; Hahamovitch, *No Man's Land*, 54–55.
48. Vernal and Barnett, "Sydney Barnett Oral History," 17.
49. Vernal and Barnett, "Sydney Barnett Oral History," 52.
50. "Minute Book, Ladies Auxiliary of the West Indian Social Club, 1954," West Indian Social Club Archives.
51. "Olga Mele Interview," Chatfield, O. Mele, Virg Lewis, Frank Barrows, roll #5A–8A, Hartford Studies Project Collection.
52. "Una Conversación," Hartford Studies Project Collection.
53. Giacomo, Sandberg, and Muniz, "Institution Called Sanchez," 20.
54. US Congress, House, Select Committee Investigating National Defense Migration, *National Defense Migration. Committee Print. Select Committee Investigating National Defense Migration, House of Representatives, Seventy-Seventh Congress, First Session, Pursuant To H. Res. 113* (Washington, DC: US Government Printing Office, 1941), 23.
55. US Congress, House, Select Committee Investigating National Defense Migration, *National Defense Migration*, 24.
56. Vernal and Mann, "Willie Mann Oral History."
57. Vernal and Mann, "Willie Mann Oral History."
58. "Edna Negron Interview," Hartford Studies Project Collection.
59. Carrie McCully, "From the South Up to Hartford: The Story of Earlene Nelson," *Hartford Courant*, July 29, 1980, 27.

PART IV

SHANNON KING

What Did Rockefeller Do about the Crooked Cop Who Sell You Drugs?

Black Protest and the Politics of Safety in the Early 1970s

Recently, historians, political scientists, and others have illuminated how Black protest politics have contributed to the making of the modern carceral state. While many scholars have concentrated on liberal and conservative "law and order" and "get tough" legislation as a countermeasure to the rise of Black political rights and power, others have anchored Black anti-crime activism as the engine of mass incarceration. Political scientist Michael Fortner's *Black Silent Majority* offers such an argument. Fortner asserts that "mass incarceration had less to do with white resistance to racial equality and more do with the Black silent majority's confrontation with the 'reign of criminal terror' in their neighborhoods." Fortner centers Black grassroots activist Reverend Oberia Dempsey's decades-long campaign against drug-related crime, spotlighting Dempsey's and others' generative role in undergirding New York governor Nelson Rockefeller's support for tougher drug legislation in 1973. Fortner's argument is, in part, premised on the determining roles of the so-called Black silent majority, characterized as a group that held "traditional Black values" and that shifted from "structural problems to individual behavior." In this political environment, when Black New Yorkers' relative social mobility made them less concerned about whites' perceptions of them—what he calls the "white gaze"—the Black community "prioritized public safety over economic and racial inequality."[1]

Although there is an uneasy consensus that African Americans supported punitive politics in the 1970s, Fortner overstates Black New Yorkers' responsibility in and support of Rockefeller's crime policy, understating the roles of race and racism.[2] Historian Jessica Neptune, describing Rockefeller's strategy, argues that Rockefeller used "Harlem" as a proxy for race. She writes, "Such language signaled to white upstate voters that the new laws were not aimed at them—that it would not be their children or loved ones who would be facing life sentences." Historian Julilly Kohler-Hausmann's *Getting Tough* finds a spectrum of Black responses to the governor's drug policy. Kohler-Hausmann notes, "Even among those advocating a hard line, calls for harsh punishment for drug sellers were often paired with demands for more systemic reforms and greater social supports." Legal scholar James Forman Jr.'s *Locking Up Our Own*, like Fortner's book, centers the Black community's support of punishment, this time in Washington, DC. But in agreement with Kohler-Hausmann, he contends, "Racism shaped the political, economic, and legal context in which the Black community and its elected officials made their choices." This essay builds on Forman and Kohler-Hausmann by taking a more granular look at Black New Yorkers' support for punitive politics.[3]

In this essay, I place Black New Yorkers' battles against unlawful policing at the center of the debate around the development of mass incarceration. This approach, what I call Black "politics of safety," proffers a more nuanced and historical understanding of Black New Yorkers' support of punishment in the wake of the Rockefeller drug laws.[4] The politics of safety speaks to the range of experiences, political views, decisions, and solutions that Blacks put forth to make sense of and ensure their safety. Because their politics emerged from the community's diverse network of institutions, leadership styles, and ideologies, Blacks held multiple, often conflicting views about how to bring about safety. In the late 1960s and early 1970s, New York City was in the middle of a drug crisis *and* a police crisis, and Black New Yorkers were often at the center of these. Undoubtedly, there were Harlemites who identified with Fortner's "Black silent majority," but it is unlikely they constituted the "majority" position on punishment. Black New Yorkers, especially those serving as public officials and in law enforcement, had rarely been "silent" about their support for anti-crime policies.

As Harlemites complained about widespread drug abuse and drug-related crimes, Congressman Charles Rangel and others spotlighted how corruption within the New York City Police Department (NYPD) worsened the drug crisis. Rangel's criticism overlapped with public hearings of the Commission to Investigate Alleged Police Corruption. In the spring of 1970, Mayor John Lindsay formed the commission, chaired by Whitman Knapp, former district attorney and later judge for the United States District Court for the Southern District of New York. The hearings unearthed widespread police corruption in Harlem—to no surprise to the city's Black community. When Knapp submitted the report to Lindsay in late December 1972, police graft remained on the mind of Harlemites as they considered the governor's drug policy throughout 1973. Ubiquitous cases of police brutality, particularly the police killing of Black youth and Black police officers, exacerbated the problem of police corruption and the drug crisis.

The Guardians Association—a Black police organization established in the late 1940s and led by Sergeant Howard Sheffey—and other Black police associations mobilized on behalf of the Black community.

By September, when the law took effect, and as more cases of police brutality hit the front pages of newspapers, the Black community remained divided about the governor's drug laws. There was no consensus in 1973 or thereafter. Like all citizens, Black New Yorkers rightfully expected and demanded the protection of the criminal legal system. But for many Blacks, supporting punishment was neither controversial nor the same as supporting the governor's new drug laws, and they said so, repetitively. Thus, instead of signaling the insignificance of race, Black politics of safety articulated an anti-racism that endeavored to transform a criminal legal system enduringly committed not to protect them.

"Dope State, a Population of Sedated Addicts"

By the spring of 1973, when Rockefeller signed his notorious drug bill into law, Reverend Oberia Dempsey had been involved in local politics for about twenty years. Born in Paris, Texas, he fought for his country in the Second World War and upon return attended Brooklyn College.[5] Before he became a grassroots leader in 1962, Dempsey had served at the historic Abyssinia Church in Harlem under Adam Clayton Powell Jr. and in Brooklyn's Mt. Lebanon Baptist Church.[6] Dempsey diagnosed the drug crisis in Harlem and across the nation as a problem of drug abuse, crime, and public policy. Known for his aggressive approach to addressing the drug crisis, he charged that drugs and dope pushers were "killing a generation of young Americans." Dempsey was a soldier in a drug war battling dangerous criminals committed to making money by any means necessary. He infamously brought the Bible and a gun, a .32 caliber, hitched to his belt holster, to church. Like other Black Christian ministers before him in the city and across the nation involved in race work, Dempsey viewed the streets as his battlefield, but instead of a nonviolent march, he promised to target the "fabulous late-model cars" that the drug pushers drove.[7] He declared, "In every block on every street, it makes no difference if it is Wall St., Park Avenue, Greenwich Village or Harlem, we will brand the dope pushers for what they are, killers, the ruination of a generation." He promised to rid Harlem of drug dealers, particularly the nondrug users, announcing, "As we get proof of the pushers ... we the people will put up large signs on street poles, hallways, and on homes identifying these peddlers of a product which can only destroy."[8]

Dempsey also directed his criticism toward federal and state government and supported foreign policy that prevent the drugs from entering the country. He urged the Nixon administration to use the Federal Bureau of Investigation, as well as other relevant federal agencies, to put a stop to the flow of drugs stealing into the country. As he noted in May 1970, "I'm all for rehabilitation programs, ... but before we mop up the floor, we must stop the leak."[9] In the spring of 1970, Dempsey complained that Rockefeller's antidrug policy was a "dismal failure." He offered to give the governor a tour of Harlem so Rockefeller could see the streets as he saw them but also to highlight that the governor's "programs ha[d] not in any way scratched the surface of the problems of narcotics and environment." According to Dempsey, the governor's policy was creating a "dope state, a population of sedated addicts who are being maintained on methadone, perhaps forever and ever."[10] Dempsey's criticism of state and federal policy led him to Washington, DC.

In the spring of 1970, Dempsey and the National Concerned Citizens against Narcotics joined the Parents' Foundation against Drug Abuse and announced a march on Washington, DC, against drug abuse and narcotics. On April 10, approximately 2,000 people represented by organizations from New England and the New York metropolitan area marched past the Capitol and the Supreme Court Buildings. At the rally at the National Mall, they demanded a federal narcotics hospital in the metropolitan area and economic sanctions against narcotic-producing nations. Speakers included representatives from the National Concerned Citizens against Narcotics, the Parents' Foundation against Drug Abuse, and Mothers against Drugs; Reverend Jerry Moore, the principal organizer of the march; and representatives from the Nixon administration, including James Farmer, assistant to the treasurer; Robert Finch of the Health, Education, and Welfare Department; and presidential aid Robert Brown. Brown stated that "President Nixon wants me to inform you that we are very much concerned with the drug problem in this country.... We are here to wage an intensive war on narcotics. The president intends to do just that and we intend to do it with your help."[11]

"Any Kid on a Ghetto Street Could Have Issued Such a Statement"

While Dempsey was a central figure in Harlem fighting drug addiction and demanding a more aggressive police presence and punitive legislation, his approach to punishment was not representative of Harlem's politics of safety. Harlem congressman Charles Rangel fought against drugs from his offices in Harlem and Washington, DC. Like Dempsey, Rangel believed that the federal government needed to stop the flow of drugs at their source. In February 1971, Rangel proposed legislation that would sever military and economic aid to nations unwilling to end the illegal production of opium.[12] In mid-July, he testified before the Senate Special Subcommittee on Alcoholism and Narcotics and called for a joint federal, state, and local attack on the illegal importation of heroin.[13] Later that month, on the steps of the Capitol, Dempsey presented Rangel with petitions requesting that the federal government designate drug abuse the nation's number one domestic priority and commit resources to the crisis.[14] By 1972, because of the inactivity of the Nixon administration and the nation's refusal to cut off aid to opium-producing nations, the congressman described the State Department as a "co-conspirator" with heroin importers. At a press conference, after the *Pittsburgh Courier*'s Sixth Annual Top Hat Award Dinner, Rangel explained that the Congressional Black Caucus "consider[ed] [narcotics] a threat to our national security." Months later, he claimed that the Nixon administration and the Central Intelligence Agency had been keeping secrets from the American public about US economic support of heroin-producing countries. He complained, "Congress and the American people are being kept in the dark while our government pours billions of dollars in foreign aid into these corrupt drug-trafficking Southeast Asian dictatorships." He concluded, "How can we intelligently legislate and deal with this menace unless we have all the facts?"[15]

Rangel also directed his antidrug politics toward law enforcement. While he supported more law enforcement in Harlem and the punishment of nonaddict drug sellers, he complained that police corruption exacerbated the drug crisis in Harlem. At a press conference in early February 1971, Rangel disclosed police involvement in the policy numbers operation and the narcotics traffic in Harlem and took reporters on a walking tour of Harlem identifying neighborhood-known narcotics trading spots. Harlem residents' letters and calls corroborated Rangel's contention. Mrs. Virginia Bell, Rangel's Harlem office manager, was overwhelmed with calls and letters from the community supporting the congressman. According to Bell, while some Harlemites witnessed police participation in the drug trade, others declared that "there had been a complete lack of response by the police when a community drive was launched to clean up neighborhoods of graft and corruption."[16] Other Black leaders supported the congressman's stand against police corruption, including Percy Sutton, Manhattan borough president; Assemblymen Hulan Jack, Mark Southall, and George Miller; both assemblymen and members of the Harlem Ministerial Interfaith Association; Charles Kenyatta, former bodyguard to Malcolm X and antidrug activist; and Captain Winston Clark of the New York Department of Correction.

Beyond the accounts of Harlem eyewitnesses, Rangel's allegations were corroborated by the Knapp Commission.[17] The *New York Amsterdam News* kept Harlemites abreast of the commission's findings. Commenting on the commission's interim report in July 1971 that found "a substantial number" of police officers involved in corruption activity, the *New York Amsterdam News* stated that "any kid on a ghetto street could have issued such a statement."[18] In November 1971, the Black weekly believed that the commission should be made a permanent body "with many more Blacks and Puerto Ricans as members" and asserted "that the findings of the Commission have created sufficient public awareness to once again demand . . . the creation of a strong civilian review process independent of the police departments."[19] The problem of police corruption threatened the safety of Harlemites and Black neighborhoods across the city. The police held them hostage to a criminal legal system that brought crime rather than prevented it. Among Blacks, reported Les Matthews for the *New York Amsterdam News*, there was little optimism that the commission's findings would effect any change. One Black store owner in the Bronx stated that "a couple [police officers] retired but not one went to jail. I doubt if there will be any conviction." The Black weekly acknowledged that there were many police officers who were "a credit to the department" but noted police graft, drunkenness, and reckless cursing in the streets sullied the NYPD's reputation and left Harlemites unsafe.[20]

Rangel also took antidrug politics to the Rockefeller administration. At the State Commission of Investigation in April 1971, he testified that Harlemites "view the police force as an occupation army which prowls the streets with a badge and a gun, but never does anything to really help them." Like the Black weekly, the congressman believed that "most of New York's 30,000-man police force [are] honest," but "an unusually high percentage of police assigned to Harlem were corrupt." Police corruption not only precluded cops from protecting citizens but also criminalized those citizens and an entire community. As Rangel noted, "The people of Harlem can't go to the police when they witness a [drug] sale because they are treated like the criminal."[21] The community's lack of trust in the police, combined with the threat of police violence, pushed Rangel to offer his constituency a narcotics line to report not only criminal activity but also police misconduct. Rangel's campaign continued throughout 1972, and in late June he noted, "To [e]nsure that the police end their corruption, it is now essential that residents of the community vigilantly keep watch over police patrols in their neighborhoods to make sure they're doing their job."[22]

"To Make the Police Service More Compatible to the Black Community"

The problems around the drug crisis and police corruption overlapped with Black New Yorkers' long-held view of the NYPD as "an occupation army." This was no hyperbole. In March 1964, Governor Rockefeller signed two bills—known as "stop and frisk" and "no-knock"—into law that targeted Black and Puerto Rican neighborhoods. The expansion of police discretion set the stage for the so-called Little Fruit Stand Riot on April 17, 1964, the arrest of several Black and Puerto Rican men and boys, and the charge of murder and subsequent trial of six Black boys, known as the Harlem Six. In mid-July, Harlem exploded after a white off-duty policeman, Lieutenant Thomas Gilligan, fatally shot James Powell, a fifteen-year-old. In the wake of the assassination of Martin Luther King Jr. in April 1968 came the surveillance, raids, subsequent arrests on April 2, 1969, and imprisonment and trial of twenty-one members of the city's Black Panther Party, known as the New York Panther 21. The overlap of the Harlem Six, the defanging of the Civilian Complaint Review Board, and New York Panther 21 trials, as well as the Black community's distrust and disregard for the district attorney, cast a shadow on the NYPD and the criminal legal system. These local stories of racial injustice paralleled similar stories across the nation, especially the police murder of Fred Hampton, the charismatic leader of the Illinois Black Panther Party, on December 4, 1969.[23]

With clamor for law and order from the Nixon administration and rising crime rates, police departments across the country, with the support of the Law Enforcement Assistance Administration, expanded their foot patrols and tactical decoy squads. The NYPD's was extensive. In the NYPD 1969 annual report, Police Commissioner Howard R. Leary wrote that it was an "epoch-making year . . . [with] increased manpower and equipment." The augmented manpower included a tactical patrol force in plainclothes, a community relations motor patrol, and several others. Another patrol created to cater to Blacks and Puerto Ricans was the Preventive Enforcement Patrol, which focused on reducing "street crime with major emphasis on narcotics law enforcement."[24] In 1970, Police Commissioner Patrick Murphy introduced the Citywide Anticrime Section, a 100-man volunteer force of armed plainclothes officers, which focused on increasing arrests. By 1972, the Anticrime Section had doubled in size. The NYPD formed these foot patrols to provide "community-oriented" policing but also to place these neighborhoods under surveillance with patrols ready to infiltrate. Thus, the expansion of police discretion and patrols in the mid-1960s and early 1970s not only aided police graft but also made Blacks feel like they were living in a police state.[25]

Black police organizations, long committed to fighting crime and cultivating better police-community relations, thrust themselves into the battle against police violence. In New York City, police sergeant Howard Sheffey, leader of the Guardians Association and chairman of the National Council of Police Societies (NCOPS), was a central figure in this effort. In November 1970, NCOPS, a New York–based council of twenty-two predominantly Black police associations, traveled around the country evaluating the police departments of major cities. Sheffey and Alphonso Deal, a Philadelphia policeman, assessed Pittsburgh's police department and its relationship with the Black community and found it wanting.[26] During the summer, NCOPS held a conference in Philadelphia. At the four-day meeting that began on June 9, police organizations mainly from the Northeast assembled in the city of Brotherly Love and put forth a political agenda. The attendees heard speeches from an array of Black leaders, including Newark's mayor Kenneth Gibson, federal judge Leon Higginbotham of the US District Court, and Minister Louis Farrakhan. Influenced by the testimonies of undercover agents at the New York Panther 21 trial, members of NCOPS stated that they would no longer support a Black police officer working as a spy or an undercover cop in "politically-oriented" cases unless unlawful activities occurred. NCOPS pledged to take action against any police officer who abused any citizen and supported a civilian review board to "offset the rubber stamp punishments now being carried out." Mayor Gibson complained about police corruption in his city and warned against any involvement in graft. Minister Farrakhan chastised Black police officers for being aggressive against their community to "stay in the favor of the white establishment."[27]

More than a month later, the *New York Amsterdam News* began a series called "The Black Policeman and the Black Community," featuring several guest columnists, including Howard Sheffey; Leonard Weir of the Afro-American Police Association in New York City; Derek Ackeridge, chairman of the Bronze Shields in Newark; Gerald Fraser of the *New York Times*; and William Strickland of the Institute of the Black World in Atlanta.[28] Sheffey contended that it was the responsibility of Black policemen "in [their] very Blackness to strive to make the police service more compatible to the Black community" and discussed the critical work that the Preventive Enforcement Patrol Squad had been doing in the community but noted the "subtle effort by some department members to stifle and block any effectiveness they may have with the Black and Hispanic community." Newark's Ackeridge advocated for the Black policeman as a Black nationalist, while Strickland pushed for Blacks as police commissioners in majority-Black cities. These articulations regarding the roles of Black policemen represented the ideological spectrum of Black police organizations influenced by Black Power politics. All spoke of the roles of the "Black policeman" in either open or veiled nationalist language, even as they pushed for inclusion and reform.[29]

Conversations about the roles of Black cops and community politics naturally moved to the pressing issue of police violence. In the late winter of 1970 into the spring of 1971, David J. Billings III, chairman of the New York City Council against Poverty, complained about police harassment and violence toward himself and his employees at the council. This was followed in April 1971 by the brutal beating of David Burston Jr. on the street, while under arrest in the squad car, and later in the police station in Brooklyn. In mid-May, police in Bedford-Stuyvesant fatally shot Rudy Simms in the back, and in late July the grand jury chose not to indict the white police officers involved.[30] Black New Yorkers read about, experienced, and witnessed other cases of police brutality throughout the year. Thus, as Black cops attempted to bring about greater comity between the Black community and the NYPD, multiples cases of police abuse and news of police corruption and even the killing of police reinforced the combustible relationship between the police and the Black community.

Complaints about police brutality overlapped with the killing of two police officers, Waverly Jones, who was Black, and Joseph Piagentini, white, on May 21 in Harlem. On their way back to their patrol car after answering a call from a sick woman at 159th Street and Harlem River Drive, Jones and Piagentini were shot in the back. Edward Kiernan, the president of the Patrolmen's Benevolent Association, instigated violence, telling his men to "shoot to kill" because "'revolutionaries' had declared war on the Police Department."[31] On May 26, Patrolman Harry Nelson of the Transit Police, Lenny Wier of the Afro-American Policemen, and Sergeant Howard Sheffey of the Guardians led a rally at 116th and Lenox Avenue to protest the shooting of the officers. Their joint statement read, "While we deplore the recent injuries and deaths to members of the force, we as policemen call all police officers to use the judgement and discretion of office which is service to the community." The statement directed a veiled criticism at Kiernan: "We also take to task the use of inflammatory statements which single out individuals or groups for public censure without proper legal sanctions." Though the responses of Harlem's Black leadership varied, they collectively echoed the Black police organizations' statement. While all condemned the killings, others complained about the absence of police protection and the irresponsibility of the NYPD. Percy Sutton, Manhattan borough president, described the killings as "senseless." Reverend Dempsey explained that there had been a "complete breakdown of law enforcement in the Harlem area," and because of that, Harlemites had lost respect for the police.[32]

Harlem's Black leadership directed blame at Kiernan. William H. Johnson Jr., president emeritus of the Guardians and president of the Federation of Negro Civil Service Organizations, asserted, "What no one is admitting is that the New York City Police Department does not come into court with clean hands. In this case 'court' is Harlem and like ghettos." While "no decent, honest hardworking citizen wants to see policemen shot down, . . . by the same token he does not want to see graft freely taken, prostitutes allowed to work, [and] dope freely peddled."[33] As Black leaders condemned the violence, they articulated the dilemma that Black Gotham had long faced regarding the safety of their communities: that regardless of their countless demands for police protection, police presence in Black neighborhoods was often a deadly brew of inaction, corruption, and aggression. This killing of police officers, including a white police officer shooting a Black veteran officer, further exposed and exacerbated this dilemma.

In late January 1972, a pair of cops, Patrolmen Gregory Foster, Black, and Rocco Laurie, white, partners who had served together in Vietnam, were fatally shot in the back while on patrol in the East Village. Allegedly three Black men shot the officers as they left the Shrimp Boat luncheonette after inquiring inside about an illegally parked car. Edward Kiernan, the Patrolmen's Benevolent Association president, lambasted Mayor Lindsay for failing to stop the "slaughter" of cops and called for mandatory death sentences for the culprits.[34] On April 3, 1972, off-duty white patrolman Robert Kenny, twenty-two years old, fatally shot nineteen-year veteran Detective William Capers, a fifty-one-year-old African American, in Jamaica, Queens. Capers and his partner, Detective Raymond Godley, assigned to the Sixteenth Division Burglary Squad, had followed three young men carrying shopping bags—Leotis Troutman, twenty-two; Bruce Underdoe, seventeen; and Thomas Scott, twenty-two—to a car and asked the driver for his identification. They found a .25-caliber gun in the car and managed to handcuff Underdoe and Scott, but Troutman escaped. Capers ran after him and fired a warning shot into the air. Nearby, Kenny heard the shot and hurried to the scene, where he found Capers with his gun kneeling over Troutman. While the white press reported the story as a mistake, as Chief of Detectives Albert Seedman called it, Les Matthews of the *New York Amsterdam News* described the incident as a pattern of white police officers killing and beating Black ones.[35] Queens' Black community and the Capers family blamed racism. Sergeant Sheffey complained that Capers's death was the result of a "'shoot-first-and-ask-questions-later' philosophy" that had been advocated by Kiernan.[36] The late detective's stepsister, Mrs. Joy Capers, declared, "We should make it clear this was nothing but a case of murder." At a meeting at the Baisley Daycare Center, Mrs. Capers doubted that the shooting was a mistake. She charged that Kiernan "is running around telling these cops to shoot to kill, and that's what this young cop did." As the *New York Amsterdam News* reported, she believed that Kenny "wouldn't have shot if Capers had been white."[37] Despite this protest, the Queens grand jury absolved Kenny.[38]

By the fall of 1972 and throughout 1973, as Governor Rockefeller's drug policy shifted and transitioned into state law, the city's police department was in the middle of a crisis. And because law enforcement was so critical to the drug crisis, Black New Yorkers were deeply invested in the efficacy and fairness of law enforcement.

"Would Put Our Youths in Jail for Life"

In early January 1973, when Governor Rockefeller gave his annual State of the State speech and introduced his new drug policy, he received a mixed response from the Black community.[39] On January 22 in Albany, Rockefeller held a press conference on the drug policy and introduced the reporters and audience to several "Harlem leaders," including Dempsey; Glester Hinds, founder of the People's Civic and Welfare Association in Harlem; Dr. George W. McMurray, pastor of the Mother African Methodist Episcopal Church; Reverend Earl B. Moore of St. Paul Baptist Church in Harlem; and Dr. Robert W. Baird, founder of the Haven Clinic for addicts in Harlem, all of whom supported the governor's harsh life sentences mandate. According to the *New York Times*, they endorsed the bill to protect the Black community from "blood-thirsty, money-hungry, death-dealing criminals."[40]

The *Daily News* described Dempsey as "the most eloquent, forceful and convincing case for the governor's recommended legislation." Dempsey focused on the safety of the "nonaddict" and averred that "it's time to start thinking about the people who are victims of these crimes by addicts . . . , time to worry about our children before they are reached by the dope pusher, time to stop listening to bleeding hearts." From Dempsey's perspective, all of Harlem's and Black New Yorkers' problems stemmed from drug abuse and the drug sellers, and because of the coddling of liberals, the "hard drug non-addict pushers" had transformed Harlem schools and housing projects into jungles. Dempsey charged, "We must pass this legislation now, today. We should have passed it yesterday. If we don't do it today, there will be no tomorrow."[41] In February, Vincent Baker, president of Citizens Mobilization against Crime, complained, like Dempsey, that the innocent and vulnerable needed protection. According to the former NAACP leader, "The hooded terrorists of Mississippi are no more to be feared than the terrorists of Harlem. A hoodlum has neither race, color, creed or national origin."[42]

Black New Yorkers had long debated and offered solutions for the city's drug crisis. Dempsey's and Baker's aim to protect victims of the drug crisis echoed the sentiments of Black New Yorkers and their leaders across the political spectrum. Black New Yorkers demanded safety, and for some, Rockefeller's life sentence mandate was a legitimate solution. But for others, especially those concerned about the welfare of the addicts but also about the targeting of Black and Brown youth, the governor's bills appeared excessive. From the very beginning, the *New York Amsterdam News* was critical of the bill. In an editorial from mid-January, "Rockefeller and Narcotics," the Black weekly summarized the bill's sentencing guidelines. While admitting that government action was "long overdue," the *New York Amsterdam News* believed the bill was excessively harsh and unnecessarily indiscriminating and stated that distinctions should be made between the youthful offender and the adult, the addict and the "nonaddict pusher," and "hard drugs" and "soft drugs," among others.[43]

During the spring, the Black weekly held a forum sponsored by radio station WLIB. James Allen, the director of the Addicts Rehabilitation Center, was concerned about how prisons might harden Black youth and pushed for great community responsibility in creating a society where citizens would not purchase stolen goods. William Johnson, coordinator of the NYPD's Community Affairs Division Narcotics Program, encouraged community members not to enable unlawful behavior and endorsed the coordination of civic, religious, and community institutions with the NYPD to support drug addicts. Other Black leaders questioned the use of the criminal legal system as an effective solution to the problem. Leroy Clarke, law professor at New York University, stated that he was not optimistic about law enforcement. He asserted, "I think his [Rockefeller's] proposal is an abuse of the Black community." Rockefeller "would put our youths in jail for life, since the people policemen arrest when they want to pretend they're doing something about the problem are Blacks and Puerto Ricans." Similarly, Diane Lacey, who coordinated the National Conference on Drug Abuse, questioned the policy side of the drug crisis, especially its lack of Black involvement.[44] Jay Swift, commissioner of the Addiction Services Agency, brought up the connection between assault and drug-addict-related crimes, a connection that Dempsey, Baker, and others made as a rationale to support the governor's bill. Swift noted that property crimes by addicts had declined during 1972 and lamented the governor's decision to prioritize punishment by "increase[ing] funds for more courts, detention centers and jails."⁴⁵

At the *New York Amsterdam News*–WLIB forum in March, Congressman Rangel suggested an alternative, to mandate life sentences of drug sellers convicted twice, which he had proposed in the past as a member of the Assembly of New York State. This approach offered the drug seller, especially the "addict pusher," the opportunity to rehabilitate. As he noted, "With 300,00 addicts in New York City alone, it would be a tragic waste of Black and Hispanic youth to give up on them completely."⁴⁶ Black New Yorkers framed safety not only through punishment but also through anti-racism and understood that they had to operate in a racist, corrupt legal system that had ineffectively rendered them justice. For many Black leaders, such as Rangel and Lacey, this meant opening up law enforcement and the criminal legal system in general to African Americans and Puerto Ricans at all governmental levels. The Black community endorsed punishment, but there was no easy consensus that the majority of Black New Yorkers supported the Rockefeller drug laws; there *was* a consensus that they distrusted law enforcement and believed that it required reform from the inside. In January 1973, Rangel complained that Blacks had been excluded from federal agencies responsible for drug abuse policy and referenced specifically the paucity of Blacks in the Special Action Office for Drug Abuse Prevention and in the Division of Narcotic Addiction and Drug Abuse of the National Institute of Mental Health. As he lamented, "Long before it became fashionable to speak of the heroin epidemic in the national media, minority communities knew the ravages of heroin addiction and understood the nature of its menace." Indeed, they understood and offered multiple solutions, but Rockefeller chose the "toughest anti-drug problem in the nation" because it fit his political agenda and ambitions for the presidency.⁴⁷

"Governor Rockefeller Should Declare a 'War on Corruption'"

A week or so before Rockefeller introduced his new drug policy and Dempsey and others began endorsing it, Judge Whitman Knapp submitted the full commission's report to Mayor Lindsay in late December 1972. Since the Knapp Commission and especially the hearings began, the *New York Amsterdam News* had reported on the commission's findings, and a year later the Black weekly condemned police corruption and noted that none of the commission's findings were new. In late February 1972, Michael Keating admitted, "Listening day after day to that testimony, . . . I often felt angry, not anger at the existence of dishonesty, but anger at the massive hypocrisy that's been laid on us over the last five years or so during all that debate about law and order and support your local police."[48] In mid-August, the Black weekly agreed with the Knapp Commission, which charged that "Governor Rockefeller should declare a 'war on corruption' to clean up the New York City justice system—police, prosecutors and judges."[49] Thus, as Harlemites, public officials, and community leaders criticized Rockefeller's drug laws for their severity, Black New Yorkers continued to pay close attention to the commission's findings, especially as they related to crime in Harlem. As reported in the press, dismissed Black patrolman and former member of the Preventive Enforcement Patrol Waverly Logan testified before the Knapp Commission that theft and the confiscation of money and drugs for police officers in Harlem were normal. According to Logan, "When you're new, you turn in all the money. But when you're working on the job awhile, you turn in no money." According to Logan, among police officers in the narcotics division, theft from drug dealers was considered "clean." Since the drug dealer was going to jail, he did not need any money and "didn't deserve no rights since he was selling narcotics."[50]

Keating's commentary on the hypocrisy of "law and order," especially around the support of the police, rang true not only in the area of police corruption. On January 27, 1973, Patrolman Robert Milano shot and killed a Black teenager, Rita Lloyd, sixteen years old, in Canarsie, Brooklyn. Milano and his partner, Edward Roach, witnessed a group of girls appearing to fight. The girls ran, but Denise Bethel, Lloyd's friend, according to the police, pointed a sawed-off shotgun at Milano's head, and the patrolman "ducked, drew his revolver and fired two shots." Both girls ran—Bethel fled around the corner and was arrested, and Lloyd hurried home, where she collapsed. Her parents called the police and an ambulance, but she died in Kings County Hospital from a bullet wound in her chest.[51] The Survival Action Committee, supporting the Lloyd family, released a statement questioning the facts of the incident and lamented that Rita was a victim of the "historically callous police force."[52] Then, on March 5, two patrolmen fatally shot Irving Wright, an off-duty Black police officer who was trying to apprehend Charles Small, who had just robbed a store at gunpoint. According to the police, the officers commanded Wright to drop his gun, but he "accidentally discharged" his gun in their direction and they shot him. The deceased was the brother of Assemblyman Samuel D. Wright; one Wright brother was a Supreme Court officer and two were members of the NYPD.[53] Police brutality that spring was unceasing.

On April 28, around five o'clock in the morning, Edward Armstead, a mechanic, and his son, Clifford Glover, walked to work. That morning, plainclothes patrolman Thomas Shea, a white officer with a record of gun mishaps, shot the ten-year-old in the back, alleging that he fired the gun in self-defense after Glover shot at him and tossed the gun to Armstead.[54] The Queens district attorney's office charged Shea with murder. On April 30, Blacks and some whites from across the city gathered with Blacks in Queens to protest the shooting of Glover. Young and old joined picket lines with some carrying placards that read "Books not Bullets!," "Stop the Racist Genocide," and "Stop Trigger Happy Cops' War Against The Poor and Working People!" As tensions arose and emotions boiled, violence erupted later in the evening and the next day. On May 1, Roy Wilkins, the executive director of the National Association for the Advancement of Colored People, called the killing of Glover "a case of police murder." To ease the tensions that evening, Sergeant Howard Sheffey sent three dozen members of the Guardians to South Jamaica to operate as a buffer between the Black community and "the increasingly edgy white cops" and help keep them "from losing perspective."[55]

Conclusion

On May 8, a week after the uprising in Queens and despite protests from Mayor Lindsay, New York City brass, the Conservative Party, and the majority of Black public officials and many others, Governor Rockefeller signed into law his signature and most controversial legislation—what he proudly called "the toughest anti-drug program in the nation."[56] In its August 11 editorial, "A Warning," the Black weekly asserted, "The *Amsterdam News*, opposed, but could not prevent, the passage of Governor Rockefeller's stringent new drug law which takes effect September 1." In unveiled language, the newspaper made clear the target of the law's sentencing guidelines: "This law is drastic and it is going to be enforced by the state—make no mistake about that. And it is going to hit heavily among Black and Puerto Ricans—make no mistake about that."[57] The Black weekly interviewed drug users in Harlem about their opinions on the new law. In lucid language, they all distinguished themselves from drug sellers, asserted that the laws were harsh, and advocated for their humanity. Eddie David lamented, "Addicts are sick people and should be treated like sick people." Others brought up police corruption and the hypocrisy of the criminal legal system. Hezekiah Felton believed that the law was unfair and recalled that he read about police stealing millions of dollars and selling drugs on the street. He advanced, "I am willing to bet that those same bums will come around to lock you up regardless if they find drugs on you or not." James Shepard directed his criticism at the governor, charging, "Tell me, what did Rockefeller do about the crooked cop who sell you drugs and then come out and lock you up after putting drugs in your pocket?"⁵⁸

Shepard's criticism of the governor, as well as the reportage by *New York Amsterdam News*, reflected the range of views that Black New Yorkers held about the antidrug laws and the criminal legal system. Harlemites were well aware of the connections between police graft and the drug crisis and questioned the integrity of Rockefeller, who knew the depths of police corruption in the city. The staff of the *New York Amsterdam News* knew this, too. By interviewing Black drug users, the Black weekly gave voice to the most vulnerable, communicating to its readership that drug addiction did not disqualify them from the community. No one could challenge the newspaper's support for anti-crime policies, and yet it vociferously criticized police violence and opposed Rockefeller's drug policy. This was uncontroversial. The "Black silent majority" did exist in Harlem, but it was not representative of the Black community or of Blacks supportive of punishment. Racism mattered—in the streets, in the political arena, and in the police department. Harlemites' demands for safety were only half heard by Rockefeller, who had set his sights on the White House.

Throughout 1973 and 1974, Black police organizations continued to fight crime and racism in law enforcement. In December 1973, John White, another Black cop, would fall victim to a white police officer. Sergeant Sheffey promised action: "We plan to take drastic action to get our point across. We will take our case to the people. We will engage in massive and continuous picketing and strategic demonstrations at key places by members, families, communities, and sympathizers."⁵⁹ For Sheffey, this was no longer a local matter. He demanded an audience with Rockefeller. While he heard Reverend Dempsey's pleas for punitive laws, Rockefeller was conspicuously silent regarding the killing of Black citizens and Black cops. Six months later the jury of the state supreme court acquitted Thomas Shea, and two years later, while now Vice President Rockefeller entertained guests at Number One Observatory Circle, Congressman Rangel was still fighting police corruption in Harlem.⁶⁰

Notes

1. For some recent scholarship on the nexus between Black protest and the making of the carceral state, see Vesla M. Weaver, "Frontlash: Race and the Development of Punitive Culture," *Studies in American Political Development* 21 (Fall 2007): 230–56; Elizabeth Hinton, *From the War on Poverty to the War on Crime: The Making of Mass Incarceration in America* (Cambridge, MA: Harvard University Press, 2016); Julilly Kohler-Hausmann, *Getting Tough: Welfare and Imprisonment in 1970s America* (Princeton: Princeton University Press, 2017); Carl Suddler, *Presumed Criminal:*

Black Youth and the Justice System in Postwar New York (New York: New York University Press, 2019); and Michael Fortner, *Black Silent Majority: The Rockefeller Drug Laws and the Politics of Punishment* (Cambridge, MA: Harvard University Press, 2015), 23, 9.

2. Noel K. Wolfe, a historian, has also contributed to this scholarship; see "Battling Crack: A Study of the Northwest Bronx Community and the Clergy's Coalition Tactics," *Journal of Urban History* 43, no. 1 (January 2017): 18–32. For a nuanced appraisal of the drug crime crisis and the Black community's response by a historian, see Donna Murch, "Crack in Los Angeles: Crisis, Militarization, and Black Response to the Late Twentieth-Century War on Drugs," *Journal of American History* 102, no. 1 (June 2015): 162–73. Murch frames the Black response within the context of police violence but also discusses how Blacks supported both punitive politics and what she calls an "anti-drug war sentiment" that explained the drug crisis in socioeconomic and political terms related to Reagan era politics.
3. Jessica Neptune, "Harshest in the Nation: The Rockefeller Drug Laws and the Widening Embrace of Punitive Politics," *Social History of Alcohol and Drugs* 23, no. 2 (Summer 2012): 175; Kohler-Hausmann, *Getting Tough*, 56; James Forman Jr., *Locking Up Our Own: Crime and Punishment in Black America* (New York: Farrar, Straus and Giroux, 2017), 11–12.
4. For more on "politics of safety," see Shannon King, *The Politics of Safety: The Black Struggle for Police Accountability in La Guardia's New York* (Chapel Hill: University of North Carolina Press, 2024).
5. Alfred E. Clark, "Rev. Oberia Dempsey Is Dead," *New York Times*, October 4, 1982, D13.
6. Fortner, *Black Silent Majority*, 98.
7. Edward Benes, "Cleric Bares Plans to Fight Dope Pushers," *New York Daily News*, June 11, 1970, 236.
8. Edward Benes, "Gun-Toting Minister Vows to Unmask Dope Pushers," *New York Daily News*, March 27, 1970, 5.
9. Edward Benes, "Drug-Related Deaths Total 11 for Weekend," *New York Daily News*, May 5, 1970, 194.
10. Edward Benes, "Harlem Pastor Derides Rocky's Drive on Dope," *New York Daily News*, April 9, 1970, 251.
11. "Parents' Drug Unit Scolds TV 'Silence' on Washington March," *Paterson (NJ) News*, April 15, 1970, 47.
12. "Rangel Moves Fight on Heroin," *New York Amsterdam News*, February 20, 1971, 2.
13. "Cong. Rangel Seeks All-Out Drug Battle," *New York Amsterdam News*, July 17, 1971, A7.
14. "Rangel Receives Signatures vs. Dope: Dope fighters," *New York Amsterdam News*, August 21, 1971, C12.
15. "Rangel Moves Fight on Heroin," 2; "Rangel Blasts Nixon," *New York Amsterdam News*, July 22, 1972, B4.
16. "Community Backs Rangel on Drugs," *New York Amsterdam News*, February 13, 1971, 1.
17. Eric C. Schneider, *Smack: Heroin and the American City* (Philadelphia: University of Pennsylvania Press, 2008), 106–14.

18. "Interim Report," *New York Amsterdam News*, July 10, 1971, A6.
19. "Knapp Attackers," *New York Amsterdam News*, November 6, 1971, A6.
20. Les Matthews, "Black Areas on Knapp Action: Pay Your Money and Take a Pick," *New York Amsterdam News*, November 6, 1971, C15.
21. "Rangel Testifies on Dope in Harlem," *New York Amsterdam News*, April 17, 1971, 43.
22. Charles B. Rangel, "Call Free Heroin Clinics an Absurd Suggestion," *New York Amsterdam News*, June 24, 1972, A5.
23. For "stop and frisk" and "no-knock" laws, the "Little Fruit Stand Riot," and the Harlem Six, see Suddler, *Presumed Criminal*, 124–50. For New York Panther 21, see déqui kioni-sadiki and Matt Meyer, *Look For Me in the Whirlwind: From the Panther 21 to 21st-Century Revolutions* (Oakland, CA: PM Press, 2017). For the Civilian Complaint Review Board, see Christopher Hayes, *The Harlem Uprising: Segregation and Inequality in Postwar New York City* (New York: Columbia University Press, 2021), 219–40; and Jakobi Williams, *From the Bullet to the Ballot: The Illinois Chapter of the Black Panther Party and Racial Coalition Politics in Chicago* (Chapel Hill: University North Carolina Press, 2015). For Fred Hampton, see Floyd McKissick, "Panthers—Another Comment: From a Black Point of View," *New York Amsterdam News*, January 10, 1970, 5; Whitney M. Young Jr., "The Panthers and the People: To Be Equal," *New York Amsterdam News*, January 10, 1970, 4; and Leroy Clark, "District Attorney Hogan: A Man Out of Step with His Time," *New York Amsterdam News*, May 19, 1973, A5.
24. Howard R. Leary, *Annual Report* (Police Department, City of New York, 1970), 5–7.
25. Hinton, *From the War on Poverty to the War on Crime*, 188–91.
26. "National Police Group Supports Guardians' Drive," *New Pittsburgh Courier*, November 14, 1970, 1.
27. Les Matthews, "Black Cops Vow Changes," *New York Amsterdam News*, June 19, 1971, 1.
28. "The Black Policeman and the Black Community," *New York Amsterdam News*, July 31, 1971, A1.
29. Howard L. Sheffey, "The Black Officer: Inform, Assist"; Derek T. Ackeridge, "The Policeman: A Black Nationalist"; and William Strickland, "Control Your Local Police," all in *New York Amsterdam News*, July 31, 1971, A-7.
30. "Poverty Unit Accuses Cops," *New York Amsterdam News*, November 14, 1970, 1; David J. Billings III and Major R. Owens, "CAP vs NYC Police," *New York Amsterdam News*, February 20, 1971, 14; "Billings, Flowers Case before Review Board," *New York Amsterdam News*, May 15, 1971, 25; Dick Edwards, "Lame Youth Beaten; Jailed on Pitkin Ave.," *New York Amsterdam News*, April 17, 1971, 23; "CORE Demands Report on Killing by White Cop," *New York Amsterdam News*, July 24, 1971, B13.
31. "2 Cops Die in Harlem Ambush," *New York Daily News*, May 22, 1971, 3.
32. "Cop Killings Hurt: What They're Saying about It," *New York Amsterdam News*, May 29, 1971, 1.
33. "Cop Killings Hurt," 43.
34. "Kiernan Asks Sure Death for Killers of Police," *New York Daily News*, January 29, 1972, 16.
35. Peter McLaughlin and Harry Stathos, "Cop Mistakenly Kills Detective," *New York Daily News*, April 4, 1972, 3; Les Matthews, "Black Cop Dies in a 'Tragic Mistake,'" *New York Amsterdam News*, April 8, 1972, A2.

36. Edward Kirkman, "Blames Cop's Slaying on Race," *New York Daily News*, April 14, 1972, 32.
37. "Family Angry at Cop's Death," *New York Amsterdam News*, April 22, 1972, A6.
38. Willie Hamilton, "Queens Jury Clears Cop," *New York Amsterdam News*, June 3, 1972, A1.
39. Kohler-Hausmann, *Getting Tough*, 96–98.
40. Francis X. Clines, "Harlem Leaders Back Life Terms for Drug Sale," *New York Times*, January 1973, 43.
41. "Witness for the Prosecution," *New York Daily News*, January 24, 1973, 87.
42. Donald Flynn, "Rock's Drug Plan Given Boost by Community Bigs," *New York Daily News*, February 24, 1973, 125.
43. "Rockefeller and Narcotics," *New York Amsterdam News*, January 13, 1973, A4.
44. "The Drug Crisis," *New York Amsterdam News*, February 24, 1973, B5.
45. "Excerpts from WLIB–*Amsterdam News* Drug Forum," *New York Amsterdam News*, March 3, 1973, A5; Francis X. Clines, "Governor's Drug Bill Splits Black and Puerto Rican Legislators," *New York Times*, March 4, 1973, 38.
46. "Excerpts from WLIB–*Amsterdam News* Drug Forum," A5.
47. "Rangel Urges Black Voice in Setting Drug Abuse Policy," *Call and Post*, January 6, 1973, 1B. After Rockefeller signed the bill into law, Rangel and others demanded the desegregation of law enforcement at all government levels. Charles B. Rangel, "Racism and Drug Enforcement," *New York Amsterdam News*, July 21, 1973, A16; "Rocky Told to Include Blacks among 100 Narcotic Judges," *New York Amsterdam News*, June 30, 1973, D7; H. Carl McCall, "Living with the New Drug Law," *New York Amsterdam News*, September 8, 1973, A5.
48. Michael Keating, "Knapp Panel Revealed Nothing New on Cops," *New York Amsterdam News*, February 26, 1972, A5.
49. "Knapp Blows Whistle on Graft-Taking Cops," *New York Amsterdam News*, August 12, 1972, A1.
50. *The Knapp Commission Report on Police Corruption* (New York: George Braziller, 1973), 100–101.
51. Philip McCarthy and Paul Meskil, "Cop Fires at Girl, Kills Another," *New York Daily News*, January 28, 1973, 232.
52. George Todd, "Girl, 16, Shot by Police, Dies in Her Mom's Arms," *New York Amsterdam News*, February 3, 1973, C1.
53. Mel Greene and Edward Kirkman, "2 Cops Kill 3rd in Accidental Shootout," *New York Daily News*, March 6, 1973, C3; J. Zamgba Browne, "Three Thousand Attend Services for Slain Cop," *New York Amsterdam News*, March 17, 1973, C1.
54. Bernard Rabin and Paul Meskil, "Cop Kills a Boy, 10, as Robbery Suspect," *New York Daily News*, April 29, 1973, 3; Thomas Hauser, *The Trial of Patrolman Thomas Shea* (New York: Seven Stories Press, 2017), 63, 94–95.
55. Rabin and Meskil, "Cop Kills a Boy, 10, as Robbery Suspect," 3; "Blacks Seething over Slaying of Boy, Ten," *New York Amsterdam News*, May 5, 1973, A1; Hauser, *Trial of Patrolman Thomas Shea*, 116, 117.
56. Gene Spagnoli, "Rocky Signs Stiff Anti-Drug Law He Asked," *New York Daily News*, May 9, 1973, 146.
57. "A Warning," *New York Amsterdam News*, August 11, 1973, A4.

58. "Drug Users Speak Out on State's New Drug Measure," *New York Amsterdam News*, August 25, 1973, B8.
59. Don Rojas, "Black Cops Threaten to 'Tie Up This City,'" *New York Amsterdam News*, December 15, 1973, 1.
60. Police corruption scandals continued into 1974 and thereafter. Paul L. Montgomery, "12 in Police Narcotic Unit Charged with Corruption," *New York Times*, March 9, 1974, 61; Bob Wiedrich, "New York City's Police Corruption," *Chicago Tribune*, March 22, 1974, 14. For Rangel on police corruption, see *Hearings before the Select Committee on Narcotics Abuse and Control, House of Representatives, Ninety-Fourth Congress, Second Session, November 19 and December 10, 1976* (Washington, DC: US Government Printing Office, 1977).

LASHAWN HARRIS

They Chained Me to a Refrigerator Like a Dog

New York Black Women,
Police Violence, and Resistance
during the Reagan Era

In November 1987, Black high school cheerleader Tawana Brawley of Dutchess County, New York, accused six white men, including cops, of several heinous crimes. The fifteen-year-old claimed the men kidnapped and brutalized her over four days. She was taken to an unknown location, where "one man showed me his badge and told me to shut up [and] I was hit in the head. When I woke up there were lots of men around." According to Brawley, the men scrawled racial epithets and dog feces on her body, ripped out her hair, and repeatedly sexually assaulted her. Because of the horrific nature of the alleged crime and the victim and men's races, genders, ages, and class statuses, the case became part of 1980s New York's highly racialized cases and one of the nation's most reported incidents of sexual and police violence. For Black New Yorkers, Brawley's assault resurrected historic scenes of white men viciously attacking Black women and girls and going unpunished. Brawley's story became a cause célèbre, going viral 1980s-style via newspapers, television and radio broadcasts, and barbershop and beauty shop conversations. National support for Brawley came from political activists, civil rights lawyers, and celebrities, including boxer Mike Tyson. The 1986 heavyweight champion donated $50,000 for the formation of a foundation for young victims of violence. Thousands of New Yorkers protested Brawley's assault, demanding legal justice for the teenager. City activist Lenora Fulani "organized a political march of 300 women of color throughout the streets of Poughkeepsie to protest the campaign to discredit Brawley by politicians and law enforcement officials." And social activist and singer Peter Seeger and nearly 200 activists stood in front of New York governor Mario Cuomo's Albany mansion demanding that state politicians hold accused assailants accountable for Brawley's rape. At the same time,

Civil rights activist Rev. Al Sharpton, Tawana Brawley, and attorney C. Vernon Mason hold hands outside the New York State Supreme Court building in New York City, July 20, 1990. (Photo by New York Times Co., courtesy Getty Images)

New Yorkers were divided on the Brawley case, especially given its controversial legal outcome. In 1988, a New York State grand jury determined that claims of police brutality, kidnapping, and sexual assault were a hoax.[1]

In this polarizing legal case, Tawana Brawley's charges of white and sexual violence and police brutality, whether real or imagined, highlighted a troubling issue plaguing 1980s New York Black women and girls' lives: wanton police violence. The Brawley story, along with the 1980s police murders of Eleanor Bumpurs and other city women, intensified New Yorkers' long-standing frustrations with women "becoming targets of brutal and abusive members of the New York City Police."[2] Racially repressive policing complicated and threatened women's existence and futures, signaling their vulnerabilities and disposability and lack of legal protection. Employing newspapers and congressional and legal records, this essay examines the violations and indignities women experienced at the hands of the New York City Police Department (NYPD). On the front lines of national domestic campaigns aimed at the surveillance and criminalization and containment of underprivileged citizens, police brutally assaulted and murdered women on crowded thoroughfares and subway stations; in police cars, precincts, and city jails; and in their homes. Part of a culture of white supremacy, police violence functioned to exert power and control over women's lives while reinforcing race, gender, and class hierarchies. Horrific encounters with the NYPD also underscored Black women's long-standing exclusion from the privileges of femininity. Gender did not shield them from police abuse. In a 2015 online editorial titled "ABWH Statement on the Modern Day Lynching of Black Women in the U.S. Justice System," the Association of Black Women Historians asserted that Black women "have never been afforded a femininity that deemed them innocent. [They] are readily blamed and maligned rather than assisted or protected."[3]

Unfettered police repression hardly went unchallenged. Equally important to histories of pervasive state and anti-Black violence are narratives about political struggles against it. Embracing a long tradition of resistance against societal inequalities, late twentieth-century political activists, cultural producers, and ordinary urbanites were critical actors in the city's multiethnic anti–police brutality movement, a movement rooted in African Americans' transnational political campaigns for equality. Women's open anarchy against police brutality encompassed a broad range of tactics. Public testimonies, civil lawsuits, complaint letters, and physical and verbal defenses became weapons against the NYPD. Collectively, women aimed at eradicating state-sanctioned abuse while demanding public and private safety, police reform and accountability, equitable distribution of city resources, and an independent civilian complaint review board. And some women, espousing a politics of refusal and rejecting the legitimacy of the state, "called for an entirely different social and economic order in which prisons and police would not exist."[4] Diverse initiatives toward addressing urban policing exposed women's enduring struggle to dismantle socioeconomic and political structures invested in their delimitation, containment, and exploitation. Moreover, radical acts against state violence motioned to women's investments in their survival and futures.

Black Women and Reaganomics

Tremendous socioeconomic and political and cultural challenges and opportunities characterized 1980s New York City. The decade is widely remembered as a period of urban decay and disorder, crime and violence, homelessness, extreme wealth and poverty, and the emergence of the acquired immunodeficiency syndrome (AIDS) epidemic and a highly potent new drug: crack cocaine. Significant cultural transformations also took "The City That Never Sleeps" by storm. Emerging out of late twentieth-century South Bronx block and houses parties, an ethnically diverse group of working-class youth pioneered new musical styles and artistic expressions that enthralled New Yorkers. Clive "Kool Herc" Campbell and other cultural producers created hip-hop, a cultural aesthetic that birthed an influential genre of music, dance, fashion, and art and offered insightful political commentary on urban America. Pioneering hip-hop artists and groups such as Grandmaster Flash and the Furious Five produced engaging songs about economic hardship, urban America, the widening gap between the rich and poor, and Reaganomics. And no doubt, the fortieth US president's economic vision of American prosperity dominated the decade, shaping working-class Black and Brown New Yorkers' quality of life.

Working-class women endured financial instabilities under the Reagan administration. According to veteran civil rights leader Bayard Rustin, Blacks "suffered a serious erosion in their standard of living." Embracing supply-side and trickle-down economic theories, Republicans lowered marginal tax rates on wealthy earners and proposed massive reductions in spending for welfare programs. Federal disinvestment from social programs pushed working-poor Black families deeper into poverty. African Americans viewed the administration's politics as a cruel assault on the poor. Congressional leader Augustus F. Hawkins accused Reagan of reversing "the role of Robin Hood completely by taking from the poor and giving to the rich." Similarly, New York congresswoman Shirley Chisholm criticized Reagan's economic policies, calling it a "disaster for lower income Americans. Reduced government spending will reduce living standards for millions of Americans."[5] Working-class New York women had much to say about reduced welfare programs. "It is foolish," reasoned cultural anthropologist Vertamae Smart-Grosvenor. "It will make life much harder. The working people will go from a rock to a hard place."[6]

Monetary cuts from welfare programs exacerbated some women's already precarious economic lives. Coming into the 1980s, working poor women were still feeling the devastating economic effects of New York's previous decade of austerity. The Big Apple was on the brink of bankruptcy during the 1970s. A fiscal crisis resulted in budget cuts, limited public services, and massive job loss. Some working-class women's economic statuses hardly improved during the 1980s. African Americans insisted that the working poor's economic conditions worsened under Mayor Edward Koch. Reflecting on Koch's leadership in 1986, Manhattan borough president and future city mayor David Dinkins articulated that New Yorkers "face a crisis that can be best described as a struggle for survival [and they] have never recovered from the ravages of the city's 1970s fiscal crisis."[7] Elected mayor in 1977, Koch was determined to bring the city out of bankruptcy. A pro-business leader, Koch's economic revitalization plan prioritized the financial interests of real estate developers and affluent residents. He failed to restore social services that were lifelines for poor residents.[8] Intending to control the city budget, Koch lowered the operating cost of city agencies between 1978 and 1983. Through hiring freezes, reducing welfare eligibility and overpayments, and employee attrition, Koch reduced city spending by an estimated $174 million.[9] New Yorkers felt the impact of city cuts. The numbers of urban citizens living below the federal poverty line increased from 1.4 million (23.9 percent) in 1979 to 1.8 million in 1985 (20.4 percent).[10]

Budget cuts and a tight labor market made it difficult for working-class women to care for themselves and their families.[11] Part of New York City's estimated 25 percent Black population throughout the 1980s, working-class Black women labored in various employment sectors, negating neoconservative arguments that women were noncontributors to American labor markets. Many secured employment positions as municipal laborers, retail clerks, janitors, data processors, and security guards.[12] Some women, particularly the elderly, worked as household laborers. In a 1980 *Afro-American* editorial, historian Gerald Horne, paralleling 1980s Black women's labor experiences to that of Great Depression era women highlighted in political activists Marvel Cooke and Ella Baker's 1935 "Bronx Slave Market" article, wrote that "the days when suburban housewives examined the knees of an elderly black woman applying for a job to ensure that they're properly scarred are not yet behind us."[13] Some women turned to New York's informal job market. Combining formal work or unemployment benefits with underground labor, women hosted pyramid scheme parties, traded food stamps for money, and peddled subway tokens, counterfeit designer handbags, cherubic-faced Cabbage Patch Dolls, and crack cocaine.[14] A highly addictive form of cocaine, crack opened up unprecedented economic possibilities for women. One Brooklyn woman moonlighted as a drug trafficker, earning $500 a day cooking crack in her kitchen. Profits from drug trafficking augmented her $114 per week file clerk salary.[15] Those unable to secure formal or informal employment relied on public assistance.

Nationwide economic cuts and urban inequalities altered New York women's lives. City policymakers and journalists condemned women for their economic conditions, advancing mid- and late twentieth-century political rhetoric that marked unprivileged women as domineering matriarchs, proverbial welfare leeches, and progenitors of disorder and a culture of poverty. Scathing public portrayals made women prime recipients for carceral and punitive interventions: those logics and practices that centered on bodily injury and harm, incessant regulation and containment, and excessive policing.

They Do Whatever They Want: Everyday Geographies of Police Violence

Carceral regimes of domination and violence expanded during the 1980s. Building upon the legacies of their Republican and Democratic predecessors, the Reagan administration's war against crime and drugs contributed to a modernized carceral state. Conservatives poured federal funds into the militarization of local police forces and prison construction projects; increased the scale of the police supervision and raids in urban communities; and established new partnerships between domestic law enforcement and defense agencies. Nationwide, Black women bore the brunt of draconian federal and state tough-on-crime and drug policies.[16] Many were subjected to no-knock warrants, mass roundups and strip and cavity searches, militarized raids, and repeated stop-and-frisks. For New York women, frightening encounters with the NYPD were a constant issue. Like other urban cities, New York's "local level policing apparatus [was] thoroughly racialized, profoundly discriminatory, and deeply punitive."[17] Authoring a series of 1980s *New York Amsterdam News* editorials on Black women's police interactions, journalist Charles Baillou wrote that women were too often victims of the NYPD.[18] As a particular iteration of state-sanctioned and anti-Black violence, police brutality disrupted women's daily worlds. Policing jeopardized women's existence, generated unexpected social and emotional costs, and threatened dreams of happiness and safety. Moreover, police violence infringed upon women's civil rights and liberties, forcing them to navigate the unpredictable terrain of city life.

Police brutality appeared in a myriad of forms, serving as an incessant source of frustration, rage, and fear for women. "There is a pervasive fear that every Black person in this city feels when they encounter a police officer. Fear that they will be the next victim of police violence and abuse solely because they are Black," commented one political activist. "This fear is fueled by incident after incident of savage, inhuman, and cruel police behavior that is unchecked."[19] While socializing with friends in public and private spaces, spending time or sleeping in their homes, requesting police assistance, traveling on public thoroughfares and transportation, or questioning policing tactics, women were racially profiled and harassed and physically and verbally violated by police. Equipped with federally funded military-style gear, officers pulled their guns and nightsticks out on unarmed women, hurled racial epithets at and intimidated them, and conducted militarized raids on their homes. And women like twenty-four-year-old New York Telephone Company employee Gale Saunders were severely beaten in police cars and jails and on city streets and public transportation.

Cops wait for a matron to search a fur-clad woman at a social club in Bedford-Stuyvesant, Brooklyn, 1982. (New York Daily News Archive, courtesy Getty Images)

Saunders was brutally attacked on the Eighty-Sixth Street subway station platform. In February 1983, Saunders and a coworker mistakenly entered the wrong subway entrance. Hoping to receive police assistance, the women approached white officer Kenneth Monsees. The officer, according to Saunders, became frustrated with the women's pleas for help. He sarcastically addressed them, claiming that their mistake was not his problem. Infuriated with Monsees's unprofessional manner, a persistent Saunders approached him a second time. In a matter of seconds, Monsees's rude demeanor escalated to violence. The officer "pushed her down to the ground," striking blows to her head and other parts of her body with his nightstick. The officer also held her in a chokehold. A battered Saunders was treated for a fractured skull at a nearby hospital. While hospitalized, Saunders was arrested for assault and resisting arrest. Eventually police charges against Saunders were dismissed. She later filed a complaint with the city's Civilian Complaint Review Board, the post–World War II police-controlled review board that many Blacks considered ineffective and functioned to delegitimize plaintiffs' grievances while masking police misconduct.[20]

Gale Saunders's public attack was not an isolated incident. Brooklyn resident Florence Coates spoke with the *New York Amsterdam News* about her violent encounter with police. In 1988, Coates, a secretary at Brooklyn's Jackie Robinson Center for Physical Culture, took her family to Manhattan Beach to celebrate Father's Day. What started out as a joyous family gathering quickly turned into a nightmare. Brooklyn police officers approached the Coates family, ordering them to take down their screenhouse. Not violating any beach regulations, Coates dismissed the officers' directive. Failure to comply with police resulted in Coates's arrest for disturbing the peace. Her real crime was rebuffing officers' authority. Coates's terrifying experience with police continued at the precinct. A woman officer strip-searched Coates in front of the entire precinct. Strip searches and other forms of legally sanctioned sexual assaults permitted officers to search individuals when there was reasonable suspicion that the individual was concealing evidence or a weapon. Irrespective of legal justification and shared gender identities, the female officer subjected Coates to a demeaning and humiliating physical search: "She opened me up in front of everybody." The cop ordered Coates to undress, bend over, and expose her genitalia. She poked and prodded at Coates's body, imposing control over her body. "I felt I was raped right then and there."[21]

Not all police violence was public. Life-threatening police interactions were not limited to attacks on the streets, in subway stations, or in police precincts. Police violence occurred beyond the public gaze in women's homes. Domestic spaces, those embodying love, caregiving, and creativity, became sites of injury and terror and human violation. Police home intrusions upended Black intimate life. It interrupted women's efforts at cultivating beautification projects and maintaining safe spaces. Cops' lack of respect for Black households was wrapped in twentieth-century racist stereotypes and political rhetoric about women and their interior spaces. Moreover, national anti-crime and drug campaigns that targeted underserved, racially diverse communities informed officers' impressions regarding Black households. Black homes were seen as ground zero for criminality, and the bodies that inhabited such spaces were considered progenitors of lawlessness.

Invasive police visits were the "worst thing that ever happened" to women. Police presence fractured inhabitants' visions of safety, bodily control, and autonomy over their households. According to one woman, "Police have no respect for you or your property. They do whatever they want to your house."[22] Entering Black households, police busted down front doors, damaged furniture and family mementos, and rummaged through women's bedroom drawers. Reflecting on a terrifying police visit, one woman noted that when the officers showed up at her door, "the banging was so hard that it seemed like the door was going to come down. The hinges were coming off the door."²³ Similarly, another woman articulated that "cops just tore up everything. They threw my new clothes on the floor and walked on them. And tore the phone off the wall."²⁴ Black women had no say in their own homes. Police disregarded women's pleas of innocence, berated them for needing assistance, and ignored their inquiries about officers' presence in their homes. When former model and homeowner Karen Griffith questioned officers about their uninvited visit to her Brooklyn brownstone, they pushed her aside and walked into her home. "I saw this white man going down the hallway. I asked if he had a warrant. He said: 'no I don't have a warrant nor do I need one.'"²⁵ Cops like the individuals Griffith encountered dismissed women's legal rights and claims of authority over their interior spaces. NYPD officers hardly cared about women's vehement demands for civility and to be treated as citizens.

Presumptive criminality, mistaken identity, gross negligence, and a constellation of other circumstances brought heavily armed officers to women's doorways. In May 1986, Bronx nurse Madeline Stovall and her twenty-year-old daughter were shocked when six "overzealous and racist" NYPD officers kicked down their apartment door. A horrific crime had brought police to the forty-three-year-old mother's home in Co-op City. Stovall was stunned when officers entered her home without a search warrant, demanding she answer questions about the kidnapping of a two-month-old white baby. Several individuals including the toddler's white mother claimed that a "light-skinned black woman" resembling Stovall committed the crime. The mother asserted that Stovall kidnapped her daughter after she refused to sell her the baby. According to Stovall, the "police were very aggressive and racially motivated because it was a white baby. They handcuffed me to my refrigerator and refused to let me call a lawyer and harassed my deaf daughter. They chained me to a refrigerator like a dog." Stovall was arrested for kidnapping. To make matters worse, Stovall's arrest was photographed and featured in the popularly read *New York Daily News*. Accompanying an editorial in that paper titled "Nurse Nabbed in Kidnapping" was an image of a distraught Stovall with arresting officers. Stovall was in disbelief about the arrest, "praying to God [that police] find the baby alive." And police did locate the toddler. A day after Stovall's arrest, police found the baby in a Connecticut businesswoman's apartment. Subsequently, criminal charges against Stovall were dropped. Threatening to initiate a civil suit against the city for false arrest, Stovall demanded a public apology from the NYPD. Her apartment was raided;

she was erroneously detained for several days; and her arrest made the local news. "I wanted a public apology from the city, from the police. I want them to hold a press conference calling all the same press together as when I was arrested. This is not the days of *The Color Purple* where black people are pulled off the street because a white person accuses them." The NYPD refused to admit any wrongdoing. "An apology," reasoned a Bronx chief of detectives, "means we did something improper. We didn't."[26]

Emergency phone calls for assistance also resulted in police abuse. As urban citizens entitled to full access to city institutions and services, Black women, halfheartedly viewing the NYPD as a safeguarding public agency, phoned police when they were in need of assistance with family disputes, neighborhood protection, and crime reporting. When calling the police, women hoped that their claims of victimhood would be read as credible and taken seriously. But expectations of fairness and compassion were far from reality. Acknowledging New York City's extensive histories of state-sanctioned violence against nonwhite residents, women hardly knew what to expect when the NYPD arrived at their doorsteps. They understood that police assistance came with unexpected consequences and that calling the cops was potentially hazardous to their existence. New York NAACP lawyer Laura Blackburne reasoned that calling the police for assistance was perilous for Black people. "Police rudeness," noted Blackburne, "has escalated to total disrespect and violence. If you are a black New Yorker, you automatically read indelibly but invisibly written 'caution' when you pick up the phone to call the police. Calling a police officer can result in death, serious physical injury, and almost certain spiritual abuse of your person and your dignity."[27] Seeking police assistance, women wondered how they would be treated. Would they be seen as victims or as assailants, and would their lives be preserved or threatened? In 1987, Brooklyn senior citizen Violet Johnson pondered such life-or-death questions. Suffering from a heart attack, Johnson begged two officers to transport her from her home to a nearby hospital. They refused, claiming that "if they took her and her heart stopped in the police car, they would be liable." Pleading for her life, Johnson asked the officers, "Are you going to let me die?" Those were some of Johnson's last words.[28]

Laura Blackburne's comments resonated with Evelyn Howard. The Brooklynite observed how her family was "treated worse than hardened criminals" when police responded to an emergency at her home. In 1982, Evelyn summoned police after an intense argument with her brother. According to Evelyn, her brother Fred Howard locked her out of their shared Bedford-Stuyvesant apartment. Feeling helpless after communications with her brother became violent, Evelyn turned to police, hoping that they would assist her in gaining entrance to the apartment. Affirming Evelyn's lockout claim, Fred informed Utica Avenue station house officers that such course of action was necessary because his sister "was being disruptive and threw a bottle at their second-floor apartment window." A call for assistance quickly turned into a terrifying ordeal. Officers went on a violent rampage, flexing their authority and brutalizing the Howard family. Evelyn watched in dismay as police assaulted her brother and his fiancée, Gwen Morris. Police yelled at Morris when she inquired about their visit, telling her to "mind your business, bitch." Officers also walked through the apartment breaking dishes and glasses and other furniture with their batons. Determined not to let the officers get away with such conduct, Morris filed an official complaint. "They just can't do these things to Black people. They should not be walking around in blue uniforms."[29]

Gwen Morris and other women luckily survived violent police attacks. But they did not emerge unscathed. Police attacks traumatized women. In the aftermath of explosive police brutality, women experienced incremental modes of violence that were imperceptible and played out over time. This kind of violence, what scholar Rob Nixon calls slow violence, was also "exponential, operating as a major threat multiplier." It "fuels long-term, proliferating conflicts in situations where the condition for sustaining life becomes increasingly but gradually degraded."[30] "Victims of brutal police attacks are anything but numbed. They are still suffering the pain and psychological trauma from their unfortunate encounters with 'New York's Finest,'" wrote one journalist.[31] Women worried about repeated attacks. And they agonized over the impact police violence had on their physical and emotional well-being. "This is one thing in my life that I will never forget," noted one Manhattan secretary and police brutality victim. "You know, being a female, I am going through physical changes right now, with my menstrual cycle like crazy. I can't even keep up with it, the doctors don't even know, they told me it is my nerves."[32]

"Naturally, I Fought Back": Women's Fight against Police Abuse

Late twentieth-century New York Black women contested state violence at every turn. Survivors and anti–police brutality activists denounced oppressive and violent structures that circumvented visions of equality and the chance to live safe and meaningful lives. They critiqued unfettered and expanding police power and over- and under-policing, exposing the less visible violations and harms that impacted their daily lives. Contesting and delegitimizing police brutality was not new for African American women. Fighting police abuse was part of Black women's historic struggles against anti-Black and state violence, as well as part of broader political campaigns centered on police accountability, legal justice and protection, and transforming and improving life for city residents. At the same time, women's commitment toward upending police violence encompassed imagining, as scholar Marisol LeBron suggests, "alternative understandings of justice, safety, and accountability."[33]

Mobilization against police brutality took on varying political and cultural expressions. Women launched and sustained anti–police brutality organizations, penned grievance letters and opinion editorials to politicians and newspaper editors, and created poems, songs, and other imaginative visual representations. Women writers such as feminist Audre Lorde employed poetry to render visible the emotional toll of police violence and Black death on Black communities. Writing out of a "sense of urgency and dread," Lorde's powerful works including "Power" (1976) and "For the Record" (in memory of Eleanor Bumpurs, 1986) exhibits communal outrage and pain over the 1973 and 1984 NYPD police killings of ten-year-old Queens resident Clifford Glover and Bronx senior citizen Eleanor Bumpurs.[34] Other women like forty-eight-year-old college student Cornelia Muamba engaged in heated public confrontations with police.

In May 1984, Muamba entered the 125th Street subway. After purchasing her subway tokens, she observed two transit officers "roughing up" a Black teenage fare violator and "cursing him out." Attempting to "protect the Black youth," Muamba intervened, giving the teen money for the subway. Instead of leaving the teen, Muamba decided to stay on the scene, wanting to make sure that police did not assault the boy. Officers were not impressed with Muamba's act of generosity. They viewed the monetary deed and public observation as a challenge to their authority and an impediment to their work. In response, police instructed Muamba to "move on and mind your business. You are going to get arrested." Muamba refused to comply with police. Nor did she mind her own business. She questioned officers' tactics and reason for harassing the teenager, especially since she had paid his fare. Noncompliance and questioning officers resulted in Muamba's arrest and a brutal attack. One "cop rushed me. I turned to the side to face him and he said, 'I should kick your ——.' I was thrown to the wall, I was handcuffed, they kept throwing me to the wall, trying to fracture my head." Alleging claims of discourtesy and injury, Muamba filed a complaint with the Transit Authority Civilian Complaint Unit.[35]

Opposition to police violence appeared in women's public testimonies. Reliving painful moments of abuse was overwhelming for women. But survivors of police assault, to borrow from Audre Lorde, had "come to believe over and over again that what is most important to [them] must be spoken, made verbal and shared, even at the risk of having it bruised or misunderstood."[36] Disclosure about state violence was a way to reclaim one's body, advocate for legal justice, and mobilize communities on behalf Black womanhood.[37] Testimony generated the opportunity to publicly document victimization, as well as publicly share with listeners the aftershocks of police violence. And for many survivors, "healing takes place," according to bell hooks, when they "speak the truth" about their trauma.[38] New York women unveiled stories of police abuse and violations with friends and family, journalists and community activists, and politicians during congressional hearings.

Women's testimonies about the NYPD were on full display at the 1983 congressional hearing on police misconduct. Headed by subcommittee chairman and Detroit congressman John Conyers, the congressional hearings were sparked by nationwide incidents of excessive and deadly police force. The New York subcommittee on police misconduct was one of several 1980s federal probes on policing.[39] In 1980, congressional leaders held hearings on the Los Angeles Police Department. Community outrage over the 1979 police killing of working-class mother Eula Love and long-standing struggles against the department's use of excessive force sparked two days of hearings.[40] Three years later, federal hearings focused on Miami police, as well as on the 1982 police killing of twenty-year-old Floridian Neville Johnson.

Convening at the Harlem State Building on 125th Street, the 369th Division Armory on 142nd Street, and the Eastern District Courtroom in Brooklyn in the summer and fall of 1983, congressional leaders heard over 300 testimonies from religious and community leaders, Black police officers, lawyers, and city officials such as Mayor Edward Koch and NYPD police commissioner Robert McGuire. Black and Brown women also appeared before the committee.[41] They courageously presented their stories as evidence of victimization and survival. Testimonies revealed the humiliation and powerlessness women felt at the hands of police. NYPD officer Warena Brown offered attendees a powerful testimony. Breaking the so-called blue wall of silence, Brown recalled how white officers brutalized her. In June 1983, Brown, who was off duty on childcare leave, witnessed a burglary while taking a walk with her baby. Brown immediately called 911 and officers showed up at the scene. While Brown aided the apprehension of two suspects, she was arrested. "I was suddenly surrounded by four to five white officers. A white police officer grabbed my baby carriage, spinning it around [and] almost throw [my baby] in the street. I explained. I am police officer Brown. I am on childcare leave without pay. I was arrested for impersonating a police officer and handcuffed. My daughter was left in the carriage on the streets of New York totally unattended. I was held in the 67th precinct for 4 hours and

2 of which it took them to ascertain my identity."⁴² Brown's charge of police impersonation was eventually dropped. Feeling outraged and in need of professional and legal advice, Brown shared what happened to her with the NYPD Guardians Association, a fraternal organization representing Black and Latinx officers and a group that was no stranger to the NYPD's history of racism.⁴³

Former sex worker Deborah Cobb also appeared before the subcommittee. Her testimony was shrouded in narratives about sex work, sexual exploitation, and shame and silence. For years, Cobb, like some survivors of police abuse, had remained quiet about her attack. She did not disclose the horrors of the assault to civil rights groups, journalists, or family and friends. Nor did she report the assault to police. Like many Black women, Cobb, as historian Darlene Clark Hine writes about women's interiority, purposely "shield[ed] the truth of [her] inner life and self from oppressors." Moreover, the possibility of having one's interior life scrutinized and documented in legal records left Cobb scared and uninterested in sharing her story with others. Cobb may have felt like 1970s sexual assault survivor Joan Little. Testifying about being sexually assaulted, according to Little, was the "toughest thing." No "woman enjoys talking about being sexually attacked."⁴⁴ But at the 1983 hearings, Cobb did one of the most difficult tasks of her life: she testified about a horrific police attack. In December 1978, Cobb was raped by a white plainclothes officer. He "forced [me] at gunpoint into his car. I wanted to run but he told me he would shoot me in the back of my head and put the gun next to my body. So, I let him have his way." Informal economy women like Cobb and others "in the life," those involved in sex work, were prime targets for carceral violence and confinement and ideal victims for abusive officers. Police understood that individuals with histories of arrests were less likely to report crimes committed against them and less likely to be viewed as victims. Few cops took seriously the "grumblings of junkies and prostitutes."⁴⁵ Cobb informed the committee that she was afraid to report her rape, fearing another attack by the officer. And Cobb had good reason to be scared. Months after the assault, she saw the officer board a city bus on which she was a passenger. He trailed her until she reached her destination. After the bus incident, Cobb never saw the man again. But she would never forget his face or what he did to her.⁴⁶

New York women employed the criminal justice system to expose police mistreatment, filing civil lawsuits against the NYPD. City courtrooms became legal battlegrounds for women. Many believed that the judicial system was a possible venue to guard against infringement of rights and articulate personal stories of civil and human rights violation. Moreover, women plaintiffs employed the courts to pursue justice against their attackers through a system that routinely denied them fairness and rebuffed their claims of victimhood.[47] At the same time, plaintiffs took a chance going to court. Few NYPD officers accused of assault or murder faced legal and professional repercussions. Their actions were often decriminalized and protected under a cloak of legal statutes. Several 1980s New York State and US Supreme Court cases made it difficult to prosecute officers accused of brutality. New York's *People v. Benjamin* (1980) and the Supreme Court's *Tennessee v. Garner* (1985) and *Graham v. Connor* (1989) established the constitutional standards for police use of force.[48] City officials, police unions, and internal NYPD investigations also cleared and sanctioned officers' use of excessive or deadly force. Cops were rarely reprimanded for abuse. If city prosecutors and grand juries did indict officers, many were often acquitted by predominantly white juries and monetarily supported by police fraternal orders. For instance, the NYPD's Patrolmen's Benevolent Association union posted the bail for white officers accused of murdering ten-year-old Clifford Glover and teenager Randolph Evans during the 1970s.[49] And in the mid-1980s, the Transit Patrolmen's Benevolent Association spent more than $300,000 in legal fees to defend the six officers charged in the 1983 death of twenty-five-year-old artist Michael Stewart.[50]

Legal challenges to police power generated real consequences for women. Many faced media scrutiny and incessant harassment, as well as police and city officials' coordinated efforts to publicly discredit them and halt their civil suits. And throughout legal proceedings, plaintiffs were subjected to invasive background investigations and portrayed as liars looking for a payday and attempting to frame good cops. For example, a few months after the October 1984 police killing of Bronx grandmother Eleanor Bumpurs, the Bumpurs family filed a multimillion-dollar lawsuit against the City of New York. In response to the legal suit, NYPD union members organized a well-orchestrated media campaign against the family, accusing them of being dysfunctional and "money hungry."[51] According to New York Civil Liberties Union and Puerto Rican Legal Defense and Education Fund attorneys Richard Emery and Hector Soto, "Civil lawsuits line up the city and the Police Department and the Corporation Counsel's office against the person who complained of police abuse. They [try] to kill the civil action."[52]

No doubt, potential judicial setbacks, public condemnation, and histories of legal injustice jeopardized women's willingness to pursue legal channels. But such obstacles did not deter women like Clara Speller from initiating legal suits. Their "well-stocked arsenal of anger," sampling from Audre Lorde, against their victimization became transformative fuel for taking on the NYPD.[53]

In 1983, thirty-eight-year-old engineer Speller filed a lawsuit against the NYPD Transit Authority. The civil suit stemmed from Speller's arrest at Manhattan's

Union Square train station in July 1980. Searching for a token booth, Speller accidently entered a restricted area in the subway. Observing Speller's behavior, transit officer Raymond Connolly approached and arrested her. Speller verbally protested her arrest, claiming she had done nothing wrong. According to Speller, Connolly and another transit officer used racial epithets and wrestled her to the ground and attacked her with a nightstick. Taken to a nearby police precinct, Speller was charged with trespassing, failure to obey an officer, and disorderly conduct. She was later acquitted of all charges. But Speller wanted more than an acquittal. She wanted legal retribution. In 1984, Speller filed *Speller v. NYCTA, et ano.* (#19234). In February 1988, a Manhattan jury awarded Speller $1.25 million, arguing that Speller's civil rights were violated.

Speller's case was one of many 1980s lawsuit cases against the NYPD that resulted in payout. Payouts rose from $599,000 in 1971 to $2.1 million in 1980. The city paid an estimated $5.8 million in out-of-court settlements between 1983 and 1984. And between 1987 and 1992, city officials paid a little over $50 million in damages to plaintiffs.[54] Speller and her family were elated about the verdict. Speller's father, Joseph, commented that "she was fairly rewarded." But the family did recognize the legal system's limitations. They reasoned that "it would only be fair if some action would have been taken against Connolly."[55] Unsurprisingly, the city failed to reprimand Connolly for assaulting Speller. By the time Speller initiated the civil suit, Connolly had retired from the NYPD.

Not all civil suits resulted in a legal victory. On April 19, 1980, residents of Harlem's 92 Morningside Avenue experienced a terrifying predawn Federal Bureau of Investigations raid. This police invasion was part of decades-long surveillance campaigns against politically engaged Black women.[56] That morning, federal agents along with NYPD officers were in search of Black Liberation Army leader Assata "Joanne Chesimard" Shakur. In 1977, Shakur was convicted of a series of crimes including first-degree murder, assault, and armed robbery. Sentenced to life imprisonment, Shakur escaped from New Jersey's Clinton Correctional Facility for Women in 1979. Shakur's escape prompted a nationwide woman-hunt. And 92 Morningside Avenue was a place of interest. More than fifty heavily armed officers tore their way through the apartment building between 1:00 and 4:00 a.m. They broke down apartment doors, pointed military-style weapons at sleeping tenants, and handcuffed residents. Agents also inspected women's bodies, forcing them to "lift their [clothes] to bare their upper legs to agents looking for a scar that Chesimard is supposed to bear." In their pursuit of Chesimard, authorities targeted several apartments, including that of Violet Hyman and Ebun Adelona. A political activist, Adelona raised money for Shakur's 1970s legal defense and socially associated with members of

Shakur's legal team. Agents ransacked Adelona's apartment. "They pulled out my linen, the bathroom door was off the hinges, and my sofa was in the middle of the floor. They grabbed me and took me into the hallway where they put my hands behind my back. It was a terrorizing experience." Violet Hyman endured a different experience. In Hyman's absence, police destroyed her home. New York activist and photojournalist Kwame Brathwaite photographed Hyman's ransacked apartment. Coming home to a horrific scene, Hyman found clothes and papers scattered on the floor and destroyed furniture. Echoing the sentiments of Hyman, Adelona, and other building residents, one woman yelled to police: "Who's gonna pay for the damage to my apartment?"[57]

Residents insisted that federal agents were responsible for apartment damages. And they asserted that the predawn raid violated their legal rights. Seeking legal justice, Ebun Adelona and other Morningside Avenue tenants filed *Adelona v. Webster* in 1981. "We must all take a stand to see to it that this kind of outrageously illegal behavior does not happen again. We feel that law enforcement agencies must be held accountable and be subject to public scrutiny when they act in a manner totally inconsistent with the guarantees of the U.S. Constitution." Legally represented by National Conference of Black Lawyers and New York Civil Liberties Union attorneys C. Vernon Mason and Richard Emery, plaintiffs sued the City of New York, the NYPD, and FBI agents, including Director William H. Webster, for $92 million. Defended by the US attorney for the Southern District of New York, Rudolph Giuliani, defendants were charged with a series of violations, including invasion of privacy, intentional and negligent infliction of emotional distress, illegal wiretaps, and false imprisonment.[58]

Morningside residents' legal battle for police accountability ended in 1987. A federal judge dismissed defendants' charges of conspiracy, illegal surveillance, and violation of constitutional rights. The legal outcome was disappointing for Morningside residents. Lack of legal culpability gave the impression that the apartment raid was unworthy of judicial retribution. Dismissed charges signaled the decriminalization of police violence and served as a reminder of the "legacies of an exclusionary politics of protection whereby [African Americans] were not entitled to the law's protection."[59]

Conclusion

Little has changed for Black women since the 1980s. For many, police violence remains a life-threatening issue, resulting in mistreatment and neglect, premature death, or loss of civil liberties. In the 2010s, NYPD officers stopped and frisked over 16,000 women, many whom were women of color. In 2016, Bronx resident Deborah Danner was fatally shot in her home by police. And in 2018, a detained Brooklyn pregnant woman while in active labor was subjected to a humiliating vaginal inspection inside a precinct. Incidents of state violence against women reveal what some Black historians have called a "modern-day Red Record of anti-Black female violence."[60]

Contesting police brutality and the structural inequalities at the heart of such violence is an ongoing battle for activists. Yet, women from New York and beyond the Big Apple are deeply committed to employing a wide range of self-defense strategies against state violence. Galvanizing around narratives about women whose lives have been lost to police violence, women's political groups such as Angela Davis and Ruth Wilson Gilmore's Critical Resistance and Kimberlé Crenshaw's African American Policy Forum and Center for Intersectionality and Social Policy Studies are committed to dismantling carceral structures and raising visibility about gender-specific stories of victimization.[61] Likewise, women continue to publicly testify about police misconduct and abuse, as well as file civil suits against abusive cops and police departments. For instance, Chicago social worker Anjanette Young sued the city and twelve Chicago police officers for wrongfully raiding her apartment in 2019. In 2021, city officials awarded Young a $2.9 million settlement.[62]

Anjanette Young, Angela Davis, and the other women's testimonies, political work, and legal pursuits remain critical to eradicating police brutality and all forms of state violence. It is this important work that will ensure women's survival and futures.

Notes

1. J. Zamgba Browne, "Tyson Sets Up $50,000 Fund to Educate Tawana Brawley," *New York Amsterdam News (NYAN)*, February 20, 1988, 3; Lenora Fulani, "One Black Woman's Thoughts as We Revisit Tawana Brawley Affair," *New Journal and Guide*, December 10, 1997, 2; "Pete Seeger Arrested at Brawley Protest," *New Pittsburgh Courier*, April 16, 1988, 3.
2. Charles Baillou, "Women Claim Brutality," *NYAN*, November 5, 1988, 11.
3. "ABWH Statement on the Modern-Day Lynching of Black Women in the U.S. Justice System," Association of Black Women Historians, July 28, 2015, http://abwh.org/2015/07/28/abwh-statement-on-the-modern-day-lynching-of-Black-women-in-the-u-s-justice-system.
4. Garrett Felber, "The Struggle to Abolish the Police Is Not New," *Boston Review*, June 9, 2020, http://bostonreview.net/race/garrett-felber-struggle-abolish-police-not-new.
5. Simon Anekwe, "Poor Folks Are High on President Reagan's Hit List," *NYAN*, February 28, 1981, 3.

6. Bill Price, "Blacks React to Reagan's Proposed Cuts," *NYAN*, February 28, 1981, 4.
7. Simon Anekwe, "Dinkins Accuses Koch of Betraying Workers," *NYAN*, June 7, 1986, 5.
8. Lee Dembart, "Koch, Criticized by Many Blacks, Seeks to Repair Ties with Them," *New York Times* (*NYT*), February 27, 1979; Jonathan Soffer, *Ed Koch and the Rebuilding of New York City* (New York: Columbia University Press, 2010).
9. Themis Chronopoulos, "The Making of the Orderly City: New York since the 1980s," *Journal of Urban History* 46, no. 5 (2017): 5.
10. Josh Barbanel, "New York City's Economy Booms, and the Poor Begin to Profit," *NYT*, May 16, 1988, B1.
11. Peter Noble, "Unemployment: Hell for Minorities," *NYAN*, September 1, 1981, 4; Doug Rossinow, *The Reagan Era: A History of the 1980s* (New York: Columbia University Press, 2015), 143.
12. Rosemary Bray, "Managing as a Black Woman," *New York Daily News* (*NYDN*), February 27, 1987, 7; "City Jobs Off Limits to Blacks, Hispanics," *NYAN*, April 6, 1985, 1; Michael Oreskes, "Census Traces Radical Shifts in New York City's Population," *NYT*, September 20, 1982, A1.
13. Gerald C. Horne, "Poverty Hits Elderly, Black Women the Hardest," *Afro-American*, September 20, 1980, 5.
14. Elizabeth Kolbert, "Illegal Workers as Domestics: Uneasy Alliance," *NYT*, October 30, 1985, C1; "Woman Pleads Guilty to Selling 31,200 Slugs for Subway Tokens," *NYT*, December 9, 1980, D23.
15. Celestine Bohlen, "Number of Mothers in Jail Surges with Drug Arrests," *NYT*, April 17, 1989, A1.
16. Elizabeth Hinton, *From the War on Poverty to the War on Crime: The Making of Mass Incarceration in America* (Cambridge, MA: Harvard University Press, 2016); Andrea J. Ritchie, *Invisible No More: Police Violence against Black Women and Women of Color* (Boston: Beacon Press, 2017).
17. Simon Balto, *Occupied Territory: Policing Black Chicago from Red Summer to Black Power* (Chapel Hill: University of North Carolina Press, 2019), 5.
18. Baillou, "Women Claim Brutality."
19. Subcommittee on Criminal Justice of the Committee on the Judiciary, US House of Representatives, Ninety-Eighth Congress (Second Session), *Report of Hearings in New York City on Police Misconduct* (Washington, DC: US Government Printing Office, 1984), 8; Subcommittee on Criminal Justice of the Committee on the Judiciary, US House of Representatives, Ninety-Eighth Congress (Part 1), *Police Misconduct* (Washington, DC: US Government Printing Office, 1984), 473.
20. Les Matthews, "Woman Cleared in Police Assault," *NYAN*, March 24, 1984, 3; Clarence Taylor, *Fight the Power: African Americans and the Long History of Police Brutality in New York City* (New York: New York University Press, 2019).
21. Baillou, "Women Claim Brutality"; Ritchie, *Invisible No More*, 121–22.
22. Toni Anthony, "Mother Hits Cops on 'Gun' Raid," *Chicago Daily Defender*, February 17, 1971, 1.
23. Subcommittee on Criminal Justice of the Committee on the Judiciary (Part 1), *Police Misconduct*, 801.

24. Anthony, "Mother Hits Cops on 'Gun' Raid."
25. "DA to Probe Cop Assault on Family," *NYAN*, April 1, 1989, 1.
26. John Melia and Thomas Raftery, "Nurse Nabbed in Kidnapping," *NYDN*, April 30, 1986, 7; "Police Try to Unravel Apparent Kidnapping," *NYT*, May 1, 1986, D27.
27. Subcommittee on Criminal Justice of the Committee on the Judiciary (Part 1), *Police Misconduct*, 472.
28. Simon Anekwe, "Dying Woman Asks Police: Are You Going to Let Me Die," *NYAN*, July 25, 1987, 3.
29. Angela Jones, "Cop Goes Berserk in Bklyn Apt.," *NYAN*, November 27, 1982, 9; Cheryl Hicks, *To Talk with You Like a Woman* (Chapel Hill: University of North Carolina Press, 2010), 184.
30. Rob Nixon, *Slow Violence and the Environmentalism of the Poor* (Cambridge, MA: Harvard University Press, 2011).
31. Charles Baillou, "Ladies Group Deplores Violent Police Attacks on City Women," *NYAN*, June 24, 1989, 4.
32. Subcommittee on Criminal Justice of the Committee on the Judiciary (Part 1), *Police Misconduct*, 476.
33. Marisol LeBron, *Policing Life and Death: Race, Violence, and Resistance in Puerto Rico* (Chapel Hill: University of North Carolina Press, 2019), 4.
34. Audre Lorde, *The Collected Poems of Audre Lorde* (Latham: Kitchen Table/Women of Color Press, 1986).
35. Barbara Kantrowitz, "Minority Leaders Accuse N.Y. Police of Brutality," *Philadelphia Inquirer*, September 20, 1983, 9; Sam Roberts, "When Police Are Accused of Brutality," *NYT*, October 27, 1983, B1; Subcommittee on Criminal Justice of the Committee on the Judiciary (Part 1), *Police Misconduct*, 477–79.
36. Audre Lorde, *Sister Outside: Essays and Speeches* (Berkeley: Crossing Press, 1984), 40.
37. Danielle McGuire, *At the Dark End of the Street: Black Women, Rape, and Resistance: A New History of the Civil Rights Movement from Rosa Parks to the Rise of Black Power* (New York: Vintage Books, 2010), xix.
38. bell hooks, *Sisters of the Yam: Black Women and Self-Recovery* (New York: Routledge, 2015), 11.
39. Marilynn Johnson, *Street Justice: A History of Police Violence in New York City* (Boston: Beacon Press, 2004).
40. David Johnston, "2 Congressmen Will Conduct Hearings in L.A. on Police Shootings of Civilians," *Los Angeles Times*, March 7, 1980, D2.
41. Sam Roberts, "Hearing on Police Cut Off in Harlem," *NYT*, July 19, 1983, A1; David W. Dunlap, "Hearings on Police to Resume Sept. 19," *NYT*, July 29, 1983, B3.
42. Subcommittee on Criminal Justice of the Committee on the Judiciary, US House of Representatives, Ninety-Eighth Congress (Part 2), *Police Misconduct* (Washington: Government Printing Office, 1984), 1638–39.
43. Subcommittee of Criminal Justice of the Committee on the Judiciary (Part 2), *Police Misconduct*, 1188–89, 1668; Andrew T. Darien, *Becoming New York's Finest: Race, Gender, and the Integration of the NYPD, 1935–1980* (New York: Palgrave Macmillan, 2013).
44. McGuire, *At the Dark End of the Street*, 277.

45. Ritchie, *Invisible No More*, 108.
46. Subcommittee of Criminal Justice of the Committee on the Judiciary (Part 2), *Police Misconduct*, 1638–39; Peter Noel, "Woman Claims Cop Sexually Attacked Her," *NYAN*, December 3, 1983, 10.
47. Rae Dawn Flood, "They Didn't Treat Me Good: African American Rape Victims and Chicago Courtroom Strategies during the 1950s," *Journal of Women's History* 17 (Spring 2005): 40.
48. Alex Vitale, *The End of Policing* (New York: Verso Books, 2017).
49. Neal Hirschfeld, "Blacks Urged to Quit PBA over Bail Posted for Cop in Shooting," *NYDN*, December 2, 1976, 5.
50. Isabel Wilkerson, "Jury Acquits All Transit Officers in 1983 Death of Michael Stewart," *NYT*, November 25, 1985; "100% behind Cop," *NYDN*, February 8, 1985, 12.
51. Frank J. Prial, "Amid Protest, Bumpurs Case Nears Its End: Summations Interrupted by a Demonstration," *NYT*, February 18, 1987, B1.
52. Subcommittee on Criminal Justice of the Committee on the Judiciary (Part 1), *Police Misconduct*, 11, 615.
53. Lorde, *Sister Outside*, 127.
54. Marshall Miller, "Police Brutality," *Yale Law and Policy Review* 17, no. 1 (1998): 156; Selwyn Raab, "City Now Suing Some Who File Brutality Cases: New Tactic in Brutality Cases," *NYT*, February 20, 1985, B1; Frank Lombardi, "Cops on Trial," *NYDN*, March 28, 1982, 6.
55. Natalie P. Byfield, "Woman Claimed Brutality at Union Square," *NYDN*, February 6, 1988, 2; Manhattan Civil Court #19234 / 1983 (*Clara Speller v. NYCTA, et ano.*).
56. Ashley Farmer, "Tracking Activists: The FBI's Surveillance of Black Women Activists Then and Now," *American Historian*, September 2020, 24–29.
57. "Gestapo Tactics in USA," *Afro-American*, May 10, 1980, 4; "FBI: Didn't Overreact in Chesimard Search," *NYDN*, April 22, 1980, 5; Simon Anekwe, "$92 Million Suit Filed against the FBI," *NYAN*, January 31, 1981, 2; "Photo Standalone—No Title," *NYAN*, April 26, 1980, 1; Kathleen Cleaver and George Kataiaficas, *Liberation, Imagination, and the Black Panther Party: A New Look at the Black Panthers and Their Legacy* (New York: Routledge, 2014), 16.
58. Simon Anekwe, "$92 Million Suit Filed against FBI," *NYAN*, January 31, 1981, 2.
59. Kali Gross, "African Women, Mass Incarceration, and the Politics of Protection," *Journal of American History* 102, no. 1 (June 2015): 26.
60. "ABWH Statement on the Modern-Day Lynching of Black Women in the U.S. Justice System."
61. African American Policy Forum, *Say Her Name: Resisting Police Brutality against Black Women* (New York: Center for Intersectionality and Social Policy Studies, 2015), 2.
62. Heather Cherone, "Chicago to Pay $2.9M to Anjanette Young to Settle Botched Raid Lawsuit," WTTW News, December 15, 2021, https://news.wttw.com/2021/12/15/chicago-pay-29m-anjanette-young-settle-botched-raid-lawsuit.

MELANIE D. NEWPORT

A Bigger, Better Jail

From Jail Overcrowding to the
Shackling of Black Chicago
during the War on Drugs Era

"Who would not be for a bigger, better jail, with more cells and safer streets?" the *Chicago Tribune* queried in 1988.[1] After over three decades of persistent jail overcrowding, police, sheriffs, judges, and criminal justice reformers alike were calling for the expansion of Cook County Jail. There was nothing race-neutral about this project: in the same years that Black political power in Chicago had achieved the culminating success of electing the city's first Black mayor, Harold Washington, Black people made up nearly 80 percent of Cook County Jail's population.[2]

As a political and legal paradigm, jail overcrowding took on new meaning in the 1980s as municipal governments looked to rationalize incarceration and surveillance to an increasingly influential Black polis. Crucially, county politics allowed policymakers to circumvent the demands of urban anti-carceral activists for improved welfare services. County governments embraced technologies of carceral space-making to meet the political demand for local mass incarceration.

Situating the escalation of drug and gang policing in relationship to the deeper history of jail reform and rising Black political power, this chapter asserts that an unheralded consequence of the War on Drugs was the extension of carceral technologies and labor into the neighborhoods of Black Chicago. Abandoning the focus on resolving jail overcrowding, policymakers' embrace of electronic monitoring—a practice often referred to as shackling—reconfigured private homes as carceral spaces during the 1990s. Instead of curbing new jail construction, electronic monitoring sustained Cook County's commitment to new jail construction and fueled the dismantling of progressive bail policies that had allowed people to remain free before trial. In tandem with other punitive practices such as saturation patrols in so-called high-crime neighborhoods, removal of Black citizens to rural state prisons, and proposals to build a "supermax" prison in rural Illinois, electronic monitoring and other pretrial and posttrial surveillance programs became central to the control of Black movement in Chicago.

As a major destination for Black migrants of the early and mid-twentieth century, Chicago looms large as a center of African American life in the United States, defined by St. Clair Drake and Horace Cayton as a veritable "black metropolis."[3] Studies of Chicago have demonstrated the fragility of Black freedom across the city's history, from the criminalization of Black children during the Great Migration, to the centrality of police violence in Black neighborhoods during the interwar era, to the rise of a majority-Black jail system by the mid-twentieth century, to the construction of prisons to sustain the removal of Black Americans from the city.[4]

These transformations were irrevocably intertwined with the rise and fall of public housing, the hardening of neighborhood segregation, and assaults on homeownership that have been defining challenges for Black residents in Chicago.[5] Recent scholarship on the history of urban criminal justice systems has emphasized the role of policing and incarceration in constraining and forcing Black movement within American cities and to rural prisons. Interdisciplinary research has found that what Heather Ann Thompson calls "the criminalization of urban space" collapses the boundaries between formal carceral spaces like prisons and jails and schools, housing, neighborhoods, and other sites of community life, creating what sociologist Carla Shedd calls a "carceral continuum."[6] While a new wave of critical scholarship has considered the contemporary operations and implications of electronic monitoring and other "alternatives to incarceration," there is a need to situate the emergence of such monitoring in the deeper history of the development of carceral controls designed explicitly for Black Americans manifested through forced migrations extending from enslavement to convict leasing to incarceration across American history.[7] Amid contemporary abolitionist calls to avoid reforms that strengthen carceral power, historicizing the transformation of the city into part of the "bigger, better jail" is essential for understanding how constraining Black movement through perpetual unfreedom became embedded in recent urban policy.

Among the contributors to *Ebony*'s landmark August 1979 issue, "Black on Black Crime," was Winston Moore, former warden of Cook County Jail and chief of security for the Chicago Housing Authority. Moore's approach was distinct in an issue that included perspectives from politicians, police chiefs, and pastors offering various social solutions—hope found in religious community, economic revitalization and full employment, community organizing around specific crimes, building trust in neighborhoods. Moore distinguished himself by arguing that Black Americans needed an "aggressive, national campaign" to demand "severe punishment" for Black people who committed crimes against other Black people, on par with how the criminal justice system treated Black criminals who committed crimes against white people. Doing so, he argued, would affirm the value of Black life.[8]

Moore blamed Black "tolerance toward the growing army of Black criminals who have turned life in the nation's ghettos into a veritable hell."[9] Arguing that incapacitation in prison was the best means of dealing with Black criminality marked a hard turn from his earlier supposition that rehabilitation and individual transformation might be the goals of incarceration. Although Moore had overseen the 1969 merger of the Chicago House of Correction with Cook County Jail into the Cook County Department of Corrections and directed the massive expansion of jail space at the ninety-six-acre site, he was fired from his position as executive director of the Cook County Department of Corrections after he was accused of abuses by both prisoners and staff.

Moore's new job as head of security in Chicago's housing projects emphasized that his tough-on-crime politics were palatable both to the white politicians who kept him employed and to constituencies of Black women living in the housing projects who had supported Moore as warden. That the predominantly Black housing projects were understood as carceral space was affirmed by the mere presence of the former jail warden.[10]

Moore was among over 500,000 African Americans who moved to Chicago between 1900 and 1980. During and following World War II, the city held the promise of jobs, although for many, exclusion from federal lending and equitable housing rapidly reproduced the poverty they had sought to escape in the American South.[11] For working-class people who made their lives in the Black neighborhoods labeled "delinquency areas" by social scientists, the pendulum of criminal justice swung between two extremes: negligence from police ambivalent about gambling and property crime in the neighborhood, and extreme punishments meted out by police accused of torture through "third degree" interrogation techniques and in the county jail's electric chair.[12]

Intensified policing of narcotics and property crimes had a profound impact on Black communities: between 1940 and 1960, the population of the Chicago House of Correction had jumped from 25 percent to 52 percent Black. Although 65 percent of jailed Black people had been born outside of Illinois, mostly in the Midwest and southern states, 90 percent of Black people in jail had lived in Chicago for more than five years.[13] During the Chicago Freedom Movement, as Martin Luther King Jr. joined local organizers in the streets to protest segregation in the city's schools and housing, white politicians repeatedly derided local protesters as outside agitators. There was a certain truth to it: regardless of origin or class, to live as a Black person in Chicago meant always being an outsider to the city's politics and paths to mobility.[14]

Such constraints shaped the currents of Black life and the relationships people had to crime. For many Black Chicagoans, "drug capitalism" and participation in informal economies provided a space for earning a living and asserting power over neighborhoods amid rampant unemployment, which approached 40 percent among African Americans in Chicago in the mid-1970s.[15] While the press was most infatuated with celebrity gangsters like Blackstone Rangers leader Jeff Fort and the turf they controlled—including a McDonald's—jailed people expressed the meaning they found through life in urban space in more mundane ways.[16] A 1976 poetry anthology comprising poems written by women in Cook County Jail depicted the streets as sites of power and sources of identity. Prisoner Carolyn X described the joy she had felt when she was free, walking down the street. "I was a woman then," she mourned. "A Beautiful Black Woman." Jail and the experience of going to "court, always to Court," had compromised her whole self: "I am now #7302473 / Neither male nor female." As she imagined herself in the world beyond jail walls, she wrote wistfully, "I'd like very much to be a woman again . . . a Black woman, that is."[17]

The wholeness that Carolyn X felt in her community was contrasted against other depictions of urban worlds where Black safety was compromised. The Chicago Urban League, in its 1970 report "Action for Survival," advocated for a capacious definition of crime that included slumlords, vendors extorting Black patrons, police brutality, white drug sellers and gun merchants, and the racism of the courts, state's attorneys, and jails as it called for a "WAR ON ALL CRIME IN BLACK CHICAGO" where crime-control solutions had left communities "over-policed and under-protected."[18] Whether crime represented an opportunity or a threat, it was a persistent problem. When crime surged in 1974, a peak year for homicides in the city, residents of the Robert Taylor Homes begged for a stronger police presence and surveillance cameras. Community advocates like *Chicago Defender* journalist Ethyl Payne, an organizer with Chicago's Coalition of Concerned Women in the War on Crime, demanded police reform and cooperation with citizens.[19]

To people like Moore, whose jail included job programs for prisoners and gave Black community members an entry point into public service, and Renault Robinson, founder of the Afro-American Patrolmen's League, urban carceral employment held real promise for getting people off the streets and into the middle class. As Chicago's Black population reached its all-time high in 1980, there was no clear consensus on how best to curb crime in Black neighborhoods in the face of so many structural challenges.[20]

The political difficulty of mobilizing against persistent criminalization of Black people and their homes and neighborhoods was a central issue in Chicago's 1983 Democratic mayoral primary. Among the candidates were Congressman Harold Washington, a longtime Afro-American Patrolmen's League ally, and Mayor Jane Byrne, who in 1981 briefly moved into the Cabrini-Green housing projects after ten murders had been committed there. Byrne had struggled to manage the police and experimented with a range of tough-on-crime tactics, including bringing eviction proceedings against 800 Cabrini-Green residents who illegally sheltered friends and relatives on parole.[21] State's Attorney Richard M. Daley, son of former mayor Richard J. Daley, was having trouble gaining traction due to his record as an incompetent and ineffective legislator. After Washington's campaign took off following a Christmas visit with prisoners at Cook County Jail that recalled his short 1972 incarceration at the jail, his run came to signify the boundless possibility of Black political capacity. Washington's primary victory over white Democrats who had struggled to marshal the forces of tough-on-crime politics, and his landslide in the general election over a Republican who had mobilized many previously Democratic policemen against him, suggested that anti-Black carceral politics were losing their foothold in the city.[22]

Despite this victory, however, the diffused nature of the criminal justice system meant that the mayor's path to influence the workings of a rapidly expanding carceral system across city streets, police stations, and county jail spaces was narrow, at best. The city controlled the police; the county had its sheriff's department, jail, and courts; the state operated the prison system; and federal agencies and courts were interested in oversight of all of these. The Chicago Police Department had seen its budget rise from $72 million in 1960 to $362 million in 1980.[23] On the verge of Washington's victory, Chicago had been awash in allegations of police brutality and torture; among the most serious were that policemen, led by Detective Jon Burge, had applied electric shocks to the people they detained.[24]

Black Chicagoans experienced nearly 70 percent of all arrests.[25] "It's nothing more than harassment," Reverend Jorge Morales, president of the West Town Concerned Citizens Coalition, told the *Chicago Reporter* of the ripple effects of such arrests. "The poor have to pay bail, lose a day's work and then the cop does not show up in court."[26]

The jail too faced rising tension over its management. Between 1970, after the city and county jails had merged, and 1983, the average daily population of the Cook County Department of Corrections had risen from 3,500 to 6,900.[27] Despite near constant construction of new buildings since the early 1970s, the jail was under fire from the federal courts over prisoners sleeping on the floors.[28] Jailers scrambled for staff and to head off a union-organizing effort among its predominantly Black staff. Facing the limited ability of family to support them while incarcerated, prisoners embraced a short-lived scheme to sell their blood to a contractor in return for commissary script. The contractor then paid the county money it used to pay for the jail building the program was housed in. The program was stopped amid concerns that prisoners' blood was contaminated with drugs and disease.[29] With other barriers to freedom, it was no wonder that fifty men commandeered a bus to escape the jail in 1980.[30] Whether jail walls could hold the growing number of Black prisoners and whether the city would be safe if Black men were free were defining questions during this era. Despite the promise embodied by Harold Washington, Black Chicagoans faced a 1980s where their ability to move freely in the city, and escape it if they chose, was becoming ever more restricted.

The War on Drugs reconfigured the struggles over Black incarceration in Chicago. As Peter Pihos has argued, public discourse often collapsed distinctions between the "interrelated phenomena" of drugs, violence, and gangs, particularly in the minds of "residents of Black neighborhoods" who appealed to their aldermen for police to respond to all three issues.[31] While the proportions of Black prisoners in Cook County Jail were relatively unchanged and actually dropped at points between the 1970s and 1990s, increased arrests and a growing enthusiasm for pretrial punishment intensified the preexisting jail overcrowding problem.

In the mid-1980s, preventive detention became a central tactic for waging the War on Drugs. The long-standing practice of keeping people in jail to prevent commission of future crimes while they awaited trial was formalized through legislative changes such as the Bail Reform Act of 1984, a federal law that empowered judges to consider the criminal histories of defendants as they made decisions about how much bail to set or whether bail should be set at all. Shifting away from the bail reforms of the 1960s that had emphasized whether people accused of crimes were too poor to pay bail and could be released without bail based on the merits of their community support, the bail reforms of the 1980s emphasized that jail could be used to eliminate any and all risk of commission of more crimes before trial. For people who had been perpetual targets of police harassment and senseless arrest, taking criminal histories into account intensified their impact over time. Imagining courts as having the capacity to anticipate the future represented a powerful expansion of judicial power. In a scathing dissent after the Supreme Court affirmed the law in *United States v. Salerno* in 1986, Justice Thurgood Marshall argued that the court's support for bail reform amounted to an "ominous exercise in demolition" of the constitutional rights of due process and protection against excessive bail through "imprisonment upon prediction."³² At the state level, bail reform took even more insidious forms as defendants were effectively jailed on the basis of their presumed guilt. After the passage of a 1985 Illinois bill legalizing the practice, the Illinois State Legislature amended the Illinois State Constitution in 1986 to allow judges to deny bail "where the presumption of guilt is great and if the defendant would pose a risk to the community if released."³³

Political demands for more pretrial incarceration only intensified with the emergence of crack and the discourse around its attendant "epidemic." In Illinois, fifty changes were made to state criminal law between 1986 and 1989 that made sentences stricter and created new offenses. By 1988, the number of people serving drug sentences in Illinois state prisons doubled.³⁴ That year, Jesse Jackson, a Chicago minister and civil rights activist who had long advocated for jailed people, declared himself a "general" in the War on Drugs as he ran for president. Of neighborhood drug sellers, he proposed, "We must drive them out."³⁵

Driving them out, of course, required somewhere to put those people. As the *Chicago Tribune* made its demands for a "bigger, better jail," it featured the complaints of Chicago Police Department superintendent LeRoy Martin prominently. "I am generating narcotics arrests out of my eyeballs," he said. "I need a building, with some bars on the windows, and someone to say, 'That is a jail.'"³⁶ Waiting on the jail to finish construction on two new buildings and the sheriff's use of releases to reduce the population were placing him in a bind. "What good does it do for us to come out and arrest if they have no place to put them?"³⁷

Electronic monitoring appeared to be a perfect solution. People were shackled with waterproof, tamper-proof bracelets or anklets equipped with a short-range transmitter that alerted authorities if the signal went outside of the 150-foot radius of a transmitter located in the wearer's home. Only 1,000 of the 1.9 million people under correctional supervision in the United States were electronically monitored when Sheriff James O'Grady began the program in Cook County in 1988.³⁸ Compared with jailing, which required costly buildings, provisions for prisoners, and staffing, electronic monitoring offered incredible value to Cook County policymakers, who relished being able to reduce the costs of $38.00 a day for jail detention to $9.94 for surveillance.³⁹

Questions of who would profit from electronic monitoring animated the implementation of the program in Cook County. In 1991, debates raged on the Cook County Board of Commissioners over whether the lowest bidder for the county's electronic monitoring contract worth $2.5 million, a Black-owned firm from Washington, DC, was qualified to carry out the shackling of 1,200 to 1,500 people. "Race is exactly what this is about," Jerry Butler, a Black member of the county board, asserted.⁴⁰ Within months, the Cook County Sheriff's Office moved to take over the contract so that the jobs would go to the sheriff's predominantly white, patronage-based staff.⁴¹

Electronic monitoring shifted responsibility for jailing from the county to family members. Portrayals of the program depicted people on electronic monitoring as deeply embedded in family life and dependent on mothers, sisters, and wives for support. As Yvonne Jones, a pregnant South Side resident facing $70,000 bail on a retail theft charge, expressed her relief at dodging incarceration in Cook County Jail to the *Chicago Tribune*, she recalled her sister tossing her a pack of Starburst. If she wanted Skittles, her sister had said, "Go get them yourself." "See what I mean?" Jones laughed. "She knows I can't go nowhere." The lighthearted story wasn't the full story: fearful of missing a nighttime visit from deputies, Jones slept by the front door in her sister's house. Jones and her family experienced perpetual carceral contact because of her electronic monitoring, including three to five surprise visits from county officials each week and four phone calls a day from the contractor managing the program. Nonetheless, Jones appreciated the time it allowed her to spend with her three children. "I get to hold them, to hug them," she said. But just as important to Jones, her sister's home offered her a sense of safety she couldn't find in the jail. "I don't have to worry about beatings."⁴²

The electronic monitoring program presumed that families had the resources to carry out in-home jailing. In 1990, the county negotiated purchase of a city-run rehab facility so it could house homeless people who were eligible for release on electronic monitoring.⁴³ In a 1994 child neglect case involving a Black extended family of twenty-eight people living in a single two-bedroom apartment on Keystone Avenue, one of the mothers in the case failed to show up for court. She was found in jail, having been arrested for her shackle turning off because the power to the apartment had been cut due to nonpayment of the bill.⁴⁴

While policymakers viewed electronic monitoring as appealing because of the increased level of scrutiny from the sheriff's office that participants received before entering the monitoring program, in contrast to judges who allowed people to go free without supervision or bond and required little screening beforehand, families tasked with home incarceration faced risks that they might not otherwise have faced if a family member had free movement.⁴⁵ This was evident in a unique incident when a South Side man on electronic monitoring was arrested on allegations of "raping two young girls at a relative's home . . . both in the home where he was confined." Spencer Leak, head of Cook County Department of Corrections, feeling exasperated that electronic monitoring provided any modicum of freedom, said, "We can't sit in the house with them all day and night."[46] Neither could family members.

Even with thousands of people wearing electronic shackles in Chicago homes, Cook County Jail was making more plans to expand. The 1990 Long-Range Master Plan projected that admissions would rise from 75,000 people a year to 111,500 a year by 2010. The jail would need to nearly double its staff from 2,300 to 4,133 and increase its budget "five-fold" to $500 million.[47] It was impossible to ignore that this was a jail expansion for Black people. The 1990 Master Plan acknowledged that 30 percent of Black men between the ages of twenty and twenty-nine had been to jail in the previous year.

While there was little connection made between the fact that the government had enlisted large numbers of Black citizens as the jailers of their loved ones at home and what the criminalization of families through intensive home surveillance might be doing to their belief in the legitimacy of the rule of law, Black public officials were called to account for solutions that might curb the upward trend in incarceration. Randolph Stone, the county's public defender, said young people turned to crime because of the "hopeless and depressed condition of many urban communities."[48] He called for a turn from crime control to crime prevention, suggesting that addressing child abuse and providing adequate housing, health care, and drug abuse support might help. The Cook County Department of Corrections' director, Spencer Leak, implemented a "Scared Straight" style program, Project Inside Out, that brought eighth graders to the jail to convince them that going to jail was a "big deal." Something had to be done to stigmatize going to jail, Leak said, because the numbers were "an indictment on the black community."[49] The tendency to blame Black communities for hyper-incarceration persisted throughout the 1990s. Harold Bailey, a well-known Black minister and chair of the Cook County Board of Corrections, believed it was incumbent upon people like him to work with communities of color "to find out what we can do to stop this madness of incarceration." Tasked with a solution, he suggested, "I want the young people to cease crime."[50]

The wide appeal of electronic monitoring's racialized rationales fueled perceptions of its success. To local observers, the possibilities seemed endless. Blaming crimes by teenagers on inattentive parents, the *Chicago Tribune* mused that "short of attaching an electronic monitoring device to every kid between 13 and 20, there's little anyone can do to guarantee they won't get into trouble."[51] With great confidence in the deterrent and incapacitating qualities of surveillance, Cook County created a vast network of service provision to control the movement and behavior of those waiting for their day in court.[52] Day reporting, or what one reporter called "invisible jail," aimed to extend "traditional in-jail services" to people who came to jails for short periods during the day.[53]

Participation in the day reporting program represented a significant commitment. In an early iteration of the program, participants were required to appear at Division IX of the jail between 9:30 a.m. and 11:30 a.m., seven days a week; carfare was provided. Over time, however, it expanded into a program from 9:00 a.m. to 3:00 p.m. that included substance abuse treatment, literacy classes, GED classes, violence prevention classes, and job skills training.[54]

For people coming from major population centers such as the city's inner-city housing projects, travel to the remote jail complex required a commitment of at least forty minutes by car. From Cabrini-Green, which was about nine miles northeast of the jail, the bus trip, which included a transfer, could take seventy-five minutes, making for a two-and-a-half-hour round trip, if all the buses ran on time.[55] For those coming to the jail by car from the farthest reaches of the county, the drive could take at least an hour. Parking at one of the paid parking lots of the jail complex and walking to the Day Reporting Center (DRC) took still more time. All of this came with a certain amount of stress: absenteeism and tardiness could be grounds for dismissal from the program and re-arrest.[56] With travel, day reporting was effectively an unpaid, full-time job.

That the predominantly Black cohort of people awaiting trial were presumed to have an implied defect or guilt that could be resolved through programming was a key assumption of programs at the DRC. Operated by TASC, Inc., a social service contractor, the DRC was "a community based facility at which pretrial detainees receive a new start through enhanced supervision along with supportive rehabilitative services."[57] Treatment Alternatives to Street Crime (later changed to Treatment Alternatives for Safe Communities) was formed as a Law Enforcement Assistance Administration pilot program in 1972 as an initiative of the Special Action Office for Drug Abuse Prevention. By the 1990s, the Chicago branch was among the largest of the 125 TASC units across twenty-five states.[58] TASC characterized its day reporting program as an "opportunity" to "help you get on the right track and support your constructive integration in the community."[59]

Blending the punitive and welfare logics of neoliberal social policy popular in the Clinton years, the *Cook County Day Reporting Center Hand Book* suggested that pretrial participants were in the program because they had failed to take personal responsibility. The program offered regular and random drug testing and access to GED programs in addition to a comprehensive counseling program. Such counseling included "reframing culture," "anger management," "violence prevention," "intensive training," "stress management," and group therapy.

Most of the nine tracks ranged from commitments of fifteen to thirty-five hours a week for 45 to 120 days; the tracks included special programming for "accountability," "resistance," "work," and "drug traffickers." In the "drug traffickers" program, participants adhered to a "Rites of Passage" "Training for Manhood program" in which "role models and counselors... guide the young male participants toward responsible adulthood" using "Afrocentric, Latino, [and] European philosophies... to provide a new lifestyle direction." Once participants had completed all tracks and had shown "social awareness, responsibility, acceptability and the ability to stay sober," they could call in to the DRC daily while continuing to await their day in court. Only after "intensive surveillance" could people accused of crimes earn their pretrial freedom.[60]

TASC and the Cook County Sheriff's Office relied on testimonials from Black men to legitimate the program. George, a forty-four-year-old man from Chicago, narrated his transformation from drug user and seller to getting work in a warehouse and looking toward the goal of becoming a "cross-country truck driver." Hasan, twenty years old, found that the DRC was a critical stop on his journey from gang affiliation and cocaine dealing to work on an electronics assembly line. "Life in the streets is short compared to the long life I can live by using the control I realized I had at the DRC," he said, attributing his transformation to becoming "aware of the personal responsibility I had."[61] The narratives did not explain the outcome of the men's trials or whether they had served sentences in jail or prison. Presented as divorced from physical incarceration, the promise of Black men's personal transformation and mobility from the informal to the formal economy would make the trek to the jail worth it.

Programs like day reporting were part of a broader punitive shift that made freedom for Black people increasingly precarious. Imprisonment for violating the terms of freedom for parole, a program to surveil people after release from prison, added to the strain on the state's prisons. The increased criminalization and policing of parole violation had risen from 17 percent of all prisoners sent to Illinois prisons in 1980 to 31 percent in 1991.[62] Parole violations were part of the larger increase to Illinois's prison population by 40 percent between 1985 and 1989, with drug crime incarcerations representing a 300 percent increase among the state's 33,000 prisoners.[63] On average, between 1978 and 1993, Illinois had spent over half a billion dollars building a prison each year. Lavishly, the state spent $16,000 a year to incarcerate each person.[64] With the proportion of Black prisoners by 1997 hovering around 70 percent, the state was spending over $370 million a year on the incarceration of Black people.[65]

To manage the overwhelming numbers of incarcerated people, state officials drew on the concept of the "invisible jail" as they created yet more pliable carceral space in Chicago. The state of Illinois established Community Drug Intervention Units in four metropolitan areas across the state, which relied on teams of two parole officers and a substance abuse counselor to supervise people at "high risk for returning to a pattern of substance abuse" after release from prison.[66]

That the staffing was weighted toward parole officers signified the function of this "treatment" program: the state had innovated a new pathway for urban, ostensibly Black drug users back to prison. That "high intensity" programs in cities were located where Illinois's largest concentrations of Black people population resided—Chicago, Aurora, East St. Louis, and Springfield—added to the spatial project of ensuring that urban African Americans lacked freedom of movement after doing their time.[67] Such projects created what Reuben Jonathan Miller has called "afterlives of incarceration" that extended surveillance and potential for criminalization and reincarceration and introduced rampant logistical challenges into the lives of people released from prison, many without money, identification, or full citizenship.[68]

While community-based treatment programs were framed as potential alternatives to incarceration in local jails and remote prisons—and cost was always a driving imperative in introducing such programs—they were intertwined with the massive expansion of prison and jail space. Black communities bore the brunt of these carceral expansions that demanded they traverse cities and states to maintain and manage degrees of unfreedom both before trial and after prison.

In February 2021, multimedia artist Mohawk Johnson began posting to social media about his struggles with his electronic monitoring equipment. Johnson was arrested by the Chicago Police Department during a Black Lives Matter protest in August 2020. The electronic monitoring system was straining as the program was rapidly expanded amid COVID deaths in Cook County Jail and rampant court delays due to the pandemic. From inside his apartment, Johnson made video after video as he received alerts that he was violating the terms of his monitoring; each time he was accused of a violation, he had to report the false alarm lest it negatively impact his court proceedings. On Twitter and Instagram, Johnson's viral videos made him a national symbol of the stress and frustration that come with meeting the terms of arbitrary terms of surveillance, particularly when that system relies on faulty equipment. "I can't even sleep in my own fucking bed without getting accused of shit," he said in a video after he received an alert while asleep.[69]

By 2021, at least 300,000 people had been shackled through electronic monitoring in Cook County.[70] Always calculated apart from the official population numbers of the county jail, electronic monitoring and other programs operating under names such as "community corrections" or "alternatives to incarceration" have distorted perceptions of the scale and scope of urban mass incarceration. Developed as a stopgap for jail overcrowding amid the War on Drugs, electronic monitoring and pre- and posttrial surveillance programs flourished as modes of criminalizing Black families tasked with jailing family members and in curtailing the freedom before and after trial that previous generations had more easily enjoyed. The development of new carceral technologies and contingencies for freedom was achieved with widespread political awareness of their disparate racial impact. As the decimation of the welfare state under neoliberalism engendered shifts toward rhetoric of "personal responsibility" in the 1990s, so too were Black Chicagoans among the majority of people impressed into "do it yourself" jailing in their homes and charged with convincing each other not to commit crime amid rampant economic and racial inequality. As such programs have consolidated carceral authority under the dominion of white county sheriffs, they have become a means of circumventing community demands for more robust social services. Destroying the boundaries between home and jail, freedom and incarceration, the normalization of surveillance and unfree movement in American cities is fundamental to the operation of "the New Jim Crow" in the twenty-first century.

Notes

1. "As the Jail Bulges, Where Is George?," *Chicago Tribune*, September 9, 1988, 26. Some of the material from this chapter has been published previously; see Melanie D. Newport, *This Is My Jail: Local Politics and the Rise of Mass Incarceration* (Philadelphia: University of Pennsylvania Press, 2023).
2. US Department of Justice, Bureau of Justice Statistics, *Census of Local Jails, 1988*, vol. 3, *Data for Individual Jails in the Midwest* (Washington, DC: US Government Printing Office, 1991), 34–35, 168.
3. St. Clair Drake and Horace R. Cayton, *Black Metropolis: A Study of Negro Life in a Northern City*, 4th ed. (1945; Chicago: University of Chicago Press, 2015); James R. Grossman, *Land of Hope: Chicago, Black Southerners, and the Great Migration* (Chicago: University of Chicago Press, 1991); Davarian L. Baldwin, *Chicago's New Negroes: Modernity, the Great Migration, and Black Urban Life* (Chapel Hill: University of North Carolina Press, 2007); Christopher Robert Reed, *Black Chicago's First Century: Volume 1, 1833–1900* (Columbia: University of Missouri Press, 2017).
4. Tera Eva Agyepong, *The Criminalization of Black Children: Race, Gender, and Delinquency in Chicago's Juvenile Justice System, 1899–1945* (Chapel Hill: University of North Carolina Press, 2018); Cynthia M. Blair, *I've Got to Make My Livin': Black Women's Sex Work in Turn-of-the-Century Chicago* (Chicago: University of Chicago Press, 2010); Simon Balto, *Occupied Territory: Policing Black Chicago from Red Summer to Black Power* (Chapel Hill: University of North Carolina Press, 2019);

Toussaint Losier, "'Prison House of Nations': Police Violence, Mass Incarceration, and the Long Course of Black Insurgency in Illinois, 1953–1987" (PhD diss., University of Chicago, 2013); Newport, *This Is My Jail*.

5. Arnold R. Hirsch, *Making the Second Ghetto: Race and Housing in Chicago, 1940–1960* (Cambridge: Cambridge University Press, 1983); Beryl Satter, *Family Properties: How the Struggle over Race and Real Estate Transformed Chicago and Urban America* (New York: Picador, 2010); Amanda Seligman, *Block by Block: Neighborhoods and Public Policy on Chicago's West Side* (Chicago: University of Chicago Press, 2005); Keeanga-Yamahtta Taylor, *Race for Profit: How Banks and the Real Estate Industry Undermined Black Homeownership* (Chapel Hill: University of North Carolina Press, 2019).

6. Heather Ann Thompson, "Why Mass Incarceration Matters: Rethinking Crisis, Decline, and Transformation in Postwar American History," *Journal of American History* 97, no. 3 (December 2010): 703–34; Carla Shedd, "Countering the Carceral Continuum: The Legacy of Mass Incarceration," *Criminology and Public Policy* 10, no. 3 (2011): 865–71; Jessica T. Simes, *Punishing Places: The Geography of Mass Imprisonment* (Berkeley: University of California Press, 2021); Erin Eife and Gabriela Kirk, "'And You Will Wait . . .': Carceral Transportation in Electronic Monitoring as Part of the Punishment Process," *Punishment and Society* 23, no. 1 (2021): 69–87.

7. Ruth Wilson Gilmore, *Golden Gulag: Prisons, Surplus, Crisis, and Opposition in Globalizing California* (Berkeley: University of California Press, 2007); Adam Malka, *The Men of Mobtown: Policing Baltimore in the Age of Slavery and Emancipation* (Chapel Hill: University of North Carolina Press, 2018); Sarah Haley, *No Mercy Here: Gender, Punishment, and the Making of Jim Crow Modernity* (Chapel Hill: University of North Carolina Press, 2019); Talitha L. LeFlouria, *Chained in Silence: Black Women and Convict Labor in the New South* (Chapel Hill: University of North Carolina Press, 2015); Dan Berger, *Captive Nation: Black Prison Organizing in the Civil Rights Era* (Chapel Hill: University of North Carolina Press, 2016); Robert Chase Smith, *We Are Not Slaves: State Violence, Coerced Labor, and Prisoners' Rights in Postwar America* (Chapel Hill: University of North Carolina Press, 2020); Garrett Felber, *Those Who Know Don't Say: The Nation of Islam, the Black Freedom Movement, and the Carceral State* (Chapel Hill: University of North Carolina Press, 2020); John M. Eason, *Big House on the Prairie: Rise of the Rural Ghetto and Prison Proliferation* (Chicago: University of Chicago Press, 2017); Anne Gray Fischer, *The Streets Belong to Us: Sex, Race, and Police Power from Segregation to Gentrification* (Chapel Hill: University of North Carolina Press, 2022).

8. Winston Moore, "Going Easy on Criminals Encourages Crime," *Ebony*, August 1979, 118.

9. Moore, "Going Easy," 118.

10. Edmund Rooney, "I Won't Quit Fight, Moore Tells Rally," *Chicago Daily News*, September 22, 1976, 2; Newport, *This Is My Jail*, 158.

11. Taylor, *Race for Profit*, chap. 1, 27–35.

12. Elizabeth Dale, *Robert Nixon and Police Torture in Chicago, 1871–1971* (DeKalb: Northern Illinois University Press, 2016); Clifford R. Shaw, *Delinquency Areas: A Study of the Geographic Distribution of School Truants, Juvenile Delinquents, and Adult Offenders in Chicago* (Chicago: University of Chicago Press, 1929).

13. Charles O'Reilley, Frances Cizon, John Flanagan, and Steven Pflanczer, *Men in Jail: A Study of the Sentenced Minor Offender* (New York: Florham Park Press, 1968), 19–20.
14. Alan Anderson and George W. Pickering, *Confronting the Color Line: The Broken Promise of the Civil Rights Movement in Chicago* (Athens: University of Georgia Press, 2008), 258–59.
15. Will Cooley, "Jim Crow Organized Crime: Black Chicago's Underground Economy in the Twentieth Century," in *Building the Black Metropolis: African American Entrepreneurship in Chicago*, ed. Robert E. Weeks Jr. and Jason P. Chambers (Urbana: University of Illinois Press, 2017), 157–58; "Statement of James W. Compton," in *Jobs and Prices in Chicago: Hearing before the Joint Economic Committee, Congress of the United States, Ninety-Fourth Congress, First Session, October 20, 1975* (Washington, DC: US Government Printing Office, 1976), 25–26.
16. Marcia Chatelain, *Franchise: The Golden Arches in Black America* (New York: Liveright, 2020).
17. Carolyn X [White], "#7302473," in *Lyrics of Locked Up Ladies*, ed. Walter Bradford (Chicago: Women's Educational Resource Center, 1976), 81–83.
18. "Position Paper for Action for Survival," July 6, 1970, series 3, box 170, folder 1857, Chicago Urban League Papers, University of Illinois at Chicago Special Collections, 4.
19. Balto, *Occupied Territory*, 235–41.
20. "Fact Sheet: Black Population Loss in Chicago," Great Cities Institute, University of Illinois at Chicago, July 2019, https://greatcities.uic.edu/wp-content/uploads/2019/08/Black-Population-Loss-in-Chicago.pdf.
21. David Axelrod, "800 Face Eviction, Mayor Says," *Chicago Tribune*, March 23, 1981, 1.
22. Gary Rivlin, *Fire on the Prairie: Harold Washington, Chicago Politics, and the Roots of the Obama Presidency*, rev. ed. (Philadelphia: Temple University Press, 2013), 84, 91.
23. City of Chicago, *House of Correction Annual Report* (Chicago, 1961), Municipal Reference Collection, Chicago Public Library–Harold Washington Library Center, 26.
24. Andrew S. Baer, *Beyond the Usual Beating: The Jon Burge Police Torture Scandal and Social Movements for Police Accountability in Chicago* (Chicago: University of Chicago Press, 2020), 101–3.
25. Office of the Superintendent of Police, *Statistical Summary 1980* (Chicago: Chicago Police Department, 1982), 12; Campbell Gibson and Kay Jung, "Table 14. Illinois—Race and Hispanic Origin for Selected Large Cities and Other Places: Earliest Census to 1990," in *Historical Census Statistics on Population Totals by Race, 1790 to 1990, and by Hispanic Origin, 1970 to 1990, for Large Cities and Other Urban Places in the United States, by Population Division*, Working Paper No. 76 (Washington, DC: US Census Bureau, 2005).
26. Wilfredo Cruz, "Minority Leaders Charge Police with 'Disorderly Conduct,'" *Chicago Reporter*, October 1, 1982.
27. Cook County Department of Corrections, *Building Program and Master Plan* (Chicago: A. Epstein and Sons, 1971), Hans W. Mattick Papers, Chicago History Museum Research Center, 30; US Department of Justice, Bureau of Justice Statistics, *Census of Jails, 1983: Vol. II, The Midwest Data for Individual Jails* (Washington, DC: US Government Printing Office, 1981), 15.

28. Newport, *This Is My Jail*, 154.
29. John Howard Association, "Cook County Jail: Blood Still for Sale," *Prison Law and Advocacy*, November–December 1981, 1.
30. Manuel Galvan and Mark Starr, "50 Flee Jail on Bus," *Chicago Tribune*, September 9, 1980, 3.
31. Peter C. Pihos, "The Local War on Drugs," in *The War on Drugs: A History*, ed. David Farber (New York: New York University Press, 2021), 144.
32. United States v. Salerno, 481 US 739 (1987); Al Kamen, "Court Upholds Preventive Detention," *Washington Post*, May 27, 1987, A1.
33. Illinois Criminal Justice Information Authority, "Crowding at the Cook County Jail: Historical Perspective and Current Strategies," October 1989, Municipal Reference Collection, Chicago Public Library–Harold Washington Library Center, 10; Civia Tamarkin, "The Judge Who Wore a Wire," *American Bar Association Journal* 70, no. 2 (February 1984): 76–80; Christine Devitt and James Coldren, *The Pretrial Process in Cook County: An Analysis of Bond Decisions Made in Felony Cases during 1982–1983* (Chicago: Illinois Criminal Justice Information Authority, August 1987), 29.
34. Peter Manikas, Mindy Trossman, and Jack Doppelt, *Crime and Criminal Justice in Cook County: A Report of the Criminal Justice Project* (Evanston, IL: Center for Urban Affairs and Policy Research, 1989), 154–55.
35. Cheryl Devall, "Jackson Calls Himself 'General' in Drug War," *Chicago Tribune*, May 23, 1988, 2.
36. "Cook County Needs Another Jail," *Chicago Tribune*, September 6, 1988, 16.
37. Matt O'Connor, "Jail Forced to Free Accused Robbers," *Chicago Tribune*, September 11, 1988, 1.
38. Matt O'Connor, "Monitor Testing Set for Freed Inmates," *Chicago Tribune*, December 9, 1988, 6; "Electronic Devices Tracking Parolees," *New York Times*, April 22, 1987, D7. For a contemporary critique of electronic monitoring, see James Kilgore, *Electronic Monitoring Is Not the Answer: Critical Reflections on a Flawed Alternative* (Urbana-Champaign, IL: Independent Media Center, 2015).
39. Tom Gibbons, "Electronic Monitoring OKd to Cut Jam at Jail," *Chicago Sun-Times*, April 4, 1989, 3; Matt O'Connor, "Bracelets Replace Bars in Jail Release Program," *Chicago Tribune*, July 4, 1989, 1; "Audit of Prisoner Monitoring Sought," *Chicago Tribune*, September 28, 1990, 3.
40. Charles Mount, "Black-Owned Firm Gets Monitor Pact," *Chicago Tribune*, June 18, 1991, 23.
41. Andrew Fegelman, "Panel Oks More Electronic Monitors," *Chicago Tribune*, March 11, 1993, 105.
42. O'Connor, "Bracelets Replace Bars in Jail Release Program," 13.
43. Matt O'Connor, "Group Warns of Shortages at Jail," *Chicago Tribune*, March 10, 1990, 5.
44. Tom Pelton, "6 Keystone Adults Are Found Guilty," *Chicago Tribune*, April 22, 1994, 17.
45. O'Connor, "Bracelets Replace Bars in Jail Release Program," 13.
46. "Freed Inmate Accused of 2 Rapes," *Chicago Tribune*, June 6, 1990, 58.

47. Matt O'Connor, "15,000 Seen at County Jail by Year 2010," *Chicago Tribune*, September 21, 1990, N1.
48. Matt O'Connor, "29% of Young Black Men Jailed in '89," *Chicago Tribune*, September 23, 1990.
49. Rosalind Rossi and Tom McNamee, "3 of 10 Young Black Men Here Jailed in '89," *Chicago Sun-Times*, September 23, 1990, 3.
50. Chinta Strausberg, "Bailey Re-elected Corrections Board Chair," *Chicago Defender*, June 11, 1996.
51. Editorial, "More Teens, More Violence," *Chicago Tribune*, September 18, 1995, 12.
52. On the welfare state origins of mass incarceration, see Elizabeth Hinton, *From the War on Poverty to the War on Crime: The Making of Mass Incarceration in America* (Cambridge, MA: Harvard University Press, 2016).
53. S. D. Williams, "Invisible Jail: Day Reporting Centers," *Corrections Compendium* 15, no. 7 (September 1990): 1, 4–7.
54. John Howard Association, "Court Monitoring Report of *Duran v. Sheahan et al.*," February 5, 1993, Municipal Reference Collection, Chicago Public Library, Harold Washington Library Center, 31–32; Cook County Sheriff's Office, *The Cook County Day Reporting Center* (brochure), n.d., box 7, folder 3, Charlotte E. Senechalle Papers, Chicago History Museum Research Center, 2.
55. Chicago Transit Authority, Chicago Transit Map, "CTA Surface System History," May 1996, Illinois Railway Museum, http://irm-cta.org/RouteMaps/FullMaps/051 -060/CTA-Map056_Front.jpg.
56. Cook County Sheriff's Office, *DCSI's Day Reporting Center* (brochure), n.d., box 7, folder 3, Charlotte E. Senechalle Papers.
57. Sheriff's Office of Cook County, *Cook County Day Reporting Center Hand Book*, n.d., box 5, folder 8, Charlotte E. Senechalle Papers, 4. TASC, or Treatment Alternatives to Street Crime, was a national program founded in 1972 and established in Illinois in 1976; see www.tasc.org/content/tasc-history (accessed February 25, 2015, site discontinued); and J. J. Robinson and A. J. Lurigio, "Responding to Overcrowding and Offender Drug Use: How about Community Corrections Approach?," *Perspectives* 14, no. 4 (Fall 1990): 22–27.
58. M. Douglas Anglen et al., *Studies of the Functioning and Effectiveness of Treatment Alternatives to Street Crime (TASC) Programs, Final Report* (Los Angeles: UCLA Drug Abuse Research Center, 1996), 3, 12.
59. Sheriff's Office of Cook County, *Cook County Day Reporting Center Hand Book*, 4.
60. Sheriff's Office of Cook County, *Cook County Day Reporting Center Hand Book*, 14–22.
61. Cook County Sheriff's Office, *DCSI's Day Reporting Center*.
62. Brian Fairchild, "Illinois 'Gets Smart' on Crime," *Insight into Corrections*, July 1993, 3.
63. Fairchild, "Illinois 'Gets Smart' on Crime," 3.
64. Fairchild, "Illinois 'Gets Smart' on Crime," 5, 12.
65. Karen S. Levy McCanna, "Illinois Prison Population Trends," *Trends and Issues Update* 4, no. 1 (July 1999): 1–4.
66. Fairchild, "Illinois 'Gets Smart' on Crime," 9.
67. "Illinois Task Force on Crime and Corrections: Final Report," March 1993, 37, US

Department of Justice, Office of Justice Programs, www.ojp.gov/ncjrs/virtual-library/abstracts/illinois-task-force-crime-and-corrections-final-report.
68. Reuben Jonathan Miller, *Halfway Home: Race, Punishment, and the Afterlife of Mass Incarceration* (New York: Little, Brown, 2021).
69. Leor Galil, "On House Arrest with Mohawk Johnson," *Chicago Reader*, March 31, 2021.
70. Chicago Appleseed Center for Fair Courts and Chicago Council of Lawyers, "10 Facts about Pretrial Electronic Monitoring in Cook County," September 2021, 2, Chicago Appleseed Center for Fair Courts, www.chicagoappleseed.org/2021/09/22/10-facts-about-pretrial-electronic-monitoring-in-cook-county.

J. T. ROANE

Topology of Flames

The Political Ecology of Fire in Late Twentieth-Century Philadelphia

On May 13, 1985, Ramona Africa commandeered the airwaves of the Cobbs Creek neighborhood. Taking up the loudspeaker that she and other members of MOVE used to broadcast the group's beliefs, its biting criticism of the system—for the group, including markets, the state, and normalizing civil society—and its demands for the immediate release of the group's political prisoners, Ramona Africa denounced Philadelphia's first Black mayor, Wilson Goode, in what proved to be a chilling prediction of the violence the Philadelphia Police Department later unleashed with the tacit support of Mayor Goode: "In 1985 we gonna make Wilson Goode look ten times worse than [former mayor] Frank Rizzo.... He gonna get a whole bunch of Black folks killed."[1] Later that day, police acting under orders of Police Commissioner Gregor Sambor dropped from a helicopter federal-grade plastics explosives procured from local Bureau of Alcohol, Tobacco, Firearms and Explosives agents on the top of the home where MOVE members lived while the fire department stood in inaction. All of the MOVE family members in the Osage Avenue home were killed except for Ramona and the young Birdie Africa. Although police and city officials justified the escalation in violence against the group in the name of protecting MOVE's neighbors, the horrific bombing combined with the fire department's inaction incinerated the neighborhood of sixty-one homes, displacing the residents the city had ostensibly sought to protect.[2]

Critical to recognize within the timing of Ramona Africa's statements is that her prediction that the city's first Black mayor could lead the forces of anti-Black violence preceded the extrajudicial state murder of the eleven MOVE members and the clearing of the neighborhood by fire. While perhaps earlier Black mayoral regimes had diminished the radical hopes and aims of Black Power's electoral transition, Goode's administration underscored the reality that Black political interests could align themselves seamlessly with anti-Black violence in the urban context. Goode, through his personal capacity to serve as the face of the local state in its transition and as the embodiment of reasoned interlocutor between corporate real estate interests and the interests of the city's Black communities—flattened through the projection of Black "middle-class" home-owning interests as all Black residents' interests—facilitated the motley urban reterritorialization by fire, not as a contradiction but as a complement from the perspective of the city's Black working-class and other vulnerable communities inhabiting the core neighborhoods. Rebranding the city from a deindustrializing manufacturing center to a site of corporate real estate investment required the "aesthetic emplacement of Blackness," the city's sublimation of the creative energies of its Black communities through various references to a Black history of place combined with the violent dislocation of multiple valences of fire that literally and metaphorically consumed Black working-class neighborhoods.[3] While promoting measures of symbolic and business-oriented inclusion, ranging from the promotion of the Odunde Festival to increasing the hiring of Black city contractors, Goode also shunned the squatter movement seeking to transform housing in the early 1980s, focused attention and resources on punitive anti-graffiti efforts in the name of cleaning up the city, facilitated public-private partnerships for large-scale redevelopment projects such as the convention center and the city's sport's stadiums, and committed capital to the attraction of media companies to the city as part of his efforts at raising the economic tide and tax base in order to lift all the city's communities out of poverty—the precondition of which was the general removal or disposability of those viewed as hindrances to accumulation through financialization and development.

In the remainder of this essay, I partially excavate the wider matrix of infrastructural volatility that followed the fragmentation of the shared infrastructures of living, especially the post-1981 fiscal crisis spurred by federal housing austerity that set the conditions for the escalation of social and political tensions in the 1980s, forming part of the terrain for the city's deadly assault on MOVE. Before reconstructing the political ecology of fire in 1980s Philadelphia, I first consider Black writers' responses to the destruction of MOVE. These artists contextualized the Philadelphia Police Department's attempts to annihilate MOVE within the wider social and political terrain of the city and nation that made the bombing of a row house and the fiery destruction of an entire community conceivable and justifiable. This sets the coordinates for my engagement with the scorched archive of extant municipal records related to house fires in the year before the attempts to destroy MOVE as well as with newspapers that document significant losses of life in the deindustrializing city. Beyond simply measuring death, I analyze the peculiar kind of work that internal-facing city documents did in the reconfiguration of the state and in relation to its legitimation within majoritarian community formations and local alternative community formations, performed in naturalizing and challenging the political ecology of deadly fires through the recursive emphasis on individual culpability as well as the rejection of this paradigm. The Detective White Papers in the Philadelphia Department of Records and City Archives in particular illustrate the ways that insinuations and tropes of irresponsibility related to smoking and "playing with matches" helped to hide the collective vulnerability of Black communities to infrastructural disintegration in the era around the attempted destruction of MOVE.

By "majoritarian," I am distinguishing my characterization of communities from simply saying "white majorities." While this terminology does include politicized versions of the majority-European-descended demographic at its center, it also encompasses some Black and other non-white groupings with overlapping and allied interests—especially in this context, social formations centering homeownership and reinforcing real estate value as the governing logic of the city in a complex interplay between top-down and bottom-up social formations shaped by the rise of vengeance politics in the 1980s and 1990s.[4] This is not to conflate holding of a title for a home and a broader ideological outlook securing the values associated with capitalist value in land but to point to the particular affiliations and associations that helped to reterritorialize the city in this fiery context, critically in the 1980s increasingly including significant Black public figures and the interests for which they came to stand.

Black Writers' Responses to the Bombing

Philadelphia's attempt to annihilate MOVE under Mayor Goode brought to a head the ways that the group came to serve as the living embodiment of perilous hindrances to producing and sustaining value in the sense of speculation in land and accumulation through members' anti-normative reproduction of the city, their commitment to deurbanizing the cityscape, and their disruptive abolition politics. Through their actions, MOVE members politicized a significant contradiction within this context as direct, vocal, and antagonistic interrupters to the political status quo and in particular as disruptors of Goode's careful efforts to steward the city's economic order from deindustrializing manufacturing center to a site of corporate real estate investment and support for the development of the city's infrastructures, underscoring the city as a site of tourism, entertainment, and mass media capital.

Sonia Sanchez, Joseph Beam, Essex Hemphill, Michelle Parkerson, and Wayson Jones used their writing to contextualize the disregard for MOVE members' basic right to life as part of a matrix of anti-Black political and social violence extending across time and related to the unfolding of the present in the city as well as its critical other coordinate, its geography—the neighborhood, region, country, and diaspora in the context of global repression and apartheid. Writing in the weeks that followed the bombing, Joseph Beam recalled and helped to situate the violence of "gunfire, a deluge of water, and finally, a catastrophic fire" that had nearly obliterated MOVE. Beam connected this imagery of racialized modes of destruction with a longer history of racist violence when he cited the lingering "stench of Black flesh turning blacker." The author used this disturbing imagery resonant with accounts of burning related to lynching and destructive forms of anti-Black arson to index blackening as the rhetorical and material power of racism to generate disposability, exposure, and death. Beam's accounting of blackening flesh connected the bombing and its aftermath—"11 Black people dead," the "53 families homeless"—to the history of normalizing bureaucratic and surveillance power in Philadelphia that he also recognized as dangerous to the possibilities for his life as a Black queer subject, describing forces that had sought the annihilation of MOVE as "agents of normalcy and decency." He went further to note that the bombing caused him "psychic scars" and made him "deeply afraid," as "a Black gay man who is a writer," for his "life and [his] home."[5]

In August 1986, Michelle Parkerson, Essex Hemphill, and Wayson Jones performed *Voicescapes: An Urban Mouthpiece* at the Painted Bride Art Center in Philadelphia. Their set included various choreo-poems that, according to reviewer Kimmika Williams, "recreated almost profound poetic profiles of some of the common people one might encounter in the city."[6] This description is apt given the complex ways in which Hemphill's poetry, written or performed, searingly captures the possibilities of Black and Black queer life in US cities during the decades of the 1980s and 1990s, part of the aliveness entangled with death that shapes the contours of his poetry.[7] As part of their larger set, Parkerson, Hemphill, and Jones also performed one of Hemphill's urgent pieces, "What Will Be Bombed Today?," which, along with other instances of global political violence, highlighted the violence on May 13, 1985, that ended with the deaths of eleven of MOVE's members on Osage Avenue in West Philadelphia.

A recording of the "What Will Be Bombed Today?" from 1987 in Washington, DC, posted on YouTube by Hemphill's longtime collaborator Wayson Jones, sounds the power that most certainly punctuated the previous Philadelphia performance. Hemphill and Jones began the piece by setting its rhythm through the repetition of "What will be, be bombed bombed, bombed?" Parkerson overlaid this with a set of sharp and critical rhetorical questions related to the primary one, "What will be bombed today?" The effect was to highlight the constitutive nature of violence to the American and global apartheid social order and therefore to connect the violence demonstrated in the Philadelphia Police Department's bombing of MOVE to the profusion of destructive force animating US power historically and into the recent receding of the smoke along Osage Avenue. Parkerson, through Hemphill's words, connected the "cindered" house where "firemen will stand around watching the block burn to the ground" with lynching—"a ni——er" in a tree do you see?"—and the burning of a Salem witch. Parkerson's performance connected to the political violence associated with anti-Blackness and gendering violence beyond the United States, as well, particularly to the 1980s intensification of apartheid in South Africa through the reference within the performance poem to a bombing of "another funeral in Soweto" and an abortion clinic.

Like Parkerson, Hemphill, and Jones, Sonia Sanchez's poem "Elegy (for MOVE and Philadelphia)" used poetic verse to situate the bombing within a longer history and wider economy of anti-Black violence, rhetoric, and ideology. She dissected the character of the nature of the life-ending force outside MOVE itself and located the capacity to kill as the maiming and murderous capaciousness of mainstream American institutions, those reproducing whiteness. Sanchez described Philadelphia as "a disguised southern city" replete with a motley cast of characters that invoke imperial domination, including cowboys, a "phalanx of parsons and auctioneers," "modern gladiators erasing the delirium of death from their shields," and puritans. Sanchez highlighted the geographic differences between West Philadelphia's predominantly Black sections in the period, including Cobbs Creek, where the city bombed MOVE, and downtown, where the majoritarian public took "sanctuary in taverns and corporations." Here Sanchez poetically explored the geographic separation that helped to render Black people beyond a right to life in the landscape, the bifurcated city of tourist and corporate reproduction and the "over there" that is a cognitive, discursive, and material outside where bombing people and burning homes can find legitimacy to the majority. Sanchez underlined the work of the media in inoculating the city's and the world's conscience for the "dreadlocks and blk/skins roasting in the fire." She described journalists as chloroforming the city, invoking a chemically induced unconsciousness to highlight the subtle and surreptitious treachery of reporters in shaping discussions of the bombing. Given the poem's mood, Sanchez's refusal of the passivity of chloroform as a substance, invoking an anesthetic ease to pain, and her employment of "chloroforming" suggests sinister incapacitation.

Sanchez's interpretation of the media's role as violent if superficially bloodless was further buttressed in the aforementioned 1987 Painted Bride and Washington, DC, live performances of Hemphill's "What Will Be Bombed Today?" Parkerson asked a twinned question that highlights the violence of the media: "Do the newspapers panic you? Do YOU sleep with a gun under your pillow?"[8] Parkerson through Hemphill as well as Sanchez named the media as the producers of the kind of panic informing quotidian acts of supposed self-protection, from violence to "sleeping with" a murderous weapon.

Later in her poem, Sanchez articulated the violent and mystifying narrations provided by the media as extending beyond periodicals to sites of official remembering and collective self-articulation: the "tourist roadhouses," which she described as trading in lobotomies. Here Sanchez indicted the media and a larger apparatus of official truth for their role in justifying and further perpetuating the violence, their actions akin to severing of connections between points of the brain in order to render one incapacitated through surgically induced debilitation. Sanchez reworked the radical alterity of MOVE established through the scorching flames as exception and driven further by the "chloroforming" of the media by naming dense sites of white racial formation—the "tourist roadhouses" as the sites of incapacitation—locating violence with the white majority who remained passive or who actively embraced the deaths of MOVE members.

Black writers and artists provide a critical opening for thinking about the ways that the reprehensible bombing of MOVE was possible within a wider economy of anti-Black, pro-apartheid, misogynist, and homophobic violence in the mid-1980s. In the next section, I partially examine a critical analysis through political ecology of proliferating fires in the period around the police bombing of MOVE.

Scorched City

On March 20, 1984, a fire that began at 41 N. Peach Street in West Philadelphia spread to the two adjoining houses, 39 and 43 N. Peach. Five Black children—three-month-old Taymar Kennedy, three-year-olds Edith Davis and Tayron Kennedy, five-year-old Shelina Guy, and eight-year-old Artavius Guy—remained trapped in the blaze and succumbed to it. Additionally, five other inhabitants—Beverly Davis, Patricia Thompkins, Lester Kennedy, Terrell Guy, and Cecil Guy—also sustained serious injuries due to smoke inhalation and burns despite narrowly escaping with their lives. All of those injured during the fire, despite damage to all three properties, were inhabitants of 41 N. Peach, where the fire originated.[9]

On April 18, 1984, Paula Benson and her children—twelve-year-old Monique, eight-year-old Monica, and four-year-old Marquika Benson—were settled into their North Philadelphia row house at 5239 N. Warnock Street for the night. The filling of the second floor with dense black smoke and the crackle of wood in the growing inferno alerted Paula to the danger. Unable to reach her children in the rear bedroom on the second floor, she ran out to a neighbor's house to call the fire department. When officers arrived, they found the first floor engulfed by flames and heavy smoke. Alerted by Paula of the danger facing her children, officers broke open the windows to the back bedroom on the second floor and removed the children. Despite suffering second-degree burns and smoke inhalation, the Bensons escaped the deadly fate of many others who succumbed in this context to the proliferation of fire.[10]

Earlier in March 1982, a fire erupted in a small apartment on the first floor of a building at Twenty-Second and Diamond Streets in North Philadelphia. The thick smoke trapped people on the third floor of the building, including a two-year-old, Yusef Kelly. Three young boys, Kevin Kelly, Kynatta Hughston, and "Benie" Jordan, found the toddler in the smoke and took him safely from the building. In their March 23, 1982, article covering the story, Deborah A. Vickers and Nashormeh Wilkie honored the young boys as heroes and announced that they would be honored with certificates of bravery by the Richard Allen Hildebrand Community Center and Jones Tabernacle AME Church. The heroics of the youth, for Vickers and Wilkie, offset the youth stories common to the era, "the age of widespread delinquency and juvenile crime."[11]

As this macabre recalling of the infrastructural violence of deindustrializing Philadelphia suggests, the row house is a form burdened by the orienting and intensifying effect of gravity on fire with the row house appropriating and enclosing three and four stories along a narrow articulation alongside a front-facing street connecting this living space primarily with sites of work through roads, sidewalks, bus lines, subways, and other infrastructures of transit. With the emergence of industrial factories of scale in the nineteenth century, the row house tracts expanded as the primary space for housing workers in Philadelphia as the "kind of space of classical or market capitalism in terms of a logic of the grid, a reorganization of some older sacred and heterogenous space into geometrical and Cartesian homogeneity, a space of infinite equivalence and extension," with Philadelphia extending most faithfully forms of "mechanical reproduction."[12] Extending living space in the limited spatial economy of the narrow parcels derived from the rationalization over the coordinates of geology and nature into private property in urban land; dense, unplanned tracts in the industrial metropolis shaped by historical rounds of speculation; and verticality in the form of basements and two to four stories that begin from the entry floor enhance susceptibility to fire.

Marcus Hunter has underscored gravity's vulnerability for urban residents through his recounting the collapse of a row house near the South Street district.[13] The dangers of gravity with poorly maintained and overburdened housing extend to gravity's effect on combustion. As Robert A. Altenkirch discusses in an interview with *Scientific American* regarding experiments with how alternative gravitational fields affect combustion on earth, gravity tends to anchor fire, reinforcing its intensity as hot gases move upward, drawing oxygen toward the lower portion of the fire.[14] This microclimate of the fire oriented vertically by gravity creates a suction that amplifies the temperature of the material serving as the fire's primary source of fuel and allowing it to spread. Fire is intensified by gravity such that while fires are sometimes easier to start under similar conditions of oxygenation with less gravitational force, they tend to dissipate rather than intensify outside a dense gravitational field.

As the deadly and traumatizing profile above suggests, living quarters in row houses are often on the second floor or above. And in row houses subdivided by landlords into apartments, the concentration of living space above the first floor is further concentrated. The vertical enclosure of the row house intensifies the fueling of fire and draws smoke upward, causing those who live above the first floor to be injured or killed in their exposure to the smoke. It is the ideal condition for fire to spread along both this vertical axis and, with enough intensity, horizontally between row houses if given enough time.

Black communities who succumbed to fire lived disproportionately in tracts of row houses built speculatively to house nineteenth-century workers and their families, and without an overarching adaptive plan for the creation of neighborhoods beyond the basic parameters of reproduction of nineteenth-century industrial workers. This landscape of living harbored the past imperatives of industrial titans long since dead, compounding the new vulnerabilities of postindustrial life with the old vulnerabilities associated with the mechanically reproduced city. Nineteenth-century forms of housing as a vertical enclosure associated with reproducing workers was overlaid by the intensified anti-Black gravity orienting the violent reterritorialization of Philadelphia in the era of working-class Black communities' displacement from industrial labor. The gravity of anti-Blackness oriented and enhanced social combustion in the urban reterritorializations of the late twentieth-century United States, marking the social location of the city's housing stock vulnerable along with other working-class neighborhoods where former factories and other abandoned housing remained vulnerable to owner arson-for-profit and deteriorating infrastructure enhanced by retrenchment of housing programs.

In the context of the 1980s infernos engulfing the city and taking a disproportionate number of vulnerable Black people and the other communities marked as disposable, city leadership embraced violent and effacing descriptions whereby they absolved landlords for the recklessness of abandonment, contempt, and neglect while blaming the victims for their own injuries and deaths. In addition to the enhancing effects of anti-Black gravity on infrastructural vulnerability, Black fire victims remained as well subject to a form of double victimhood through the form of nefarious inscription. A pie chart encoding data from 1982 created by the fire commissioner's office ranked the categories "careless smoking" and "children playing with matches" as the two leading causes of fire deaths, together composing 60 percent of Philadelphia's deadly fires.[15]

There is no way to determine definitively the nature of these fires and their origins, given the nonpublic and subsequent regular destruction of fire records, according to an official I contacted in order to seek access to fire department records. In documents that the city has retained within White Papers from the 1980s in the city archives, including this data, the language used by the fire investigators insinuate and naturalize carelessness on the part of Black victims, casting aspersion on these statistics. Carelessness, indifferent child-rearing, and the insinuation of arson served the general effect of papering over the violent social murder enacted by retrenchment in state allocations for housing as well as the effects of absentee landlordism.

Data on fire deaths by month from 1983 reveal by the department's own reporting that November, December, and January, three of the coldest months of the year, reported forty-nine deaths, or more than half of the total eighty-nine deaths due to fires in the city. There is another peak, perhaps unanticipated in one of the hottest months of the year, July, which had a total of eight deaths, compared with June's three and August's four deaths. This distribution of fire deaths with the largest peaks in the coldest months as well as a smaller upsurge in one of the hotter months suggests the proliferation of house fires was related to the matters of heating, cooling, and electrical wiring. If careless smoking and children with matches represent the most likely causes of fire according to the fire department, this does not neatly correspond to the uneven distribution of fire deaths per month.

The use of bureaucratic insinuation to hide the violence of neglect on the part of absentee landlords is evident in a report from 1984 following the death of a Black youth in Southwest Philadelphia. At two o'clock in the afternoon on Sunday, March 11, 1984, Jacqueline Wheeler and the child in her care, eight-year-old

George Gaskins, sat to watch television in the front room of Wheeler's apartment. George went to the back room of the apartment when suddenly Wheeler noticed the front of the apartment filling with dense black smoke. Although she and other residents of the apartments attempted to rescue Gaskins, the boy succumbed to smoke inhalation. The documentation of the incident in the city's White Papers shows a disconcerting contempt and disregard for vulnerable Black people, particularly children, within the outlook of these agents of the state. Rather than condemning the apartment owner and his lack of accountability for "faulty electrical wire," detectives suggested that Gaskins "may have been playing" with the wiring, implying that he may have caused his own untimely demise. Despite Wheeler's statement that George had gone to the back room only three minutes before the apartment filled with smoke, detectives cast aspersions on the boy and his caretaker while carefully avoiding any language that might indicate the responsibility of the landlord in the youth's untimely perishing.[16]

In the context of this vulnerability, the city's "firsts" in Black political leadership redoubled commitments by the city's chief agencies to formulations for fire safety that avoided the question of a political ecology of fire in vulnerability. During Harold Hairston's tenure as Philadelphia's first Black fire commissioner for Mayor Ed Rendell's administration, smoke detectors came to serve as the antidote for the unsound infrastructures of housing in public discussions as promoted by fire officials and the city. As early emphases on "adaptive architecture," smoke detectors did not address faulty wires or explosive boilers but simply alerted residents to leave a structure in the case of a fire already in progress.

Smoke detectors are fickle, themselves subject to deterioration and dead batteries. Often the heat of an intensive fire obscures whether they were functional prior to a blaze. As technologies, they preserve and enhance the unevenness of vulnerability of the city's declining housing stock in neighborhoods of disinvestment shaped by discrimination in real estate and mortgage markets on top of the racist labor market and exacerbate the vulnerability of disoriented youth, disabled persons, seniors, or any others who might not process the shrill alert in what's embedded within their use as a rational plan for escape. This is compounded during sleeping hours and for those with limited or absent mobility. Hairston's use of press conferences to criticize the parents of lost youth and caretakers for elders for the improper use of the devices, or their absence, naturalized the vulnerability of the city's housing stock and located the onus of responsibility of death by fire on residents and tenants. As technological solutions, smoke detectors dislocate responsibility for succumbing to smoke and flames onto vulnerable residents, especially those not having procured a functioning one. Their installation anticipates the escape hatches and other architectural novelties proposed as additions to homes in New Orleans following Hurricane Katrina that address individual survivability but that anticipate mass vulnerability. They moved from a technological novelty in the 1960s to a feature that all responsible residents were tasked with upkeeping in the same period of the state's retraction from responsibility for housing, coming to serve as a commonsense fix for the rapidly exacerbating unevenness of the metropolis under a shifting political economic regime.

In the wake of a number of high-profile fires that resulted in the deaths of children, Hairston underscored lapses in responsibility for the upticks in deaths in the mid-1990s. In the wake of a 1997 fire that killed forty-one-year-old Ronald Davenport as well as twenty-three-year-old Fatima Bonner; her three children, six-year-old Sherrell Bonner Roberson, four-year-old Kareem Fittimon, and two-year-old Ki-ara Fittimon; and their cousin eleven-month-old Devin Leatherberry Jr., Commissioner Hairston gave a press conference emblazoned with two large signs depicting tombstones with the child victims' names and an inscription that read "Fire is killing our children. It's not their fault, it's our responsibility." While producing the children as victims, this rhetoric of "fault" and "responsibility" suggested the culpability of Bonner and the elder victim as well as the others who sustained injuries, including Bonner's brother, twenty-five-year-old Mark Bonner. Rather than an innocuous lament of the children's death, Hairston used the press conference to reinforce an ostensibly harmless pronouncement about children's safety that indicted the families of youth victims of the city's infrastructural hostility for the preponderance of death. During the press conference, Hairston used the tragic circumstances to advance criticism for parents rather than for the city's housing authorities: "My experience tells me that children do not get themselves out. It's as simple as that. They get confused in a fire. And, although you may have a very, very precocious child, they cannot save themselves if you don't get them by the hand and if you don't march them out of the place. That's the way you save your children." Although this pronouncement had no bearing in the facts of the particular fire, the tragedy provided an opening and cover for hiding infrastructural vulnerability in plain sight. The reporter covering Hairston's press conference following the fire concluded that "smoke detectors could have prevented the tragedy. So might have careful smoking."[17]

Arson

Beyond these directly identifiable cases, the insinuation of arson along with the quotidian demarcation of fires and fire-related deaths as the result of residents' "irresponsibility" helped to create uncertainty about the nature of fires and their relationship to the deterioration of the infrastructures of living and cohabitation and the tyranny of value in an anti-Black political economy exacerbated by evaporating industrial jobs met with retrenchment and state austerity. Accusations of arson served to truncate in public discourse the nature of house and industrial fires to a "type" of antisocial behavior associated with "intentional fires" often concerning behavioral issues related to anger and revenge generated in response to familial life. Despite the growing public awareness of the proliferation of arson driven by antisocial behavior, the accusation of intentional fire was difficult to prove without eyewitness evidence by court standards, making the ultimate culprit in life-altering and devastating blazes nearly impossible to resolve. It is in this hazy zone created through journalistic profiling—including a kind of late twentieth-century popularization of criminological-inflected reporting, regular public accusation of arson without public resolution of cases, and the sensationalizing of certain cases—that arson as a discourse gained its power through its capacity for clouding and disorientation, much like the smoke itself.

This spread of fires was characterized by then mayor Frank Rizzo's brother, the fire commissioner, in 1976 as an "epidemic of arson." In a front-page story from July 1977, *Inquirer* journalist Elizabeth Duff compiled a composite arsonist through the stories of a boy of twelve, Tim, who endured his parents' ubiquitous fighting; a twenty-seven-year-old man, Jim, who "seems perpetually angry" and jealous of his wife; and fifty-year-old John, whom Duff described as an "alcoholic of low intelligence [and] with a long criminal record." These sequential narratives together outline the arsonist along a pathological life-course and suggest that the "societal sickness" of arson might appear anywhere along the development of the boy to the more senior man convicted of intentionally setting destructive fires toward various ends but most often driven by rage associated with interpersonal insecurity and violence. This depiction casts arson as a formulation of social delinquency emerging from individual family dynamics.[18]

By the early 1980s Philadelphia, "arson for profit" emerged as a recognized tactic employed by landowners seeking to recover insurance from properties destroyed by fires they set or paid to have set, consuming old factories as well as buildings inhabited by vulnerable Black and Blackened communities. These cases, such as the one described by journalist Dick Cooper in 1981, provided ample material to condemn those involved in destroying other peoples' residences for crass financial gain. Following a tenant-led rent strike at Monterey Apartments at Forty-Third and Chester Avenue, co-owner of the apartments Frederick Sturm hired Michael Raffa to burn the inhabited segment of the complex down in order to collect the insurance, displacing all of the families and attempting to defraud insurance companies through the $480,000 claim in insurance covering fires. This kind of case had a double effect on the residents of Black and Blackened communities in the era of deindustrialization. This fire directly displaced residents who possessed enough social and political connections to stage a rent strike over heat and hot water. Additionally, the tactic of burning down buildings and collecting insurance on residential and former industrial properties contributed to the zeroing out of value in core city neighborhoods by rendering whole segments virtually uninsurable. As the federal court formulations suggests, the primary concern of the courts was never the displaced residents, despite Cooper's mention of them, but rather the issues related to conspiracy to commit insurance fraud.

The heinousness of this condemnable action by landowners to profit from calculated destruction and an individual's willingness to accept cash to do it must not obscure the new urban federal reconstruction and resource allocation that cases receiving attention facilitated and through which "arson for profit" became identifiable within public discourse and naturalized through reporting on new partnerships between policing agencies that directly set the scene for the city's bombing of MOVE. As Cooper's reporting centers foremost, the prosecution of Sturm and Raffa and the ability to identify "arson for profit" emerged through a partnership between the city's fire investigators, Philadelphia police, and agents of the federal ATF, with the "Monterey Apartments case" unlikely to "have gone to trial if traditionally rival agencies had not begun sharing information and investigating here during the mid-1970s."[19] Arson was both a material reality and a figuration facilitating the recalibration of state power in the deindustrializing urban context, providing new collaborative relationships between the agents conspiring in 1985 to immolate MOVE.

Again, Black city officials, this time Wilson Goode acting prior to his mayoral administration, as city managing director under Mayor William J. Green, helped to reinforce a vision of enforcement anticipating key reterritorialization of the urban political economy and geography with long-term effects on the demographic and political composition of Philadelphia and the formulation of budget, property, and a form of majoritarian, proprietary citizenship associated with small business owners and homeowners that inaugurated new forms of urban power. Goode helped to establish, along with members of Kensington Action Now, the arson task force to address and manage cases of suspected intentional fire in the neighborhood. Kensington Action Now joined with churches, an insurance company, and foundations to establish a plan for revitalizing Kensington. In order to protect and insure this interest in the neighborhood, the members of the association envisioned that they would augment the city's fire investigations primarily through an arson prevention program. The arson task force would work with police and fire officials as well as building inspectors to note "likely" "arson targets," including "buildings that are heavily insured, have changed hands recently, are in poor repair and whose owners have not paid city taxes." Kensington Action Now also included in its proposal a "patrol" of the neighborhood conducted by city fire officials in the area between Front Street and Lehigh and Erie and Aramingo Avenues. According to the group's plan, the Department of Licensures and Inspections would seal buildings that burned and also ones identified as future fire threats. The organization itself received a $7,000 foundation grant to build a computer system to maintain a registry of potential arson target properties and also committed to run an "arson hot line" whereby residents could report "problem buildings and fire hazards."[20]

Kensington Action Now, with Goode's support, brings to the fore a novel political social formation that I hesitate to term "neoliberal" for fear of what that term's inelasticity might do to obscure the specificity of this kind of integration between anticipatory action related to potential arson, nongovernmental-governmental partnership, foundation financing, early computing technology, intracommunal and vertical surveillance, and an organizational drive for additional police-like patrols. Kensington Action Now was founded in 1975 and by 1980 integrated thirty-six organizations, including block clubs, churches, and civic groups. In 1980 the organization's treasurer, Fred Weber, identified Kensington Action Now's two primary objectives in an interview with *Inquirer* journalist Connie Langland—housing rehabilitation and "policeman to walk beats" in Kensington—and said the organization had helped to raise thousands of petition signatures supporting a foot patrol.[21] In the same year, the organization had partnered with insurance company Aetna, which invested $2 million in order to finance a profit-oriented housing program to symbolically ameliorate charges of the company's exclusion of neighborhoods like Kensington from insurance coverage.[22]

In 1982, the group's anti-arson committee hosted Michael Brown, the state of Pennsylvania's insurance commissioner. The group, including the commissioner, set out from the organization's offices on Frankford Avenue and took a walking tour of the burned-out buildings in Kensington, paying closest attention to "buildings the group said it thought were set on fire for profit." The organization sought the investment of premiums on the large, burned buildings by the insurance companies "to help turn them around" and requested that Brown send letters to insurance executives to encourage their investment in Kensington. Brown asked in reciprocity for the organization to support and pressure state legislators for one of the anti-arson bills they were hosting in Harrisonburg at the time. Kensington Action Now hoped to attract investments similar to the $2 million received from Aetna for housing rehabilitation and in collaboration with Goode's actions as managing director to "pilot [an] anti-arson task force that could by" the following year "be expanded throughout" Philadelphia.[23] This was under Mayor Green's administration, which also made layoffs of firefighters and other city workers his solution for the city's growing budgetary issues.[24]

In a short segment of *Squatters: The Other Philadelphia Story*, a July 1984 public broadcast production for WNET Thirteen New York, then mayor-elect Goode's contemporaneous statements about squatting marked it as illegal and contrary to "property rights": "The issue really is not one of desire or will; the issue really is one as I see it of what's legal. Keep in mind that property right is still fundamentally a right in this country and in this city." Goode, who sat for his interview with WNET Thirteen reporters for the production in the weeks after his electoral victory, denounced the mass movement organized by ordinary people to publicly commandeer livable properties, citing the unlawfulness of such an appropriation. In a subsequent interview included in the same program, Goode suggested that he anticipated that squatters would continue their demonstrations despite his recent election. He acknowledged that they would pressure him and anticipated that the protesters' expectations of his mayoral administration would exceed his capacity to act but also that in a year's time, his policy ingenuity would deflate the squatters' demands: "I expect there will be pressure and there will be expectation that exceeds my ability to perform. I expect that there will be demonstrations and pickets and all of those things, but I expect to be a responsive mayor. I expect after a year to put demonstrators out of business in this town."[25] Given his preliminary cabinet meetings' emphasis on cleaning up graffiti, attracting a major cable corporation to wire Philadelphia, and moving forward the city's partnership to develop the convention center, his agenda suggests that either Goode was disingenuous with his claims to address the city's housing crisis or he was swayed by the rising tide of growth ideology.

In the same recording, founding pastor of a storefront congregation L. M. McClain made a powerful statement that confronted the city's inaction in the rapidly deteriorating conditions of the 1980s housing crisis. "We've been trying to get the city to help the poor. That's what we've been trying to do for the last four years," she noted. Moving among her congregants as she preached, McClain pointed to the contradictions of those seeking to exclude the de-housed from shelter: "You may have a house, yes, but there's somebody don't have a house. Is that right?" McClain went on to justify and encourage the city's burgeoning squatters' movement, characterizing the people appropriating abandoned homes across Philadelphia as in line with her critical exegesis of the Bible's

New Testament: "Jesus didn't have anywhere to live either, so we could typify him as a squatter, amen."

McClain, who founded Emmanuel's Temple of Deliverance in 1964, extended the tradition of preaching gospel singers and singing preachers, from Charles A. Tindley to Shirley Caesar, using the pulpit to spread a message in which the resounding power of Jesus's direct engagement with and special interest in those dispossessed of a place to live.[26] McClain articulated support for squatters in recognition of their wretchedness—their conditioning as the damned, condemned, enclosed, or removed as part of the city's late twentieth-century transformation. McClain embraced and extended Black liberation theology, and with it an ethics of the city that identified radical inclusivity, underscoring a commitment to analyzing, assessing, and remaking society in consideration of those marked as the disposable and displaceable within the political economic recalibrations at the turn of the twenty-first century precipitated in response to deindustrialization. Radical inclusivity rather than a liberal project of inclusion premised on regularization and the dissolution of difference through spatial policing and management names a modality for drawing the despised through a revolt against the premises of sanitization, linked with conditional inclusion and its structural relationship to broad disposability. Centering the squatter and placing her or him in line with the biblical account of Jesus, McClain expressed a faith in the power of the poor for redefining the present and future conditions of the city through their marked inhabitance of unused property.

If MOVE directly confronted value in the sense of accumulation through members' politicization of dereliction and their abolitionist outlook, and if McClain expressed commitment to a vision of just housing distribution irrespective of legality, then Goode's vision derived from an interpretation of housing as property and commodity. The Goode administration as well as those before and after it privileged property and the expansion of real estate interests over the interests of working-class Black people in the city, those who were renters as well as those in the transformed political economy who could not maintain their aging houses. Goode embraced a vision of "responsible governance" that equated with fiscal restraint and a respect for property with generative governance and, through the faulty logics of late twentieth-century capitalist ideology, suggested the expansion of corporate profit subsidized through tax incentives, including tax abatement or commercialization of public land, would drive investment that would subsequently lift the fortunes of all urban residents by curtailing the city's economic devastation precipitated by more than a decade of economic transformation.

MOVE's case is significant in its distinction with the direct action that police took with support from federal authorities to destroy the group. Outside the acute act of bombing by the state, however, it shared material and discursive underpinnings with the deadly effects meted out, primarily in the vulnerability experienced by working-class Black communities and other immiserated groups in the city at the end of the twentieth-century reterritorialization in the context of democratic mayoral administrations' effort to violently reterritorialize the postindustrial city. The 1985 bombing unfolded along a continuum with other forms of quotidian infrastructural violence through which federally imposed and locally enforced austerity was lived and felt in the city's Black communities. The death of poor Black children and other vulnerable people evidenced the broader immolation of urban residents who succumbed to the conditions of "social murder" produced by deindustrialization and violent retrenchment that undermined the primary infrastructures of living and further eroded the geographies of working-class Black social reproduction.[27]

Bureaucratic city agencies charged with investigating the effects of vulnerability helped to recast victims as perpetually irresponsible, denying the social-geographic realities of the condemnation of working-class Black communities and deindustrializing neighborhoods. In order to reinvigorate accumulation in urban land and to distract from the primary causes of fire deaths, Black officials in complementary fashion reinforced the toxic matrix of vulnerability and false culpability.

Notes

1. Ramona Africa v. Commonwealth, trial transcripts, box 10, folders 3 and 4, Philadelphia Special Investigation (MOVE) Commission Records, SCRC 605, Special Collections Research Center, Temple University Libraries, Philadelphia, PA.
2. Ramona Africa v. Commonwealth, trial transcripts.
3. Rodrick Wallace, "A Synergism of Plagues: 'Planned Shrinkage,' Contagious Housing Destruction, and AIDS in the Bronx," *Environmental Research* 47 (1988): 1–33; Elizabeth Hinton, *America on Fire: The Untold Story of Police Violence and Black Rebellion since the 1960s* (New York: W. W. Norton, 2021); Ansfield Bench, "Born in Flames: Arson, Racial Capitalism, and the Reinsuring of the Bronx in the Late Twentieth Century," *Enterprise and Society* 23, no. 4 (2022): 923–27, https://doi.org/10.1017/eso.2022.40. Also see Brandi Summers, *Black in Place: The Spatial Aesthetics of Race in a Post-Chocolate City* (Chapel Hill: University of North Carolina Press, 2019).
4. J. T. Roane, "Spitting Back at Law and Order: Donnetta Hill's Rage in an Era of Vengeance," *Signs: Journal of Women in Culture and Society* 46, no. 4 (2021): 853–82, https://doi.org/10.1086/713303.
5. MOVE manuscript, Joseph Beam Papers, Sc MG 455, box 8, folder 11, Schomburg

Center for Research in Black Culture, Manuscripts, Archives and Rare Books Division, New York Public Library.
6. Essex Hemphill and Wayson Jones Collection, Sc MG 832, box 2, folders 3–5, Schomburg Center for Research in Black Culture.
7. Kevin Everod Quashie, *Black Aliveness, or a Poetics of Being* (Durham, NC: Duke University Press, 2021), https://doi.org/10.1515/9781478021322.
8. Here Parkerson through Hemphill doubles back to an interpretation of the relationship between the media and violence at least as old as Ida B. Wells's practice of "writing dynamically." As Jaqueline Goldsby develops, Wells used her pamphlets to challenge the fundamental ways that journalism helped to drive Black death, especially lynching, by making it a "routine, habit-forming reading event" or something that people came to consume regularly as the violent exception confirming the warm and pulsing white center of normative vitality. Jacqueline Goldsby, *A Spectacular Secret: Lynching in American Life and Literature* (Chicago: University of Chicago Press, 2006), 49.
9. Police Department Detective Bureau, White Papers, April 18, 1984, Philadelphia Department of Records and City Archives.
10. Police Department Detective Bureau, "Rescue of Children: 5239 N. Warnock St.," White Papers, April 18, 1984, Philadelphia Department of Records and City Archives.
11. Deborah A. Vickers and Nashormeh Wilkie, "Youths Snatch Child from Fire," *North Philly Free Press*, March 23, 1982.
12. Frederic Jameson, "Cognitive Mapping," in *Aesthetic Theory: Essential Texts for Architecture and Design*, ed. Mark Foster Gage (New York: W. W. Norton, 2011), 251.
13. Marcus Hunter, *Black Citymakers: How The Philadelphia Negro Changed Urban America* (New York: Oxford University Press, 2015).
14. Robert A. Altenkirch, "How Would Fire Behave in a Zero-Gravity, Normal-Atmosphere Environment?," *Scientific American*, October 10, 1997, www.scientificamerican.com/article/how-would-fire-behave-in.
15. Fire Reports, 1970–90, Philadelphia Department of Records and City Archives.
16. Police Department Detective Bureau, White Papers, November 1983–December 1984, 37.
17. Thomas J. Gibbons Jr., "Fatal Fire Puts Focus on Safety: After Six People Died, Commissioner Hairston Spoke Out—Again," *Philadelphia Inquirer*, May 27, 1997.
18. Elizabeth Duff, "Arson: U.S. Burns with a Societal Sickness," *Philadelphia Inquirer*, July 10, 1977, A1.
19. Dick Cooper, "Cooperation Cuts Arson for Profit in Phila.," *Philadelphia Inquirer*, April 26, 1981, B1, B4.
20. Paul Horvitz, "Arson Task Force Nears Completion: Group Wants to Halt Fires and Revitalize Kensington," *Philadelphia Inquirer*, November 15, 1982, B8.
21. Connie Langland, "In Kensington, Looking to a Local Boy Made Good," *Philadelphia Inquirer*, January 31, 1980, 3B.
22. Neil Pierce, "Target Neighborhood: Aetna's Experiment in Kensington," *Philadelphia Inquirer*, April 28, 1980, 11.
23. Metropolitan Section Editors, "Anti-arson Group's Work Encouraged," *Philadelphia Inquirer*, September 19, 1982, 32.

24. Langland, "In Kensington, Looking to a Local Boy Made Good."
25. *Squatters: The Other Philadelphia Story*, Communication Excellence to Black Audiences (CEBA) audio and moving image collection, Schomburg Center for Research in Black Culture.
26. *Squatters: The Other Philadelphia Story*. For more about the formation of McClain's church, see Samaria Bailey, "Emmanuel's Temple of Deliverance: Spirited Worship Invigorates the Faithful," *Philadelphia Tribune*, September 17, 2016, www.phillytrib.com/religion/emmanuels-temple-of-deliverance-spirited-worship-invigorates-the-faithful/article_2ca3fbbd-e5e8-5ad7-97e1-d016a9bb68c9.html. See also Claudrena N. Harold, *When Sunday Comes: Gospel Music in the Soul and Hip-Hop Eras* (Urbana: University of Illinois Press, 2020).
27. Frederich Engels, *Condition of the Working Class in England*, ed. Mark Harris, Marxists Internet Archive, 2010, www.marxists.org/archive/marx/works/download/pdf/condition-working-class-england.pdf.

PART V

STEFAN M. BRADLEY

Chasing Angels

Black Life in Los Angeles since 1965

Out here, it was supposed to be different.
—**Black Oklahoma migrant in Los Angeles**

Upon arriving in Los Angeles in 2017, I was astonished by two things: the sheer beauty of people and places in the city and the entrenched racial segregation that existed in the metropolis. My immediate family stayed in a quiet neighborhood called Westchester, which bordered Inglewood and was near the airport. The next-door neighbors, two of whom included a retired teacher and policeman, were extremely welcoming and friendly. Despite their kind generosity and hospitality, we immediately stuck out as residents in the enclave because of our beautiful Black skin. We never felt threatened, but we were always conscious of our presence in that space. We were often engaged in conversations about whether we were new and where precisely we lived in the neighborhood. That there were few Black families and children in the predominantly white and upper-middle-class neighborhood was not at all surprising or accidental. Even by Los Angeles standards, rent there was high and mortgages were prohibitive, which likely kept most working-class Black and Brown people out of the area. Pricing has historically been a way to fortify against racial integration. In the case of Westchester, many of the older residents had been there for more than three decades, so there had been little turnover in terms of housing.

Pricing alone, however, was not to blame for the paucity of Black families. That neighborhood, like so many others in Los Angeles, once enforced racial restrictive covenants throughout the mid–twentieth century and beyond. Until the 2020s, home deeds in Westchester maintained language such as "No part of any lot shall ever at any time be used or occupied or be permitted to be used by any person not of the white or Caucasian race, excepting that persons not of the Caucasian race may be kept therein by such Caucasian occupant strictly in the capacity of servants or such occupant."[1] In that way, Westchester, like so many other Los Angeles neighborhoods, was designed to be white.

Although there were few Black children who lived in the neighborhood, there were many Black youth who came to the enclave via bus to attend Westchester High School. Many of those students came from Compton, South Central, and other areas where Black people lived en masse. Famed rapper Roddy Ricch was a student who traveled from Compton to Westchester to attend high school. Similarly, Latasha Harlins, a fourteen-year-old girl whose killing was an impetus for the 1992 Los Angeles Rebellion, navigated on a bus from South Central to Westchester. In the locale, one would not see the Black students if one did not go to the campus. And, often disturbingly, when those young learners of color happened to walk around the neighborhoods, there was chatter on Internet apps like Nextdoor, querying as to whether anyone knew those teenagers who seemed to be out of place. If one were to drive two miles east on Manchester Boulevard from Westchester into Inglewood, few would question whether the students belonged. The demographic disparities of neighborhoods in Los Angeles are as stark as they are historically intentional.

In a city that features Hollywood, the Magic Kingdom of Disneyland, and ubiquitous plastic surgery, things are not always what they seem in Los Angeles. After years of listening to "gangsta rap," I visited Compton for the first time in decades. There, instead of members of the Crip and Blood gangs, I saw Black people riding atop horses down the middle of the street. Apparently, they were part of a group called the "Compton Cowboys." I was assured that gangs still existed in Compton, but if one only went by what one saw on television or heard on the radio, one's impression of the suburban enclave would be exclusively that of violence and destruction rather than that of community and resilience. By the way, some of the gangs that friends mentioned were the Executioners and Banditos, which they said exist among Los Angeles County sheriff's deputies.[2] Again, Los Angeles can be deceiving.

Situating Black Los Angeles

I have first cousins who live in the Watts section of Los Angeles. When I was a child in the 1980s, my family visited from Washington State. At the time, I was too young to be aware of the challenges of the neighborhood; I could only recall the sheer joy of the birthday parties I attended across the street from my aunt Susie's house. She loved to tell the story of how she was in Watts before most Black people arrived. Originally from Port Gibson, Mississippi, she and her husband left the former Confederate state shortly after the gruesome murder of Emmett Till to find work in Southern California. Aunt Susie found employment as a maid in a white Jewish family's home. She and her husband were eventually able to amass enough capital to purchase a home in Watts with orange trees in the backyard.

"Anywhere but here" was the right place for many Black Americans who grew weary of the political, racial, and cultural violence they faced in the southern states. While they decried the Jim Crow of the South, a version of Jim Crow also awaited them in the West. Scholars like Brian Purnell, Jeanne Theoharis, and Komozi Woodard discuss the concepts of Jim Crow North and West.[3] No region was as physically violent as the South, but the principles of racial oppression associated with Jim Crow proliferated in all areas of the United States.

The Black population that resided in Los Angeles was typical of other Black Americans who left all that they knew in the South to explore opportunities in unfamiliar urban environs. History has done well to focus on the arrival of Black migrants to New York, Philadelphia, and Chicago, but the Great Migration to the West is equally significant. In the mid-twentieth century, Black southerners arrived in California for work in the airline industry and on the docks. As scholars have well noted, the prospect of jobs was not enough to pull these southerners away from the region where their ancestors' blood had enriched the fertile soil; there were catalyzing push factors. The inability of Black citizens to engage the democracy, enjoy public schools, and maintain a decent quality of life was enough to move some. Still others felt impelled to move because of the specter of violence that overshadowed every day. Living in and rearing children in a city that did not have the outward signs of extreme racism was quite attractive to many Black people. With that in mind, throngs of Black southerners made their way west between 1940 and 1970. Although life was markedly better in Los Angeles, the new residents faced major societal obstacles that challenged advancement.

Black Youth and the Results of Policy

Few states have witnessed the rise of mass incarceration like California. Los Angeles, in particular, was a locus for many reasons to expand punitive policies. The threat from street gangs, more than anything, served as a key driver of violence. Scholars have thoroughly covered the various aspects of incarceration as it related to youth in Los Angeles. Regarding the state, there were gradations for the punishment and bad behavior of young people. Youth who were found on the other side of the law had to attend juvenile court. If youths were convicted of violating the law for the first time, the courts typically released them to their families or potentially a community organization with some sort of required behavior modification. If the violating behavior continued and the young person had to return to court, there was the likelihood that the court would remand the young person to the juvenile detention center or juvenile hall, which housed youth offenders for brief periods of time as a form of punishment and encouragement to correct the behaviors. The next steps for offending youth who had committed egregious violations were the youth forestry camps and the California Youth Authority. At the camps, young people were removed from the city as they served longer terms of time. When district or state's attorneys sometimes charged youth offenders as adults, the offending young person was sent to county jail but placed in what was called the "juvenile tank." Those who experienced the juvenile system referred to the California Youth Authority as "Gladiator School."[4] Prison was the next rung on the ladder of incarceration.

Although the Division of Juvenile Justice had rehabilitation as a goal, stories abound regarding the negative attributes of these forms of imprisonment. Young people, upon arrival, often faced violence and dangerous provincialism that led to forms of tribalism. Even as some counselors attempted to steer the young people toward positive outcomes, the supervision of the authorities was not enough to prevent the rise of a co-curriculum that reinforced negative behaviors. Often, when youth left or termed out of the camps, their experience hardened them, making them susceptible to gang life on the streets. When under the supervision of the Division of Juvenile Justice, they became "gladiators," learning to fight, improvise weaponry, identify a clique, and defend territory in a confined space. Those were all useful skills for life in a society that had all but given up on urban youth development. "Monster" Kody Scott, who was a member of the Eight Tray Gangsters set of the Crips gang, remembered that "the juvenile tank has got to be the most blatant exercise the state has ever devised for corrupting, institutionalizing, and creating recidivism in youths." Young people are "dropped into a prisonlike setting with not so much as an inkling of counseling or adult support," he remembered.[5]

If the 1960s was a decade of hope, then the theme of the 1970s was skepticism. Granted, activists and legislators made crucial steps in the way of achieving policy and codifying freedom rights. The Civil Rights Act (1964), Voting Rights Act (1965), and Fair Housing Act (1968) recognized the struggles of Black citizens who sought to live out the American dream, and life improved for many. The Great Society, War on Poverty, and liberalism helped advance life chances for some Black people in the 1960s and early 1970s. Black homeownership in the city (and nation) increased, as did the attainment of secondary and higher education. During that period, a larger contingent of Black Angelenos ascended into the middle class than ever before. For many on the margins, however, the progressive policies were not adequate; an entrenched underclass remained in Los Angeles in the 1970s. The American response to the debilitating OPEC oil embargo of 1973 underscored seemingly fixed economic disparities between the races. In a city that relied almost exclusively on automobile transportation, the crisis was crippling for those who could barely survive on their wages and the costs associated with traveling back and forth to their jobs. As the nation transitioned from a heavily industrialized to a more service-based economy, the financial concerns of many Black Angelenos endured in spite of some progress.

For some young people in Los Angeles, gang life seemed to be the most viable option. Nationally, the unemployment rate of Black youth ages sixteen to twenty-one was between 45 and 55 percent in the 1970s and 1980s, which was the highest it had been since 1954.[6] There is some context to the rise in percentage. For instance, more Black secondary students were persisting in school and not dropping out to supplement their families' income by taking a job, which technically meant they were unemployed. Those who needed employment, however, still faced difficulty. Government officials at every level defunded youth development programs. At the same time, schools were unable to reach young people through the curriculum and wraparound services they offered. These factors made gang life seem reasonable to some young people. "Monster" Kody Scott, who later changed his name to Sanyika Shakur, discussed his decision to join the Crips gang in the 1970s as a prepubescent youth in his memoir, *Monster*. He recalled a conversation he had with Tray Ball, his assigned mentor in the gang: "Bangin' ain't no part-time thang, it's full-time, it's a career. It's bein' down when ain't nobody else down with you. It's gettin' caught and not tellin'. Killin' and not caring, and dyin' without fear. It's love for your set and hate for the enemy."[7] Tray Ball's admonishment about the life resembled that of a recruitment officer for the US military during the Cold War.

It appeared that some young people in the streets of South Central were becoming citizens of their own sovereign nations and seeking to defend the territory of those nations through a violence similar to that used in Cold War skirmishes abroad and with a rhetoric familiar to war hawks throughout history. Scott noted that the gangs of South Central recruit[ed] more people than the four branches of the U.S. Armed Forces did. Crack dealers employ[ed] more people . . . than AT&T, IBM, and Xerox combined." Further, he added, South Central was "under more aerial surveillance than Belfast, Ireland." There was no wonder, according to Scott, why "everyone is armed, frustrated, suppressed, and on the brink of explosion."[8]

Similar to those who experienced trauma in conflicts abroad, violence also scarred the psyches of Black youth in South Central. Scott discussed the post-traumatic stress syndrome that people in his neighborhood endured as violence intensified. In Los Angeles, gang life became more lethal when higher-powered internationally made weapons and crack cocaine entered the fray. Of course, gang conflicts had existed for decades and sparring between organizations was typical, but by the end of the 1970s and early 1980s, the skirmishes became deadly. In 1980, there were 192 gang-related deaths in Los Angeles.[9] Police officials and civilians alike were clear about the reason for such heightened violence: a mix of deadly firearms and narcotics. A 1985 *Los Angeles Times* article reported that in addition to handguns, weapons like the Israeli Uzi submachine gun, the Russian AK-47, the TEC-9, the MAC-10, and other rapid-fire instruments appeared in the hands of young people who had never before been outside of city limits.[10] Surviving in war-torn neighborhoods forced young people to grow up too quickly. "At sixteen I felt twenty-four.... We grew and died in dog years," Scott soberly remembered.

The illicit drug trade greatly intensified gang life in Los Angeles. By the 1970s, American leaders at each level of government attempted to deal with the narcotics epidemic by declaring a "War on Drugs" during the Nixon administration. Republican New York governor Nelson Rockefeller (1959–73) oversaw the passage of laws imposing mandatory minimum prison sentences of up to fifteen years for the possession or sale of marijuana, cocaine, and heroin, making the punishment of those crimes on par with murder in terms of sentencing. California followed suit.

Ronald Reagan, the former "law and order" Republican governor of California who was nemesis to Black Panther Party members and college student activists alike, finally made a successful bid for the presidency in 1980 after two failed attempts. In the midst of a deep recession and foreign policy crises, Reagan campaigned on the economic fears of the white working class, the desires for extensive tax breaks for the business class, and anxieties surrounding crime. He stigmatized those in need of assistance by invoking images of a Black "welfare queen" while claiming that affirmative action was "reverse discrimination" that issued jobs to undeserving Black candidates. Underneath the veneer of the jovial, B-level actor dwelled a cold warrior who sought to cut government resources, privatize essential industries, and institute practices of globalization that harmed American working people. Reagan was willing to employ whatever tactics necessary to contain communism.[11]

To be sure, cocaine had always been prominent among elite classes of Angelenos. By the 1980s, however, "America was awash with cocaine, . . . thanks to

Colombian cartels," explained historian David Farber.[12] The Colombian cartels, along with the drug trafficking organizations from Mexico and the American appetite for escapism, created an alternative economy regulated only by violence and the market itself. To provide weapons and munitions for the US-backed Contras in Nicaragua during the Cold War, the US government negotiated the sale of Colombian cocaine in the United States for funds.

A wider market was necessary to significantly increase the anti-communism resources. To assist in that effort, former Dorsey High School tennis player Rick Ross scaled up his California-based business model to work directly with Colombian suppliers and sell millions of dollars' worth of crack in South Central. Proceeds from those sales benefited Reagan's anti-communism goals.[13] Crack exponentially expanded the user network of cocaine.

Despite the federal government's entanglement with the business of drugs, when cocaine reached the masses in the form of crack, many elected officials and residents alike looked to imprisonment as the solution to the health epidemic of rising addiction and the crime associated with the illicit drug. Not surprisingly, the incarceration of Black and Latino/a people skyrocketed. Legal scholar Michelle Alexander referred to this form of mass incarceration as the "New Jim Crow."[14]

The War on Drugs left certain segments of Los Angeles in a perpetual state of martial law. "The state applied militarization unequally by focusing on historic African American and Latino neighborhoods in the south central part of the city," historian Donna Murch asserted. "Los Angeles exemplified how the drug war intensified the militarization of domestic policing."[15] In Los Angeles, law enforcement exercised free reign with regard to policing those suspected of consuming and selling narcotics.

As a result of an escalating Cold War and a national campaign to curb crime, the methods of incarceration became more militarized in the 1980s. Congress passed the Military Cooperation with Civilian Law Enforcement Agencies Act of 1981.[16] The act established official lines of collaboration between the US military and local law enforcement agencies in combating drug trafficking, civil disturbances, and terrorism. It also helped make the transfer of militarized equipment to civilian police departments a regular practice. The entrance of military-grade weaponry eventually had major implications for Black people living in urban and suburban areas. By 1982, former Harvard law professor James Q. Wilson and former criminologist George L. Kelling published an article in *The Atlantic* on what they termed the "broken-windows" theory. It supported a form of policing in which officers detained, arrested, and rousted citizens for minor violations in search of larger crimes.[17]

A major impetus for eradicating gangs and drugs in 1980s Los Angeles was the arrival of the Olympics. The city's first Black mayor, Tom Bradley, helped win the bid for America and the metropolis. Narcotics and violence greatly concerned Olympic committee officials. The behavior of law enforcement provided some solace to those who worried for the safety of the world-class athletes and fans who were coming to enjoy the games. Those sentiments led to more brutal policing tactics. By the summer of 1984, deaths associated with gang activities decreased.[18]

With the games complete, Los Angeles rapper Toddy Tee, in his hood-famous song "Batterram," discussed how the Los Angeles Police Department employed SWAT teams with their mini-tanks to penetrate the homes of those suspected of violating drug laws. He rapped: "And the chief of police says he just might flatten out every house he sees on sight because he say the rock man is taking him for a fool."[19] Of all things, Chief Daryl Gates, who had taken the reins in 1978, could not tolerate disrespect, as he considered himself to be the stalwart representative of law and order. From his point of view, disrespecting him or the police department may have well been an attack on the American way. Never shying away from a battle, the chief (who, like former police chief William H. Parker, was a veteran) militarized the police and commenced to invading domiciles to root out drugs and pushers. South Central was occupied territory.

Although the 1984 Summer Olympics placed pressure on law enforcement, the decision to aggressively police suspected drug dealers and locations where drugs were prominent was not the exclusive decision of government legislators and executives. Residents of South Central and other areas with high Black populations lobbied for an increased police presence and the extirpation of drugs. Many of the homeowners and longtime residents intimately witnessed the ravaging effects of crack. Discussing New Yorkers' struggle to prevent drugs from entering Black enclaves in an earlier era, historian Michael Fortner asserted that the majority of people in the neighborhoods despised the drug activity and wanted to see the users and dealers punished. He described that group of people as the "Black Silent Majority."[20] Lawmakers, Fortner claimed, took their cues from those afraid or unable to effectively confront the onslaught of drugs. As a result of their appeals, Democrats and Republicans alike endorsed incarceration in an escalating fashion. That eventually led to federal legislation like the Anti–Drug Abuse Act of 1986, which instituted mandatory minimums for federal terms for possession of relatively small amounts of crack.[21] In contrast to the minimums associated with the powder form of cocaine, the punishments regarding crack were inequitable. In terms of sentencing, 1 gram of crack cocaine was treated the same as 100 grams of powder cocaine. If one were convicted of distributing 5 grams of crack cocaine (which in the eyes of the courts was the equivalent of 500 grams of powder cocaine), then one would have to serve a mandatory sentence of five years in prison. This formula resulted in extremely high sentences for offenders.

With the support of some neighborhood residents and the Congressional Black Caucus, California legislators passed nearly eighty anti-gang laws during the 1980s and 1990s that coincided with increased antidrug legislation. The rash of laws did not end well for Black youth, young men in particular. In an article covering the effects of crack on Los Angeles, Donna Murch found that by the end of the 1980s, the sheriff of Los Angeles County "listed 47 percent of all Black men in Los Angeles County between the ages of twenty-one and twenty-four as gang members."[22] That was impossible, but that data provided fuel for abusive and exploitative policing practices. The movie *Training Day*, which was in part filmed in South Central and the surrounding Black communities, highlighted some of those practices of a corrupt drug unit.

The Los Angeles Police Department placed the craftily named Community Resources against Street Hoodlums unit, or CRASH, in the vanguard of its offensive against gangs and drugs. It was created in 1979 as a tactical squad that focused on neutralizing known youth offenders. Data collection played a significant part of the unit's efforts, as officers gathered as much biographical information as possible on the young people they rousted for crimes, such as curfew violation. In that way, CRASH, which was the subject of the Hollywood movie *Colors*, created a database of gang members and young people whom officers believed were affiliated with gangs. With this method, the police knew precisely who "Monster" Kody Scott was, where he stayed, and with which set he affiliated before the boy became a teenager. The unit often booked young people from areas like South Central on minor violations, which began their journey into the juvenile justice system. As historian Elizabeth Hinton pointed out, the police department rarely enforced curfew laws on young people outside of those Black and Latino/a neighborhoods.[23] Because the unit arrested mostly Black youth, when it reported on its efforts to lawmakers, legislators assumed that young Black people broke the law the most and needed to be corralled. Resources flowed away from youth development toward the capture and punishment of children. In essence, CRASH specialized in criminalizing Black youth, which set the stage for the more intense and invasive police tactics in the neighborhoods.

Aside from the brutal police practices and mass incarceration, crack had terribly deleterious effects on the psychological and physical well-being of those in working-class and poverty-stricken neighborhoods. Women addicted to crack were incredibly vulnerable. Some turned to sex work, while others did whatever they could to get the drug. Men took advantage of these women's (many of whom were Black) addictions and kidnapped, raped, or killed them. The *Los Angeles Times* found that from the mid-1980s to the early 1990s, there were at least five serial killers targeting drug-addicted women, and over 100 women, most of whom were addicted sex workers, met death.[24]

Affirmative Action, Political Ascendancy, and AIDS

As the underclass grew, the beneficiaries of affirmative action programs who gained access to higher education and professional job spaces made some progress. Additionally, the Black entertainment class shined especially bright in Los Angeles. Athletes and actors received worldwide attention for their "showtime" lifestyles. Taking advantage of the relative privilege they enjoyed, those with disposable income moved to neighborhoods where the homes were assessed at higher values than those in working- and poverty-class areas.

Affirmative action made it possible for Black students to attend flagship institutions like the University of California, Los Angeles, in higher numbers than ever. Black Panthers like Elaine Brown and Angela Davis were able to take advantage of UCLA as a student and an employee, respectively, but not without controversy, of course. Other students benefited from the work of civil rights and Black Power advocates who paved the way for the Ralph J. Bunche Center for African American Studies. Soon Black students were achieving in all aspects of college life; a Black woman even won the presidency of the undergraduate student body.[25] By 1980, Black student admissions reached a high point in the university's history. That year, the UCLA School of Law admitted almost fifty Black students, which was a 40 percent increase from 1970. Affirmative action was working in education, but white backlash strengthened in California. In 1996, Proposition 209 outlawed the consideration of race in all public university admissions. Within two years of the proposition passing, the percentage of Black students admitted to UCLA's law school dropped precipitously from 7.4 to 2.6.[26] This was a setback in terms in the face of steady racial progress in higher education.

In the decades after the 1960s, elected office provided opportunities for Black advancement in Los Angeles. Tom Bradley was among the Black politicos who ascended in the post–civil rights era. US representative Maxine Waters, like Bradley, attempted to make life better for Black people in the wake of the 1965

Watts Rebellion. Waters began as a Head Start instructor in Watts and eventually won a place in the state assembly. As did so many other Black activists, Waters demonstrated and protested against the investment of US businesses in apartheid South Africa. In 1990, she was elected to the US House of Representatives and has since convincingly won reelection each cycle. Famously and controversially, the congresswoman highlighted the collusion of the CIA in the proliferation of crack in South Central. Waters, who at one point chaired the Congressional Black Caucus, won her most recent campaign by in part promising to torment and neutralize the efforts of former president Donald J. Trump. Westchester, where my family once resided, was in her district.

Recently elected mayor Karen Bass was on a similar trajectory as that of Congresswoman Waters. Bass was an activist and institution builder who helped develop the Community Coalition of South Los Angeles, a stalwart organization that advances justice and equity in neighborhoods throughout South Central. She too ran and won a spot in the state assembly and eventually was elected to the US House of Representatives. Bass's election to the highest executive office of the city extends Bradley's legacy, as well as the legacies of the Black officeholders elected before the modern civil rights era. It also represented an upward trend in the elections of Black women as mayors of major US cities.[27]

In the 1990s, there was a stark contrast between lived experiences of Black Angelenos who appeared on movie and television screens and those who struggled to exist. Michigan transplant and renowned Laker point guard Earvin "Magic" Johnson was one of the most visible examples of the entertainment class. By day, he dazzled crowds with his smile and uncanny athletic abilities at the Great Western Forum in Inglewood, helping his team of all-stars to win five championships over the Boston Celtics and other East Coast rivals. By night, however, he enjoyed the famous Los Angeles nightlife. In November 1991, at the height of Johnson's brand recognition, he contracted HIV via heterosexual relations and retired from his career in the National Basketball Association.[28]

That a man of Johnson's stature had a disease that ravaged the queer male and intravenous drug-consuming communities in Los Angeles drew much media attention and fueled rumors.[29] Johnson made it clear that he was heterosexual but had been unfaithful to his spouse, who fortunately tested negative. Unlike most Angelenos who had been infected, Johnson could afford the best possible care. Between 1980 and 1990, there were almost 9,000 confirmed cases of AIDS in Los Angeles, and fear ravaged the city.[30] Johnson, with the best care that money could buy, began an outlined health regimen coupled with a routine schedule to consume established and experimental drugs. He lived to become a Laker executive and thriving businessman. During that period, however, most Black people in the city with HIV eventually died of AIDS.³¹ That Johnson no longer shows traces of HIV is, indeed, magic.

Black Beverly Hills to the LA Rebellion

Many Black Angelenos avoided the travails associated with AIDS, drugs, and gang life; they instead navigated the upper echelons of society. Some participated in selective groups like the Boulé, Jack and Jill of America, the Links, and the Black Greek-letter organizations of the Divine Nine. Their children often did not attend Los Angeles Unified School District schools but instead went to private institutions like the Marlborough School, Archer School for Girls, and the network of Catholic schools.³² These families lived in high-value homes in places like Ladera Heights, View Park–Windsor Hills, and Baldwin Hills, above the apartments in "the Jungle" neighborhood (Baldwin Village).³³ More than 75 percent of the residents in those "Black Beverly Hills" neighborhoods were Black. To get to and from their domiciles, they had to see those Black Angelenos who were less fortunate in terms of housing and employment.

Some of the Baldwin Hills families tried to keep their children from the troubles down the hill in South Central, but in 1991, trouble was never too far away. The Black community, irrespective of class status, was greatly angered when a store owner of Korean descent shot and killed Latasha Harlins, a teenage Black girl, after accusing her of shoplifting. The relationship between the Black consumers and Korean business owners in South Central was already fragile, and Harlins's death did more damage. Days later, videotape of Rodney King, a Black motorist who led police on a chase outside the city limits, surfaced. The images were wretched, showing white police officers brutalizing King. Surely, thought Black people in South Central and Baldwin Hills, the violating officers would be punished because there was video evidence. In 1992, they, and so many others, were proved categorically wrong, as none of the officers was convicted of committing a crime against King.

In a 1996 song titled "To Live and Die in LA," rapper Tupac Shakur reflectively contemplated the 1992 LA Rebellion. He wrote, "We might fight with each other, but I promise you this: we'll burn this bitch down, get us pissed."³⁴ South Central Los Angeles erupted in anguish, anger, and frustration in April 1992. Much wider in scope than the Watts Uprising, the destruction associated with the rebellion was not left to the Black ghetto. Further, members of the Latino/a community, in solidarity, joined in the rebellion. Of the more than sixty people who died in the uprising, a third were Latino, and members of that community represented more than 50 percent of the arrests that police made. Protesters of all classes and colors rose up to show their dismay with the dispensability of Black and Brown people in the justice system. By the time the uprising ended in May, more than $775 million of destruction had occurred. People from a diverse array of communities reacted to poverty, poor policing, and racial oppression.[35]

Housing Crises

Housing values in Los Angeles typically go in one direction: up. That is why the national housing crisis of 2008 was catastrophic for so many. As Keeanga-Yamahtta Taylor explained in *Race for Profit: How Banks and the Real Estate Industry Undermined Black Homeownership*, Black aspiring homeowners were financially punished for falling victim to improper lending practices. In 2002, President George W. Bush stated that he wanted the United States to become an "ownership society" and emphasized his desire for citizens to purchase homes. According to a White House press release, the president encouraged financial institutions to assist in closing the homeownership gap between people of color and white owners. Taking heed, lenders pushed subprime loans to low-income Black and Brown first-time buyers. The new homeowners took advantage of down-payment assistance and other programs designed to get them to the point of acquisition. The problems arose when it came time for the actual loans, which eventually included "balloon" payments and were often linked to the rise and fall of fluctuating federal rates. Three years after President Bush made his ownership challenge, over half the loans that Black and Latino purchasers received in Los Angeles County were subprime.[36]

Between 2000 and 2020, Black people who purchased homes in densely populated Black neighborhoods were especially vulnerable to the fragility of the national housing market and economy. Between 2007 and 2012, Black homeowners in Los Angeles County experienced foreclosure rates three times higher than that of white owners.[37] That was not surprising, considering that in Los Angeles County, the loan-to-income ratio for Black borrowers was 9 percent higher than that of white borrowers.[38] This had significant and disparate wealth implications for the Black families whose homes were foreclosed. The value of homes in those neighborhoods fell drastically after the Great Recession of 2008. For many Black families in Los Angeles, the wealth they imagined amassing with homeownership evaporated, leaving them only with crushing debt and less desirable housing options. As housing values rebounded, many Black would-be buyers were priced out of the market. That led to racial shifts in neighborhoods.

Housing opportunities for would-be Black buyers in the Los Angeles metro area market has remained relatively slim. According to a 2022 *Stacker* article based on the US Census data of 2020, the national rates of Black homeownership remain lowest of all other racial demographics.[39] Nationally, Black homeownership lagged behind white homeownership by more than 30 percentage points. In Los Angeles, the homeownership gap is significant, as the Black homeownership rate is 34.6 percent, in contrast to the white homeownership rate of 51.7 percent. When compared nationally, according to the article, the Black homeownership rate in Los Angeles is ranked #124 among all metro areas in the United States. In areas just outside of Los Angeles, such as Riverside and Orange County, Black homeownership rates saw slight increases between 2016 and 2021, but the homeownership rate in Los Angeles has remained stagnant.[40] That data makes it difficult for potential homebuyers in Los Angeles to dream.

Recently some Black Angelenos have indicated that Los Angeles no longer maintains the allure it once did. A 2020 article in the *Los Angeleno* observed that the "destabilizing force of the 21st century—the cost of housing—threatens" Black access to the good life.[41] Furthermore, gentrification is eating away at the ability of older and vulnerable Black residents to even exist in the neighborhoods that white people once fled. Before the arrival of hipsters, Black residents of those neighborhoods contended with the arrival of Latino/a homebuyers who were also looking for reasonably priced domiciles. Then, although gang activity dropped precipitously from the levels it had been at in the 1980s and 1990s, the violence associated with street warfare in the second decade of the 2000s has been enough to push longtime Black Los Angeles residents outside of the city.[42]

During the winter of 2020–21, my family committed to house hunting in Los Angeles. In an exciting moment, we came upon a three-bedroom, two-bath home of 1,500 square feet in the city of Inglewood, not far from where the Los Angeles Rams had recently completed the So-Fi Stadium and where the Los Angeles Clippers were set to play at the Great Western Forum. To our chagrin, the relatively paltry home was listed at the "meager" price of $950,000. Not surprisingly, our story was not unique. Kenya McClendon, a Black woman who grew up in Inglewood, finally became eligible for a home loan only to find herself outbid every time.[43] Time and again, the costs of homes during the bidding wars quickly stretched beyond the amount her bank approved. Sadly, McClendon noted, "I feel that people who are not from the community, it's easier for them to come and purchase a home than it is for me, and I grew up in the community." McClendon observed a demographic shift in her neighborhood away from the predominantly Black working-class people she saw as a child to those who are not Black or working-class.

Housing costs place immense pressure on those who choose to live in the Los Angeles area. The 2019 United Ways of California's "Real Cost of Living Measure" indicated that for a family of two adults and one child, it required $95,112 a year to cover housing, transportation, and other costs. The combined wages for the average family in Inglewood, however, amounted to $49,063 a year. In a city of 100,000 that is 37.8 percent Black, the cost of housing has made it prohibitive to live.[44] My family left Los Angeles the summer of 2021 for a better opportunity, and we were not alone. In what some call California's Black Exodus, people who once lived in South Central and cities like Inglewood and Compton are moving to less expensive residences outside of the metro area or out of the state altogether. Often, those Black residents leaving the city move to Lancaster and Palmdale, but some relocate south to the states of Texas and Georgia, where they search for the same amenities that their grandparents sought in Los Angeles. As eviction restrictions associated with COVID-19 loosen or expire, there will undoubtedly be more migration out of Los Angeles.[45]

Not all recent real estate news is bad for Black people. In June 2022, the County of Los Angeles, in an atypical act of reparation, returned waterfront land that had once belonged to the family of Charles and Willa Bruce, a Black couple who had been defrauded of their property in Manhattan Beach during the Jim Crow era. That tract of land and the edifices included were worth upwards of $20 million. The county, initially, leased part of the property for $413,000 a month. By January 2023, however, the county officially purchased the land and buildings for $20 million.[46] The Bruce family is not representative of most Black Angelenos in that they were able to take advantage of restorative justice; however, their history with Los Angeles adequately represents the travails of Black people striving to enjoy the life that the City of Angels boasts.

The remnants of the Black southern migration exist today in restaurants like La Louisianne, Harold and Belle's, and Louisiana Fried Chicken. There is even a Louisiana to Los Angeles (or LALA) Organizing Committee that marches in the Kingdom Day Parade to reflect the undeniably strong connection to the South that still exists for Black people in the City of Angels. On the radio, one can still jam to "oldies but goodies" on Art Laboe's show on KDAY. In the past half century since the civil rights movement, many Black Los Angeles residents have fared well, growing families, accumulating wealth, and enjoying political access at the highest levels. The city is not, however, the same refuge it was for

Black people decades ago, as housing and the cost of living can be daunting. Unless Black newcomers find themselves in the professional or entertainment class, they will, by and large, need angels to prosper in Los Angeles.

Notes

1. Alysha Conner, "'No Colored People Allowed': Housing Covenants, Still, Present Racial Barriers in 2021," *Our Weekly Los Angeles*, August 27, 2021.
2. Jaclyn Diaz, "Alleged Gangs in LA Sheriff's Department to Be Investigated by Oversight Panel," NPR, March 25, 2022, www.npr.org/2022/03/25/1088905429/lasd-gangs-investigation-los-angeles.
3. Brian Purnell and Jeanne Theoharis, eds., with Komozi Woodard, *The Strange Careers of the Jim Crow North: Segregation and Struggle outside the South* (New York: New York University Press, 2019).
4. David William Reeves, "Gladiator School: Stories from Inside YTS," *Medium*, October 15, 2020, https://gladiatorschool.medium.com/gladiator-school-stories-from-inside-yts-b6ac0f683c68.
5. Sanyika Shakur, aka Monster Kody Scott, *Monster: The Autobiography of an L.A. Gang Member* (New York: Grove Press, 1993), 136.
6. John Cogan, "The Decline in Black Teenage Employment: 1950–70," *American Economic Review* 72, no. 4 (May 2017): 621; "Unemployment Rate—16–19 Yrs., Black or African American," US Bureau of Labor Statistics, retrieved from FRED, Federal Reserve Bank of St. Louis, on August 15, 2022, https://fred.stlouisfed.org/series/LNS14000018.
7. Shakur, *Monster*, 12.
8. Shakur, *Monster*, 69–70.
9. Stephan Braun and Paul Feldman, "Killing Related to Street Gangs Hits Record in '87," *Los Angeles Times*, January 8, 1988, D3.
10. Mark Stein, "Machine Guns: Firepower of Civilians Escalating," *Los Angeles Times*, September 9, 1985, vi and 3.
11. For a critical assessment of Reagan's life, see Daniel Lucks, *Reconsidering Reagan: Racism, the Republican Party, and the Road to Trump* (Boston: Beacon Press, 2020).
12. David Farber, *Crack: Rock Cocaine, Street Capitalism, and the Decade of Greed* (Cambridge: Cambridge University Press, 2019), 36.
13. Gary Webb, *Dark Alliance: The CIA, the Contras, and the Crack Cocaine Explosion* (New York: Seven Stories Press, 1998), 142.
14. Michelle Alexander, *The New Jim Crow: Mass Incarceration in the Age of Colorblindness* (New York: New Press, 2010).
15. Donna Murch, "Crack in Los Angeles: Crisis, Militarization, and Black Response to the Late Twentieth-Century War on Drugs," *Journal of American History* 102, no. 1 (June 2015): 164.
16. US General Accounting Office, *Military Cooperation with Civilian Law Enforcement Agencies*, July 28, 1983, GAO.gov, www.gao.gov/products/122004.
17. George L. Kelling and James Q. Wilson, "Broken Windows: The Police and

Neighborhood Safety," *The Atlantic*, March 1982, www.theatlantic.com/magazine/archive/1982/03/broken-windows/304465/.
18. Alex Alonso, "Out of the Void: Street Gangs in Black Los Angeles," in *Black Los Angeles: American Dreams and Racial Realities*, ed. Darnell Hunt and Ana-Christina Ramon (New York: New York University Press, 2004), 155.
19. Toddy Tee, "Batterram," Jim-Edd Music (BMI), 1985.
20. Michael Fortner, *Black Silent Majority: The Rockefeller Drug Laws and the Politics of Punishment* (Cambridge, MA: Harvard University Press, 2015).
21. H.R. 5484—*Anti-Drug Abuse Act of 1986*, August 19, 2022, Congress.gov, www.congress.gov/bill/99th-congress/house-bill/5484.
22. Murch, "Crack in Los Angeles," 167.
23. Elizabeth Hinton, *From the War on Poverty to the War on Crime* (Cambridge, MA: Harvard University Press, 2017), 219.
24. Scott Gold and Andrew Blankstein, "'It Was a Terrifying Time,'" *Los Angeles Times*, August 4, 2010, A1.
25. "Black Bruin History at UCLA," Alumni Newsletter, February 2021, https://newsletter.alumni.ucla.edu/connect/2021/feb/black-bruin-history/default.htm.
26. Jerome Karabel, "The Rise and Fall of Affirmative Action at the University of California," *Journal of Blacks in Higher Education*, no. 25 (Autumn 1999): 110.
27. Jennifer Harlan and Giulia McDonnell Nieto del Rio, "8 Black Women Form Sisterhood of Power as Big-City Mayors," *New York Times*, November 2, 2021, A10.
28. Magic Johnson, "I'll Deal with It: HIV Forced Me to Retire, but I'll Still Enjoy Life as I Speak Out about Safe Sex," *Sports Illustrated*, November 18, 1991, https://vault.si.com/vault/1991/11/18/ill-deal-with-it-hiv-has-forced-me-to-retire-but-ill-still-enjoy-life-as-i-speak-out-about-safe-sex.
29. Richard Stevenson, "Magic Johnson Ends His Career, Saying He Has AIDS Infection," *New York Times*, November 8, 1991; Jennifer Brier, *Infectious Ideas: U.S. Political Response to the AIDS Crisis* (Chapel Hill: University of North Carolina Press, 2009), 62, 76, 88–89.
30. Jonathan Lloyd, "30 Years Ago: First AIDS Cases Reported in LA," NBC Los Angeles, June 2, 2011, www.nbclosangeles.com/news/local/30-years-later-first-aids-cases-reported-in-los-angeles/1899759/.
31. See Renata Simone, "Endgame: AIDS in Black America, 2012," PBS/*Frontline*, www.pbs.org/wgbh/frontine/documentary/endgame-aids-in-black-america/.
32. Kimberly Baker Guillemet, *Black Prep: Life Lessons of a Perpetual Outsider* (Los Angeles: Ransom and Baker Publishing House, 2021), 123–31.
33. Hadley Meares, "Baldwin Hills, 'The Black Beverly Hills': The Life and Times of the Community," LAist, March 17, 2022, https://laist.com/news/la-history/baldwin-hills-the-black-beverly-hills-the-life-and-times-of-the-community.
34. Tupac Shakur and Val Young, "To Live and Die in LA," *The Don Killuminati: The 7 Day Theory*, Death Row Records, 1996.
35. Cora Cervantes and Edwin Flores, "Latinos Recall L.A. Riots' 30th Anniversary and a 'Levantamiento.' What Has Changed?," *NBC News*, April 29, 2022, www.nbcnews.com/news/latino/latinos-recall-l-riots-30th-anniversary-levantamiento-changed-rcna26358.

36. Keeanga-Yamahtta Taylor, *Race for Profit: How Banks and the Real Estate Industry Undermined Black Homeownership* (Chapel Hill: University of North Carolina Press, 2019); Paul M. Ong, Chandara Pech, and Deirdre Pfeiffer, "The Foreclosure Crisis in Los Angeles," *California Policy Opinions* (2014): 44.
37. Ong, Pech, and Pfeiffer, "Foreclosure Crisis in Los Angeles," 47.
38. Ong, Pech, and Pfeiffer, "Foreclosure Crisis in Los Angeles," 45.
39. "The Black Homeownership Gap in Los Angeles," *Stacker*, March 22, 2022, https://stacker.com/california/los-angeles/black-homeownership-gap-los-angeles.
40. Ashley Collins, "Black Homeownership Is Growing Slowly but Surely," FirstTuesday Journal, March 10, 2023, https://journal.firsttuesday.us/black-homeownership-is-growing-slowly-but-surely/89465/.
41. Erin Aubry Kaplan, "For Many Black People, L.A. Is No Longer the Last Best Place to Live," *Los Angeleno*, January 30, 2020.
42. Ann Brenoff, "Behind LA's Dramatic Decline in Gang Violence," HuffPost, December 6, 2017, www.huffpost.com/entry/gang-violence-decline_n_6656840; Ailsa Chang, Jonaki Mehta, and Christopher Intagliata, "A Window of Opportunity: Black Flight from Compton to the Inland Empire," NPR, March 6, 2021, www.npr.org/2021/05/06/994376649/a-window-of-opportunity-black-flight-from-compton-to-the-inland-empire.
43. Anabel Munoz and Grace Manthey, "Black Families Own Homes at a Lower Rate Than White Families in SoCal. Here's Why That Matters," *ABC Eyewitness News*, July 16, 2021, https://abc7.com/black-homeownership-gap-in-southern-california-real-estate-inglewood-los-angeles/10884320/.
44. United Ways of California, "The Real Cost Measure in California 2021," Tableau Public, accessed August 19, 2022, https://public.tableau.com/app/profile/hgascon/viz/TheRealCostMeasureinCalifornia2021/RealCostDashboard.
45. Lauren Hepler, "California's Black Exodus Comes with a Hidden Toll for Transplants," Cal Matters, July 15, 2020, https://calmatters.org/projects/california-black-population-exodus/.
46. Rosanna Xia, "Unprecedented Plan to Return Bruce's Beach to Rightful Black Heirs Revealed by Officials," *Los Angeles Times*, June 23, 2022, www.latimes.com/california/story/2022-06-23/los-angeles-county-releases-plan-to-return-bruces-beach; Bill Chappell, "The Black Family Who Won the Return of Bruce's Beach Will Sell It Back to LA County," NPR, January 4, 2023, www.npr.org/2023/01/04/1146879302/bruces-beach-la-county-california.

CHANELLE ROSE AND BENJAMIN H. SARACCO

Camden Rising?

The Black Struggle for Racial Justice, Equity, and Inclusion in the Age of Urban Revitalization, 1971–2020

In July 1989, Mayor Melvin "Randy" Primas, the Black People's Unity Movement (BPUM), and the New Jersey Department of Corrections proposed a site for the construction of a second prison in Camden on the twenty-acre Delaware River waterfront property owned by BPUM. The state also recommended a $30 million, 350-bed addition to the Riverfront State Prison (built in 1985), located just north of the Benjamin Franklin Bridge and approximately ten blocks from the site of the second prison. The new multistory, minimum-security facility would be surrounded by guard towers and fences topped with razor wire, adjacent to the rowhouse streets of the North Camden neighborhood. If accepted, North Camden's total prison population would exceed 1,800, approximately 25 percent of the neighborhood's residents.[1]

Primas, a former employee of BPUM and Camden's first African American mayor, attempted to subdue mounting local resistance to the second prison. On July 13, 1989, Primas told the *Courier-Post*, a daily newspaper serving the South Jersey region, that the city currently received $1 million from the Riverfront prison and the state would provide $2.8 million in payments in lieu of taxes for the second one. He declared, "I view the prison as an economic development project. In addition, I think surveillance from the two prison towers might stop some of the overt drug dealing in North Camden."[2] This response to strong opposition from several faith-based, multiracial community organizations not only failed to assuage residents' concerns but also angered many. Bertha Aytch, an African American member of Residents against the Prison and also Concerned Citizens of North Camden (CCNC, a progressive grassroots organization of white, Latino, and Black community organizers founded in 1978), viewed the Riverfront Prison Phase II as a collusion with the mayor and BPUM. In response to Primas's remarks about surveillance and drugs, Aytch said, "We find such ignorance amazing. Drug trafficking is not so much a result of social ills as it is economic ills. Until poor folks in places like Camden have access to a decent education and a guarantee of a decent job that pays a living wage, they will continue to supplement their income by what means are available."[3] On July 26, twenty-five demonstrators from the CCNC protested outside BPUM's Cooper Street headquarters, chanting, "No Prison," while some bore handwritten signs that read, "The Rich Get Richer and the Poor Get Prisons."[4] Many feared their North Camden neighborhood—a geographic island cut off from downtown by the Benjamin Franklin Bridge, already crippled by drugs, dilapidated houses, and a negative image—would become a "cage." Talk of racism also fueled opposition from those who argued that the state would never envision having two state prisons built in a predominantly white, suburban area like Cherry Hill.[5]

Despite the financial constraints facing newly elected African American mayors like Primas, community activists accused him and BPUM of betraying the Black community. The second prison was never built. However, the controversy surrounding its construction provides insights into the complicated legacy of Black political representation in Democrat-led cities like Camden, where Black mayors endorsed policies rooted in civil rights liberalism while adopting a neoliberal approach to urban revitalization that often conflicted with the interests of local people.

Over the past several decades, African Americans have dominated Camden's mayoral leadership, but their governance illustrates the limits of politics by representation—especially since the city's poor and working-class Black and Brown residents (despite small victories) seldom reaped the benefits of county-driven urban revitalization. In fact, control of the Camden County Democratic Party, alongside state-level oversight that led to a complete takeover of the city in the early years of the twenty-first century, has received harsh criticism from those who claim it undermined the civic engagement of the community. Even though scholars have examined the city's decline and revitalization efforts, a social history of Camden's African American leadership and communities since the 1980s requires more attention. Focusing on Black Camdenites raises questions that not only shed light on the urban crisis in other northern cities but also reveal the unique challenges facing local residents during the post–civil rights era. How did machine-bred Black politicians' neoliberal approach to addressing poverty, education, and urban decay affect African Americans? How has the city's post-1970s demographic shift to mostly African Americans and Puerto Ricans illuminated the complexities of Black-Latino relations in the United States? This chapter will attempt to answer these questions by highlighting the voices of primarily African American residents who worked alongside whites and Latinos to make more democratic the decision-making processes that affected their lives.

In this essay, we examine the complicated history of Black politics and neoliberalism in a city where the African American leadership played a complicit role in the disenfranchisement of local residents by accepting increasing state and county oversight. Notwithstanding some of the benefits of state oversight and revitalization efforts since the 1980s, we argue that the lives of most Black and Latino Camdenites (particularly poor residents) have not significantly improved because of the Black leadership's failure to address chronic structural inequalities: poverty, public health disparities, poor education, and inadequate housing. Despite the African American–Puerto Rican solidarity that emerged following the 1971 racial uprisings, also known as the "Puerto Rican Race Riots," their alliance (particularly at the political level) has occasionally become fraught with tension over competition for more resources and representation.

Much has been written on the significant rise in Black political power since the 1970s, as African American mayors (mostly Democrats) had the extraordinary task of governing economically depressed cities beset with deindustrialization, white flight, and fiscal crises.[6] But the relatively new scholarship on how neoliberalism has shaped Black politics offers new insights into the challenges facing mayors burdened with reviving cities in decline while addressing the socioeconomic needs of residents. What began under President Richard Nixon's administration but became more firmly established during Ronald Reagan's presidency was a neoliberal shift in urban politics. Geography professor Nicholas Blomley argues that this change led to "cities competing aggressively to attract capital, tourists, and government funds," which has been identified "with a consequent shift from an emphasis on local livability and the life opportunities of local residents to an externally oriented logic of the bottom line."[7] This "urban neoliberalism" prioritized public-private partnerships, deregulation, and fiscal austerity (often resulting in cuts to government social programs), and it favored market solutions to social problems. Moreover, the "neoliberal racial order" deemphasized the importance of addressing systemic racism as an integral part of urban reform and gravitated toward the "culture of poverty" explanations for drugs and crime in inner cities.[8] As political scientist Lester K. Spence observes, some Black elected officials' pathologizing of African American culture as the main cause of social ills "in the wake of a neoliberal turn" has given them more "latitude to criticize their Black constituencies in ways their white counterparts arguably couldn't."[9] The study of the Black experience in Camden provides a window into how the transformation in urban politics under state and local

Democrat control fostered resilience and resistance from primarily poor and working-class African Americans (alongside Latino residents) who fought for meaningful electoral representation.

The Postwar Urban Crisis and Election of Mayor Randy Primas

Although the urban crisis devastated postindustrial metropolises across the nation, Camden's loss of nearly half its industrial job base surpassed other deindustrializing cities in the Northeast and Midwest.[10] By the 1940s, Camden had a population of approximately 117,000, and its big three manufacturers—Campbell Soup Company, New York Ship Building Company, and RCA Victor—employed most of its residents. These major industries helped to solidify Camden's regional importance as an industrial powerhouse, but the city also boasted a thriving business district with commercial corridors, particularly along Broadway, Kaighn, Haddonfield, and Westfield. However, in a single decade, before the 1971 race riots, Camden's manufacturing based had declined by 48 percent.[11] Bridget Phifer, an African American executive director of Parkside Business and Community in Partnership, recalled the significant impact of these changes on Parkside, a neighborhood just southeast of downtown. According to Phifer, "Parkside became an African-American community because of white flight, because of de-industrialization, because Campbell Soup and others decided to pack up, and the naval shipyard, they decided to relocate. And with that, the jobs went. And so when the jobs . . . leave, you know, people follow."[12] The 1971 racial uprisings (which occurred after a Puerto Rican motorist was brutally beaten by two white police officers) hastened the final migration of whites and businesses from the city, a process that had begun a decade earlier with the growth of racially exclusive suburbs in Cherry Hill, Pennsauken, and Voorhees.[13] By the end of the decade, Camden was no longer a manufacturing center or a predominantly white working-class city.[14]

The conventional story of Camden's urban heyday invariably chronicles its downtown amenities (including the Walt Whitman Hotel and the Stanley Theatre), culturally rich neighborhoods, and three large manufacturing companies. However, the glamorous depiction of the city's glory days tends to obscure the lived experiences of people of color who faced racial and economic discrimination. Prior to World War II, mostly white ethnics (Italians, Jews, Poles, Germans, and Irish) resided and worked in the city, but it had small pockets of African Americans and Puerto Ricans whose racialized experiences were daily reminders of their second-class citizenship. Even though Charles "Poppy" Sharp (founder of the Black Believers of Knowledge in 1968, later renamed the Black People's

Unity Movement) lived in a racially mixed neighborhood, he remembered that schools and other facilities were segregated in Camden. Much like the Jim Crow South, Sharp was forced to sit in the balcony of the Lyric Theater. "We had to go upstairs," he recalled.[15] In addition, during the late 1970s, Minister Wasim Muhammad, a fifty-four-year-old native of the city and president of the Camden Advisory Board of Education, vividly remembered his father telling him when he was a fourth-grader to walk the long way home from football practice by not going through Whitman Park because "it was such a racist area." Looking back on this experience, he explained, "I either got chased by white boys or chased by the white police saying, 'Niggah, don't you come through here.' They didn't want you to walk through their community."[16] Local efforts to maintain the racial order were reinforced by housing discrimination and urban renewal, commonly referred to as "Negro Removal," during the 1960s. Like other parts of the country, urban renewal displaced Black Camdenites from their neighborhoods.[17]

Under the leadership of Poppy Sharp, BPUM waged a fierce battle against racial injustice and the lack of Black political power in Camden.[18] The group demanded more Black representation at a time when African Americans and Latinos were excluded from political leadership. BPUM leader Malika Chaka recalled, "At that time in Camden (circa 1960s), even though none of the white leaders lived in the ward, they couldn't get the party to put any Blacks on the ticket. We were told it wasn't time."[19] By the 1970s, however, Sharp developed a reputation as a "sellout" in the African American community after forming a political coalition with Mayor Angelo J. Errichetti in the 1973 municipal elections. As the director of public works and chairman of the city's Democratic Party, Errichetti wielded significant control of the party, due to his staunch loyalty from state legislators, handpicked men elected to the Freeholder Board, and early backing of Brendan Thomas Byrne, who became governor of New Jersey in 1974.[20] The *Courier-Post* described Errichetti as a "super power" in Democratic ranks despite his state grand jury indictment for misconduct while serving as the director of public works.[21] Democratic city boss Errichetti recruited Sharp and later appointed him to serve as his Youth Council director following his landslide mayoral victory. By this time, Sharp and BPUM had adopted a less radical ideology that viewed electoral politics and Black capitalism as the most effective way to improve the racial plight of African Americans. Indeed, it was BPUM's Economic Development Corporation, which focused heavily on developing minority businesses, that attracted Randy Primas to the organization. Primas, an East Camden native and 1971 business graduate of Howard University, later credited Sharp for his early entrance into politics.[22] Primas said, "Because he [Sharp] stood up and did what he did, I had the opportunity to run for city council at age 23."²³ Even though Sharp and BPUM played an integral role in developing Primas's race consciousness and paving the way for Black political leadership in the city, Mayor Errichetti's mentorship played a significant part in his emergence as Camden's first Black mayor.

The Technocratic Mayor, Neoliberalism, and Community Organizing

Mayor Randy Primas faced many of the internal and external factors that plagued Black urban mayoral politics during the post–civil rights era. By the 1980s, Camden had become a poster child for urban decline as deindustrialization, population loss, and crime beleaguered the city. The exodus of whites to the suburbs precipitated a dramatic decline in Camden's tax base as local businesses shut down, leaving the city with no hotels, major retailers, or movie theaters during this period.²⁴ The city's fiscal crisis exacerbated already dire conditions, and Mayor Primas inherited a $5 million budget deficit from the Errichetti administration. During his first year in office, Primas offered glaring statistics in a speech he delivered to an audience of approximately 150 students at an event sponsored by Rutgers University's Black Student Union and political science department. He told students and faculty that only 17,000 of 85,000 Camden residents were employed, and 55 percent of the population received some form of public assistance.²⁵ The majority of these residents were Black and Latino, even though the city also had a small Vietnamese community that was forced to leave Saigon after the Americans departed in 1975. Although rising crime rates affected other cities in New Jersey and across the country, Camden's small size and extreme poverty concentrated in Black and Brown communities intensified the problem. Addressing the crime issue would become one of Primas's main challenges, alongside the city's fiscal crisis and negative image, which made attracting businesses and middle-class residents extremely difficult.

In contrast to the "civil rights" mayors of the late 1960 and 1970s, Primas had more in common with a new generation of Black elected officials that J. Phillip Johnson calls "technocratic mayors." Thompson distinguishes technocratic mayors from African American politicians like Kenneth Gibson (Newark) or Harold Washington (Chicago), who were elected in racially polarized elections and challenged the Democratic establishment to make significant changes to the racial and social order. In his book on the complicated legacy of Black mayors in urban communities, Thompson argued, "New, younger, black mayoral candidates replaced mayors of the civil rights era, promising to deemphasize race, promote efficient government, and offer strategies to lure investors to strengthen downtown businesses and create jobs."²⁶ While African American mayors like Gibson and Washington encountered racially divided elections, Primas had a smoother transition because he joined the established interracial political coalition of ex-mayor Errichetti. Primas mostly continued the politics of Errichetti's Democratic Party machine, even though the city had lost its influence as the center of county politics. Indeed, Errichetti had helped Primas secure his two terms in office as a city councilman and later assured Primas he would receive support from the thirty-four-member Democratic City Committee in his candidacy for mayor.²⁷ His ascendancy as part of the city's Democratic machine evoked criticism from Camden's social activists, who assailed him for being ostensibly more beholden to county Democratic leaders than to the local people during his mayoral run in 1981. During the municipal election, some of the most vitriolic attacks came from opponents who criticized Primas's machine-backed politics—especially mayoral candidate Roy Jones, a community activist and outspoken founder and chairman of the Camden Citizens Coalition (CCC) who ran on an anti-machine platform.

The CCC, a predominantly African American organization, worked on behalf of local residents supporting direct-action protests that addressed the city's housing crisis and poor living conditions. In January 1981, Jones and other members of the CCC, along with Concerned Citizens of North Camden, joined twenty-five protesters who emptied a truckload of trash from the Roosevelt Manor housing project and then formed a human blockade at the intersection of Broadway and Federal Street.²⁸ They aimed to bring attention to the lack of trash collections and the deplorable living conditions in the projects. During the same month, the CCC and several public housing tenants' associations— including Roosevelt Manor's—laid out plans to organize a rent strike to put a spotlight on the lack of heat, hot water, trash collections, security, and general maintenance.²⁹

Unsurprisingly, Jones announced his run for mayor in front of a vandalized vacant house to underscore the housing crisis in Camden. This thirty-three-year-old native of Parkside had a history of civil rights organizing in the city that dated back to the 1960s, and he pledged to run on an independent ticket to maintain some political autonomy. "I'm not going to Erichetti [*sic*] or Florio [US representative James Florio, D-NJ] for anything," he declared. "I'm only going to the people."³⁰ In addition to improving the plight of local residents' housing conditions, Jones's campaign focused on ridding the city of corruption, mismanagement, and Democratic Party machine politics. Primas distanced himself from Errichetti following the FBI's Abscam investigation that ultimately led to Errichetti's conviction on bribery and conspiracy charges, but Jones pointed out that Primas was a protégé of Errichetti's and remained silent on corruption in the city. "It so happens that Primas is a part of the machine structure," Jones asserted.[31] Some residents of Camden praised Jones for taking a stand. In a letter to the *Courier-Post*, one person wrote,

> I would like to applaud and thank Roy Jones and the Camden Citizens Coalition for their commitment and dedication to the City of Camden, especially at a time when there is a lack of voices crying out against the corruption and lack of concern for poor people. We had a few voices in the '60s, but the vast majority of them blended in with the Erichetti [*sic*] administration and therefore have been silent. We need people of Mr. Jones' intelligence, honesty and strength, who along with Mongolisa [*sic*]. Davis and others of the C.C.C. have stood up against the power structure from the mayor's resignation to mismanagement in public housing and the affirmative action ordinance.[32]

During his first official act as mayor, Primas unveiled a plaque dedicating the new county's $12 million waterfront park to the late Ulysses S. Wiggins, a prominent Camden doctor and head of the local chapter of the National Association for the Advancement of Colored People.[33] The following year he established a seven-member Affirmative Action Review Council to ensure the implementation of Camden's affirmative action law (adopted in August 1980), which required the hiring of minorities on construction projects. As Primas explained, one of the main goals of his administration was "to revitalize the Affirmative Action Council so that the city's affirmative-action ordinance can be vigorously enforced and achieve the goals set forth in that ordinance."[34] Despite his strong backing of a symbolic government policy emerging from the hard-fought battles of the civil rights struggle, his administration did not focus on building coalitions with the city's progressive white, African American, and Puerto Rican organizers to make radical changes to the city's Democratic establishment. Primas won a landslide victory with the support of the Democratic Party and African American voters, but he soon came under increasing attack from community activists who spoke out against his urban revitalization efforts.

On March 20, 1983, CBS aired its top-rated *60 Minutes* episode, "Father Doyle's Camden," which broadcast Camden's urban crisis to a national audience and seemingly undermined Mayor Primas's urban revitalization efforts. The thirteen-minute segment showed a city beleaguered by vacant, dilapidated buildings, empty storefronts, and extreme poverty. During the interview, Father Michael Doyle, a Catholic priest of Sacred Heart and a leading activist in the city, told CBS's Harry Reasoner, "This country should not, with all its money and ingenuity and professional ability and indeed goodness, should never ever be responsible for the fact that thousands of children are born in Camden in ugly situations."³⁵ Doyle's statements were a moral indictment of America as he criticized the deplorable living conditions of Camden residents in a country rich in wealth and resources. Father Doyle also implicated the increasing power of the suburbs and criticized the building of a new prison that Mayor Primas and city officials had endorsed. He described the city as a receptacle for trash, sewage, the unwanted poor, and finally criminals who would be housed at the new state prison that was under construction. Yet the city's business and political leaders derided the CBS program for its biased, one-sided view of Camden that only showed its worst conditions. Nevertheless, many residents criticized Primas's administration as the city became a dumping ground for surrounding suburban municipalities' unwanted pollution, prisoners, drug addicts, and affordable housing commitments.

Increasing state oversight, alongside a shift in power from the city to suburban powerbrokers, shaped Primas's controversial support of upgrading the city's sewage treatment plant and trash incinerator, completed in 1987 and 1989, respectively. According to W. Dennis Keating and Norman Krumholz, Camden's upgraded sewage plant replaced forty-six local treatment plants that were shut down after suburban residents voiced concerns about the degraded environmental conditions in their communities.³⁶ In addition, the incinerator not only burned trash from all of Camden's suburbs but also serviced over 200 trucks driving through the city. Keating and Krumholz's study on rebuilding urban neighborhoods underscores the price Camden had to pay for financial support from the state. They observed, "In exchange for state aid that by 1990 would amount to one quarter of the city's budget, Camden was forced to accept projects that no other municipality in southern New Jersey would take."³⁷

Camden's fiscal dependence on the state significantly influenced Mayor Primas's decision to support several urban renewal projects that undermined the interests of Black and Hispanic residents—the most controversial being the construction of a $30 million medium-security state prison on a thirteen-acre tract between Delaware Avenue and the Delaware River in North Camden. During his mayoral campaign of 1980, Primas took a public position against building a medium-security prison and pointed to his vote against it while president of the city council during Errichetti's administration as proof of his commitment. However, pressure from Trenton along with the city's financial troubles made the mayor vulnerable to the state's overtures, which included $2.5 million in bailout funds to avert another fiscal crisis, $1 million in subsidy payments for hosting the prison, and state control over the city's finances.³⁸

Mounting opposition from the Concerned Citizens of North Camden thwarted Primas's early efforts. This politically active grassroots organization had a history of engaging in direct action and using disruptive tactics to demand concessions from the city government.[39] In fact, the CCNC began devising a strategy to fight against the state's proposal for the new prison site after Mayor Primas announced his plans. Although Brian Medley, a Black native of North Camden and graduate of Rutgers University–Camden, acknowledged the problem of overcrowding in the state's prisons, he affirmed, "If necessary, I'm sure residents would put their bodies on the line. This is serious. This is the most striking blow in terms of trying to eliminate a residential area."[40] On July 22, 1981, members of the CCNC met at the Grace Lutheran Church on State Street in North Camden to voice their concerns about the prison and develop a plan of action. While the CCNC had hundreds of members, only thirty-four people attended the meeting, and they disagreed over support of or opposition to the state's proposition.[41] Some residents remained open to accepting the prison if city officials agreed to install more traffic lights, invoke the city's affirmative action ordinance, and provide more funding for housing rehabilitation and playgrounds in North Camden. CCNC member Christine Boswell viewed the prison as a way to maintain a closer connection to incarcerated family members. "I do not see the prison as a monster. I see it as a place where our people—our brothers, fathers and sons—are incarcerated," she said. Similarly, Doris Campbell said that the CCNC could become involved in prison reform, an important issue that many local residents supported. Even though Boswell and Campbell agreed with those who had strong reservations, they also saw this as an opportunity for residents to negotiate with Primas and the state.

Strong opposition to the prison came from CCNC members like Samuel Benson, a Black resident of North Camden. "They [East Camden] don't want it. Cramer Hill doesn't want it. Fairview doesn't want it and we don't want it," he declared.[42] Benson had served as president of the CCNC in 1979 while working closely with the organization's urban planner, Tom Knoche. Knoche was a leftist white native of Baltimore who helped to spearhead the CNCC's board-up program that prioritized rehabilitation over the demolition of vacant houses.[43] In May 1981, Knoche, Benson, and other members of the CCNC met privately with Mayor Primas and William Fauver, the New Jersey State Department of Corrections commissioner, in city council chambers to discuss the impact of the prison on their community. In an effort to secure some benefits for their community, CCNC members asked for police protection, cleaner streets, and more assurance that Camden residents would be guaranteed a fair share of the jobs created by the prison.[44] Few of their demands were met, and some of them failed to dissuade Primas or city officials from accepting the bailout bill signed by Governor Brendan Byrne, which ultimately resulted in the construction of the state prison in 1985. During Primas's tenure as mayor, historian Howard Gillette surmised, "Primas found himself increasingly at odds with his natural black constituency. Forced to improve the city's finances, he accepted compromises and pursued goals that inevitably put him in opposition to a range of city activists."[45]

As a technocratic mayor who ultimately viewed himself as a city manager tasked with revitalizing Camden's waterfront downtown area, Primas adopted a neoliberal agenda that promoted market-driven solutions to the fiscal crisis and worked to attract businesses. This approach resulted in less support to neighborhood revitalization. The mayor and local civic elite looked to private industry and downtown revitalization as the best way to solve Camden's economic crisis and social problems. Primas adopted Baltimore's approach to revitalizing its Inner Harbor by partnering with Campbell Soup, RCA, and Cooper University Healthcare to develop the downtown waterfront. As market-based solutions became the dominant paradigm for national economic policy during the 1980s, Primas supported President Reagan's new urban initiative for enterprise zones, which he saw as an opportunity to lure businesses and the middle class back to the city. On March 23, 1981, Reagan gave a message to Congress that outlined the enterprise zone concept, stipulating that the federal government would provide tax breaks and regulatory relief to businesses willing to locate in distressed cities, thus spurring commercial and industrial investment. This idea had become increasingly popular in Britain, and Prime Minister Margaret Thatcher's conservative government established several enterprise zones in England.[46] The US Congress failed to enact meaningful enterprise zone legislation, but state legislatures across the country proposed their own enterprise bills, and cities competed to receive federal enterprise zone status.

Even before Republican governor Thomas Kean signed the state's urban enterprise law, Primas wrote a telegraph to Reagan requesting that the president designate Camden as one of the country's first federal urban enterprise zones. Primas explained, "As our factories closed, many of our people became part of that social service bureaucracy which you have said has a vested interest in the poverty business."[47] He also discussed Camden's high unemployment rate of 20 percent (nearly two and half times the state average and nearly double the national average); minority youth unemployment that exceeded 50 percent; and the number of the city's children living in households that received welfare or Aid to Families with Dependent Children (60 percent). The mayor expressed reservations about the controversial part of the proposed bill that would allow employers to pay below minimum wage, but he strongly supported the majority of the plan. Commenting on bipartisan support for the enterprise zones, especially at the local level, Alan H. Peters and Peter S. Fisher explained that inner-city politicians saw them as "the only policy game in town—traditional inner-city programs were most unlikely to expand during the early Reagan years." They added, "The zones took an essentially optimist view of the residents of depressed neighborhoods: given the opportunity, inner-city residents could be as entrepreneurial and hard working as the rest of Americans."[48]

On August 15, 1983, Governor Kean signed the urban enterprise law at Ulysses S. Wiggins Waterfront Park in Camden as a symbolic gesture to honor his pledge that Camden "would be the first city in New Jersey to benefit from the program." (Newark, the state's largest city, also qualified as one the first target areas for New Jersey.) The new legislation included employee training to help reduce Camden's unemployment rate and boost economic incentives for businesses, including corporate tax credits; state sales tax exemption for construction materials in the zone; lower unemployment costs for hiring lower-income employees; and retail sales tax exemption.[49] Primas identified the industrial Waterfront South (approximately eighty acres) as the enterprise zone's designated area, and two years after Governor Kean signed the law, the mayor gave an upbeat speech before the Cherry Hill Chamber of Commerce that emphasized his administration's "small successes." Like other mayors, he presented a downtown-centric model of urban revitalization that included several projects under construction—specifically, a downtown transportation center and a new medical office building near the Cooper University Healthcare. He told the chamber of commerce that corporations were expressing more interest in establishing businesses in the city, and the urban enterprise zones could help to provide employment for local residents who desperately needed jobs.[50] However, the efficacy of enterprise zones and their ability to revitalize America's blighted areas had mixed results. In Florida, for example, the state established enterprise zones in 1981 to attract new businesses and provide more job opportunities in Miami's historically Black Liberty City after the notorious 1980 "McDuffie riots," but little progress had been made. US senator Frank Raleigh Lautenberg (D-NJ), owner of a multimillion-dollar processing business, said the zones created "a crazy competition in which the winner loses most." Specifically, "lower taxes and more services in the zone mean higher taxes and fewer services elsewhere," he observed.[51] This proved to be true for Camden, and enterprise zones ultimately failed to make a significant dent in the city's urban crisis and may have even led to additional nuisance industries in already overburdened environmental justice neighborhoods.⁵² In addition, Camden's reputation as a crime- and drug-ridden city in crisis deterred businesses from investing in the city.

Conclusion

Even though Mayor Primas was complicit in the usurpation of power by both Camden County and the state of New Jersey governments, the control exerted by the majority-white, suburban Democratic machine over Black and Brown politics set a precedent for mayoral elections in the city. To maintain its influence, the Democratic machine endorsed African American and Latino politicians with limited experience to be either appointed to finish a term or nominated to run for mayor. Moreover, the huge financial support of county-backed Democratic candidates along with New Jersey's unique ballot design laws made it nearly impossible for opposition candidates to win in Democratic primaries.⁵³ When Mayor Aaron Thompson, Primas's immediate successor, chose to defy the powerful Camden County Democratic organization's party boss, George Norcross, he lost the support of the Camden City Democratic Committee and served only one term (1990–93). In an interview, Jose Delgado, a longtime resident who lost to then party nominee Dana Redd in the 1990 mayoral primary, explained his plans to make changes that would not require approval from the city council because of its loyalty to Norcross. He recalled, "If I had won the mayorship, I would have had a council that was almost completely controlled by the political machine, by George Norcross."⁵⁴ Mayor Arnold Webster (1993–97) lost the party's endorsement after seeking more independence from its control. But Webster's decision to challenge the power structure has been overshadowed by his conviction of wire fraud for illegally accepting $20,000 from his former position at the financially strapped Camden City School District.⁵⁵ Similarly, Mayor Milton Milan, Camden's first Latino mayor, who succeeded Mayor Webster, served time in prison after an FBI investigation found him guilty of a variety of crimes detailed in a *Courier-Post* article. His offenses included "taking mob payoffs, using city contractors to perform free work on his home, laundering money from a drug dealer, committing insurance fraud, using vehicles supplied for free by a towing contractor and selling a stolen computer to an intern."⁵⁶ Although both mayors left a legacy of corruption, they also came to office during a shift of political power in the city from Black to Hispanic voters.

Black-Latino alliances began to fray as the City of Camden's Spanish-speaking population increased and Latinos fought for more political representation in local government. Historian Laura Lahey's study of Camden during the post–civil rights era examines the fusion of Black Power militancy and Puerto Rican nationalism in the city, documenting the solidarity that emerged between both groups after the 1971 racial uprising.[57] Additionally, during the 1980s, African Americans and Puerto Ricans formed a united front against the construction of two state prisons in North Camden. However, tensions grew as Latinos began demanding more political power and access to the city's limited resources, especially during Mayor Arnold Webster's tenure. In March 1994, former city councilman Santiago Ilarraza, who seemingly spoke on behalf of a newly formed group—the Puerto Rican and Hispanic Committee for Equality and Good Government—charged Webster's administration with perpetuating "a policy of exclusion" toward Camden's Hispanic community.[58] The following year, Hispanic leaders organized an all-day conference to discuss the lack of Hispanic representation in multiple areas of city government/civic affairs and Mayor Webster's failure to adequately address their concerns. The meeting triggered a series of news conferences and confrontations.

Bomb threats, accusations of racism, and even physical altercations at city council meetings intensified racial/ethnic tensions. In response to the charges against Mayor Webster, his administration released a report to demonstrate his strong record. According to the June 1995 report, Blacks made up 56 percent of Camden's population and held 44 percent of jobs; whites composed 13 percent and held 39 percent of jobs; and Latinos represented 31 percent of the population but held only 17 percent of jobs. Of nineteen department heads, only one was Latino, and of 184 employees in the city housing department, only 38 were Latino.[59] The report also pointed out that the seven-member city council had three Blacks, two Hispanics, and two whites.[60]

Even though parts of the study substantiated their claims, Hispanic leaders criticized its alleged inaccuracies. A few weeks later the Greater Camden County Reinvestment Corporation for Concerned Leaders of Camden City published a booklet, *An Analysis of Blacks and Hispanics in Camden County Government*, which accused Hispanic critics of racial prejudice. Roy Jones, executive director of the reinvestment corporation and author of the booklet, argued, "The clearest and most immediate example of Hispanic prejudice is the insistence by Hispanic leaders that the Webster Report on Camden City Hispanic Inclusion is inaccurate." But the disparities in other areas heightened public scrutiny and compelled Webster to make some concessions. In August 1995, a thirty-member Hispanic Steering Committee secured an agreement from the mayor to ensure its community benefited from the $21 million in empowerment zone money and $42 million in funding to rehabilitate a housing development with a significant Latino population.[61] Webster also agreed to appoint more Hispanics to several crucial boards, including the city's Empowerment Zone Trust Commission. Interestingly, Roy Jones characterized the Hispanic Steering Committee's complaints and charges of racism as part of a larger effort to divide and conquer the Black and Hispanic communities in Camden. He lamented, "Hispanic leaders have purposefully ignored white racism and white dominance. Hispanics are fighting ... in the wrong arena, and the charges of racism are hypocritical and contrived." He also accused "white Hispanics" of trying to divide and conquer and being part of a white-controlled Democratic machine. But Hispanic activist Carlo Perazo assailed Jones for trying to divert attention away from Webster's poor record.[62] Nevertheless, Jones maintained that city government was Black and Brown in appearance, but in practice elected officials from both groups were completely beholden to largely white suburban outsiders in county and state government and in powerful nonprofits and anchor institutions that created policy decisions for the city behind closed doors.

Cooper's Ferry Partnership (CFP), a politically connected private nonprofit organization, played a leading role in advancing the county and state government's neoliberal economic development projects in Camden. The CFP, originally created through a partnership by the City of Camden, Campbell Soup Company, and RCA in 1984, focused primarily on creating planning documents for the city's waterfront during the first ten to fifteen years of its existence.[63] However, the CFP became a driving force behind private-public initiatives to spend a significant amount of public funding on entertainment-oriented waterfront developments aimed to attract Camden outsiders (white) to the city during the early 1990s and next two decades. The CFP helped to establish the Adventure Aquarium in 1992 (a $23 million project), a large outdoor concert venue, the Camden Children's Garden, the now-demolished minor league baseball stadium, and luxury apartments that most Black residents cannot afford to rent in a city where the median household income is $27,000. The aquarium development promised jobs for city residents that would trickle down, but shortly after it opened many Black city residents complained about not being called back from job interviews, and some advocated an all-out boycott of the facility.[64] Similarly, Campbell's minor league baseball field, publicly funded by the Delaware River Port Authority, cost $18 million but was recently demolished in 2021 in order to make way for an expansion of Rutgers University–Camden's athletics fields. (The Delaware River Port Authority was later the subject of a federal investigation for using economic development funds for political purposes and today no longer conducts any economic development activity as a result.)[65] Moreover, the rise of PILOTs (payments in lieu of [property] taxes) awarded to developments such as the New Jersey State Aquarium, the Victor luxury apartments, Eds and

Meds institutions such as Rutgers University–Camden and Rowan University, and corporations also became more prominent during this period.

Although the CFP has been credited for helping to revitalize the city, many Black residents chided the organization for carrying out corporate gentrification and being beholden to outside interests. (Cooper's Ferry Partnership changed its name to Camden Community Partnership in late 2021.) Juan Gonzales commended downtown waterfront investment, portraying it as a "sign of progress." "You need attractions, you need revenue, you need a tax base," he noted. But the CFP has been described as a "shadow government" by both residents and some elected officials who claim that these developments have largely served a function of attracting white suburban workers and visitors to the city while simultaneously extracting wealth and resources into outside private interests' coffers. Longtime city resident and activist Vida Neil explains that politicians were creating a "bubble city," or a city within a city. She contends the "bubble city" is being created for other residents and employees who work at local universities, hospitals, or any of the businesses recently recruited to build corporate headquarters in the city.[66] In the article "'They're Not Building It for Us: Displacement Pressure, Unwelcomeness, and Protesting Neighborhood Investment," Stephen Danley and Rasheda Weaver draw on interviews from Camden residents to demonstrate the alienating effects of the waterfront's high parking prices, explaining, "The result is residents receive a clear message: this space is designed to protect visitors to waterfront sites from Camden residents. Because of the surrounding communities' sharp segregation, the unwelcomeness is often visible in starkly racial terms. The waterfront is white space. It is not designed for the residents themselves."[67] Echoing these sentiments, Kevin Barfield declared, "Camden is rising in new buildings. But the most important investment is the people. The people are not rising. Until the people have quality housing, education, stability within their communities, safe neighborhoods, jobs for the youth and even jobs for you, how do you rise?"[68]

City officials adopted a neoliberal approach to improving the quality of education in Camden after the 2012 Urban Hope Act, sponsored in the senate by state senator Donald Norcross (D-Camden) with the strong support of his brother, George Norcross. In 2013, the New Jersey State Department of Education's takeover of Camden's school system at the request of Mayor Dana Redd strengthened the push toward public alternatives to traditional K–12 through the Charter School Program Act of 1995. In his study of Camden residents' response to the state-imposed charter and renaissance schools, Keith Benson argued that "many Camden projects bear the [George] Norcross name, are affiliated with Cooper Hospital, or appear to benefit individuals with ties to Norcross," which has caused an important number of residents to "doubt whether any of Camden's current changes, including renaissance schools, is anything other than a profit or power-grabbing endeavor executed by Norcross."[69] Moreover, the privatization of public education has led to a loss of experienced Black educators in the city, which potentially caused a lack of representative teachers in schools and led to more middle-class Black professionals leaving the city altogether. In a 2020 interview, Bridget Phifer lamented, "There's really a push against the charter schools because, again, it's just that economic political privatized power base is coming to control who's hired." Furthermore, she explained, "Very often when the charter schools come in, you don't see black and brown people. You see young white females and perhaps in some instances men who are in those classrooms."[70] A study published by the New Jersey Policy Perspective found that the percentage of Black teachers in Camden had fallen over the last two decades from 52 percent in 1999 to 30 percent in 2019.[71] Even though Mayor Dana Redd and other African American elected officials touted the charter schools as a welcome alternative to the city's failing public school system, many Black families spoke out against their impact on the rash of closures or acquisition of public schools. Certainly, the success of these schools has become a deeply divided issue in the city, sometimes fracturing residents along ethnic/racial lines. In fact, a significant number of Latinos support charter and renaissance schools.

The neoliberal economic development model of using public funds to subsidize most of these projects, instead of potentially using the funds to positively and directly impact the lives of Black and Brown residents, has had a deleterious effect on the community. Specifically, the lack of investment in public education, libraries, job training, and housing has contributed to the socioeconomic disparities impacting Black residents to this day. However, Camden's Black community is not monolithic, and a significant number of residents view revitalization efforts as a clear sign of progress. Others have persevered despite the myriad challenges facing their communities.

To demonstrate the resilience and progress within Camden's Black community, several recent grassroots initiatives have emerged in the areas of business, education, the arts, and environmental activism. For instance, the Camden We Choose Coalition—comprising organizations such as the Camden Parents Union, the New Jersey Working Families Party, and other labor and advocacy groups—has focused on promoting employment equity. Utilizing the provisions of the state's Faulkner Act, the coalition introduced an ordinance requiring private employers in Camden with twenty-five or more full-time employees to disclose local hiring practices and salary ranges via a petition-driven ballot initiative, fostering greater transparency and economic opportunity for residents.

In business and the arts, Black entrepreneurs and cultural organizations are increasingly establishing a presence downtown. Artist Erik James Montgomery has opened a photography studio, while Cynthia Primas, through the IDEA Center for the Arts nonprofit, offers art-focused programming for youth. Additionally, Camden-based environmental justice organizers, after years of advocacy, played a key role in the implementation of New Jersey's Environmental Justice Law. This legislation has enabled residents to participate in New Jersey Department of Environmental Protection (DEP) permit hearings concerning polluting industries, such as the Covanta trash incinerator and Eastern Metal Recycling. These hearings have allowed Camden residents to lobby for community benefits in exchange for air quality permit renewals, giving them a stronger voice in the environmental and public health decisions affecting their neighborhoods. Together, these initiatives reflect a growing commitment to cultural, economic, and environmental empowerment within Camden.

Notes

1. Valerie Sweeten, "Residents: No to Second Prison Protestors March against Proposed Facility," *Courier-Post* (Cherry Hill, NJ), August 21, 1989.
2. "State Talking with City Group about Land on Riverfront Prison," *Courier-Post*, June 13, 1989.
3. Bertha Aytch, "Another Prison: State, City and BPUM Are Betraying North Camden," *Courier-Post*, June 22, 1989.
4. Kevin Riordan, "Prison Protest Leads to Argument," *Courier-Post*, July 26, 1989.
5. "Residents Oppose Second State Prison," *Courier-Post*, July 15, 1981.
6. See J. Phillip Thompson III, *Double Trouble: Black Mayors, Black Communities, and the Call for a Deep Democracy* (New York: Oxford University Press, 2005); Kevin Mumford, *Newark: A History of Race, Rights, and Riots in America* (New York: New York University Press, 2007); Roger Biles, *Mayor Harold Washington: Champion of Race and Reform in Chicago* (Champaign: University of Illinois Press, 2018).
7. Nicholas Blomley, *Unsettling the City: Urban Land and the Politics of Property* (New York: Routledge, 2004), 30.
8. Michael C. Dawson and Megan Ming France, "Black Politics and the Neoliberal Racial Order," *Public Culture* 28, no. 1 (2016): 44, https://read-dukeupress-edu.ezproxy.rowan.edu/public-culture/article/28/1%20(78)/23/82909/Black-Politics-and-the-Neoliberal-Racial-Order.
9. Lester K. Spence, *Knocking the Hustle: Against the Neoliberal Turn in Black Politics* (Brooklyn: Punctum Books, 2015), 45.
10. Howard Gillette, *Camden after the Fall: Decline and Renewal in a Post-Industrial City* (Philadelphia: University of Pennsylvania Press, 2006), 42–43.
11. By 1967, industrial employment had dramatically dropped by 12,000, and the following year the New York Ship Building Company closed, resulting in the loss of another

7,000 industrial jobs. This rate exceeded that of other cities, such as Philadelphia, Detroit, or Cleveland, going through deindustrialization at the same period.
12. Bridget Phifer, interview by Michael Denton, October 24, 2020, WHYY/Rowan University Camden Oral History Project.
13. Jeffery M. Dorward and Philip English Mackay, *Camden County, New Jersey, 1616–1976: A Narrative History* (Camden Co., NJ: Camden Co. Cultural and Heritage Commission, 1976), 155.
14. Gillette, *Camden after the Fall*, 43.
15. Kevin Riordan, "City to Honor Controversial Voice of the Black Community," *Courier-Post*, March 14, 1993.
16. Wasim Muhammad, interview by Chanelle Rose, October 26, 2021, WHYY/Rowan University Camden Oral History Project.
17. Urban renewal in south Camden's Centerville–Liberty Park neighborhood displaced over 1,000 families, including African American and white working-class residents. While many of these white residents moved to racially exclusive suburbs, federal housing discrimination policies forced an increasing number of Black Camdenites who migrated from the South, alongside Puerto Rican migrants recruited by Campbell's Soup, to live in the inner city's overcrowded neighborhoods. Interstate 676 led to more than 6,000 units of housing being either bulldozed or scattered by renewal projects in the city. The FHA's discriminatory appraisal system redlined communities of color, resulting in entire cities being labeled ineligible for loan guarantees, including Camden. See Kenneth Jackson, *Crabgrass Frontier: The Suburbanization of the United States* (New York: Oxford University Press, 1985), 213.
18. Sharp, a self-described Black freedom fighter, preached a message of Black self-determination similar to other Black Power activists while working closely with white suburban allies in Friends of the Black People's Unity Movement to fight for decent housing, better schools, and an end to police brutality. In 1968, BPUM joined a coalition of progressive organizations, including the Friends of the Black People's Unity Movement, to find adequate housing for the Shields family, a Black family in North Camden displaced by urban renewal. Sharp's confrontational tactics and BPUM-led demonstrations led to altercations with the local police, harassment, and surveillance. See Gary Hunter, *Neighborhoods of Color: African American Communities in Southern New Jersey, 1638–2000* (Thorofare, NJ: Slack Incorporated, 2015), 175.
19. Virgil P. McDill and Harry C. Silcox, eds., *Camden Then and Now: An Intergenerational History Project* (Philadelphia: Brighton Press, 1997), 34, Camden County Historical Society, Camden, NJ.
20. "A Crisis of Power in Camden," *Courier-Post*, December 14, 1973.
21. Ronald Sullivan, "Mayor of Camden Indicted in Bid-Rigging Conspiracy," *New York Times*, December 14, 1973.
22. Ken Shuttleworth, "Black Activist Helps Camden Center Celebrate," *Courier-Post*, March 31, 1985.
23. "City to Controversial Voices of the Black Community," *Courier-Post*, March 14, 1993.
24. Ronald Alsop, "Urban Rescue Blighted Camden, N.J., Digs Out of Its Rubble, but Big Task Remains," *Wall Street Journal*, February 8, 1982.

25. William W. Sutton, "Lecturing on Problems of Camden," *Philadelphia Inquirer*, September 16, 1982.
26. Thompson, *Double Trouble*, 6.
27. Ken Shuttleworth, "Jockeying Starts for 1st Position in Mayoral Race," *Courier-Post*, November 30, 1980.
28. "Trash Used in Protest," *Courier-Post*, January 21, 1981.
29. "Rent Protest Feared," *Courier-Post*, January 15, 1981.
30. "Camden Activist to Seek Mayor's Seat," *Courier-Post*, February 22, 1981.
31. "Candidate Jones Focuses Campaign on Machine Politics," *Courier-Post*, May 5, 1981.
32. "As Readers See It Camden City Must Blame Itself, Not the Suburbs," *Courier-Post*, April 1, 1981.
33. "Melvin Primas Sworn In as Mayor," *Courier-Post*, July 2, 1981.
34. William Sutton, "Panel Chosen to 'Vigorously' Enforce Camden's Affirmative Action Law," *Philadelphia Inquirer*, October 12, 1982, Camden County Historical Society.
35. *60 Minutes* quoted in "Father Doyle's Camden Has Been There All Along," *Courier-Post*, March 24, 1983.
36. W. Dennis Keating and Norman Krumholz, eds., *Rebuilding Urban Neighborhoods: Achievements, Opportunities, and Limits* (California: SAGE Publications, 1999), 58.
37. Keating and Krumholz, *Rebuilding Urban Neighborhoods*, 58.
38. "Prison Site: State Won't Be Asking Much Longer," *Courier-Post*, May 17, 1981.
39. In September 1979, for example, members of the CCNC carried a bag of fleas to the mayor's office and put them on his desk after no action had been taken to address millions of biting fleas that had taken over one section of North Camden near Byron Street. But most of their efforts focused on neighborhood rehabilitation, especially the board-up program that was established to deter vandalism and ultimately provide homeownership for local residents. See Linda Jankowski, "Citizens Battle Bites, Blight, and Bars," *Courier-Post*, February 16, 1981.
40. "Residents Opposed to Prison Site," *Courier-Post*, July 15, 1981.
41. Linda Jankowski, "Protestors to Storm Primas' Office," *Courier-Post*, July 22, 1981.
42. Jankowski, "Protestors to Storm Primas' Office."
43. Mary Pembleton, "Group to City: Halt Wrecking," *Courier-Post*, July 28, 1979.
44. Ken Shuttleworth, "Two Prison Sites Still on Holding List," *Courier-Post*, July 25, 1981. In 1981, the CCNC organized a squatting campaign, a by-product of its homeowner program, with thirteen families (mostly Latino) that took over abandoned houses for five years before city officials reluctantly conceded to some of their demands See Tom Knoche, "Organising Communities," from *Social Anarchism*, 1993, 6, https://ia800904.us.archive.org/14/items/OrganisingCommunities/organizing _communities-2008_version.pdf.
45. Gillette, *Camden after the Fall*, 102.
46. Robert Benenson, "Reagan and the Cities," *Editorial Research Reports* 2 (1982): 1–11, https://library-cqpress-com.ezproxy.rowan.edu/cqresearcher/document.php?id =cqresrre1982072300.
47. "Primas Asks Reagan to Include City in Plan," *Courier-Post*, January 29, 1982.
48. Alan H. Peters and Peter S. Fisher, *State Enterprise Zone Programs: Have They Worked?* (Kalamazoo: W. E. Upjohn Institute for Employment Research, 2001), 26.
49. "Law Boosts Camden for Business, Jobs," *Courier-Post*, August 16, 1983.

50. Kevin Riordan, "Primas: City on Brink of Boom," *Courier-Post*, February 27, 1985.
51. "Enterprise Zone Offers City the Chance to Thrive," *Courier-Post*, August 17, 1983.
52. In fact, Mayor Primas cited the urban enterprise zone in Waterfront South as being a reason to build the trash incinerator; see Andrew Maykuth, "Camden's Leaders Are Pushing Idea of a Trash-to-Steam Plant," *Philadelphia Inquirer*, November 11, 1984.
53. These laws allow for county parties to play an oversize role in the creation of the layout of ballots for primary elections. They have the power to award the party "the line" and bracket candidates together into a single column, which provides a significant advantage to whomever the party selects as its endorsed candidates. As a result, nonparty-endorsed candidates are pushed over to the extreme edges of the ballot, which has the effect of suppressing votes for these candidates. See Julia Sass Rubin, "Toeing the Line: New Jersey Primary Ballots Enable Party Insiders to Pick Winners," *New Jersey Policy Perspective*, June 2020, 1–5, www.njpp.org/wp-content/uploads/2020/06/NJPP-Report-Toeing-the-Line-New-Jerseys-Primary-Ballots-Enable-Party-Insiders-to-Pick-Winners.pdf.
54. Jose Delgado, interview by Khan Aktas, November 3, 2020, WHYY/Rowan University Camden Oral History Project.
55. See Clint Riley, "Camden Ex-Mayor Guilty of Fraud," *Courier-Post*, April 21, 1999.
56. Riley, "Camden Ex-Mayor Guilty of Fraud."
57. Laura Lahey, "Justice Now! ¡Justicia Ahora! African American–Puerto Rican Radicalism in Camden, New Jersey," in *Civil Rights and Beyond: African American and Latino/a Activism in the Twentieth-Century United States*, ed. Brian Behnken (Athens: University of Georgia Press, 2016), 152–71.
58. "Camden Leader Accuses Mayor of Hispanic Exclusion," *Courier-Post*, March 11, 1994.
59. "Webster to Increase Latino Representation," *Philadelphia Inquirer*, August 17, 1995; "An Analysis of Blacks and Hispanics in Camden County Government" (infinished), June 1995, Camden County Historical Society, Camden, NJ.
60. Roy Jones, *An Analysis of Blacks and Hispanics in Camden County Government*, June 20, 1995, Blacks and Hispanics, Camden County Historical Society.
61. Monica Rhor, "Webster Says He'll Give Bigger Role to Latinos," *Philadelphia Inquirer*, August 17, 1995.
62. "Two Black Activists Repudiate Hispanics' Charges of Racism," *Courier-Post*, June 21, 1995.
63. "Cooper's Ferry Development Association (CFDA)," Discover the Camden Waterfront, Wayback Machine, October 10, 2000, https://web.archive.org/web/20001010231341/http://www.camdenwaterfront.com/cfda/.
64. "Camden Isn't Swimming in Newly Created Jobs," *Philadelphia Inquirer*, February 23, 1992.
65. Peter Samuel, "Another Philly Corruption Scandal Unfolding," Camden Civil Rights Project, April 5, 2013, https://camdencivilrightsproject.com/another-philly-corruption-scandal-unfolding-drpa-federal-grand-jury-investigation/.
66. Stephen Danley and Rasheda Weaver, "'They're Not Building It for Us': Displacement Pressure, Unwelcomeness, and Protesting Neighborhood Investment," *Societies* 8, no. 3 (2018): 8.
67. Danley and Weaver, "They're Not Building It for Us," 9.

68. Kevin Barfield, interview by Jake Brodbeck, November 3, 2020, WHYY/Rowan University Camden Oral History Project. The Camden Library System became a casualty of the increase in PILOTs, shutting down completely in 2011 under the leadership of Mayor Dana Redd due to a $26.5 million city budget deficit. "Library Shutdown in Camden, N.J.," Governing, February 25, 2011, www.governing.com/archive/library-shutdown-camden-new-jersey.html. CFP planning decisions have contributed to massive environmental and health disparities in the city such as significantly higher asthma rates and the city being designated an overburdened environmental community. New Jersey Department of Environmental Protection, *Overburdened Communities under the New Jersey Environmental Justice Law in Camden City, Camden County*, June 1, 2022, www.nj.gov/dep/ej/docs/communities/camden-camden-city-maps-obc.pdf.
69. Keith Benson, *Education Reform and Gentrification in the Age of #Camdenrising: Public Education and Urban Redevelopment in Camden, NJ* (New York: Peter Lang, 2019), 168.
70. Phifer interview by Denton.
71. April Saul, "'There's No Simple Answer': Can the Whitening of Camden's Teachers Be Reversed?," WHYY/PBS NPR, February 26, 2021, https://whyy.org/articles/theres-no-simple-answer-can-the-whitening-of-camdens-teachers-be-reversed.

JEFFREY O. G. OGBAR

The Black Mecca

Atlanta and Twenty-First-Century Black Movement

Atlanta was the Mecca, building railroads and trains /
Bear with me for a second, let me put y'all on game.
—**Kendrick Lamar,** "Not Like Us" (2024)

In what is widely considered the biggest rap battle in the history of hip-hop, two titans of the art, Kendrick Lamar (Kendrick Lamar Duckworth) and Drake (Aubrey Drake Graham), exchanged a series of musical salvos in the spring of 2024. The former, a native of Compton, California, accused the latter, who hails from Toronto, of being an inauthentic interloper who, eager for cultural bona fides and commercial access, would "run to Atlanta." The Pulitzer Prize recipient, who holds more Grammys than all rap artists but two (Jay-Z and Kanye West), offered a biting critique of Drake. In the song "Not Like Us," Kendrick argued that his Canadian adversary headed to "the Mecca" in his thirst for "street cred," current "lingo," and "a few dollars." Ultimately, Kendrick accused Drake, the *Billboard* "Artist of the Decade" who holds the most number one singles on the Hot R&B/Hip-Hop Songs chart, of using Atlanta in the way that imperialists exploit countries. According to Kendrick, the most precious commodity in Drake's extraordinary wealth— African American musical culture—finds its richest deposits in the Gate City. Kendrick dropped a powerful line: "You not a colleague, you a f——in' colonizer." In what became the week's most streamed song in the world (including in Toronto), Kendrick Lamar's "Not Like Us" highlighted—to a global audience—the significance of Atlanta as a site for conspicuous Black enterprise and artistic creativity.[1] This popular culture reference highlights the degree to which post–Great Migration movement to the South, and to the Atlanta area in particular, has upended decades-long non-southern expressions of African American culture. The Motown sound, the Sound of Philadelphia, midwest funk, or even the birthplace of hip-hop (the Bronx, New York) did not capture the zeitgeist of Black musical dominance like the veritable capital of the South did. What had been the "Imperial City" to the Ku Klux Klan exactly a century earlier, Atlanta has drawn more Black migrants than any city in the United States since the end of the Great Migration, creating a rich social, economic, political, and cultural locus for Black achievement and visibility.

Atlanta's place as a metonymic reference for African American business, politics, and culture is not without merit. The city has the highest concentration of Black millionaires, Black-owned businesses, and Black colleges and universities and consistently lands at the top of various rankings of "best of" lists for Black people in cities.[2] Black people within the city are not sequestered in only a few areas; instead they occupy every class stratum and neighborhood and public venue in highly visible fashion, from jazz concerts in the city's largest park to upscale restaurants and high-rise luxury condos. Even the Atlanta Hawks owner, in 2012, lamented that the team had an overwhelming Black attendance rate that was "four to five times all other [NBA] teams," which frightened some whites from attending games, despite the absence of any reported crimes or trouble.[3] Politically, local African American leaders have resonated nationally, from US representative John Lewis and US senator Raphael Warnock to former mayor Keisha Lance Bottoms and gubernatorial candidate Stacey Abrams. In January 2024, Atlanta became the first major city to have fifty years of an unbroken line of African American mayors. If any city can claim the moniker of "Mecca" for Black people, this sprawling city carved out of Georgia's forests and red clay is it.

In the half century after the end of the Great Migration and the election of the first Black mayor of a major southern city, African American national political ascendance across a range of spaces has been remarkable. New York, Chicago, Los Angeles, Philadelphia, Houston, Seattle, Baltimore, and Dallas, as well as hundreds of small cities and towns, have elected Black mayors since 1973. What had once been heralded as a remarkable political feat, a Black mayor of Atlanta had come to be expected—and accepted—by most Atlantans by the start of the twenty-first century.

The election of Shirley Franklin in 2001 was distinguished by her being the first woman mayor of any major southern city. Her success led her to national acclaim. In 2005, *Time* named the Howard University alumna as one of the five best big-city mayors in the country, among other national awards, including recognition for elevating Atlanta to one of the cities with the most LEED (Leadership in Energy and Environmental Design) buildings. Foreign and national corporations continued to expand investment in the city under her administration. She was even in contention for a World Mayor honor. Franklin rode a tidal wave of support to a second term with an astounding 90 percent of votes cast.[4] Crime rates continued to track a national trend downward. In Franklin's last year of office, 2009, Atlanta saw the lowest number of homicides in the city since 1963.[5] By many measures, the racial tensions, violence, and wave of big city problems appeared to give way to the sort of progress, stability, and opportunities for which many had longed. No Atlanta mayor in history could boast a record of garnering such electoral popularity across gender, racial, and class lines.

In 2009, Franklin's former campaign manager, state senator Mohammed Kasim Reed, another Howard alum, decided to run as her successor. Among other candidates, his major opponent was Mary Norwood, a white city council member and Buckhead resident. A white mayor of Atlanta had seemed out of reach decades earlier, but the racial landscape of the country had shifted considerably since Maynard Jackson's first victory. Many majority-white cities had Black mayors, while the mostly white country had a Black president. Majority-Black cities like Detroit and Gary had elected white mayors. But, in the Black Mecca, what would become of the decades of celebrated Black municipal leadership? What would happen to Black appointments or aggressive affirmative action programs with successful MBE records? On Election Day, November 3, 2009, Norwood, the white candidate, won more votes than anyone else in the race. At 46 percent of the votes, however, she did not secure a victory. A runoff with Reed was set for December 1. With 84,000 votes cast, the election was so close that a recount delayed the final result until December 9, when Reed was declared victor by 714 votes.

A native Atlantan, Reed nudged out a slim victory and inherited a city with a declining crime rate and an expanding metro area with growing investments from Fortune 500 companies. The city continued to make assiduous efforts to address the wide range of crises that had beset it over the past several decades. In 1987, under Mayor Andrew Young, who governed under historic crime rates, the Atlanta Police Department created a special unit, Red Dog, to target drug dealers. The aggressive police unit soon became notorious for its brutality—and possibly extralegal activities. By the end of the first decade of the twenty-first century, the complaints against the unit for verbal and physical abuse had become a cacophony of alarm from citizens across the areas where Red Dog was most active. Cristina Beamud, executive director of the Atlanta Citizen Review Board, which investigates complaints against police abuse, explained that the board had received "a disproportionate number of complaints about officers who belong to the Red Dog unit as opposed to officers involved in the [other] zones." The chief of police, George Turner, explained that "crime—and the drug trade in particular—has gotten more sophisticated, often moving indoors. We, too, have gotten smarter, using technology and intelligence-driven analysis to strategize and shift resources as needed. But let me be clear: That does not mean there still isn't a need for aggressive, street-level crime-fighting—there is."[6] In February 2011, Chief Turner, with Mayor Kasim Reed's support, announced that the Red Dog Unit would be disbanded. Even a majority-Black police force under Black administrators could not prevent allegations of abuse against Black people.

Among the other features that Reed inherited was a thriving and growing TV and film industry, which itself offered copious opportunities to extend the narrative of the city as a cultural center for Black America. There has never been any contest that the cultural landscape of Atlanta has always been extraordinarily rich. Yet, that landscape had changed dramatically with the rise of African American leadership. In 1974, Maynard Jackson created the city's Bureau of Cultural Affairs. It provided grants and other assistance for artists across platforms, including music, visual arts, drama, literary arts, and more. Created amid the Black Power movement, one cannot disentangle the influence and importance of the bureau from its historical context. A city that had trafficked in hagiographic Confederate traditions for over a century was under African American leadership for the first time. From loyal slaves of *Gone with the Wind*, to grinning and dancing magical Negroes from *Song of the South*, through Ku Klux Klan Klaverns and Stone Mountain's massive Confederate monument, the Gate City had a storied tradition of white nationalist celebrations in popular culture and leisure. Of course, from Collier Hills to Ben Hill to Grant Park, streets, neighborhoods, and parks have been institutionalized reminders of the city's Confederate heritage. Much like the mayor's efforts to open the city's closed access to Black firms in city contracts, Jackson charged the new Bureau of Cultural Affairs to widen the cultural representation of the city. Even as street names were changed to represent the fullness of Atlanta's history of Black and white citizens, the popular cultural representations shifted from the romantic homages to the Confederacy. Although not explicit, the bureau advanced Black art in particular, although white artists always received funding and support. Ultimately, the new office, in conjunction with tax incentives from the Georgia Entertainment Industry's Investment Act, "served as the expressive arm of perceived black political and economic power resulting from Jackson's affirmative action initiatives," as historian Maurice Hobson explains.[7] Transformative effects of the bureau were made across various arts. Hundreds of artists, venues, centers, theaters, and organizations received grants that facilitated programming, which elevated the city and enhanced its national reputation as a cultural hub.

In 1988, the Fulton County Arts Council and the Fulton County Commission, under leadership of Michael Lomax, founded the National Black Arts Festival. Twenty years later, after drawing millions to the city through its annual festivals, the US Congress recognized the National Black Arts Festival for its importance to the "cultural fabric of greater Atlanta and all of America." Artists across the spectrum of creativity have transformed the city into an extravaganza of Black artistry, from Maya Angelou and Wynton Marsalis to Bill T. Jones, Nikki Giovanni, and Gregory Porter. From plays at the 14th Street Playhouse in Midtown to jazz, modern dance, ballet, African dance, blues concerts, and arts and crafts in Piedmont Park, the festival has been one of dozens of anchor events that have promoted the city's Black Mecca authenticity. Music emerged as one of the most visible art forms to emanate from the city.

Alternatively called the "Motown of the South" or the "Music Capital of the South," the city has also become a center for music production, especially in R&B and hip-hop, generating over half a billion dollars a year. The city is home for a long list of artists as well as Black-owned studios, production companies, and record labels. As journalist and cultural critic Michael Harriot explained, "You can't even talk about black music without having Georgia on your mind." From Gladys Knight, OutKast, Toni Braxton, TLC, Usher, Goodie Mob, Ludacris, and T.I. to Future, 2 Chainz, 21 Savage, Migos, Ciara, Killer Mike, Lil Baby, Gucci Mane, and beyond, the impact on music is profound. Black-owned labels, such as LaFace (Babyface), So So Def (Jermaine Dupri), Konvict Musik (Akon), RBMG (Usher), Freebandz (Future), and Grand Hustle (T.I.) have shaped America's popular music. Multiple sources call the city the capital of hip-hop music. Revolt, a music-related website, ranks Atlanta number one among cities most central to the artform. VisitTheUSA.com, which calls itself the "official travel site of the USA," devotes a section to Atlanta as "the hip-hop capital of the USA."[8] Many artists who are non-Atlanta natives—Mariah Carey, Steve Harvey, Janelle Monáe—have relocated to the city, drawing other high-profile entertainers. Along with Miami, New York, and Los Angeles, Atlanta looms large as a site for glamour, leisure, and excess for African American cultural trendsetters and creatives. Given the prominence of popular music, is it not entirely surprising that TV and film production also took root in the city. To again quote Harriot, when it comes to African American cultural expressions, "Atlanta is the culture."[9]

In 2006, the breakout Real Housewives franchise debuted with an all-white cast of affluent wives in Orange County, California. Two years later, *The Real Housewives of Atlanta* debuted with the franchise's first majority-Black cast. With this show, which centered on the lives of the affluent housewives and their families in the Atlanta area, viewers were introduced to a world of conspicuous consumption and excess, on par with the franchise's shows set in other cities. The obvious difference, of course, was not only the Black cast but the Black denizens of the show's background supporting cast: real-life family physicians, lawyers, stylists, event planners, restauranteurs, personal assistants, therapists, and personal trainers. The people were not actors cast as extras in a fictional Black utopian world. Rather, the overwhelming Blackness showcased a world that is largely unseen anywhere. *The Real Housewives of Atlanta* was a great success, eventually earning higher ratings than all other shows in the franchise, and emerged as the highest-rated program on the network. Over twenty Black Atlanta-based reality shows have debuted since the first year that *The Real Housewives of Atlanta* aired, highlighting a veritable "Wakanda,"[10] or utopian space of Afro-Selfdeterminism, featuring Black physicians (*Married to Medicine, Atlanta Plastic*), Black real estate titans (*Ladies Who List: Atlanta, Married to Real Estate, Selling It in the ATL*), and Black music executives (*Love and Hip Hop: Atlanta, Growing Up Hip Hop: Atlanta*). The names of Atlanta reality shows with majority-Black casts are far too numerous to list, but it is notable that no city boasts the draw that the "Hollywood of the South" has for Black reality shows, consistently underscoring how visible the city has become as a center for Black popular culture.

By 2016, no city had as many TV and film projects in the United States, other than Los Angeles and New York. Of course, television and movie production, which grossed over $9.5 billion for the state, had been centered in metro Atlanta. This has been so impactful that Atlanta created the Mayor's Office of Film and Entertainment. Like most departments, whether legal, education, or transportation, the office is under Black executive management. In fact, two Black women, Cardellia Hunter and Phillana Williams, served as comanagers of the office in 2022.[11] Like many sectors of municipal management, Atlanta has consistently reflected a level of Black executive leadership rarely seen in other cities anywhere.

One of the largest film production studios in the country is based in Atlanta and owned by a Black billionaire, Tyler Perry. The 330-acre lot rests on the former Fort McPherson army base, which the Union army established after the Civil War. In Black-majority shows or movies, such as *Being Mary Jane, Beyond the Pole, Black Ink Atlanta*, or *ATL*, the brand of Atlanta has been conspicuous to such an extent that the immensely talented auteur Donald Glover, an area native, launched one of the most critically acclaimed TV shows of 2016, aptly named *Atlanta*. The Black Mecca narrative has become so popular that a major tourist industry developed around attracting the billions from the African American business meeting and tourist market. From the early 1990s, Black tourists have traveled to the city for leisure or business, making it the number one or number two tourist destination for the last twenty years. There is no doubt that the centrality of Atlanta in popular culture as a center of Black excellence has continued to promote the Black Mecca narrative.

Scores of thousands each year migrate to the Atlanta metro area, drawn to the same positive qualities promoted in the popular press: Black exceptional opportunities. Rodney Strong, who has long played an important role in facilitating the political economy under multiple administrations, calls the process a "virtuous cycle." This cycle, he details, follows the publicity surrounding a major Black appointment (or series of appointments): Black CEOs and heads of major segments of the city and county governments, including public safety, education, legal, and more. The visibility of these figures, Strong explains, underscores Atlanta's reputation as open to Black success and opportunity, drawing talented, ambitious, and resource-rich African Americans into the city. The process traverses industries. Most notably, tech has enjoyed this virtuous cycle. Local African Americans in tech have gained so much visibility that in 2019 *USA Today* declared the city to be the nation's "black tech capital." Per Strong's comments, the city's reputation as an educational center, tech center, and business center for African Americans would necessarily attract ambitious, highly trained Black professionals, perpetuating the virtuous cycle. Whatever the factor, Black transplants to Metro Atlanta have been significant.[12]

Over a half a million African Americans migrated into the area between 2000 and 2010 alone, pushing the total Black metropolitan population to 1.7 million. They represented the largest net gain of any racial or ethnic group in the region. And much of the migration has been of highly skilled and educated workers. The rate of African Americans with a bachelor's degree is 40 percent higher than the Black national average.[13] Atlanta in 2020 was the ninth largest metropolitan area in the United States but ranked second—just behind New York City's Metropolitan Statistical Area—in Black residents, at over 2 million people. Communities that were once known as notorious centers of racism and white supremacist activity, like Stone Mountain and Forsyth County, became integrated by the influx of Blacks from both the city and other parts of the country. Professionals—white and Black—who sought strong school systems, large homes, and affordable luxuries found these communities attractive. In 1997, Stone Mountain had become a majority-Black suburb.

As typical to the Atlanta narrative, these positive statistics are not without a complicated wider picture. Atlanta is strained by environmental and infrastructure pressures and, at least for most of the late twentieth century, extraordinarily high crimes rates and concentrated poverty. Atlanta has more Black businesses and Black millionaires per capita than any other city but the lowest rate of social mobility and greatest wealth disparity among American cities. A child born into poverty in Atlanta has only a 4 percent chance of escaping poverty in his or her lifetime.[14] While the rate of Black affluence has increased since 1970, the poverty rate has remained almost exactly the same: 29 percent. By 1990, Atlanta had one of the highest ratios of citizens—10 percent—who lived in public housing projects. These were often veritable war zones with exponentially high levels of crime. As part of what some have called the "Olympification" of the city, the Atlanta Housing Authority, under chairperson Renee Glover, secured federal funding to destroy much of the public housing and provide residents with vouchers to live in mixed-income areas. By 2011, the first American city to erect public housing became the first to tear down all public housing projects.[15]

Challenges notwithstanding, the allure of Atlanta has recently brought into the city the highest percentage of whites since the 1970s. Reflecting national trends that find that whites and Blacks are not nearly as opposed to integrated neighborhoods as earlier generations had been, the racial landscape of the city has continued to evolve. The city peaked in population in 1970 with 496,973 before experiencing a steady decline, driven mostly by whites moving to the suburbs, while Black movement out of the city moved at a slower pace. Over 120,000 whites left Atlanta between 1970 and 1990. Between 1990 and 2000, however, over 7,300 whites moved into the municipality of Atlanta, while the number of Blacks decreased by nearly 26,000. By 2010, continued influx resulted in another 9,504 white people. Simultaneously, the Black movement into spacious, middle-class, and upscale suburban areas accelerated as Black migration into the metro area continued. Clayton County, south of the city, increased from 24 percent Black to 51 percent, between 1990 and 2000, while DeKalb County increased its Black population from 42 percent to 53 percent. In all, the number of Black people who lived in the surrounding suburbs had increased by over 1 million between 1980 and 2000. Over the next twenty years, the Black population of the Atlanta metro area increased by an additional 67 percent. Explosive growth continued into the twenty-first century, where Atlanta hit 498,715 in the 2020 census—more people than at any point in its history—while the metro area ballooned to over 6 million people.[16] The city of Atlanta was, after fifty years, growing again. Moreover, it is no longer the archetypal southern city with a racial binary.

While some have argued that Black people were leaving the city (for various reasons), between 2010 and 2020 there was a net *increase* of Black people into the city—even as the Black population in the suburbs also increased. Two things were occurring at the same time: an influx of Black people into the city, and a much larger influx into Atlanta of non-Blacks. In fact, there were 21,502 additional African Americans in the city between 2010 and 2020, even as the Black percentage of the city decreased from 54 percent to 49.8 percent. The proportion of Black Atlantans dropped not because there were fewer Black people but because of the influx of whites, Latinx, and Asian Americans who, collectively, outpaced Black in-migration. During this decade, there was also the loss of scores of thousands of Black residents to secession.[17] In 2017, a middle-class area in southwest Atlanta, which included parts of Black neighborhoods such as Ben Hill and Red Oak, seceded from the city, becoming the state's eighth largest city, South Fulton. Around 90 percent of South Fulton is African American. It became, per the 2020 US Census, the Blackest city of over 100,000 people in the country. Some 67 percent are homeowners—over 59 percent higher than the national average of Black homeownership of 42 percent. Over 37 percent of the residents hold at least a college degree, 42 percent higher than the national Black average of college completion. If the city's population of over 107,000 had remained in Atlanta, 2020 would have had recorded more Black residents there than at any point in the city's history.[18]

Despite cries of Blacks being "pushed out" by white newcomers or by what has nebulously been called "gentrification," the actual data do not reflect any Black exodus—of the poor or otherwise. The destruction of public housing relocated thousands of people from blighted areas of highly concentrated poverty, drug addiction, and violence. Throughout that period (1996–2011), the overwhelming majority of former public housing residents remained in the city—between 80 and 85 percent, according to research from Georgia State University.[19] Simultaneously, crime continued to plummet, dropping to historic lows. In fact, at the start of 2011, the homicide rate had dropped around 50 percent from 1999 levels. By 2019, the rate remained roughly comparable to the 2011 level.[20] Black homeownership has also increased, as property values have increased. Black homeownership stood at 42 percent in 1980 and has since increased by 16.6 percent to 49 percent, seven points higher than the rate under the first Black mayor. It is also 16.6 percent higher than the Black national average.[21] Nationally, the city ranked in the top ten among cities with the largest increases of Black homeownership. Many of the gentrifiers have been, in fact, Black. In communities across the city, African Americans have been among the higher-income newcomers moving into new construction apartments, condominiums, or renovated homes in the West End, Adair Park, Midtown, and other areas. In fact, Atlanta in 2022 led the country in new apartment construction. A few old industrial sections of the city have been transformed, including Atlantic Station and Castleberry Hill. The latter, near the Atlanta University Center (AUC), was once home to blighted factories and shops. The area saw a new Paschal's Restaurant erected, along with a hotel and dozens of shops, art galleries, restaurants, and bars. It remains largely African American, although it, like many places in the city, enjoys a diverse clientele of whites, Blacks, Latinx, and Asians. The largest such transformation is the industrial park in Midtown that became the upscale, mixed-use community of Atlantic Station.[22]

Built on the site of the Atlantic Steel Mill Station in 1901 but largely closed in 1974, Atlantic Station is a standard example of gentrification. A partially abandoned brownfield site, the area was rundown with little housing or opportunities for commerce or leisure. The developer, Jim Jacoby, assumed an ambitious task to create a walkable district with mixed-used development of higher-end apartment rentals, a large movie theater, a bowling alley, restaurants, sports bars, and space for open-air concerts across 138 acres. This community would be anchored by high-rise office buildings and two glistening, upscale high-rise condominiums, the Atlantic and the Twelve, the latter of which was partially a hotel. Opened in October 2005, the area eventually became a significant entertainment space for the city. Most visitors are Black, but the clientele continues to be a racially and ethnically diverse one. The occupants of the two new high-rise upscale condos are largely Black and other people of color. There is probably no city in the country that can boast of creating brand-new, high-end condominium skyscrapers in prime city locations with mostly Black residents.

The diversification of the Gate City demographically reflects the increasing diversity of the country as a whole. With larger numbers of Latinx and Asians, it is no longer the archetypal racially bifurcated southern city, although it remains the second most-segregated city in the country.[23] On the other hand, some of the suburbs reflect unprecedented residential integration. The segregation index of the Atlanta Regional Commission region dropped from 77.4 percent to 46.9 percent. For the Atlanta Metropolitan Statistical Area, residential segregation declined from 68.8 to 48.3 percent. Not only is Gwinnett County, once overwhelmingly white, one of the most diverse counties in the region, but its integration index (the likelihood that two randomly selected households in the same census tract will be of different races) is the highest of any Sunbelt metro area and higher than the richly diverse Kings County, which includes Brooklyn, New York. By 2020, over seven times as many African Americans lived in the suburbs and exurbs of Atlanta than in the city. Outside of the city, African Americans have lower poverty rates than those inside, although communities are economically diverse. Eight of the eleven counties around Atlanta are majority–of color; most are majority-Black. Only Cherokee, Forsyth, and Fayette Counties have a white majority.[24] Metro Atlanta has been transformed as an extension of the Black Mecca.

A 2024 national study of property values in majority-Black zip codes found that, on average, Black home values were increasing faster than in white areas, helping to narrow the (still gaping) racial wealth gap to record lows. While Detroit's rising Black real estate values accounted for an aggregate increase of $3 billion, Atlanta's metro area dominated the national landscape, with six of the top ten Black "turnaround" zip codes in Clayton County alone. As noted above, Black migration into the county turned it majority-Black in recent years.[25] Yet, a wrinkle in these advances is the rapacity of home equity corporate investment groups that have targeted the Atlanta area by purchasing nearly 20,000 homes—critically depriving access to them to new homebuyers while driving up the price of homes.[26]

The Gate City had become a city of opportunity and achievement, especially for African Americans in the political arena. In 2017, however, the city, again, had a leading white candidate for mayor. In a crowded field of fourteen candidates, including several whites, Blacks, and an Asian American, mayoral hopefuls made appeals to Atlanta's citizens. The fall election produced a runoff between two Atlanta City Council members, Keisha Lance Bottoms and Mary Norwood. Bottoms, a native of the city, won a narrow victory against Norwood, which, like her predecessor's runoff, came down to less than 800 votes. As the sixtieth mayor of Atlanta, Mayor Bottoms was the sixth consecutive Black mayor and its second Black woman. Its sixty-first mayor, Andre Dickens, was elected in 2021. A graduate of Benjamin E. Mays High School, Dickens was born in Atlanta the same year that Maynard Jackson first took office. He is the city's first mayor to have always lived under a Black mayor. In 2024, Atlanta became the first city over 250,000 to have consecutive Black mayors for at least fifty years.[27]

A century earlier, white nationalists barred Black people from public high schools, municipal employment, neighborhoods, parks, and basic amenities. In the mid-1920s, most police officers of the all-white force were dues-paying members of the KKK. But between 1990 and 2022, only one police chief, Erika Shields (2016–20), was not Black, and the city had a mostly Black police force. The city was so successful in the degree to which the police force demographically represented the city that consulting professionals for government agencies used Atlanta as a case study.[28] In many respects, the transformation of the former capital of the KKK has been nothing short of extraordinary. In some ways, this transformation appears to be a consequence of the reverse migration that *New York Times* journalist Charles Blow advocates in his 2021 book, *The Devil You Know: A Black Manifesto*. Blow argues that, by relocating to southern states with high Black populations, African Americans can forge political majorities and, therefore, political power to enact policies that are beneficial to a racially just society. In 2020, Blow left New York City for Atlanta, where he lives amid shining towers; large, comfortable homes; universities; and businesses that were built by or mostly inhabited by Black people in a way that no other city could boast.[29]

Beyond politics, Atlanta expanded its position as a center of Black education —even beyond the Atlanta University Center. Among the thirty-six largest metropolitan areas, only Washington, DC, has a higher percentage of African Americans with college degrees (32 percent compared with Atlanta's 28 percent).[30] In addition to the storied histories of the highly rated and renowned historically Black colleges and universities in Atlanta, there are over a dozen other schools in the Atlanta metro area. Georgia State University, once a segregated whites-only school for commuter students, enrolls and graduates more Black students than any brick-and-mortar university in the country, including, of course, any HBCU. Although not an HBCU, its student government, social programs, and general student culture is unlike most traditionally white schools. Student government and homecoming courts are very diverse but also disproportionately Black. Brian Blake became its first Black president in 2021, overseeing a vast educational enterprise, at over 54,000 students, scores of degree programs, and ten schools and colleges, including law, business, arts, and sciences. Its Andrew Young School of Policy Studies is named after Atlanta's second Black mayor. Georgia State University, with several high-ranking Black administrators, by 2021, was the largest school in the state and in the top ten largest universities in the country. It is also the fifth-highest Black doctorate–granting institution in the country.[31]

Of course, the HBCUs have expanded and matured in remarkable ways since the election of one of their own alumni as the city's first Black mayor. In addition to expanded academic programs within these schools, the Morehouse School of Medicine (a fully independent institution from Morehouse College) was established in 1981, becoming one of four majority-Black medical schools in the country. Spelman College has emerged as the wealthiest wholly private HBCU in the country, drawing some of the most competitive applicants.[32] It simultaneously has the highest percentage of Black students of any college or university (around 99 percent Black) and the highest graduation rate of any HBCU, exceeding the white national average graduation rate by nearly 20 points. It has a per capita student endowment higher than nearly 90 percent of all colleges and universities, even higher than Georgetown, Tulane, and the University of Southern California.[33] Morehouse College is the fourth richest HBCU and produces more Black male graduates who eventually earn PhDs in STEM, humanities, and social sci-

The Atlanta area has drawn more African Americans than any other metropolitan area in the United States since the end of the Great Migration. Only the New York City metropolitan area has a higher number of Black people. (Photo courtesy Wikimedia Foundation)

ences than any school in the country. Both produce a higher rate of students who eventually earn MDs, JDs, MBAs, or PhDs than most white or Black schools. Notably, Spelman outperforms five of the eight Ivy League universities in the rate of Black graduates who earn doctorates in STEM.[34] Clark Atlanta University (formed from a merger of Clark College and Atlanta University in 1988) is the largest among AUC schools and attracts talented students from throughout the country in an array of programs, including its celebrated communications major and business school. Collectively, the nine accredited HBCUs in Georgia generate a total impact of $1.3 billion into the economy.[35]

Despite the successes of other schools in the AUC, Morris Brown College lost its accreditation in 2002. It was burdened by mismanagement, scandal, and a paltry endowment before reducing its operations sharply as it reorganized. When it lost its accreditation, it was removed from the Atlanta University Center Consortium, which, among other things, granted it shared resources with the member schools, including the AUC library. For years, fewer than fifty students were enrolled. The city, as well as Invest Atlanta, the city's economic development agency, provided critical financial assistance in the years following the school's precipitous decline. After twenty years, Morris Brown successfully regained its accreditation in 2022 and began a robust rebuilding campaign to draw students, faculty, and donors.

In some respects, the story of the AUC represents a microcosm of the Black Mecca. When people think of the extraordinary achievements of Black people in the city, the successes are celebrated and become the rule at the expense of the examples that belie the grand narratives of success. The growth, opportunities, and impressive feats of (primarily) Black women who lead Spelman College are deservedly praised. The extraordinary troubles of Morris Brown's mismanagement, fiscal precarity, and even criminal negligence do not neatly fit with the praises heaped upon the city's Black colleges. Yet, despite challenges with wealth disparities, social mobility, and more, the city continues to draw transplants while capturing center stage in Black popular culture.

By the 1990s, Atlanta was firmly ensconced in the popular Black imagination as the nation's veritable Black capital and, importantly, a site of Black leisure. An intersection of its concentration of Black college students and general appeal as a tourist destination for Black people produced the largest Black college-age gatherings anywhere: Freaknic. What started as a spring break picnic for Atlanta University Center students in 1982 grew in popularity within several years. By the late 1980s, AUC students hosted hundreds of friends from other colleges and universities who traveled to the renowned picnic organized by the DC Metro Club with a live go-go band in a local park. Before and after the Saturday picnic, parties sponsored by various student organizations punctuated the city's nightclubs and hotels. Typically, most Atlantans were unaware that the Freaknic weekend had actually happened, unless one lived near the host park.

By the mid-1990s, the gathering had grown considerably and was trademarked "Freaknik" (with a *k*), reaching beyond the college community with commercial promotions. Overlapping social spaces of college students, local and out-of-town youths and adults, and even dancers from local strip clubs created a curiously diverse cross-section of people. Corporate sponsors and radio promotion swelled the event to 250,000 visitors (or over half of the city's total population), who congested the highways and city streets. Reports of sexual assaults spread, and other violence increased. Some college students went as far as to provide unsanctioned (armed) security to protect attendees. The occasion was no longer the DC Metro Club's signature event. Despite the trademark, it had evolved into a leviathan, untethered to any single organization, even if some tried to claim it. Ultimately, the city, under Mayor Bill Campbell, attempted to curtail the activities with closure of highway exits, increased police presence, nuisance tickets for jaywalking, and public drunkenness. Efforts at rebranding the weekend as "Black College Spring Break" proved futile to curb the unruly, bacchanalian gathering that frustrated many Black and white Atlantans with nightmarish traffic jams and rowdy crowds. In 1998, the Atlanta Committee for Black College Spring Break reported, "We cannot support events that bring lewd activities, sexual assaults, violence against women and public safety concerns—firetrucks not being able to reach victims, and ambulances not being able to reach hospitals in a timely manner."[36] The largest annual gathering of African American young people had come to an inglorious end, yet its legend had reified the status of Atlanta as a special site of Black cultural appeal and prominence.[37] As if a foil to the rise of

Freaknik, a local music festival formed in 1994, FunkJazz Kafé, which offered a rich mélange of cultural work in an entirely novel way.

Attracting rap artists and pioneers of a new genre known as neo-soul, FunkJazz Kafé was founded by an alumnus of Clark Atlanta University, Jason Orr. Artists such as Erykah Badu, Jamie Foxx, Common, Janelle Monáe, Jill Scott, India.Arie, OutKast, and Goodie Mob performed to packed audiences, often overflowing onto outside sidewalks. While it was broader than music alone, as singer Van Hunt notes, it was the first and "only environment that welcomed and embraced" the new generation of Black artists who spearheaded neo-soul in the early and mid-1990s. Called a "legendary carnival of art and music" by *Vibe* it often assembled in a massive former warehouse and offered various rooms, each focused on a different aesthetic space: voguing models, spoken word, graffiti, MCs and the main stage with performing musicians. A marketplace had oils, incense, T-shirts, and books. In many ways, it was starkly counter to the worst of the allegations and seedy stories emanating from Freaknik, yet Ray Murray, music producer for Atlanta-based Organized Noise, called FunkJazz Kafé an authentic expression of "the Atlanta vibe." People eagerly visited from around the world to experience this avant-garde Blackness, widely considered subaltern and free from distilled corporate interests.[38]

Conspicuously grounded in Black aesthetics, FunkJazz Kafé, while running parallel with Freaknik in Atlanta for several years, exemplified the broad diversity of the cultural and political worlds of young Black people: their leisure, pleasure, joy, and music. As Nathalie Fox explains, "Orr's vision allowed him to create a festival where black musicians, sculptors, painters, poets, clothing designers, alternative medicine practitioners, and chefs could display their talent as well as educate others without the constraints they faced in Eurocentric settings."[39] Additionally, in spaces that often celebrated Atlanta for its strides in politics and business, these events highlighted the Gate City as a critical site for the production and showcasing of Black art and leisure. The city was more than Black business success; it became a veritable cultural capital.

With a robust social, political, cultural, and economic landscape open to Black people, the city itself—not any one segment of the city—has become widely perceived as Black. Unlike New York, Chicago, or Los Angeles, there were not sections (Harlem, the South Side, or South Central) relegated to the Black experience. There were no provincial signifiers of Black space for non-Atlantans. Simply "Atlanta" serves as the signifier of Black space. Even a hit rap song from the early 1990s, "Guerillas in tha Mist," which celebrated its Black nationalist bona fides, did not use the group's hometown, South Central Los Angeles, or even the nearby Compton. "J. D. is blacker than a city called Atlanta," the line proclaimed. Years later, Bay Area MC Blackalicious similarly rhymed that he was "Blacker than a panther / Blacker than Atlanta."[40] In 2015, the comedic duo of the Comedy Central TV show *Key & Peele* offered a series finale of rich social commentary (as usual). A sublime musical skit depicted a Black man being magically transported to an Edenic all-Black city. His tour guide cheerfully sings that he is in a place "where there ain't no pain and no sorrow. It's the place to be if your skin is brown ... I'm talking 'bout Negrotown." Confused about his whereabouts, the man asks his guide, "Negrotown? What, like Atlanta?" The guide smiles, "Almost." Ultimately, the city is a fiction of his imagination—prompted after a racist cop rendered him unconscious with a head injury.[41] Although multiple municipalities (Memphis, Baton Rouge, New Orleans, Baltimore, and so on) have higher percentages or higher raw numbers of Black people, saying, "Blacker than Cleveland" does not evoke the same meaning in popular culture.

Running counter to the legacies of Confederates of the Civil War, the Redeemer New South industrialists, and the Klansmen who heralded Atlanta as their Imperial City, Atlanta's most recent leadership has remade the city in astounding ways. Charles Blow, in his prescription to build Black political power, notes that the people should not expect a "Wakanda" or utopia. Humans are not perfect, and their institutions will invariably reflect their messiness, conflict, and struggle. Though not Wakanda (or "Negrotown," for that matter), Atlanta does more than any other city in the country to systematically and successfully provide space for Black advancement, opportunity, and more. The fact that the city is the capital of one of the most anti-Black states in the history of the country makes its ascendance as a veritable Black Mecca particularly striking.[42] After millions of African Americans fled the insalubrious conditions of the Deep South—including cities and towns across Georgia—in search of opportunities, the former "citadel" of the Klan became the most attractive destination to Black movement. More than anything, these strides and achievements demonstrate the degree to which drive, determination, and, importantly, bold imagination continue to inspire Black movement and, consequently, affect America in remarkable fashion.

Notes

1. The song "Not Like Us" was one of several exchanges in a lyrical battle between Kendrick Lamar and Drake. The wide consensus is that Lamar won this historic battle among titans. See Joe Coscarelli, "Kendrick Lamar vs. Drake Beef Goes Nuclear: What to Know," *New York Times*, May 6, 2024; "15 Signs Drake Lost Kendrick Lamar Beef," Complex, May 7, 2024, www.complex.com/music/a/tracewilliamcowen/drake-lost-kendrick-lamar-beef-signs.

2. "Atlanta Remains Nation's Hub for Black-Owned Businesses," LendingTree, February 5, 2024, www.lendingtree.com/business/small/black-owned-businesses-study/?fbclid=IwZXhobgNhZW0CMTAAARolzVO9NCjYxgyicHD44GnzNDStiad6nKi6kVDg19nYQTiYQMYTJUmxvGw_aem_3idnCuRCUgidGaRmBr7ewQ; "The Cities Where African-Americans Are Doing The Best Economically 2018," *Forbes*, January 15, 2018, www.forbes.com/sites/joelkotkin/2018/01/15/the-cities-where-african-americans-are-doing-the-best-economically-2018/.
3. "The NBA's Atlanta Hawks Problem," SBNation, September 11, 2014, www.netsdaily.com/2014/9/11/6126959/the-nbas-atlanta-hawks-problem; "The Atlanta Hawks' Audience Problem Is That It Isn't Black Enough," BuzzFeed, September 8, 2014, www.buzzfeed.com/errinwhack/atlanta-hawks-audience-problem.
4. "Republican Mayor Wins Convincingly in NYC, but Democrats Perform Well in Other US Cities," City Mayors, June 23, 2005, www.citymayors.com/politics/usa_elections05.html.
5. "Atlanta Homicides Second Lowest in 50 Years," *Atlanta Journal-Constitution*, January 10, 2013, www.ajc.com/news/crime-law/atlanta-homicides-2nd-lowest-years/5KZDukpRGDMGUwXb5maL4K/; "Murders in Atlanta," *Atlanta Journal-Constitution*, January 31, 2017, www.ajc.com/news/crime-law/murders-atlanta-are-way-but-overall-crime-way-down/dBSfTIdF7afBJ38yGmqVrM/.
6. Steve Visser, "Police Red Dog Unit Disbanded in Atlanta," *Atlanta Journal-Constitution*, February 9, 2011; "Atlanta Police Chief Disbands Red Dog Unit," WSBTV, February 8, 2011, www.wsbtv.com/news/atlanta-police-chief-disbands-red-dog-unit_nd9w2/241792890.
7. Maurice J. Hobson, *The Legend of the Black Mecca: Politics and Class in the Making of Modern Atlanta* (Chapel Hill: University of North Carolina Press, 2017), 205.
8. "How Atlanta Became the New Cultural Capital of America," Daily Beast, April 11, 2017, www.thedailybeast.com/how-atlanta-became-the-new-cultural-capital-of-america; Michael Harriot, "Atlanta Is the Real Wakanda," *The Root*, February 19, 2019; "From Atlanta to NYC: 11 Best Hip Hop Cities that Redefined the Genre," Revolt, March 10, 2024, www.revolt.tv/article/11-best-hip-hop-cities-that-redefined-the-genre; "Why Atlanta Is the Hip-Hop Capital of the USA," Visit the USA, accessed September 15, 2024, www.visittheusa.com/experience/why-atlanta-hip-hop-capital-usa.
9. Michael Harriot, "Atlanta Is the Real Wakanda," *The Root*, February 19, 2019.
10. Wakanda is the name of the fictional country from the Marvel Comics character Black Panther. Wakanda is an African country that had never been colonized by the West and, by the modern era, is the most technologically sophisticated country on Earth. The 2018 movie *Black Panther* was mostly filmed in Atlanta with a Black director and majority-Black cast. It became the highest grossing Black film (cast and director) in history and the third-highest grossing film in the United States and Canada. The term "Wakanda" has come to signify an unrivaled space of Black excellence, freedom, and self-determination.
11. Office of Film and Entertainment, City of Atlanta, GA website, accessed July 23, 2022, www.atlantaga.gov/government/mayor-s-office/executive-offices/office-of-film-entertainment.
12. Rodney Strong, former compliance officer for the City of Atlanta, interview with

author, May 31, 2022; "Goodbye, Silicon Valley, Hello Atlanta: Black Entrepreneurs Part of New Migration to South," *USA Today*, March 10, 2019.
13. "Atlanta," Black Demographics, accessed June 19, 2022, https://blackdemographics.com/cities-2/atlanta/.
14. Charles Jaret, "Black Migration and Socioeconomic Inequality in Atlanta and the Urban South," *Humboldt Journal of Social Relations* 14, no. 1/2 (1987): 62–105; "Economic Disparities in the Black Mecca," *Atlanta Business Chronicle*, June 26, 2020; David Sjoquist, "Racial Differences in Atlanta's Median Household Income Widespread, Deeply Rooted," SaportaReport, July 19, 2020, https://saportareport.com/?s=+Racial+Differences+in+Atlanta%E2%80%99s+Median+Household+Income+Widespread. See also "Racial Wealth Gap," Atlanta Wealth Building Initiative, accessed July 22, 2024, www.atlantawealthbuilding.org/racial-wealth-gap; and Sarah Foster and Wei Lu, "Atlanta Ranks Worst in Income Inequality in the U.S.," Bloomberg, October 10, 2018, https://atlanta.curbed.com/2013/7/23/10217118/study-atlanta-ranks-dead-last-in-upward-mobility.
15. Robbie Brown, "Atlanta Is Making Way for New Public Housing," *New York Times*, June 20, 2009.
16. Moshe Haspel, "Changing Demographics: Race and Ethnicity, 1990 to 2020," 33.7°N: Finding Meaning at 33.7°N, November 15, 2021, https://33n.atlantaregional.com/monday-mapday/changing-demographics-race-and-ethnicity-1990-to-2020; "Doubling of Nonwhite Population Leads Demographic Changes over Past 45 Years in Atlanta Region," *Georgia State News Hub*, April 24, 2017, https://news.gsu.edu/2017/04/24/nonwhite-population-demographic-changes/; "Atlanta's Nonwhite Population Doubles since 1970," *Atlanta Agent Magazine*, April 24, 2017, https://atlantaagentmagazine.com/2017/04/24/atlantas-nonwhite-population-doubles-since-1970/.
17. *Atlanta in Focus: A Profile from Census 2000*, Brookings Institution Center on Urban and Metropolitan Policy, accessed January 9, 2019, https://web.archive.org/web/20111221063813/http://www.brookings.edu/~/media/Files/rc/reports/2003/11_livingcities_Atlanta/atlanta.pdf, archived from the original on December 21, 2011; City of Atlanta QuickFacts, US Census Bureau, accessed July 6, 2022. https://web.archive.org/web/20120802165747/http://quickfacts.census.gov/qfd/states/13/1304000.html; "Profile of General Population and Housing Characteristics: 2010," Decaturish, accessed September 15, 2024, https://decaturish.com/wp-content/uploads/2014/11/Atlatna-Facts.pdf.
18. "Quick Facts," U.S. Census Bureau, accessed July 10, 2023, www.census.gov/quickfacts/fact/table/atlantacitygeorgia#; "88% of Blacks Have a High School Diploma, 26% a Bachelor's Degree," U.S. Census, accessed July 19, 2023, www.census.gov/library/stories/2020/06/black-high-school-attainment-nearly-on-par-with-national-average.html; www.cityofsouthfultonga.gov/3009/About-Us; "City of South Fulton Council Districts," FultonCounty.Gov, accessed July 8, 2023, http://share.myfultoncountyga.us/datashare/fultoncounty/maps/CityofSouthFulton_ProposedCouncilDistricts_el_v2.pdf.
19. Deirdre Oakley, professor of sociology, Georgia State University, quoted in Paul Kersey, *Black Mecca Down: Collapse of the City Too Busy to Hate* (Scotts Valley, CA: Create Space 2012), 76.

20. "Atlanta GA Crime Rate 1999–2018," Macrotrends, accessed July 19, 2023, www.macrotrends.net/cities/us/ga/atlanta/crime-rate-statistics.
21. "The Black Homeownership Gap in Atlanta," Stacker, March 22, 2022, https://stacker.com/georgia/atlanta/black-homeownership-gap-atlanta; "Black Homeownership: A Look at the 11-County Area, 1980–2019," 33°N: Finding Meaning at 33.7°N, February 18, 2022, https://33n.atlantaregional.com/friday-factday/black-home ownership-a-look-at-the-11-county-area-1980-2019.
22. "Cracking the Zip Code of Atlanta Cool," *Atlanta Journal-Constitution*, April 25, 2008; John Yellig, "Atlanta Leads U.S. in Intown Apartment Development," *Atlanta Agent Magazine*, September 14, 2022, https://atlantaagentmagazine.com/2022/09/14/atlanta-leads-u-s-in-intown-apartment-development/; "Atlantic Station Shopping a Retail Rush for City," *Atlanta Business Chronicle*, March 3, 2006.
23. Nate Silver, "The Most Diverse Cities Are Often the Most Segregated," FiveThirty Eight, May 1, 2015, https://fivethirtyeight.com/features/the-most-diverse-cities-are-often-the-most-segregated/.
24. Jim Skinner, "A Decade of Change: Population and Demographics in Metro Atlanta," 33°N: Finding Meaning at 33.7°N, August 13, 2021, https://33n.atlantaregional.com/friday-factday/a-decade-of-change-population-and-demographics-in-metro-atlanta; "Doubling of Nonwhite Population Leads Demographic Changes over Past 45 Years in Atlanta Region," Georgia State News Hub, April 24, 2017, https://news.gsu.edu/2017/04/24/nonwhite-population-demographic-changes/; "Atlanta's Nonwhite Population Doubles since 1970," *Atlanta Agent Magazine*, April 24, 2017, https://atlanta agentmagazine.com/2017/04/24/atlantas-nonwhite-population-doubles-since-1970/; Jarrod Apperson, "An Afterward to White Flight: Atlanta's Return to Community and Long Road toward Integration," The Patch, January 28, 2013, https://patch.com/georgia/eastatlanta/bp--an-afterward-to-white-flight-atlantas-return-to-cd126722ab4.
25. "Black Homeowners Start to Close Gap in Property Values," Stateline, May 1, 2024, https://stateline.org/2024/05/01/black-homeowners-start-to-close-gap-in-property-values/.
26. "Atlanta's Black Communities Lost $681 Million in Home Equity after Corporate Investors Seize on Real Estate Market," *Atlanta Daily World*, May 8, 2024, https://atlantadailyworld.com/2024/05/08/atlantas-black-communities-lost-681-million-in-home-equity-after-corporate-investors-seize-on-real-estate-market/.
27. In 1970, Newark became the first major city to elect a Black mayor in the Northeast. Luis A. Quintana, who is Puerto Rican, served as acting mayor in Newark, New Jersey, from 2013 to 2014, when Mayor Corey Booker resigned after his election to the US Senate. Quintana was succeeded by Ras Baraka. In terms of *elected* mayors, Newark would, therefore, share the distinction with Atlanta for having only Black mayors for half a century.
28. "Promising Practices for Increasing Diversity among First Responders," Department of Labor, accessed December 21, 2022, www.dol.gov/sites/dolgov/files/OASP/legacy/files/FirstResponders_APDCase_Study.pdf.
29. Charles Blow, *The Devil You Know: A Black Power Manifesto* (New York: Harper, 2021).

30. "Best and Worst Cities for Educating Blacks," *The Atlantic*, June 2015, www.theatlantic.com/politics/archive/2015/06/best-and-worst-cities-for-educating-blacks/432099/.
31. "Survey of Earned Doctorates," National Center for Science and Engineering Statistics, Directorate for Social, Behavioral and Economic Sciences, National Science Foundation, December 2020, https://ncses.nsf.gov/pubs/nsf21308/data-tables#group1; "Georgia State University Fact Book, 2020-2021," accessed October 4, 2024, https://oie.gsu.edu/document/2020-fact-book/?wpdmdl=4226.
32. Howard University, more than five times the size of Spelman College, has a larger endowment but is a semipublic school, receiving over $200 million in annual special appropriations from the federal government. If, however, one were to compare Spelman against Howard's endowment on a per capita basis, the former's endowment is over 80 percent larger than Howard's. "Howard University Fiscal Year 2021 Budget Request," Department of Education, accessed May 16, 2022, www2.ed.gov/about/overview/budget/budget21/justifications/t-howard.pdf.
33. "Spelman College," College Raptor, accessed July 24, 2022, www.collegeraptor.com/colleges/rankings/Spelman-College-GA--141060.
34. "Baccalaureate Origins of Underrepresented Minority Research Doctorate Recipients," National Science Foundation, NSF 22–335, August 9, 2022, https://ncses.nsf.gov/pubs/nsf22335.
35. "HBCUs Make America Strong," UNCF, 2018, https://cdn.uncf.org/wp-content/uploads/PDFs/fy_2018_budget_fact_sheets/HBCU_FactSht_Georgia_5-17D.pdf?_ga=2.163650175.1357827528.1658710657-499068884.1658710657.
36. "Freaknik Documentary 'The Wildest Party Never Told' in Development at Hulu," movie trailer, Complex, April 7, 2023, www.complex.com/music/a/brad-callas/hulu-freaknik-documentary-the-wildest-party-never-told.
37. In addition to an episode of NBC's *A Different World*, various hip-hop songs, and a 2010 musical, Freaknik was the subject of the documentary *Freaknik: The Wildest Party Never Told*.
38. Nathalie D. Fox, "FunkJazz *Kafé*: The Music, Marketing, and Movement" (master's thesis, Georgia State University, 2020), doi: https://doi.org/10.57709/19396471. See also *FunkJazz Kafé: A Diary of a Decade*, dir. Jason Orr (2012), extended movie trailer on YouTube, www.youtube.com/watch?v=9u_QKXAn-gE.
39. Fox, "FunkJazz *Kafé*," 1.
40. Da Lench Mob, "Guerillas in Tha Mist," *Guerillas in Tha Mist*, Street Knowledge Records, 1992; Blackalicious, "Blacka," *Imani Vol. 1*, Black Mines, 2015.
41. See Joanna Robinson, "How the Key & Peele Series Finale Paid Off: 4 Seasons of Cutting Social Commentary," *Vanity Fair*, September 10, 2015, www.vanityfair.com/hollywood/2015/09/key-and-peel-finale-2015-negrotown.
42. In Georgia in 1860, 99.7 percent of Black people were enslaved; following the nineteenth-century closure of a short-lived Black public high school in Augusta, no public high school was available to Black students until 1924. Black people, in addition to being barred from voting, hospitals, public parks, and so on, were lynched at one of the highest rates in the country in the late nineteenth century through the early twentieth century.

ACKNOWLEDGMENTS

Each scholarly project is a result of a wide community of supporters, friends, and colleagues who are often unaware of their important part in pushing it along. This project owes its existence to the patience, friendship, and intellectual space that many people provided. I thank the friends of my Ogbar Fire Pit Crew, Hartford's own Tobacco Shop, the Samson Crew, the "Good Rev. Dr." Kevin Brown, Alex Torres for the many long sessions of catching up during commuting, Adisa Iwa, Kirk Bradley, and Damon Scott. Thanks go to Andrew Woods and his leadership with Hartford Communities That Care. I've been honored to serve that organization and mission for over a decade.

Appreciation goes to the Atlanta History Center, the Library of Congress, the Robert W. Woodruff Library in the Atlanta University Center, and the University of Connecticut's Humanities Institute. I thank the many contributors who persevered through drafts, a pandemic, closed libraries, and archives and still made it happen. This work has been inspired by the remarkable scholars of Black urban space, from W. E. B. Du Bois through today's generation of scholars. The editorial vision and interest of the University of North Carolina Press is deeply appreciated.

Thanks go to my mom, dad, uncles, aunts, and cousins for the stories of growing up in Chicago. They continue to shape how I approach scholarship on and my understanding of the city. Shout outs go to Reginald Roberts, Mark Pope, Eric Anderson, Chris Wiley, Oscar Mendoza, Rosia Davis, Letitia Thompson Fox, Richard Walker, and Lorie Regalado for animating my upbringing in Los Angeles. Growing up in the big city was richer for my friendships.

More than anything, I thank my family for their patience, time, and support: Jeanna, Jeffrey Asa, and HazelAnn.

CONTRIBUTORS

Stefan M. Bradley is Charles Hamilton Houston '15 Professor of Black Studies and History at Amherst College.

Scot Brown is associate professor of history at Howard University.

Tatiana M. F. Cruz is assistant professor and interdisciplinary program director of Africana studies at Simmons University.

Tom Adam Davies is senior lecturer in American history at the University of Sussex.

LaShawn Harris is associate professor of history at Michigan State University.

Maurice J. Hobson is associate professor of Africana studies at Georgia State University.

Shannon King is associate professor of history at Fairfield University.

Melanie D. Newport is associate professor of history at the University of Connecticut.

Jeffrey O. G. Ogbar is professor of history and director of the Center for the Study of Popular Music at the University of Connecticut.

Brian Purnell is associate professor of Africana studies and history and chair of the Department of Africana Studies at Bowdoin College.

J. T. Roane is assistant professor of African studies and geography at Rutgers University.

Chanelle Rose is associate professor of history at Rowan University.

Benjamin H. Saracco is associate professor at and chair of Rowan University Libraries and instructor of biomedical sciences at Cooper Medical School of Rowan University.

Fiona Vernal is associate professor of history and Africana studies at the University of Connecticut.

INDEX

Page numbers in italics refer to illustrations and page numbers in bold refer to tables.

Aaron, Hank, 68
Abernathy, Ralph D., Jr., 64
Abrams, Stacey, 322
Abyssinia Church, Harlem, 201
Ackeridge, Derek, 206
"Action for Survival" (Chicago Urban League), 244
Adarand Constructors v. Peña, 45
Adelona, Ebun, 234–35
Adelona v. Webster, 235
Aetna (insurance company), 272–73
"affective mobilities," 186, 190
affirmative action: and Affirmative Action Review Council, Camden, 306; expansion of (1965–95), 33–41; foundations of, 30–33; in Los Angeles, 290–91
Africa, Birdie, 259
Africa, Ramona, 259–60
African American populations. *See* Black populations; Great Migration
African Hebrew Israelites, 86
Afro-American Patrolmen's League (Chicago), 244–45
Afro-American Police Association, 206
Afro-Caribbean populations, 140
Afro-self-determinism, 57, 67, 68, 326
agriculture: and guest workers, 181; impact on migration, 184–85; and migrant farmwork and camps, 182, 188; and tobacco industry, 177, 181, 182, 185
AIDS crisis, 92; in Los Angeles, 291–92
Alabama, 40
Albany Avenue, Hartford, CT, 180, 182, 188
Al B. Sure, 111
Alexander, Michelle, 140, 287

Allen, Bobby, 107
Allen, Henry, 97–98
Allen, James, 210
Allman, Arthur, 102
Allman, Derrick, 103
Allman, Georgia, 102–3
Allman, Gwen, 102
Allman Sisters, 103
Als, Hilton, 137, 166–67
Altenkirch, Robert A., 266
American Economic Association, 32
American imperialism, 64, 178, 190
An Analysis of Blacks and Hispanics in Camden County Government, 312
André 3000, 6, 89, 90–91, 93
Angelou, Maya, 325
Ansaru Allah community. *See* United Nuwaubian Nation of Moors (Georgia)
anti-Blackness, 263, 266. *See also* racial issues
anti-crime activism, 199, 200, 226. *See also* War on Drugs
Anti-Drug Abuse Act (1986), 288
antipoverty programs, 120, 125–26. *See also* poverty; welfare programs
the Apollos (band), 104
Aquí Me Quedo (Glasser), 185
Archer, Dennis, 34
archival materials, 167, 179, 189, 190
Armstead, Edward, 212–13
Arrington, Richard, 40
Arroyo, Felix, 128, 131
arson, 269–75. *See also* fire
Asian Americans, 46, 133, 329, 331
Association of Black Women Historians (ABWH), 221

Association Promoting Constitutional Rights of the Spanish-Speaking (APCROSS), 125
Atlanta (television series), 5
Atlanta, GA, 5; and Andrew Young and economic development, 40–41, 65–66; arts and culture in, 325; Black Arts movement in, 85–86; Black education in, 332; as "Black Mecca," 56–57, 70, 71–72, 83, 321–36; and Black migration, 327–29; Black-owned businesses in, 71–72; Black reality shows in, 325–26; Bureau of Cultural Affairs in, 79, 85–86, 324; child murders in, 91; as "City Too Busy to Hate," 56, 57, 58; crime rates in, 323–24; and Democratic National Convention (1988), 85; film production in, 326–27; Freaknic/Freaknik in, 334–35; gentrification in, 68–69, 330; and Hartsfield airport project, 36–37, 39, 43, 70–71; and HBCUs, 332–34; history and background of, 55–59; homeownership and property values in, 330–31; Maynard Jackson and minority business development in, 35–39; media coverage of, 66–67; migration to and economic opportunity in, 14–15; as music capital, 79, 325; and Neighborhood Planning Unit, 84; Olympic games in (1996), 67, 79, 92; and "Olympification," 80, 82–83, 91, 93, 94n3, 328; poverty rates in, 69, 91–92, 330–31; public schools in, 59–60; radical vs. reformist politics in, 64–65; rebranding of (1980s), 85; and Shirley Franklin's mayorship, 322–23; skyline and construction projects in, 67; structural racism in, 55–56; tech industry in, 327; tourism in, 326–27; and urban unrest, 61–63. *See also* Stone Mountain, GA
Atlanta Action Forum, 59, 60–61, 63
Atlanta Board of Education, 60
Atlanta Citizen Review Board, 323
Atlanta Plan, 5, 32, 36, 39, 57, 58–59, 66
Atlanta Police Department, 323–24
Atlanta Project (SNCC), 64

Atlanta Public School Board, 58
Atlanta University Center (AUC) Consortium, 57, 79, 329–30, 332, 333
The Atlantic (periodical), 287
Atlantic Records, 98
Atlantic Starr (band), 111
ATLiens (OutKast), 83, 90–91
Aurra (band), 111
Aytch, Bertha, 299–300

the Bad Bunch, 104
Badu, Erykah, 335
Bailey, Harold, 249
Bailey, Julius H., 88–89
Baillou, Charles, 224
bail reform, 246–47. *See also* incarceration
Bail Reform Act (1984), 246
Bailey, Jay, 70
Baird, Robert W., 209
Baker, Ella, 223
Baker, Vincent, 209–11
Baldwin Hills, CA, *17*, 68, 292
Ball, Tray, 285
Banditos (gang), 282
Baranco, Greg, 68
barbershops, 110, 180, 183, 189
Barfield, Kevin, 314, 320n68
the Bar-Kays, 97, 111
Barnett, Sydney, 179–83, 186–87, 191
Barnett's Clothing Store (Hartford, CT), 182
Barry, Marion, 35, 40, 43
Barthelemy, Sidney, 40
Baskins, Milton, 106
Baskins, Tony, 106
Bass, Karen, 291
The Battle with the Slums (Riis), 1
BE 100 (*Black Enterprise* magazine), 43–44
Beam, Joseph, 261, 262
Beamud, Cristina, 323
Bell, Virginia, 203
Benjamin, André. *See* André 3000
Bennett, Kenneth, Sr., 187
Benson, Keith, 314
Benson, Marquika, 265
Benson, Monica, 265

Benson, Monique, 265
Benson, Paula, 265
Benson, Samuel, 308
Berlin, Germany, 6
Bethel, Denise, 212
Beyoncé, 81
Big Jay Bush and the House Rockers, 102, 103, 104
Bilderbergers, 86, 95n25
Billings, David J., III, 207
Birmingham, AL, 40
Birmingham Plan, 40
Black Arts movement, 79, 325
Black barbershops, 110, 180, 183, 189
Black Believers of Knowledge, 302
"Black Beverly Hills," 292
"Black Boomerang," 122, 126, 135n11
Blackburne, Laura, 228
Black Enterprise (magazine), 29, 40, 42–44, 49
Black flight, 6, 7–8, 16
Black Hebrews, 80
Black-Latino alliances, 130, 158, 178, 301, 311–12. *See also* multiracial/multiethnic coalitions; Rainbow Coalition; solidarity
Black Liberation Army, 234
Black liberation theology, 80, 83, 93, 274
Black Lives Matter movement, 252
"Black Mecca" (Atlanta), 56–57, 70, 71–72
Black Metropolis (Drake and Cayton), 2
Black New South, 83–86, 94n14
"Black on Black crime," 242–43
Black Panther Party, 3, 62, 64, 205, 286, 290
Black People's Unity Movement (BPUM), 299–300, 302–3, 317n18
Black populations: and Black elites, 43–44, 63–64; and Black middle class, 5; and Black-owned businesses, 8; and Black protest, 199–214; Black silent majority in, 199–200, 214, 288; and communities as safe spaces, 189–90; cultural contributions of, 3, 5–6; diversity within, 11; education levels of, 10, 14–15; in elected positions, 4; national political influence of, 322; in post–Black Power era, 41–48; and radical and militant movements, 63–64; and socioeconomic status (SES) divide, 44, 48–49; in southern US, early twentieth century, 1; and support of drug policies, 200. *See also* Great Migration
Black Power movement, 31, 34, 41–48, 63, 324; and Afro-self-determinism, 57
Black science fiction, 79–83
Black Silent Majority (Fortner), 199
Blackstone Rangers, 244
Black Wealth/White Wealth (Oliver and Shapiro), 46
Blake, Brian, 332
Blige, Mary J., 113
Blomley, Nicholas, 301
Blood gang, 282
Bloomfield, CT, 177
Blow, Charles, 17–18, 331–32, 336
Bond, Julian, 70
Bonner, Fatima, 269
Bonner, Mark, 269
Booker T. Washington High School (Atlanta), 55
Bootsy's Rubber Band, 97, 111
Boston, Amanda T., 139
Boston, MA: and "Black Boomerang," 122, 126, 135n11; and Boston School Committee, 128; busing crisis in, 12; Charlestown neighborhood in, 11, 12, 129; Dorchester neighborhood in, 121, 122; and Freedom House, 123; gentrification in, 11–12; housing crisis in, 126–27; Mel King mayoral campaign in (1983), 127–32; and Model Cities Administration, 124; multiracial/multiethnic coalitions in, 122–27; public schools in, 124–25; racial violence in, 129; and Roxbury Multi-Service Center (RMSC), 123–24; Roxbury neighborhood in, 121, 122; South End neighborhood in, 122–23, 126–27; and Spanish Alliance, 124; and "Stop Day," 123; and Tenants Development Corporation, 126–27; Tent City in, 126, 127, 130;

Boston, MA (*continued*)
  urban crisis and Rainbow Coalition in, 121–22; and Villa Victoria, 127, 130. *See also* Rainbow Coalition
Boston, Thomas, 36, 38, 42, 45
Boswell, Christine, 308
Bottoms, Keisha Lance, 71, 322, 331
Boyz II Men, 111
Braconi, Frank, 10
Bradley, Regina, 90
Bradley, Tom, 33, 35, 48, 65, 288, 290
Branch Davidians, 88
Brathwaite, Kwame, 235
Brawley, Tawana, 219–20, *220*
Braxton, Toni, 325
Brick (band), 97
Bridgeport, CT, 165
Brimmer, Andrew, 31–32
Brimmer-Marshall Disparity Study, 32, 45
"broken-windows" theory, 287
Bronze Shields (Newark, NJ), 206
Brothers Johnson, 97
Brown, Elaine, 290
Brown, James, 110
Brown, Michael, 272
Brown, Warena, 231–32
Brown, William H., III, 31
Bruce, Charles, 295
Bruce, Willa, 295
B. T. Express, 111
Bumpurs, Eleanor, 220, 230, 233
Bunte, Doris, 128
Burge, Jon, 245
Burris, Charles, 72
Burston, David, Jr., 207
Bush, George W., 293
Butler, Jerry, 247–48
Butler, Octavia, 81
Byrd, Byron, 104–5
Byrne, Brendan Thomas, 303, 309
Byrne, Jane, 245

Cabrini-Green Homes (Chicago), 245, 250
Caesar, Shirley, 274
California: Baldwin Hills, *17*, 68, 292; and California Youth Authority, 284; Compton, 15–16, 282, 295; and Division of Juvenile Justice, 284; Inglewood, 25n36, 282, 294–95; Lancaster, 15, 295; Manhattan Beach, 295; Palmdale, 15, 295. *See also* Los Angeles, CA
Camden, NJ, 299–316; and Affirmative Action Review Council, 306; Black experience in, 299–302; "bubble city" phenomenon in, 314; and Camden Citizens Coalition (CCC), 305; elections in, 319n53; and "Father Doyle's Camden" (*60 Minutes*), 306–7; fiscal struggles in, 306–7; and Hispanic Steering Committee, 312–13; as industrial base, 302; library system in, 320n68; Randy Primas as mayor of, 302–11; public schools in, 314–15; urban renewal and displacement in, 317n17; waterfront projects in, 313
Camden Citizens Coalition (CCC), 305
Camden Parents Union, 315
Camden We Choose Coalition, 315
Cameo (band), 97, 111
Campbell, Bill, 34, 334
Campbell, Clive "Kool Herc," 222
Campbell, Doris, 308
Capers, Joy, 209
Capers, William, 208
capitalism: Black, 31–32; and *Black Enterprise*, 43–44; racism linked with, 60–61
carceral regimes. *See* incarceration
Carey, Mariah, 325
Caribbean migration, 160, **162–63**, 181; and circum-Caribbean migration, 181, 184; to Hartford, CT, 177–78; historiography of, 184. *See also* West Indian immigration
Carolyn X, 244
Carter, Jimmy, 36–37, 65
Cayton, Horace R., 2, 242
Central Intelligence Agency (CIA), 203, 291
Chain of Change (Mel King), 128
Chaka, Malika, 303
Chambers, Glenn, 184

Chance, Marshall, 88
Charlestown neighborhood, Boston, 11, 12, 129
Charles Wright and the Watts 103rd Street Rhythm Band, 97
Chicago, IL: Black communities in, early twentieth century, 2; Black flight and suburbanization in, 14; and Chess Records, 98; and Chicago Police Department, 245, 247, 252; and Cook County Department of Corrections, 243, 245–46; and Cook County Jail, 241, 242, 244, 246, 249; day reporting programs in, 249–51; electronic monitoring systems in, 247–49, 252–53; jail construction in, 247; mayoral race in, 1983, 245; and parole violation, policing of, 251; and War on Drugs and carceral state, 241–53; Harold Washington and minority business development in, 39–40
Chicago Freedom Movement, 243
Chicago House of Correction, 243
Chicago Housing Authority, 242
Chicago O'Hare International Airport, 39, 71
Chicago Urban League, 244
Chisholm, Shirley, 222
Ciara (singer), 325
circum-Caribbean migration, 181, 184
the Citations (band), 104
Citizens Mobilization against Crime (New York City), 209
civic engagement, 179, 183, 187, 190, 300
Civil Rights Act (1964), 84, 284; and Title VII, 34
Civil War: aftermath of, 99, 336; and Fort McPherson army base, 326
Clark, Winston, 203
Clark Atlanta University, 73n4, 333
Clark College, 57
Clarke, Leroy, 210
Clay Arsenal neighborhood, Hartford, CT, 188
Clerge, Orly, 139

Cleveland, OH, 29
Clinton, Bill, 45
Close, Stacey, 186
Coalition of Concerned Women in the War on Crime, 244
coalition politics, 63–64, 177, 303, 305–6. *See also* Black-Latino alliances; multiracial/multiethnic coalitions; Rainbow Coalition
Coates, Florence, 226
Cobb, Deborah, 232
cocaine, 286–87; crack cocaine, 92, 221, 288–90. *See also* War on Drugs
Cohen, William, 183
Cold War, 285, 287
Coleman A. Young Foundation, 39
Collins, John, 125–26
Collins, William, 61
Colombian drug cartels, 287
Colonial Migrants at the Heart of Empire (García-Colón), 184
Colón Sánchez, Maria, 179–83, 186, 187–88, 191
Colors (film), 289
Commandment Keepers, 88
Commission on Human Rights, 189
Commission to Investigate Alleged Police Corruption (Knapp Commission), 200, 204, 211–12
Commodores (band), 97, 111
Common (rapper), 335
community archives, 179, 190
Community Assembly for a United South End (CAUSE) (Boston), 126
Community Coalition of South Los Angeles, 291
Community Drug Intervention Units (Illinois), 252
Community Reinvestment Act (1977), 13
Community Resources against Street Hoodlums (CRASH), 289
Compton, CA, 15–16, 282, 295
Concerned Citizens of North Camden (CCNC), 299–300, 307–8, 318n39, 318n44

Con Funk Shun (band), 97, 111
Congressional Black Caucus (CBC), 289, 291
Congress on Racial Equality (CORE), 128
Connolly, Raymond, 234
construction industry: Black companies in Atlanta, 66; hiring discrimination in, 31
Contras (Nicaragua), 287
Conyers, John, 231
Cook County Department of Corrections, 243, 245–46
Cook County Jail, 241, 242, 246, 249; poetry anthology from (1976), 244
Cooke, Marvel, 223
Coolio (rapper), 113
Cooper, Dick, 270–71
Cooper's Ferry Partnership (CFP), 313–14
core-periphery frameworks, 3
Corinealdi, Kaysha, 184
The Cosby Show (television series), 5, 44, 46–47
Costa Rica, 184
Cotillion Records, 98
Cotto Nuñez, Ana, 188
COVID-19 pandemic, 252, 295
crack cocaine, 92, 221, 288–90. *See also* War on Drugs
Crenshaw, Kimberlé, 236
criminalization, 92, 220, 242, 245, 249, 251–52. *See also* incarceration
Crip gang, 282
The Crisis (NAACP journal), 8
Cuomo, Mario, 219

Daley, Richard J., 245
Daley, Richard M., 245
Danbury, CT, 165
Danley, Stephen, 314
Danner, Deborah, 236
Davenport, Ronald, 269
David, Eddie, 213
Davis, Angela, 236, 290
Davis, Beverly, 264
Davis, Edith, 264
Day Reporting Center (DRC) (Chicago), 250–51

day reporting programs, 249–51. *See also* incarceration
Dayton (band), 99, 103, 111
Dayton, OH, 97–113; Black unemployment in, 109–10; community music education in, 101–3; cultural scene in, 99–101; and funk movement, 111–13; industrial collapse in (1970s), 108–9; music performance opportunities in, 103–7; public schools in, 103, 108–9; talent shows in, 104–6
Dayton Sidewinders, 104
Deal, Alphonso, 206
DeBarge (band), 111
declension narratives, 179, 189
deindustrialization, 4, 17, 33, 301; in Atlanta, 57; and blue-collar to white-collar transition, 41–42; in Camden, NJ, 302, 304; in Dayton, OH, 109; in Philadelphia, 260, 261, 265–66, 271, 275
Delgado, Jose, 311
Democratic Party: in Atlanta, 65; in Camden, NJ, 303, 305–6, 311; and National Convention (1988), 85; and white supremacism, 55
Dempsey, Oberia, 199, 201, 202, 207–11, 214
Denton, Nancy A., 3
Denver, CO, 11
desegregation, 11–12. *See also* school desegregation
Detroit, MI: and "Black Bottom," 100; and Great Migration, 14; and Motown Records, 98; real estate values in, 331; "second wave" of Black mayors in, 34, 35, 47, 65; and Sheltered Markets Program, 39
The Devil You Know (Blow), 331–32
diasporas: African, 121; Caribbean, 177, 178; "overlapping" in New York City, 143–45, 151–52, 158–60, 164; "overlapping" in urban contexts, 137–43; among southern whites, 183; "tributary," 177, 185–86
Dickens, Andre, 72, 331
Diggs, Charles, 65

Dillard, Daria, 107–8
Dillinger, Daz, 113
Dinkins, David, 222
Dirty South sound, 79–80, 82
discrimination. *See* employment discrimination; housing discrimination
displacement, 9–10, 22n8. *See also* gentrification
DJ Quik, 113
Dominican Republic, 184
Doyle, Michael, 306–7
Dozier, Tim, 100–101
Drake (Aubrey Drake Graham), 321, 336n1
Drake, St. Clair, 2, 242
"drug capitalism," 244
drug crisis, 201–3, 212, 286, 288; in Atlanta, 323–24; and drug policies, 199–200, 209–11; and police corruption and distrust of police, 205–9; and surveillance, 299–300. *See also* War on Drugs
Du Bois, W. E. B., 1, 183
Duckworth, Kendrick Lamar, 321
Duff, Elizabeth, 270
Dutchess County, NY, 165
Dyson, Eric, 49

Early, Edmond, 107
Earth, Wind & Fire, 97, 111
Ebony (magazine), 58, 66, 242
elected officials, Black, 30, 33; and MBE programs, 39. *See also* mayors, Black
electronic monitoring (shackling), 241, 247–49, 252–53
"Elevators (Me & You)" (OutKast), 83, 90–91
Elks Club (Hartford, CT), 187
Emergency Tenants Council (Boston), 127
Emery, Richard, 233, 235
Emmanuel's Temple of Deliverance (Philadelphia), 274
employment discrimination, 31, 188–89
enterprise zones, 309–11
entrepreneurship, Black, 38, 42
En Vogue (band), 111
EPMD (hip-hop duo), 113
Equal Credit Opportunity Act (1974), 13

Equal Employment Opportunity Act (1972), 34
Equal Employment Opportunity Commission (EEOC), 31, 45
Errichetti, Angelo J., 303, 304, 305–6
Evans, Randolph, 233
Executioners (gang), 282

Fabulous Originals (band), 104, 107
Fair Employment Practices Committee, 189
Fairfield County, CT, 165
Fair Housing Act (1968), 13, 16, 284
Farber, David, 287
Fard Muhammad, 81
Farmer, James, 202
farming. *See* agriculture
Farrakhan, Louis, 206
Fatback Band, 111
Faulkner Act, 315
Fauver, William, 308
Faze-O (band), 99, 103, 105, 111, 113
Federal Bureau of Investigation (FBI), 87, 202, 234; and Abscam investigation, 305
Federation of Negro Civil Service Organizations, 208
Felton, Hezekiah, 213
Field, Kendra, 183
Finch, Robert, 202
fire: and arson, 269–75; effect of gravity and microclimates on, 266; and smoke detectors, 268–69
Fisher, Peter S., 310
Fittimon, Kareem, 269
Fittimon, Ki-ara, 269
Five Percenters, 80, 88
Florio, James, 305
Floyd, Cyndi, 109
Flynn, Raymond, 120, 129, 131, 132
Ford, Gerald, 37
Forman, James, Jr., 200
Forrest, Nathan Bedford, III, 72, 76n31
Fort, Jeff, 244
Fortner, Michael, 199, 288
Foster, Gregory, 208
Foster, Tony, 107

the Four Corners (band), 104, 107
Fox, Nathalie, 335
Foxx, Jamie, 335
Franklin, Shirley, 65, 322–23
Franklin, V. P., 63
Fraser, Gerald, 206
Freaknic/Freaknik (Atlanta), 334–35
Freebandz record label, 325
Freedom House, Boston, 123
Freeman, Lance, 9–10, 138, 139
The Fresh Prince of Bel Air (television series), 44
Frontline (PBS documentary series), 41
Fulani, Lenora, 219
Fullilove v. Klutznick, 38, 45
Fulton County Arts Council (Atlanta), 325
Funkadelic, 97, 111
Funk-Jazz Kafé, 335
funk music, 3, 79–80, 89, 321; and "battle of the bands," 103, 105; and electronic technology, 111–12; links to hip-hop, 112–13; from local experience to commercial music, 111–13; and music education, 101–3; and stage presence, 103–4; and talent shows, 104–6; women's supportive roles in, 107–10
Future (rapper), 325

gangs: celebrity gangsters, 244; in Los Angeles, 282, 283–86, 288–89, 292; and War on Drugs, 246
gangsta rap, 47, 282
the Gap Band, 111
Garcia, Frieda, 123–24, 128
García-Colón, Ismael, 184, 185
Garner, Eric, 160
Garvey, Marcus, 8, 88
Gary, IN, 30, 65
Gaskins, George, 268
Gates, Daryl, 288
Gates, Henry Louis, Jr., 41, 48–49
Gates, James, 102
Gates, Olga, 102–3
gentrification, 6–13; African Americans as drivers of, 6–7, 10; in Atlanta, 330;

definitions of, 138; and "displacement," 9–10; in Harlem, 7–10, *9*; impact of, 145, 159; in New York City, 138–39; patterns of, nationwide, 11; and wealth and racial stratification, 12–13
Georgia, migration to, 295. *See also* Atlanta, GA
Georgia Entertainment Industry Investment Act, 79
Georgia State University, 332
Getting Tough (Kohler-Hausmann), 200
"ghettos": creation of, 122; as interpretive position, 142; policies that shaped, 144–45; and tropes and stereotypes, 157
GI Bill, 21n4
Gibson, Kenneth, 33, 35, 40, 206, 304–5
Gillette, Howard, 309
Gilligan, Thomas, 205
Gilmore, Ruth Wilson, 140, 236
Giovanni, Nikki, 325
Giuliani, Rudolph, 235
Glass, Ruth, 6
Glasser, Ruth, 185
Glover, Clifford, 212–13, 230, 233
Glover, Donald, 326
Glover, Renee, 328
Godley, Raymond, 208
Goldstein, Brian D., 139
Goldthree, Reena, 184
Gonzales, Juan, 314
Goode, Wilson, 34, 259–60, 261, 271, 273, 274
Goodie Mob (band), 79–80, 86, 92–93, 325, 335
Googson, Maggie, 55
Governing (magazine), 6
GQ (band), 111
Graham Central Station (band), 97, 111
Graham v. Connor, 233
Grand Hustle record label, 325
Grandmaster Flash and the Furious Five, 5–6, 222
Graves, Earl, Sr., 43
gravity and microclimates in fires, 266

Great Migration, 2–3, 17, 80, 94n4; to Boston, 121; to California, 295–96; to Chicago, 242, 243; and economic opportunity, 14–15; to Hartford, CT, 178–79, 180–81; and industry in Dayton, OH, 99, 100–101; to Los Angeles, 282–83; and religion and spirituality, 81–82; and return to South, 321–22; and suburbs, 139
Great Recession (2008), 293
Green, William J., 271, 273
Green-Rainbow Party, 133
Gregory, James, 183–84
Griffith, Karen, 227
"groove," in recorded music, 97, 106, 111
Guardians Association (New York), 201, 206
Gucci Mane (band), 325
guest worker programs, 177, 181. *See also* labor
Guy, Artavius, 264
Guy, Cecil, 264
Guy, Shelina, 264
Guy, Terrell, 264

Hahamovitch, Cindy, 185
Hahn, Steve, 183
Hairston, Harold, 268–69
Hampton, Fred, 205
Harlem, New York City, 7–10, *9*, 22n14, 149–50; drug abuse in, 200–201; and drug crisis, 203–4, 209–12; "Harlem" as proxy for "race," 199–200. *See also* New York City
Harlem Ministerial Interfaith Association, 203
Harlem Park to Park, 8
Harlem Six, 205
Harlins, Latasha, 282, 292
Harmon, Reggie, 107
Harriot, Michael, 325
Harris, Margaret "Angel," 107–8
Harris, Oscar, 66
Harrison, Keith, 105
Hart-Celler Act (1965), 177

Hartford, CT, 177–91; churches and religious life in, 187; historiographies of, 183–86
Hartman, Saidiya, 180, 183
Hartsfield, William B., 55, 58
Hartsfield-Jackson Atlanta International Airport, 67, 70–71, 73. *See also* Atlanta, GA
Harvey, Steve, 325
Hatcher, Richard, 30, 33
Haven Clinic, Harlem, 209
Hawkins, Augustus F., 222
Hawthorne Express (band), 106, 107
Hayes, Audrey, 106
Hayes, Isaac, 106
HBCUs (historically Black colleges and universities), 57, 60, 332–34
Heatwave (band), 97, 99, 102, 103, 111, 113
Hemphill, Essex, 261, 262–63, 264
Hendrix, Jimi, 97
Herman J. Russell Company, 56, 66
Herman J. Russell Foundation, 70
heroin, 203, 211. *See also* War on Drugs
Hibbler, Dalithian, 89
Higginbotham, Leon, 206
Hill, Jesse, 59, 62
Hinds, Glester, 209
Hine, Darlene Clark, 232
Hinton, Elizabeth, 289
hip-hop, 5–6, 93, 111, 221–22, 321; Atlanta as capital of, 325; funk's influence on, 112–13; OutKast, 79–80; and sampling, 112; social justice orientation of, 82; Wu Tang Clan, 160. *See also* rap
Hispanic communities. *See* Latinx communities
historiography, 167–68n2, 178, 183–86
HIV (human immunodeficiency virus). *See* AIDS crisis
Hobson, Maurice J., 19, 324
homeownership: in Atlanta, 329–30; Black, 8; in Chicago, 14; in Harlem, 150; in Los Angeles, 284, 293–95; in Pennsylvania, 151–52
"home sphere," 100, 101, 109

Honduras, 184
hooks, bell, 231
Horne, Gerald, 223
"Hoteps," 83
house fires. *See* fire
House Yisrael of Atlanta, 86
housing crisis: and absentee landlords, 267–68; in Hartford, CT, 178–80; in Los Angeles, 293–96; and mortgage lending, 7, 13, 268; and rent-control laws, 139; and squatting, 273; and zoning regulations, 87, 178
housing discrimination, 2, 13; in Boston, 135n11; and housing stock and fire risk, 266–69; and "Negro Removal" in Camden, NJ, 303
housing projects. *See* public housing projects
Houston, Whitney, 111
Howard, Evelyn, 228–29
Howard, Fred, 228–29
Howard University, 303, 322, 340n32
How the Other Half Lives (Riis), 1
Hudson, Ronnie, 112
Hughston, Kenyatta, 265
Humphrey, Hubert, 63
Huncie and the Entertainers, 104
Hunt, Van, 335
Hunter, Cardellia, 326
Hunter, Marcus, 266
Huntley, Walter, 65
Hurston, Zora Neal, 81
Hyman, Violet, 234–35

Ice Cube, 113
IDEA Center for the Arts (Camden, NJ), 316
Ilarraza, Santiago, 312
Illuminati, 86, 95n25
immigration: from Africa, 160, **161–62**, 164; from Caribbean region, 160, **162–63**
imperialism, 64, 178, 190
the Imperials (band), 104–5
incarceration, 224; and bail reform, 246–47; and day reporting programs, 249–51; and electronic monitoring systems, 247–49, 252–53; mass, 140–41, 166, 167, 199; as "New Jim Crow," 287; and parole violation policing, 251–52; police violence as central to, 242; pretrial, 247; as preventive, 246; youth, 284. *See also* criminalization
India.Arie, 335
Inglewood, CA, 25n36, 282, 294–95
Inquilinos Boricuas en Acción, Boston (IBA), 126–27
Insecure (television series), 5
Institute of the Black World, 64, 206
Interdenominational Theological Center, 57
Internet apps: for monitoring neighborhoods, 282
Invest Atlanta, 333
Isley Brothers, 97

Jack, Hulan, 203
Jackson, Janet, 111
Jackson, Jesse, 133, 247
Jackson, John L., 139
Jackson, Maynard H., Jr., 5, 32–33, 35–39, 56–57, 65, 323; and Bureau of Cultural Affairs, 79, 85–86, 324; election, significance of, 84; legacy of, 72–73
Jackson, Michael, 106, 111
Jackson 5, 106
Jacoby, Jim, 330
jail systems, 241–42; Cook County Jail, 241, 242, 244, 246, 249. *See also* incarceration
Jamaica, 179, 181, 186, 190
James, Rick, 97, 110, 111
James, Sharpe, 40
Janey, Kim, 133
Jay-Z, 5, 113, 321
the J.B.'s (band), 97, 111
J. Croson v. Richmond (1989), 44–45
The Jeffersons (television series), 5, 44
Jenkins, Herbert, 55
Jeter, Mary, 107

Jet Stone News, 109
JFK International Airport, 71
Jim Crow laws, 186, 283, 295
Jimmy Castor Bunch, 97
Johnson, Bob, 43
Johnson, Earven "Magic," 291
Johnson, Fay Clarke, 185
Johnson, Kathy, 92
Johnson, Lyndon B., 31, 122
Johnson, Mohawk, 252
Johnson, Neville, 231
Johnson, Violet, 184, 228
Johnson, William, 208, 210
Jones, Beverly, 72
Jones, Bill T., 325
Jones, Doug, 106
Jones, Hubert "Hubie," 123, 124–25
Jones, Jim, 88
Jones, Roy, 305–6, 312–13
Jones, Waverly, 207
Jones, Wayson, 261, 262–63
Jones, Yvonne, 248
Jones Tabernacle AME Church (Philadelphia), 265
Jordan, "Benie," 265
Junie (Morrison), 99, 103, 111
juvenile justice. *See* youth policy, Los Angeles

Kean, Thomas, 309, 310
Keating, Larry, 69
Keating, Michael, 211–12
Keating, W. Dennis, 307
Kelling, George L., 287
Kelly, Kevin, 265
Kelly, Yusef, 265
Kennedy, John F., 30
Kennedy, Lester, 264
Kennedy, Taymar, 264
Kennedy, Tayron, 264
Kenny, Robert, 208–9
Kensington Action Now (Philadelphia), 271–73
Kenyatta, Charles, 203
Key & Peele (television show), 336

Khan, Chaka, 97
Kiernan, Edward, 207–9
Killer Mike, 325
Kindred (Butler), 81
King, Lonnie, 60
King, Martin Luther, Jr., 62, 64, 243
King, Martin Luther, Sr., 68, 126
King, Mel, 119–20, 122–23; on housing crisis, 127; legacy of, 132–34; mayoral campaign of (1983), 127–32
King, Rodney, 292
Knapp, Whitman, 200, 211
Knapp Commission (Commission to Investigate Alleged Police Corruption, New York), 200, 204, 211–12
Knight, Gladys, 325
Knoche, Tom, 308
Koch, Edward, 222–23, 231
Kohler-Hausmann, Julilly, 200
Konvict Musik record label, 325
Kool & the Gang, 97, 111
Koresh, David, 88
Kross, Kris, 113
Krumholz, Norman, 307
Ku Klux Klan (KKK), 55, 72, 76n31, 322, 324, 331, 336
Kusmer, Kenneth, 183

La Alianza Hispana (LAH), 124
Laboe, Art, 295
labor: and agricultural migration, 185, 187; and Black women's experiences, 223; and guest worker programs, 177, 181; and labor camps, 188; and migrant farmwork, 182, 188; and organized labor, 140; shortages of, 32, 110, 181. *See also* deindustrialization; unemployment
Lacey, Diane, 210, 211
Ladera Heights, CA, 16, 17, *17*, 25n39, 68
LaFace record label, 325
Lahey, Laura, 311–12
Lakeside (band), 97, 99, 101, 103, 108, 111, 113
Lamar, Kendrick, 6, 321
Lancaster, CA, 15, 295

Langland, Connie, 272
Latinx communities: activists in, 120; in Boston, 121–22, 125, 134–35n10; in Harlem, 8, 149–50; and La Alianza Hispana (LAH), Boston, 124; in Long Island, 158; in Los Angeles, 15; and Rainbow Coalition, Boston, 130–31; and Spanish Alliance, Boston, 124. *See also* Black-Latino alliances; Puerto Rican immigration
Laurie, Rocco, 208
Lautenberg, Raleigh, 310
Law Enforcement Assistance Administration, 205
Leak, Spencer, 248–49
Leary, Howard R., 205
Leatherberry, Devin, Jr., 269
LeBron, Marisol, 230
LEED (Leadership in Energy and Environmental Design) buildings, 322
Lemonade (Beyoncé), 81
Letson, John W., 59
Lewis, Earl, 100, 137, 141, 143, 167–68n2, 171–72n23
Lewis, John, 322
Lewis Mumford Center for Comparative Urban and Regional Research (Albany, NY), 139–40
liberation theology, 80, 83, 93, 274
Lil Baby (rapper), 325
Lindsay, John, 200, 208, 211, 213
Little, Joan, 232
Little Fruit Stand Riot (1964), 205
Litwack, Leon, 183
Lloyd, Rita, 212
Locking Up Our Own (Forman), 200
Logan, Waverly, 212
Lomax, Michael, 38, 65, 325
Long Island, NY, 153–58, **154–56**. *See also* New York City
Lorde, Audre, 230, 233
Los Angeleno (newspaper), 294
Los Angeles, CA, 15–16, 24–25nn35–36; affirmative action in, 290–91; AIDS crisis in, 291–92; and "Black Beverly Hills," 292; Black homeownership in, 293–95; Black youth and punitive policies in, 283–90; and Community Coalition of South Los Angeles, 291; and Community Resources against Street Hoodlums (CRASH), 289; Compton neighborhood in, 282; cost of living in, 295; gang life in, 285–86; housing crisis in, 293–96; and Los Angeles Rebellion, 282, 292–93; Olympic games in (1984), 288; police department in, 231; public schools in, 292; riots in (1992), 46, 48; segregation, informal, in, 281–82; and socioeconomic status (SES) stratification, 16–17, *17*; South Central, 15, 24–25nn35–36, 282, 285, 287–89, 291, 292, 335; Watts neighborhood in, 282–83; and Watts Rebellion (1965), 290–91; Westchester neighborhood in, 281–82
Los Angeles International Airport, 71
Los Angeles Times, 286, 290
Love, Eula, 231
low-rider car culture, 110
L.T.D. (band), 97, 111
Ludacris (rapper), 325

Maisel, Richard, 185
the Majestics (band), 104
Malcolm X, 203
Mandela, Nelson, 67
Mandrill (band), 97
Manhattan Beach, CA, 295
Mann, Lovely, 179–83, 186, 188, 189, 191
Mann, Willie, 189, 191, 191n7
manufacturing, 180, 182, 185, 186, 188. *See also* deindustrialization
Marable, Manning, 31
Marbury, Lester, 107
Marbury, Raymond, 107
Margo, Robert, 61
Marsalis, Wynton, 325
Marshall, Ray, 32
Marshall, Thurgood, 246–47
Martin, LeRoy, 247
the Mary Jane Girls (band), 111

Mason, C. Vernon, *220*, 235
Massachusetts Institute of Technology, 128
Massell, Samuel, 35
Massey, Douglas S., 3
mass incarceration, 140–41, 166, 167; and anti-crime activism, 199. *See also* incarceration
Mass Production (band), 111
Matthews, Les, 204, 208
mayors, Black, 29–30, 129; and Black business community, 43; elites' support for, 47; "first-wave," 33–34; and minority hiring, 35, 42; "second-wave," 34, 48; as "technocratic," 304; "third-wave," 51n13
Mays, Benjamin Elijah, 58, 68
Mbeki, Thabo, 67
McClain, L. M., 273–74
McClendon, Kenya, 294–95
McDowell, Eva Mae, 187
"McDuffie riots" (Miami), 310
McGuire, Robert, 231
McLendon, Gary, 157
McLoud, Harry, 104
McMurray, George W., 209
media: connections of, to violence, 233, 263–64, 276n8; social, 252
Medley, Brian, 308
Mele, John, 188
Mele, Olga, 188, 191
Memphis, TN, 18; Stax Records, 98
the Meters (band), 97
metropolitan frameworks, 142, 144. *See also* urban areas
Miami, FL, 310
Michney, Todd, 139
Midnight Star (band), 111
Migos (hip-hop group), 325
migrant farmwork, 182, 188. *See also* labor
migration: and "affective mobilities," 186, 190; and Black Exodus, CA, 295; and Black return to South, 80, 83–84; to New York City, 139–40, 158–59; transnational, 177–79, 184, 185, 190; as unmooring/untethering, 186–91
Milan, Milton, 311

Milano, Robert, 212
Military Cooperation with Civilian Law Enforcement Agencies Act (1981), 287
Miller, George, 203
Miller, Reuben Jonathan, 252
Minaj, Nicki, 6
Minneapolis, MN, 98
Minority Business Development Agency, 37, 45
minority business enterprise (MBE) programs, 30, 32, 35–37, 39, 47, 56; challenges to, 45; groups that benefited from, 42–43. *See also* Atlanta Plan
mobilities, affective, 186, 190
Model Cities Administration (Boston), 124
Monáe, Janelle, 325, 335
Monroe County, PA, 151–52
Monsees, Kenneth, 225
Monster (Shakur), 285
Montgomery, Erik James, 36
Moody, Robert, 182, 187
Moore, Earl B., 209
Moore, Jerry, 202
Moore, Winston, 242–43
Moorish Science Temple of America, 80, 81, 86
Morales, Jorge, 245
Morehouse College, 57, 67, 332–33
Morial, Ernest, 35, 40
Morris, Gwen, 229
Morris Brown College (Atlanta), 57, 72, 333
the Morroccos (band), 103
mortgage lending, 7, 13, 268. *See also* housing crisis
Mother African Methodist Episcopal Church (New York City), 209
Mothers against Drugs, 202
Motown format, 105, 321
MOVE (Philadelphia), 259–64, 271, 274–75
Mt. Lebanon Baptist Church (Brooklyn), 201
Mtume (band), 111
Muamba, Cornelia, 230

Muhammad, Fard, 81
Muhammad, Wasim, 303
multiracial/multiethnic coalitions, 120, 121, 122–27, 132. *See also* Black-Latino alliances; Rainbow Coalition; solidarity
Murch, Donna, 140–41, 287, 289
Murphy, Patrick, 205
Murray, Ray, 335
Mystic Order of Melchizedek, 80

narcotics, 202–3, 212, 286, 288. *See also* drug crisis; War on Drugs
Nate and the Typicals (band), 104, 106, 107
National Association for the Advancement of Colored People (NAACP), 110, 306
National Basketball Association (NBA), 322
National Black Arts Festival, 325
National Black Political Convention, 65
National Concerned Citizens against Narcotics, 202
National Conference of Black Lawyers, 235
National Conference on Drug Abuse, 210
National Council of Police Societies (NCOPS), 206
National Defense Migration, 188
nationalism, Black, 63, 86; and "nation building," 63. *See also* United Nuwaubian Nation of Moors (Georgia)
National Urban League, 177–78
Nation of Alkebulan, 86
Nation of Islam, 3, 63, 80, 81, 86, 164
Negron Cruzado, Jose, 188
Negron Rosario, Edna, 188, 189–90, 191
Neil, Vida, 314
Nelson, Carmel, 190
Nelson, Earlene, 190, 191
Nelson, Harry, 207
neoliberal policies, 48, 91, 272, 301, 315
neo-soul, 335
Neptune, Jessica, 199–200
New Britain, CT, 182, 186, 189
New Edition (band), 111
New Horizons (band), 99, 111
New Jersey: and Department of Environmental Protection (DEP), 316; and Working Families Party, 315
"New Jim Crow," 287
Newman, Kathe, 10
New Negro Renaissance, 7
New Orleans, LA, 40
Newton, Huey P., 62
Newton, Velma, 184
New Urban League of Greater Boston, 128
New York Amsterdam News, 204, 206, 208–9, 210, 211, 213–14, 224, 226
New York City: African immigrants to, 160, **161–62**, 164; Black immigration to, 139–40, 160; Black population changes in (1970–2010), 145–66, **146–48**; Black protest in (1970s), 199–214; boundaries of and communities in, 172–73n34; the Bronx, 160; Caribbean immigrants to, 160, **162–63**; and Citywide Anticrime Section, 205; and Community Affairs Division Narcotics Program, 210; drug crisis and harsh drug policies in, 209–11; gentrification in, 7–10, *9*, 138–39, 145, 159; Harlem, 7–10, 22n14; neighborhoods in, 174n43; and "overlapping diasporas," 143–45, 164; police corruption in, 200–201, 205–9; police violence in, 219–36; and Preventive Enforcement Patrol, 205, 206, 212; prison populations in, 166, 167; Staten Island, 160; and suburbanization, 139, 152–53
New York City Council against Poverty, 207
New York City Police Department (NYPD): and congressional hearing on police misconduct, 231, 236; and Guardians Association, 232; lawsuits against and payouts from, 234; and Patrolmen's Benevolent Association, 233; and police violence and Black women, 219–36. *See also* police brutality/violence
New York Civil Liberties Union, 235
New York Times, 17, 72, 131, 206, 209, 331
Nichols, Tyre, 18
Nixon, Richard M., 31, 37, 62–63, 301

Nixon, Rob, 229
"no-knock" policies, 205, 224. *See also* police corruption
Norcross, Donald, 314–15
Norcross, George, 311
Norwood, Mary, 323, 331
Nuruddin, Yusuf, 81–82
Nuwaubian Moors. *See* United Nuwaubian Nation of Moors (Georgia)
N.W.A. (hip-hop group), 113

O'Bryant, John, 128
Office of Federal Contract Compliance, 31
Office of Minority Business Enterprise, 31, 35
O'Grady, James, 247
Ohio, 99. *See also* Dayton, OH
the Ohio Players (band), 97, 98, 103, 105, 111, 113
Ohio Untouchables (band), 102
Oliver, Melvin, 46
Olympic games (Atlanta, 1996), 67, 79, 92
Olympic games (Los Angeles, 1984), 288
"Olympification" of Atlanta, 80, 82–83, 91, 93, 94n3, 328
Omnibus Small Business Act (1978), 37
oral histories, 179, 185
Organized Noise (production duo), 335
Orr, Jason, 335
Ortiz, Nilda, 188
Osborne, Jeffrey, 111
OutKast, 79–80, 82–83, 86, 89–91, 92–93, 325, 335
Overnight Low Show Band, 104

Painter, Nell, 183
Palmdale, CA, 15, 295
Pan-African Orthodox Christian Church (Shrine of the Black Madonna), 86
Panama Canal, 181, 184
Panshin, Alexei, 82
Panshin, Corey, 82
Parents' Foundation against Drug Abuse, 202
Parker, Ray, Jr., 111

Parker, William H., 288
Parkerson, Michelle, 261, 262–63, 264
Parliament (band), 97, 111
Parliament/Funkadelic, 110, 112–13
parole violation, policing of, 251–52. *See also* incarceration
Patrolmen's Benevolent Association, 207
Pattillo, Mary, 139
Patton, Antwan (Big Boi), 89, 90–91
Payne, Ethyl, 244
People's Civic and Welfare Association, 209
People v. Benjamin, 233
Perazo, Carlo, 313
periodization, 184
Perry, Tyler, 326
Peters, Alan H., 310
Phase III (band), 104
Phifer, Bridget, 302, 315
Philadelphia, PA, 206; arson in, 269–75; Black working-class neighborhoods in, 260; deindustrialization in, 265–66; fires and political power in, 259–60, 264–75; and Kensington Action Now, 271–73; and MOVE bombing, 259–64; and Philadelphia International Records, 98
Philadelphia Plan, 31
Piagentini, Joseph, 207
Pike County, PA, 151–52
Pittsburgh, PA, 206
Platypus (band), 99, 102, 103, 108
Pleasure (band), 97
Pola, Carmen, 128
police brutality/violence, 18, 200–201, 207–9, 212–13, 219–36; in Atlanta, 59; and Black homes, invasive visits to, 226–27; Black women's resistance to, 229–35; in Chicago, 242; during Reagan era, 224–29; and women, 224–29, 225. *See also* New York City Police Department (NYPD)
police corruption: in Harlem, 203–4; in New York City, 200–201; and drug crisis in New York City, 205–9

"politics of safety," 200–201, 202
Porter, Gregory, 325
poverty: antipoverty movement in Boston, 120–22, 125–26; in Atlanta, 69; impact of policies on, 144–45; and New York City Council against Poverty, 207; rates of, 47; and socioeconomic inequality, 41–42; and welfare programs, New York City, 222–23. *See also* wealth; welfare programs
Powell, Adam Clayton, Jr., 201
Pressley, Ayanna, 133
Primas, Cynthia, 316
Primas, Melvin "Randy," 299–300, 302–11
Prince (singer), 110; Prince and the Revolution, 111
prisons: construction of, 242, 299, 307–8; and prison industrial complex, 92; and prison populations, 166, 167. *See also* incarceration
Project Inside Out (Chicago), 249
public housing projects, 328, 329; in Boston, 12, 122, 129; and Cabrini-Green Homes, Chicago, 245, 250; in Camden, NJ, 305; and Robert Taylor Homes, Chicago, 244
public schools. *See* school desegregation
Public Works Employment Act (1977), 37
Puerto Rican immigration, 182; to Hartford, CT, 177–78, 187–88; and seasonal work, 185. *See also* Latinx communities
Puerto Rican Migration Division, 185
"Puerto Rican Race Riots," 301
Purnell, Brian, 283
Putnam, Lara, 181, 184

Race for Profit (Taylor), 293
racial issues: and anti-Blackness, 263, 266; in Atlanta, 55–56; and definitions of race, 171–72n23; and racial violence, 129; in South, shifts during twentieth century, 84; and structural racism, 2–3
Raffa, Michael, 270–71
Rainbow Coalition, 119–34; Boston's urban crisis and, 121–22; foundations of, 119–20; Mel King's mayoral campaign (1983) and, 127–32; prior multiracial/multiethnic coalitions in Boston, 122–27. *See also* Black-Latino alliances; multiracial/multiethnic coalitions
Rainbow Coalition Party, 133
Ralph J. Bunche Center for African American Studies, UCLA, 290
Rancifer, Ronnie, 106
Rangel, Charles, 200, 202–4, 211, 214, 217n47
rap, 47, 79, 112, 288; and Funk-Jazz Kafé, 335–36; rap battles, 321; and Tupac Shakur, 292. *See also* hip-hop
Raydio (band), 111
Reagan, Ronald, 37–38, 44, 85, 91, 286, 301; and enterprise zones, 309; and Reaganomics impact on Black women, 221–23; and War on Drugs, 46, 47–48, 224–29
The Real Housewives of Atlanta (television show), 325–26
Reasoner, Harry, 306–7
Redd, Dana, 311, 314, 315
Red Dog police unit (Atlanta), 92, 323–24
redlining, 13, 16, 122, 179, 317n17
Reed, Ishmael, 81
Reed, Mohammed Kasim, 323–24
religion and spirituality, 80–81
Rendell, Ed, 268
Renfrow, Frank, 109
rent-control laws, 139
Residents against the Prison (Camden, NJ), 299
restrictive covenants, 16, 122, 281
Revolt website, 325
Ricch, Roddy, 282
Rice, Norman, 34
Richard Allen Hildebrand Community Center (Philadelphia), 265
Richie, Lionel, 111
Rick James and the Stone City Band, 97, 111
Riis, Jacob, 1
Riverfront State Prison (Camden, NJ), 299; Phase II, 299–300
Rizzo, Frank, 259, 270

RMBG record label, 325
Roach, Edward, 212
Roberson, Sherrell Bonner, 269
Robert Taylor Homes (Chicago), 244
Robinson, Renault, 244
Rockefeller, Nelson, 199, 202, 205, 209, 286; anti-drug policies of, 213–14; drug policies of, 211–13
Rodriguez, Alex, 125, 128, 131, 132–33
Rodriguez, Ana Maria, 124
Ronnie Hudson & The Street People (band), 112
Rosario, Elena, 185
Rose, Chanelle, 20, 299–316
Rose Royce (band), 111
Ross, Michael H., 67
Ross, Rick, 287
Roxbury Multi-Service Center (RMSC), 123–24
Rufus (band), 97
Rushen, Patrice, 111
Rushing, Byron, 128
Russell, Bill, 126
Russell, Herman Jerome, 38–39, 43, 55, 56, 62, 66, 67, 68
Russell, Rogers, 55
Russell Innovation Center for Entrepreneurs (RICE) (Atlanta), 70
Rust Belt cities, 17. *See also* deindustrialization
Rustin, Bayard, 63, 222

Sade (singer), 111
Sambor, Gregor, 259
Sanchez, Sonia, 261, 263–64
San Francisco, CA, 11
San Francisco International Airport, 71
Santeria (religion), 81
Saunders, Gale, 224–26
Schlicting, Kurt, 185
school desegregation: in Atlanta, 59–60; in Boston, 11–12, 120, 123–25, 128–29, 132; and Boston's "busing crisis," 129; in Dayton, OH, 108–9; resistance to, 58; and Second Atlanta Compromise, 59–60

science fiction. *See* Black science fiction
SCLC (Southern Christian Leadership Conference), 64
Scott, Jill, 335
Scott, "Monster" Kody, 284, 285–86, 289
Scott, Thomas, 208
Seale, Bobby, 62
Second Atlanta Compromise, 59–60
Seedman, Albert, 208
Seeger, Peter, 219
segregation: among Black ethnic groups, 140; in Boston neighborhoods, 122; in Camden, NJ, 302–3; in Dayton, OH, public schools, 108–9; in Long Island, 153–58, **154–56**; in Los Angeles, 281–82; in northern urban areas, 4; residential, in Dayton, OH, 99–100
sex work, 232, 290
shackling (electronic monitoring), 241, 247–49, 252–53
shade tobacco, 177, 181, 182; and Shade Tobacco Growers Association, 185
Shadow (band), 99, 111
Shakur, Assata "Joanne Chesimard," 234–35
Shakur, Sanyika, 285
Shakur, Tupac, 112, 292–93
Shapiro, Thomas, 46
Sharp, Charles "Poppy," 302–3, 317n18
Sharpton, Al, **220**
Shea, Thomas, 213, 214
Shedd, Carla, 242
Sheffey, Howard, 201, 206, 207, 213, 214
Sheller, Mimi, 180
Sheltered Markets Program (Detroit), 39
Shepard, James, 213–14
Shields, Erika, 331
Shiloh Baptist Church (Hartford, CT), 187
Shockley, Alfred, 101
Shockley, Laura, 101
Shockley, Steve, 101
Shrine of the Black Madonna (Pan-African Orthodox Christian Church) (Atlanta), 86

silent majority, Black, 199–200, 214, 288
Simms, Rudy, 207
Sims, Walter, 55
Sipp, Kevin, 89
60 Minutes (television news program), 68
Skyy (band), 111
Slave (band), 97, 99, 100–101, 103, 108, 111, 113
slavery: legacy of, 143, 324
Sly and the Family Stone, 97, 105, 106, 110
Small, Charles, 212
Smart-Grosvenor, Vertamae, 222
Smith, Neil, 9
Smith, Virgil, 105
smoke detectors, 268–69. *See also* fire
SNCC (Student Nonviolent Coordinating Committee), 64
Snoop Dogg, 113
Snowden, Muriel, 123
Snowden, Otto, 123
social workers and activism, 120, 123, 125
socioeconomic status (SES), 6–7; and Black flight, 10; and growth of gap in inequality, 41–42; and high-status Black neighborhoods, 68–69; and race and class in neighborhoods, 16. *See also* poverty
Soldiers of the Soil (Johnson), 185
solidarity, 124, 125, 133, 178, 292, 301, 312. *See also* Black-Latino alliances; multiracial/multiethnic coalitions
the S.O.S. Band, 97, 111
So So Def record label, 325
Soto, Hector, 233
Soul Ages (band), 104
The Souls of Black Folk (Du Bois), 1
Sound of Philadelphia, 321
Southall, Mark, 203
South End Tenants Council (Boston), 126
Southern Christian Leadership Conference (SCLC), 62
Southernplayalisticadillacmuzik (OutKast), 89, 90
Southern Poverty Law Center, 86–87
Spanish Alliance (Boston), 124

Speller, Clara, 233–34
Speller v. NYCTA, et ano., 234
Spelman College, 57, 332–33
Spence, Lester K., 301
squatter movements, 260, 273–74. *See also* housing crisis
Squatters: The Other Philadelphia Story (television show), 273
Steve Arrington's Hall of Fame record label, 99, 111, 113
Stewart, Michael, 233
Stokes, Arthur "Hakim," 105–6
Stokes, Carl, 29, 33
Stone, Clarence, 40
Stone, Randolph, 249
Stone Mountain, GA, 72, 324, 327. *See also* Atlanta, GA
stop-and-frisk policies, 205, 224, 235. *See also* police corruption
Stovall, Madeline, 227–28
St. Paul Baptist Church (Harlem), 209
Strickland, William, 206–7
Stringer, Scott M., 9
strip searches, 226. *See also* police brutality/violence
Strong, Rodney, 65, 68, 70, 71, 327
Sturm, Frederick, 270–71
suburbanization, 13–18; in Atlanta, 68–69; in New York City, 139, 152–53
Sugrue, Thomas, 139
Sun (band), 99, 103, 104, 111, 113
Sun Ra and the Arkestra, 81
Supreme Court, US, 44–45
Survival Action Committee (New York), 212
Sutton, Percy, 203, 207
Sweat, Keith, 111
Swift, Jay, 210–11
Switch (band), 111

Tama-Re compound (Putnam County, GA), 92
Task Force on Children out of School (Boston), 124–25
Taylor, Delbert, 107

Taylor, Keeanga-Yamahtta: *Race for Profit*, 293
Taylor, Monique M., 139
Tee, Toddy, 288
Tenants Development Corporation (South End, Boston), 126–27
Tennessee v. Garner, 233
Tent City, Boston, 126, 127, 130
"tethering," 180, 186
Texas, migration to, 295
Thatcher, Margaret, 309
Their Eyes Were Watching God (Hurston), 81
Theoharis, Jeanne, 283
Thomas, Clarence, 45
Thompkins, Patricia, 264
Thompson, Aaron, 304–5, 311
Thompson, Heather Ann, 140–41, 242
Thompson, J. Phillip, III, 33, 47, 48
T.I. (rapper), 325
Timbaland (music producer), 113
the Time (band), 111
Tindley, Charles A., 274
Title VII, Civil Rights Act, 34
TLC (band), 325
Tolnay, Stewart, 183
Tower of Power (band), 111
Training Day (film), 289
transnational migration, 177–79, 184, 185, 190. *See also* migration
trauma: and migration, 186; police violence and, 229, 231; post-traumatic stress syndrome after gang violence, 286
Treatment Alternatives to Street Crime (TASC), 250–51
Tregar, Betsey, 124
Trenton, NJ, 307
Trotter, Joe, 183
Troutman, Leotis, 208
Troutman, Roger, 89, 97, 111–12, 113
Troutman Enterprises, 112
Trump, Donald J., 291
Trupeau, Aaron, Sr., 65, 66
Tuckel, Peter, 185
Turner, George, 323–24
21 Savage (band), 325

2 Chainz (band), 325
Tyson, Mike, 219

Ulster County, NY, 165
Underdoe, Bruce, 208
unemployment: Black, 32, 91, 122, 244, 310; Black youth, 59, 125, 285, 309; in Dayton, OH, 108, 109–10. *See also* labor
United Fruit Company, 185, 186
United Nuwaubian Nation of Moors (Georgia), 80, 81, 83, 86–93
United States v. Salerno, 246–47
Universal Negro Improvement Association, 3, 88
University of California, Los Angeles (UCLA), 290
"unmooring," 180, 181, 186
urban areas: Black population declines in, late twentieth century, 13–14; and Black urban neighborhoods, 100; business development policies in, 30–33; and "criminalization of urban space," 242; fires in, and political power, 259–60, 264–75; and inner city poverty and crime, 5, 6, 47, 91; landscapes and deindustrialization in, 265–66; and metropolitan frameworks, 142, 144; as sites for Black advancement, 4–5; and "urban crisis," 120, 121–22, 140, 300–301, 302, 306; and unrest, 61–63; white interests and elites in, 33–34
Urban Hope Act (2012), 314
Urban Institute report, 41
urban renewal: in Atlanta, 83, 85, 91–92; in Boston, 121–22, 126; in Camden, NJ, 303, 307, 317n17; and displacement, 317n17. *See also* gentrification
US Census: statistics, 140; tract-level data, 165; tract-level data, New York City, 145, 148, 149–50; tract-level data, Pennsylvania, 151–52
Usher (singer), 325

Vandross, Luther, 111
Vaughn, William "Boots," 101–2

Venable, James, 72
Venezuela, 184
Vickers, Deborah A., 265
Villa Victoria, Boston, 127, 130
Vincent, Rickey, 97
Voicescapes: An Urban Mouthpiece (performance), 262
Voting Rights Act (1965), 30, 84, 284

Wakanda (fictional African nation), 58, 336, 337n10
Walsh, Marty, 133
Wanna Make Love (Sun), 104
War (band), 111
Ward, Robert, 102
Ware High School (Augusta, GA), 73n1
The Warmth of Other Suns (Wilkerson), 183–84
Warnock, Raphael, 322
War on Drugs, 46, 47–48, 92; in Chicago, 241–53; and Colombian drug cartels, 287; and crack cocaine, 288–89; and Los Angeles gang life, 286. *See also* drug crisis
War on Poverty, 122, 284
Warren, Bobby, 102
Washington, DC: Black mayors and political power in, 30, 33, 35; Black population declines in, 14–15; Black support of punishment/incarceration in, 200; minority business development in, 40, 43
Washington, Harold, 39, 129, 241, 245, 246, 304–5, 306
Washington, Walter, 33
Wasow, Omar, 63
Waters, Maxine, 290–91
Watkins-Owens, Irma, 184
Watley, Jody, 111
Watts Rebellion (1965), 290–91
The Way We Go to School: The Exclusion of Children in Boston (RMSC report), 125
WDAO (Dayton, OH, radio station), 106–7
wealth: and racial stratification, 12; and racial gap in, 69, 75n11. *See also* poverty

Weaver, Rasheda, 314
Weber, Fred, 272
Webster, Arnold, 311, 312–13
Webster, William H., 235
Weems, Robert, 38, 44
Weir, Leonard, 206
welfare programs, 222–23; in Camden, NJ, 309–10
Wells, Ida B., 276n8
West, Kanye, 321
West Indian immigration, 181; and seasonal work, 185. *See also* Caribbean migration
West Indian Social Club (Hartford, CT), 185, 187
Wheeler, Jacqueline, 267–68
White, John, 214
White, Kevin, 119
White, Mel, 128
White, Mike, 34
white flight: in Atlanta, 59; in Boston, 121, 122; in Dayton, OH, 109; in Hartford, CT, 179
"white gaze," 199
white supremacism, 55
Wier, Lenny, 207
Wiese, Andrew, 139
Wiggins, Ulysses S., 206
Wilder, Keith, 106
Wilkerson, Isabel, 80, 183–84
Wilkie, Nashormeh, 265
Wilkins, Roy, 213
Williams, Kimmika, 262
Williams, Phillana, 326
Williams, Rhonda, 46
Wilson, James Q., 287
Windsor, CT, 177
The Wire (television series), 5
WLIB (New York City radio station), 210, 211
WNET Thirteen (PBS station), 273
women: Black women and police violence, 219–36; Black women and Reaganomics, 221–23; and crack cocaine, 289–90; roles in funk music scene, 107–10

Woodard, Komozi, 283
Woodson, Carter G., 183
The World Beyond the Hill (Panshin and Panshin), 82
World War II: defense training programs during, 188–89; West Indian contributions during, 181
Wright, Irving, 212
Wright, Samuel D., 212
Wu, Michelle, 133–34
Wu Tang Clan (band), 160
Wyly, Elvin, 10

York, Dwight "Malachi," 83, 87, 88, 91, 92
York, Jacob, 92

Young, Andrew, 39, 40–41, 43, 65–66, 84–85, 323; and Brimmer-Marshall Disparity Study, 45; on poverty in Atlanta, 91–92; and pro-business agenda, 47
Young, Anjanette, 236
Young, Coleman, 35, 39, 65
Young, Damon, 83
the Young Mods (band), 104
youth policy, Los Angeles, 283–90

Zapp Band, 89, 99, 103, 111–12, 113
zoning regulations, 87, 178. *See also* housing crisis

www.ingramcontent.com/pod-product-compliance
Lightning Source LLC
LaVergne TN
LVHW090456180925
821343LV00002B/52